Elliot G. Storke

The Domestic Animals

From the Latest and Best Authorities

Elliot G. Storke

The Domestic Animals

From the Latest and Best Authorities

ISBN/EAN: 9783337236311

Printed in Europe, USA, Canada, Australia, Japan

Cover: Foto ©Lupo / pixelio.de

More available books at **www.hansebooks.com**

THE
DOMESTIC ANIMALS:

EMBRACING

I. The Horse.—TO BREED, BREAK, FEED, MANAGE, AND CURE
II. Cattle.—THE VARIOUS BREEDS, AND HOW TO MANAGE THEM.
III. Sheep.—THEIR BREEDS, MANAGEMENT, DISEASES, ETC.
IV. The Pig.—TO BREED, FEED, CUT UP, AND CURE.
V. Poultry.—THE DIFFERENT KINDS, AND TREATMENT
VI. Bees.—THEIR HABITS, MANAGEMENT, ETC.

FROM THE LATEST AND BEST AUTHORITIES.

ILLUSTRATED.

EDITED BY E. G. STORKE.

AUBURN, N. Y.:
THE AUBURN PUBLISHING COMPANY.
E. G. STORKE, PUBLISHING AGENT.
1860.

Entered according to the Act of Congress, in the year 1859,
BY WILLIS W. SITTSER,
in the Clerk's Office of the District Court for the Northern District of New York.

INDEX TO THE DOMESTIC ANIMALS.

A.

	PAGE
Arabian	13
Alderney cattle	108
Ayrshire	99
Angus cattle	118
Abortion	164

B.

	PAGE
Bacon, to cure	233
" Wiltshire	235
Barley for the horse	40
Bantam fowls	252
Bees, classes of	281
" their wonderful instincts	282
" advantages of keeping	283
" their management	283
" " in spring	283
" " in winter	292
" transporting	295
" to stupefy	296
" driving	298
" how to feed	284
" fall feeding of	291
" composition of food for	285
" care in swarming	286
" hives and boxes for	292–305
" enemies of	293
Bee, the queen, drone and working	281, 282
" flowers	294
" feeder	284
" dress	289
Bots	90
Butter, making	137
" Orange county	143
" premium	142
Breeding the horse	19
Breaking "	22
Breeding-mares, care of	21
Backing the horse	23
Bitting "	25
Blinkers or blinders for the horse	34
Bull, the, described	123
Bakewell sheep	174
Berkshire hog	203

C.

	PAGE
Cleveland bay	17
Cruiser, how subdued	27
Carrots, for the horse	41
Congestion	79
Choking	81
Colic, spasmodic	81

	PAGE
Catarrh	82
Cheshire cattle	108
Cow, description of a good	124
" profits of	152
" spaying of, its advantages, etc.	156
Calves, to rear	125
" diseases of	166
Calving	163
Cheese, making	147
Churn	139
Cud, loss of	166
Cochin China fowls	246
Cattle, their breeds, etc.	97
" their value	97
" dairy breeds of	97
" Ayrshire	99
" Alderney	103
" Yorkshire	105
" Cheshire	108
" Dorsetshire	108
" Kerry	108
" Durham	111
" Hereford	113
" West Highland Scot	114
" Devon	116
" Galloway	118
" Angus	118
" Leicestershire	107
" breeding	119
" rearing	126
" feeding	128
" barn	135
" diseases of, etc.	162
" to estimate live weight of	241
" choking of	163
" cream-pot breed	240
Cotswold sheep	179
Cheviot sheep	179
Chinese hog	207

D.

	PAGE
Dorsetshire cattle	108
Dairy breeds of cattle	97
Dairy-house	137
Durham cattle	111
Devon cattle	116
Dorking fowl	250
Duck, domestic	262

E.

	PAGE
Exercise of the horse	46
Essex hog	206
Eggs, to ship	277

F.

	PAGE
Fat-producing breeds of cattle	108
Food of horses	39
" relative value of	40
" its effect on offspring	42
" solid, for calves	128
Feeding cattle	128
Food should be cooked	132
Food, kinds of, for cattle	132
Food as affecting milk	136
Founder	86
Founder, chronic	86
Felon	163
Foul in the foot	165
Fowls, Malay	245
" Cochin China	246
" Spanish	247
" Poland	248
" Hamburg	249
" Dorking	250
" Sussex	251
" game	251
" Bantam	252
" " game	253
" Guinea	259
" pea	261
" diseases of	273-276
" to caponize	272

G.

Grooming	45
Glanders	84
Galloway cattle	118
Gloucestershire hog	205
Game fowl	251
Guinea-fowl	259
Goose, domestic	264
Goose, wild	266
Goose, Canada	268

H.

Hams, Westphalia	235
Hams to cure	233
Horse, character of	11
" breeds of, in the United States	11
" race	11
" Arabian	13
" Canadian	14
" Norman	14
" Morgan	16
" Cleveland bay	17
" dray	17
" trotting	18
" to breed	19
" to break	22
" riding the	23
" taming, the Rarey system	26-36
" stable, management of the	36
Horses, food of	39
Horses, exercise of	46
Horses' feet, to manage	47
Horse, to shoe	48
Horse-shoes, different kinds of	50-59
Horse, fallen, to manage	59
" vices and dangerous habits of	59-69
" soundness of	69
" his purchase and sale	69-79
" diseases of, etc.	79-94
" distemper	87
" medicine for	93
Hereford breed of cattle	118
Heifer, age of, for breeding	125
Hoven or "over full"	163
Hives and boxes for bees	305
Hog, domestic	203
" Berkshire	203
" Hampshire	205
" Yorkshire	205
" Herefordshire	205

	PAGE
Hog, Gloucestershire	205
" Northamptonshire	205
" Norfolk	206
" Leicestershire	206
" Lincoln-hire	206
" Essex	206
" Sussex	207
" Chinese	207
" Suffolk	207
" to choose the	207
" house	210
" breeding	212
" feeding	212
" " chemistry of	220
" to castrate	215
" to spay	215
" to ring	215
" his diseases	222-230
" medicines for	230
" to slaughter	232
" to cut up	232-237
Hamburg fowls	249

I.

Inflammation	80
" of the lungs	82
" of the brain	85

K.

Kerry cattle	108

L.

Leicestershire cattle	107
Lactometer	152
Lambs, care of	184
" substitute	186
" twin	187
" castration of	189
" docking of	190
" spaying of	191
Lincolnshire hog	206
Leicestershire hog	206

M.

Milking	137
Milk-fever	165
Merino sheep, American	171
Merino sheep, Saxon	173
Malay fowls	245

N.

Northamptonshire hog	205
Norfolk hog	206

O.

Ox described	124

P.

Potatoes for the horse	41
Poll-evil	89
Pig, to choose	207
Pork, to cure	231-236
Poultry, domestic	245
" to feed	269
" houses, etc.	270
" to caponize	272
" to ship	286
" importance of keeping	245
" its varieties	245
Poland fowls	248
Pea-fowl	261

R.

Reproduction applied to cattle	125
Rearing calves	126
Red water	165

S.

	PAGE
Stable management	36
Stable, ventilation of the	37
" cleanliness of the	38
" floor	38
Shoeing the horse	48
Shoes, how to put on	49
Shoes, different kinds of	50-59
Spavin	86
Strangles	87
Spaying cows	155
" " its advantages	156
" " how done	159
" " care after operation	161
Stock, number to be kept	238
Spanish fowls	247
Sheep	171
" native	171
" American merino	171
" Saxon merinoes	173
" Bakewell	174
" South-Down	176
" Cotswold	179
" Cheviot	179
" comparative value of different breeds	180
" their general management	183

	PAGE
Sheep, summer management	183
" care in handling of	183
" washing	192
" shearing	192
" winter management of	193
" winter food of	193
" medicines for	193
Swine	203
Sussex hog	207
Suffolk	207

T.

	PAGE
Turnips, Swedes, for horses	41
Table of medicines for the horse	92
Turkey, domestic	253
Turkey, wild	253

W.

	PAGE
Worms in horses	81
Wind-galls	91
Wheatmeal porridge for calves	127

Y.

	PAGE
Yorkshire cattle	105
Yellows, or jaundice	166
Yorkshire hog	205

PREFACE.

THE immense advantages derived from the subjugation to our use of the Domestic Animals are perhaps not fully appreciated. Let any one carefully consider the valuable services rendered to civilized man by the horse, the ox, the cow, the sheep, the pig, the domestic fowl, and the honey bee. Let him take into view the labor they perform, the food and clothing, the comforts and conveniences which they supply, and he will at once see the importance of the *subjects* of this manual.

On each of these subjects carefully arranged treatises are given, showing the best breeds of the several animals, the true methods of breeding, feeding, breaking, working, fattening, etc., the various diseases to which they are subject, and their remedies and treatment. The matter is derived from varied and reliable sources, from the latest and best European and American writers, the object being to condense the most useful practical information within the shortest compass, and to so arrange it that any thing sought for could at once be found.

Every owner of a horse, a cow, or a pig, or the keeper of

bees or of poultry, will find in this work hints and instruction of the most valuable kind, and which, if properly observed, will save to him in a single year many times the cost of this volume, in the economy of feeding, and in the increased value to him of the products of the animals kept.

It is intended to be a hand-book, in which can at any time be found the practical directions of men of the largest experience and of the closest observation in its several departments. Such a work it is believed cannot fail of being equally acceptable and useful to a large class of readers in every section of the country.

THE HORSE:

HOW TO BREED, BREAK, FEED, AND MANAGE,

AND HOW TO TREAT HIS DISEASES;

TOGETHER WITH

THE ART OF TAMING

AS PRACTICED BY

WILLIAM AND JOHN S. RAREY.

DOMESTIC ANIMALS.

THE HORSE.

THE CHARACTER OF THE HORSE.—The horse is now one of the most universally distributed animals, and everywhere he is recognized as the most useful amongst the quadruped servants of man, yielding in intelligence to the dog alone, and perhaps not to him; for in those countries, —some portions of Arabia for instance—in which he is admitted to the full and unrestricted companionship of man, sharing his food with the family of his master, and, like him, a dweller in the tent, his sagacity far surpasses that of our stable-reared horses, however affectionately they may be treated. In the early ages of the world the horse seems to have been devoted to the purposes of war or pleasure, whilst the ox was the agricultural drudge. But the beauty, strength, and tractability of the horse have now connected him, directly or indirectly, with almost all the purposes of life. If he differ in different countries in form and size, it is from the influence of climate, food, and cultivation; but otherwise, from the war-horse, as he is depicted in the sculptures of ancient temples, to the stately charger of Holstein and of Spain, or from the fleet and beautiful Arabian to the diminutive Shetlander, there is a similarity of form and character which clearly mark a common origin.

PRINCIPAL BREEDS IN THE UNITED STATES.—The principal breeds now common to this country are the *common horse*, descended from those brought in by the early colonists, and variously mixed with varieties subsequently introduced; the *thorough-bred*, or *race-horse;* the *Arabian*, the *Canadian*, the *Norman*, the *Cleveland bay*, the dray, and the *American trotting-horse*. Of the *common horse*, no specific description can be given, as he is a compound of many races variously and incongruously mixed.

The Race-Horse.—The English race-horse is undoubtedly the finest animal of his species in the world. In swiftness and energy he surpasses even his Arabian progenitor, though on the burning sands of the desert, to which not being acclimatized, he might not be equal in point of endurance. He is always distinguished by the beautiful head of the class from which his ancestors sprung; this being as finely set on a neck of faultless contour. His oblique shoulders give as good earnest of strength as do his well-formed hind-legs of speed. By the sculptor, perhaps, the legs from the knee downward might be pronounced unfit for the *beau ideal* of a perfect animal, yet this, though admitted by judges to be sometimes the case, is, after all, a matter of little consequence. Certain it is, that whenever the English race-horse has contended on fair ground

FLYING CHILDERS.

with the finest Arabian breeds, he has invariably come off conqueror, even though he may be by no means the finest specimen of his class.

The racer, however, with the most beautiful form, is occasionally a sorry animal. There is sometimes a want of energy in an apparently faultless shape for which there is no accounting; but there are two points among those just enumerated which will rarely or never deceive, a well-placed shoulder and a well-bent hinder leg.

The Darley Arabian was the parent of our best racing stock. He was purchased by Mr. Darley's brother at Aleppo, and was bred in the neighboring desert of Palmyra.

The immediate descendants of this invaluable horse were the Devonshire, or Flying Childers; the Bleeding, or Bartlett's Childers, who was never trained; Almanzor and others.

The two Childers were the means through which the blood and fame of their sire were widely circulated, and from them descended another Childers, Blaze, Snap, Sampson, Eclipse, and a host of excellent horses.

The Devonshire, or Flying Childers, so called from the name of his breeder, Mr. Childers, of Carr House, and the sale of him to the Duke of Devonshire, was the fleetest horse of his day. He was at first trained as a hunter, but the superior speed and courage which he discovered caused him to be soon transferred to the turf. Common report affirms that he could run a mile in a minute, but there is no authentic record of this. Childers ran over the round course at Newmarket (three miles six furlongs and ninety-three yards) in six minutes and forty seconds; and the Beacon course (four miles one furlong and one hundred and thirty-eight yards) in seven minutes and thirty seconds. In 1772 a mile was run by Firetail in one minute and four seconds.

More than twenty years after the Darley Arabian, and when the value of the Arabian blood was fully established, Lord Godolphin possessed a beautiful but singularly-shaped horse, which he called an Arabian, but which was really a Barb. His crest, lofty and arched almost to a fault, will distinguish him from every other horse.

He had a sinking behind his shoulders almost as peculiar, and a corresponding elevation of the spine toward the loins. His muzzle was uncommonly fine, his head beautifully set on, his shoulders capacious, and his quarters well spread out. He was picked up in France, where he was actually employed in drawing a cart; and when he was afterward presented to Lord Godolphin, he was in that nobleman's stud a considerable time before his value was discovered. It was not until the birth of Lath, one of the first horses of that period, that his excellence began to be appreciated. He was then styled an Arabian, and became, in even a greater degree than the Darley, the founder of the modern thorough-bred horses. He died in 1753, at the age of twenty-nine.

An intimate friendship subsisted between him and a cat, which either sat on his back when he was in the stable, or nestled as closely to him as she could. At his death the cat refused her food and pined away, and soon died. Mr. Holcroft gives a similar relation of the attachment between a race-horse and a cat, which the courser would take in his mouth and place in his manger and upon his back without hurting her. Chillaby, called from his great ferocity the mad Arabian, whom one only of the grooms dared to approach, and who savagely tore to pieces the image of a man that was purposely placed in his way, had his peculiar attachment to a lamb, who used to employ himself for many an hour in butting away the flies from him.

The Arabian Horse.—By far the most beautiful variety of the Arab horse is the Barb, as he is called from his having been brought to this country from Barbary, as vague a term as is Arabia, including the country between Tunis and Morocco. The Barb is, however, small, rarely exceeding fourteen hands, and is thus considerably less than the Bedouin horse of North and East Arabia. This breed of horses was introduced long ago into England; the celebrated Godolphin Arabian, so called, was supposed to be a Barb. It is to this breed that Spanish horses owe their fire and beauty, and most of the best English race-horses have the blood of the Barb in their veins. It is, however, remarkable that, considering the lavish expenditure on improving the breed of English horses, no attempts have been made to procure any of the mares of the highest Arabian stock. We appear to have placed the chief dependence on the Arab stallion, though it is well known to Oriental breeders that the mare is of by far the greater importance. Whoever attempts further to infuse Arab blood into the English horse should go to Muscat or its vicinity for his stock; and not, as is frequently done, to Egypt or the Barbary coast, where the horses are, for the most part, small.

The Arabian horse would not be acknowledged by every judge to possess a perfect form; his head, however, is inimitable. The broadness and squareness of the forehead, the shortness and fineness of the muzzle, the prominence and brilliancy of the eye, the smallness of the ears, and the beautiful course of the veins, will always characterize the head of the Arabian horse.

His body may be considered as too light, and his chest as too narrow; but behind the arms the barrel generally swells out, and leaves sufficient room for the play of the lungs.

In the formation of the shoulder, next to that of the head, the Arab is superior to any other breed. The withers are high, and the shoulder-blade inclined backward, and so nicely adjusted that in descending a hill the point or edge of the ham never ruffles the skin. He may not be thought sufficiently high; he seldom stands more than fourteen hands two inches. The fineness of his legs, and the oblique position of his pasterns, may be supposed to lessen his strength; but the leg, although small, is flat and wiry; anatomists know that the bone has no common density, and the startling muscles of the fore-arm and the thigh indicate that he is fully capable of accomplishing many of the feats which are recorded of him. The Arab horse is as celebrated for his docility and good temper as for his speed and courage.

The kindness with which he is treated from a foal, gives him an affection for his master, a wish to please, a pride in exerting every energy in obedience to his commands, and, consequently, an apparent sagacity which is seldom seen in other breeds. The mare and her foal inhabit the same tent with the Bedouin and his children. The neck of the mare is often the pillow of the rider, and, more frequently, of the children, who are rolling about upon her and the foal; yet no accident ever occurs, and the animal acquires that friendship and love for man which occasional ill-treatment will not cause him for a moment to forget.

When the Arab falls from his mare, and is unable to rise, she will immediately stand still, and neigh until assistance arrives. If he lies down to sleep, as fatigue sometimes compels him, in the midst of the desert, she stands watchful over him, and neighs and rouses him if either man or beast approaches. An old Arab had a valuable mare that had carried him for fifteen years in many a hard-fought battle, and many a rapid weary march; at length, eighty years old, and unable longer to ride her, he gave her, and a cimeter that had been his father's, to his eldest son, and told him to appreciate their value, and never lie down to rest until he had rubbed them both as bright as a looking-glass. In the first skirmish in which the young man was engaged he was killed, and the mare fell into the hands of the enemy. When the news reached the old man, he exclaimed that "life was no longer worth preserving, for he had lost both his son and his mare, and he grieved for one as much as the other;" and he immediately sickened and died.

The Canadian Horse.—This variety of the horse is chiefly found in Canada, though they have been introduced, in considerable numbers, into the United States. They are chiefly of French descent, though many of the larger and more valuable of them are the produce of crosses with various English breeds. They are a very hardy race, easily kept, long-lived, and the larger varieties excellent farm and draught horses. Not as large as the Norman horse, they still exhibit many of his characteristics. Many stallions have been brought into the states, and crossed with our common breeds. The result has tended to give vigor and compactness of form and constitution, and a continuance of the practice is suggested.

The Norman Horse.—This is a hardy and very valuable breed of French horses of recent introduction. Mr. Harris thus speaks of them:

"Those who are acquainted with the thorough-bred Canadian horse will see in him a perfect model, on a small scale, of the Percheron horse.

THE NORMAN HORSE.

This is the peculiar breed of Normandy, which is used so extensively throughout the northern half of France for diligence and post horses, and from the best French authorities I could command (I cannot now quote the precise authorities), I learned that they were produced by the cross of the Andalusian horse upon the old heavy Norman horse, whose portrait may still be seen as a war-horse on the painted windows of the cathedral of Rouen, several centuries old. At the time of the occupation of the Netherlands by the Spaniards, the Andalusian was the favorite stallion of the north of Europe, and thus a stamp of the true Barb was implanted, which remains to the present day. If you will allow me to digress a moment, I will give you a short description of the old Norman draught-horse on which the cross was made. They average full sixteen hands in height, with head short, thick, wide, and hollow between the eyes; jaws heavy; ears short and pointed well forward; neck very short and thick; mane heavy; shoulder well inclined backward; back extremely short; rump steep; quarters very broad; chest deep and wide; tendons large; muscles excessively developed; legs very short, particularly from the knee and hock to the fetlock, and thence to the coronet, which is covered with long hair, hiding half the hoof; much hair on the legs."

Mr. Youatt, in speaking of the French horses, says: "'The best French horses are bred in Limousin and Normandy. From the former district come excellent saddle-horses and hunters; and from the latter a stronger species, for the road, the cavalry or the carriage. The Norman horses are now much crossed by our hunters, and occasionally by the thorough-bred; and the English roadster and light draught horse has not suffered by a mixture with the Norman."

In his remarks on the coach-horse, Mr. Youatt says: " The Normandy carriers travel with a team of four horses, and from fourteen to twenty-two miles in a day, with a load of ninety hundred weight."

JUSTIN MORGAN.

The Committee of the N. Y. State Agricultural Society, "on stock owned out of the state," at the State Fair at Auburn, in 1846, thus spoke of the Morgans:

"Gifford Morgan, a dark chestnut stallion, fourteen hands and three inches high, aged twenty years, was exhibited by F. A. Weir, of Walpole, N. H. It is claimed on the part of his owner, that this horse possesses the celebrated 'Morgan' blood in greater purity than any other now living. 'General Gifford,' got by the above-named horse, was exhibited by Mr. C. Blodget, of Chelsea, Vt. In his size, figure, action, and color, he closely resembles his sire. Both are exceedingly compact horses, deep-chested and strong-backed, with fore-legs set wide apart, and carrying their heads (which are small, with fine, well-set eyes) high and gracefully, without a bearing-rein. Their action attracted the marked admiration of all. This breed are reputed to possess great bottom and hardiness, and every thing about the two presented, goes to prove that their reputation in this particular is well founded. For light carriage or buggy horses, it would be difficult to equal them, and if by crossing with prime large mares, of any breed, size could be obtained in the progeny, without losing the fire and action of the Morgan, the result of the cross would be a carriage of very superior quality. Your committee are not aware of the extent or result of such crosses, in the region where the Morgans originated. Unless experience has already demonstrated their inutility, we could recommend to our horse-breeders some well-considered experiments, limited at first, to test the feasibility of engrafting the Morgan characteristics on a larger horse."

The Cleveland Bay.—This horse is thus described by Mr. Youatt:
" The produce of Cleveland mares is a coach-horse of high repute, and likely to possess good action. His points are, substance well placed, deep and well-proportioned body, strong and clean bone under the knee, open, sound, and tough feet, with fine knee action, lifting his feet high. The full-sized coach-horse is in fact an overgrown hunter.

" The old Cleveland horse is almost extinct, and his place supplied in the manner just described. The Suffolk Punch, the product chiefly of Suffolk and some of the neighbouring districts, is regenerated, but is a different sort of animal to the breed of olden times. He usually varied from fifteen to sixteen hands in height, and was of a sorrel color. He was large-headed, low-shouldered, broad and low on the withers, deep, and yet round-chested; long in the back, large and strong in the quarters, round in the legs, and strong in the pasterns. He would throw his whole weight into the collar, and had sufficient hardihood and strength to stand a long day's work. The pure breed has, however, passed away, and is succeeded by a cross between the half or three-parts bred Yorkshire with the old Suffolk. He is taller than the former horse, somewhat higher and firmer about the shoulders, with sufficient quickness of action and honesty to exert himself to the utmost at a dead pull, whilst the proportion of the withers enables him to throw immense weight into the collar. The encouragement given by the Royal Agricultural Society of England for horses of this class has been the cause of considerable increase in their numbers."

Cleveland Bays have been introduced into this country, and have spread considerably. They are very large horses; and, for their size, are symmetrical in form, and fair in action. The cross with our common mares produces an excellent farm horse, though said to be of *sullen temper.*

The Dray-Horse.—Of the heavy black dray-horses, but few have been imported into this country, and they do not seem likely to become favorites here. Mr. Youatt says of them:

" The heavy black horse is the last variety it may be necessary to notice. It is bred chiefly in the midland counties, from Lincolnshire to Staffordshire. Many are bought up by the Surrey and Berkshire farmers at two years old,—and being worked moderately until they are four, earning their keep all the while, they are then sent to the London market, and sold at a profit of ten or twelve per cent.

It would not answer the *breeder's* purpose to keep them until they are fit for town work. He has plenty of fillies and mares on his farm for every purpose that he can require; he therefore sells them to a person nearer the metropolis, by whom they are gradually trained and prepared. The traveler has probably wondered to see four of these enormous animals in a line before a plow, on no very heavy soil, and where two lighter horses would have been quite sufficient. The farmer is training them for their future destiny; and he does right in not requiring the exertion of all their strength, for their bones are not yet perfectly formed, nor their joints knit; and were he to urge them too severely, he would probably injure and deform them. By the gentle and constant exercise of the plow, he is preparing them for that *continued and equable* pull at the collar, which is afterward so necessary. These horses are adapted more for parade and show, and to gratify the ambition which one brewer has to outvie his neighbor, than for any peculiar utility. They are certainly noble-looking animals, with their round, fat carcases, and their sleek coats, and the evident pride which they take in themselves; but they eat a great deal of hay and corn, and at hard and long-continued work they would be completely beaten by a team of active muscular horses an inch and a half lower.

The only plea which can be urged in their favor, beside their fine appearance, is, that as shaft-horses over the badly-paved streets of the metropolis, and with the immense loads they often have behind them, great bulk and weight are necessary to stand the unavoidable shaking and battering. Weight must be opposed to weight, or the horse would sometimes be quite thrown off his legs. A large heavy horse must be in the shafts, and then little ones before him would not look well.

The Trotting-Horse.—The relative merits of the English and American trotting-horse, have been the subjects of careful discussion by competent judges. The New York *Spirit of the Times*, one of the best authorities on this subject, thus canvasses the matter:

"Nimrod, in admitting the superiority of our trotting-horses to the 'English,' claims that the English approach *very near* to the Americans. Possibly the characteristic national vanity would not allow him to make a further concession. But there is no comparison whatever between the trotting horses of the two countries. Mr. Wheelan, who took *Rattler* to England, last season, and doubly distanced, with ease, every horse that started against him, as the *record shows*, informs us that there are twenty or more roadsters in common use in this city, that would compete successfully with the fastest trotters on the English turf. They neither understand the art of training, driving, nor riding them. For example: some few years since, *Alexander* was purchased by Messrs. C. and B. of this city, for a friend or acquaintance, in England. Alexander was a well known roadster here, and was purchased to order at a low rate. The horse was sent out and trials made of him; but so unsuccessful were they, that the English importers considered him an imposition. Thus the matter stood for a year or more. When Wheelan arrived in England, he recognized the horse and learned the particulars of his purchase, and subsequent trials there. By his advice the horse was nominated in a stake, at Manchester we believe, with four or five of the best trotters in England, Wheelan agreeing to train and ride him. When the horses came upon the ground, the odds were four and five to one, against *Alexander*, who won by nearly a quarter of a mile. Wheelan says he took the track at the start, and widened the gap at his ease—that near the finish, being surprised that no horse was near him, as his own had not yet made a stroke, he got frightened, thinking some one might outbrush him,—that he put Alexander up to his work, and finally won by an immense way, no horse, literally, getting to the head of the quarter stretch, as he came out at the winning stand! The importers of Alexander, at any rate, were so delighted at his performance, that they presented Wheelan with a magnificent timing-watch, and other valuable presents, and sent Messrs. C. and B. a superb service of plate, which may, at any time, be seen at their establishment, in Maiden Lane."

This difference between English and American trotters is clearly attributable to superior training and jockeying. We have in this country hundreds of Rareys, who can teach not only the nobles of the realm but the common jockeys also, the mysterious arts of horse-training and managing, although they may not now be able to command for their services quite the compensation which that gentleman received.

BREEDING.—Breeders of all kinds of animals are unanimous in their opinions that it is necessary to have distinct varieties, usually distinguished as thorough-bred, for the propagation of the species, whether it be determined to carry on the unblemished pedigree, or to cross with other breeds. The high value set upon the short-horned cattle, is estimated principally by the purity of the blood; and the true Southdown or Leicester sheep by a similar criterion.

It is a general observation with those who have devoted attention to the subject, that horses and mares require much time after they have been trained, before they distinguish themselves as the progenitors of first-rate stock. This affords another argument in favor of early training. Both with mares and stallions their best foals have often not come forth till they were advanced in years. According to the presumed age of the Godolphin Arabian, he was thirteen years old when he became the sire of Regulus. Paynator and Whalebone were each of them twenty years old when their sons, Dr. Syntax and Sir Hercules, were foaled. Potooooooooo, Sultan, Langar, and Venison, were each of them sixteen years old when they became the sires respectively of Waxy, Bay Middleton, Epirus and Kingston. Melbourne was fifteen when he begot West Australian; Hap-hazard fourteen when he was the sire of Filho da Puta. Orville was the same age when he was the sire of Ebor, and twenty when he begot the still more celebrated Emilius; and an infinity of similar examples may be added. This property applies more generally to stallions than to mares: for it is sometimes apparent, that their first foals are vastly superior to their subsequent produce. This was the case in olden times with the dams of Mark Antony, Conductor, Pyrrhus, and Pantaloon; and more recently with Sultan, Touchstone, Sir Hercules, and Filho da Puta. Whether the subsequent change of partners has any prejudicial effect on the future progeny, is a subject worthy the most scrupulous attention of breeders. The case of Penelope is in favor of the assumption; for the superiority of her first seven foals by Waxy, over the others by different horses, is a fact which cannot be disputed. It is curious to remark, that when a thorough-bred mare has once had foals to common horses, no subsequent foals which she may have had by thorough-bred horses have ever evinced any pretensions to racing qualities. There may be an exception; but I believe I am correct in stating that there is not. It is laid down as a principle, "That when a pure animal, of any breed, has once been pregnant to one of a different breed, she is herself a cross ever after; the purity of her blood having been lost in consequence of this connection." This will no doubt be received by many persons as an abstruse hypothesis, but there are unequivocal incidents in favor of it; and that valuable monitor, past experience, must be received as a more convincing argument than the opinion of individuals, on subjects which are hidden from our understanding by the impenetrable veil which, on many occasions, enshrouds the secret mysteries of nature. There are events on record which prove this faculty, although they do not enlighten us as to the physical influences which control it. Sir Gore Ousely, when in India, purchased an Arabian mare, which during several seasons would not breed, and, in consequence, an intercourse with a zebra was resorted to; she produced an animal striped like its male parent. The first object being accomplished, that of causing her to breed, a thorough-bred horse was selected, but the produce was striped. The following year another horse was chosen, yet the stripes, although less distinct, appeared on the foal. Mr. Blaine relates that a chestnut mare also gave birth to a foal by a quagga, and that the mare was afterward bred from by an Arabian horse, but that the progeny exhibited a very striking resemblance to the quagga.

The progeny will, as a rule, inherit the general or mingled qualities of the parents. There is scarcely a disease by which either of them is affected, that the foal does not often inherit or show a predisposition to it. Even the consequences of ill-usage or hard work will descend to the progeny. There has been proof upon proof that blindness, roaring, thick wind, broken wind, spavins, curbs, ringbones, and founder, have been bequeathed to their offspring both by the sire and the dam.

Peculiarity of form and constitution will also be inherited. This is a most important but neglected consideration; for, however desirable or even perfect may have been the conformation of the sire, every good point may be neutralized or destroyed by the defective structure of the mare. The essential points should be good in both parents, or some minor defect in either be met, and got rid of by excellence in that particular point in the other. The unskillful or careless breeder, too often so badly pairs the animals that the good points of each are almost lost, the defects of both increased, and the produce is far inferior to both sire and dam.

The mare is sometimes put to the horse at too early an age; or, what is of more frequent occurrence, the mare is incapable from old age. The owner is unwilling to destroy her, and determines that she shall pay for her keeping by bearing him a foal. What is the consequence? The foal exhibits an unkindness of growth, a corresponding weakness, and there is scarcely an organ that possesses its natural and proper strength.

That the constitution and power of endurance of the horse are in a great measure inherited, no sporting man ever doubted. The qualities of the sire or the dam descend from generation to generation, and the excellences or defects of certain horses are often traced, and justly so, to some peculiarity in a far-distant ancestor.

It may, perhaps, be justly affirmed, that there is more difficulty in selecting a good mare to breed from than a good horse, because she should possess somewhat opposite qualities. Her carcass should be long, in order to give room for the growth of the fœtus; and yet with this there should be compactness of form and shortness of leg. What can they expect whose practice it is to purchase worn-out, spavined, foundered mares, about whom they fancy there have been some good points, and send them far into the country to breed from, and, with all their variety of shape, to be covered by the same horse? In a lottery like this there may be now and then a prize, but there must be many blanks.

As to the shape of the stallion, little, satisfactory, can be said. It must depend on that of the mare, and the kind of horse wished to be bred ; but if there is one point absolutely essential, it is "compactness" —as much goodness and strength as possible condensed into a little space.

Next to compactness, the inclination of the shoulder will be regarded. A huge stallion, with upright shoulders, never got a capital hunter or hackney. From him the breeder can obtain nothing but a cart or dray horse, and that perhaps spoiled by the opposite form of the mare. On the other hand, an upright shoulder is desirable, if not absolutely necessary, when a mere slow draught-horse is required.

From the time of covering, to within a few days of the expected period of foaling, the cart-mare may be kept at moderate labor, not only without injury, but with decided advantage. It will then be prudent to release her from work, and keep her near home, and under the frequent inspection of some careful person.

When nearly half the time of pregnancy has elapsed, the mare should have a little better food. She should be allowed one or two feeds of grain in the day. This is about the period when they are accustomed to slink their foals, or when abortion occurs; the eye of the owner should, therefore, be frequently upon them. Good feeding and moderate exercise will be the best preventives of this mishap. The mare that has once aborted is liable to a repetition of the accident, and therefore should never be suffered to be with other mares between the fourth and fifth months; for such is the power of imagination or of sympathy in the mare, that if one suffers abortion, others in the same pasture will too often share the same fate. Farmers wash, and paint, and tar their stables, to prevent some supposed infection—the infection lies in the imagination.

The thorough-bred mare—the stock being intended for sporting purposes—should be kept quiet, and apart from other horses, after the first four or five months. When the period of parturition is drawing near, she should be watched and shut up during the night in a safe yard or loose box.

If the mare, whether of the pure or common breed, be thus taken care of, and be in good health while in foal, little danger will attend the act of parturition. If there is false presentation of the fœtus, or difficulty in producing it, it will be better to have recourse to a well-informed practitioner, than to injure the mother by the violent and injurious attempts that are often made to relieve her.

The parturition being over, the mare should be turned into some well-sheltered pasture, with a hovel or shed to run into when she pleases; and if she has foaled early, and grass is scanty, she should have a couple of feeds of grain daily. The breeder may depend upon it, that nothing is gained by starving the mother and stinting the foal at this time. It is the most important period of the life of the horse; and if, from false economy, his growth is arrested, his puny form and want of endurance will ever afterward testify the error that has been committed. The grain should be given in a trough on the ground, that the foal may partake of it with the mother. When the new grass is plentiful, the quantity of corn may gradually be diminished.

The mare will usually be found again at heat at or before the expiration of a month from the time of foaling, when, if she is principally kept for breeding purposes, she may be put again to the horse. At the same time, also, if she is used for agricultural purposes, she may go again to work. The foal is at first shut in the stable during the hours of work; but as soon as it acquires sufficient strength to toddle after the mare, and especially when she is at slow work, it will be better for the foal and the dam that they should be together. The work will contribute to the health of the mother; the foal will more frequently draw the milk, and thrive better, and will be hardy and tractable, and gradually familiarized with the objects among which it is afterward to live. While the mother, however, is thus worked, she and the foal should be well fed; and two feeds of corn, at least, should be added to the green food which they get when turned out after their work, and at night.

In five or six months, according to the growth of the foal, it may be weaned. It should then be housed for three weeks or a month, or turned into some distant rick-yard. There can be no better place for the foal than the latter, as affording, and that without trouble, both food and shelter. The mother should be put to harder work, and have drier food. One or two urine-balls, or a physic-ball, will be useful, if the milk should be troublesome or she should pine after her foal.

There is no principle of greater importance than the liberal feeding of the foal during the whole of his growth, and at this time in particular. Bruised oats and bran should form a considerable part of his daily provender. The farmer may be assured that the money is well laid out which is expended on the liberal nourishment of the growing colt; yet, while he is well fed, he should not be rendered delicate by excess of care.

A racing colt is often stabled; but one that is destined to be a hunter, a hackney, or an agricultural horse, should have a square rick, under the leeward side of which he may shelter himself; or a hovel, into which he may run at night, and out of the rain.

BREAKING.—The process of breaking-in should commence from the the very period of weaning. The foal should be daily handled, partially dressed, accustomed to the halter when led about, and even tied up. The tractability, and good temper, and value of the horse, depend a great deal more upon this than breeders are aware.

Every thing should be done, as much as possible, by the man who feeds the colt, and whose management of him should be always kind and gentle. There is no fault for which a breeder should so invariably discharge his servant as cruelty, or even harshness, toward the rising stock; for the principle on which their after usefulness is founded, is early attachment to, and confidence in man, and obedience, implicit obedience, resulting principally from this.

After the second winter the work of breaking-in may commence in good earnest. The colt may be bitted, and a bit selected that will not hurt his mouth, and much smaller than those in common use. With this he may be suffered to amuse himself, and to play, and to champ it for an hour, on a few successive days.

Breaking in Harness.—Having become a little tractable, portions of the harness may be put upon him, concluding with the blind winkers; and, a few days afterward, he may go into the team. It would be better if there could be one horse before and one behind him, besides the shaft horse. There should at first be the mere empty wagon. Nothing should be done to him, except that he should have an occasional pat or kind word. The other horses will keep him moving, and in his place; and no great time will pass, sometimes not even the first day, before he will begin to pull with the rest. The load may then be gradually increased.

Riding.—The agricultural horse is sometimes wanted to ride as well as to draw. Let his first lesson be given when he is in the team. Let his feeder, if possible, be first put upon him. He will be too much hampered by his harness, and by the other horses, to make much resistance; and, in the majority of cases, will quietly and at once submit. We need not to repeat, that no whip or spur should be used in giving the first lessons in riding.

Backing.—When he begins a little to understand his business, backing—the most difficult part of his work—may be taught him; first to back well without any thing behind him, and then with a light cart, and afterward with some serious load—always taking the greatest care not seriously to hurt his mouth. If the first lesson causes much soreness of the gums, the colt will not readily submit to a second. If he has been previously rendered tractable by kind usage, time and patience will do every thing that can be wished. Some carters are in the habit of blinding the colt when teaching him to back. This may be necessary with a restive and obstinate one, but should be used only as a last resort.

Obedience.—The colt having been thus partially broken-in, the necessity of implicit obedience must be taught him, and that not by severity, but by firmness and steadiness. The voice will go a great way, but the whip or the spur is sometimes indispensable—not so severely applied as to excite the animal to resistance, but to convince him that we have the power to enforce submission. Few, it may almost be said, no horses, are naturally vicious. It is cruel usage which has first provoked resistance. That resistance has been followed by greater severity, and the stubbornness of the animal has increased. Open warfare has ensued, in which the man has seldom gained advantage, and the horse has been frequently rendered unserviceable. Correction may, or must be used, to enforce implicit obedience after the education has proceeded to a certain extent, but the early lessons should be inculcated with kindness alone. Young colts are sometimes very perverse. Many days will occasionally pass before they will permit the bridle to be put on, or the saddle to be worn; and one act of harshness will double or treble this time; patience and kindness, however, will always prevail. On some morning, when he is in a better humor than usual, the bridle may be put on, or the saddle may be worn; and, this compliance being followed by kindness and soothing on the part of the breaker, and no inconvenience or pain being suffered by the animal, all resistance will be at an end.

The same principles will apply to the breaking-in of the horse for the road or the chase. The handling, and some portion of instruction, should commence from the time of weaning. The future tractability of the horse will much depend on this. At two years and a half, or three years, the regular process of breaking-in should commence. If it is delayed until the animal is four years old, his strength and obstinacy will be more difficult to overcome. The plan usually pursued by the breaker cannot perhaps be much improved, except that there should be much more kindness and patience, and far less harshness and cruelty, than these persons are accustomed to exhibit, and a great deal more attention to the form and natural action of the horse. A headstall is put on the colt, and a cavesson (or apparatus to confine and pinch the nose) affixed to it, with long reins. He is first accustomed to the rein, then led round a ring on soft ground, and at length mounted and taught his paces. Next to preserving the temper and docility of the horse, there is nothing of so much importance as to teach him every pace, and every part of his duty, distinctly and thoroughly. Each must constitute a separate and sometimes long-continued lesson, and that taught by a man who will never suffer his passion to get the better of his discretion.

After the cavesson has been attached to the headstall, and the long reins put on, the colt should be quietly led about by the breaker—a steady boy following behind, by occasional threatening with the whip, but never by an actual blow, to keep him moving. When the animal follows readily and quietly, he may be taken to the ring, and walked round, right and left, in a very small circle. Care should be taken to teach him this pace thoroughly, never suffering him to break into a trot. The boy with his whip may here again be necessary, but not a single blow should actually fall.

Becoming tolerably perfect in the walk, he should be quickened to a trot, and kept steadily at it; the whip of the boy, if needful, urging him on, and the cavesson restraining him. These lessons should be short. The pace should be kept perfect, and distinct in each; and docility and improvement rewarded with frequent caresses, and handfuls of corn. The length of the rein may now be gradually increased, and the pace quickened, and the time extended, until the animal becomes tractable in these his first lessons, toward the conclusion of which, crupper-straps, or something similar, may be attached to the clothing. These, playing about the sides and flanks, accustom him to the flapping of the coat of the rider. The annoyance which they occasion will pass over in a day or two; for when the animal finds that no harm comes to him, he will cease to regard them.

Bitting.—Next comes the bitting. The bits should be large and smooth, and the reins buckled to a ring on either side of the pad. There are many curious and expensive machines for this purpose, but the simple rein will be quite sufficient. It should at first be slack, and then very gradually tightened. This will prepare for the more perfect manner in which the head will be afterward got into its proper position, when the colt is accustomed to the saddle. Occasionally the breaker should stand in front of the colt, and take hold of each side rein near to the mouth, and press upon it, and thus begin to teach him to stop and to back on the pressure of the rein, rewarding every act of docility, and not being too eager to punish occasional carelessness or waywardness.

Shying.—The colt may now be taken into the road or street, to be gradually accustomed to the objects among which his services will be required. Here, from fear or playfulness, a considerable degree of starting and shying may be exhibited. As little notice as possible should be taken of it. The same or a similar object should be soon passed again, but at a greater distance. If the colt still shies, let the distance be still farther increased until he takes no notice of the object. Then he may be gradually brought nearer to it, and this will be usually effected without the slightest difficulty: whereas, had there been an attempt to force him close to it in the first instance, the remembrance of the contest would have been associated with every appearance of the object, and the habit of shying would have been established.

Use of the Whip.—Hitherto, with a cool and patient breaker, the whip may have been shown, but will scarcely have been used; the colt must now, however, be accustomed to this necessary instrument of authority. Let the breaker walk by the side of the animal, and throw his right arm over his back, holding the reins in his left, occasionally quickening his pace, and at the moment of doing this, tapping the horse with the whip in his right hand, and at first very gently. The tap of the whip and the quickening of the pace will soon become associated in the mind of the animal. If necessary, these reminders may gradually fall a little heavier, and the feeling of pain be the monitor of the necessity of increased exertion. The lessons of reining-in and stopping, and backing on the pressure of the bit, may continue to be practiced at the same time.

Use to the Saddle.—He may now be taught to bear the saddle. Some little caution will be necessary at the first putting of it on. The breaker should stand at the head of the colt, patting him and engaging his attention, while one assistant on the offside gently places the saddle on the back of the animal, and another on the near side slowly tightens the girths. If he submits quietly to this, as he generally will when the previous process of breaking-in has been properly conducted, the ceremony of mounting may be attempted on the following or on the third day. The breaker will need two assistants in order to accomplish this. He will remain at the head of the colt, patting and making much of him. The rider will put his foot into the stirrup and bear a little weight upon it, while the man on the off side presses equally on the other stirrup-leather; and according to the docility of the animal, he should gradually increase the weight until he balances himself on the stirrup. If the colt is uneasy or fearful, he should be spoken kindly to and patted, or a mouthful of grain be given to him; but if he offers serious resistance, the lessons must terminate for that day. He may probably be in better humor on the morrow.

When the rider has balanced himself for a minute or two, he may gently throw his leg over and quietly seat himself in the saddle. The breaker will then lead the animal round the ring, the rider sitting perfectly still. After a few minutes he will take the reins and handle them as gently as possible, and guide the horse by the pressure of them, patting him frequently, and especially when he thinks of dismounting; and, after having dismounted, offering him a little grain or green feed. The use of the rein in checking him, and of the pressure of the leg and the touch of the heel in quickening his pace, will soon be taught, and his education will be nearly completed.

Kindness united with Firmness.—The horse having thus far submitted himself to the breaker, these pattings and rewards must be gradually diminished, and implicit obedience mildly but firmly enforced. Severity will not often be necessary. In the great majority of cases it will be altogether uncalled for: but should the animal in a moment of waywardness dispute the command of the breaker, he must at once be taught that he is the slave of man, and that we have the power, by other means than those of kindness, to bend him to our will. The education of the horse should be that of the child. Pleasure is as much as possible associated with the early lessons, but firmness, or if need be, coercion, must establish the habit of obedience. Tyranny and cruelty will more speedily in the horse than even in the child, provoke the wish to disobey and, on every practicable occasion, the resistance to command. The restive and vicious horse is, in ninety-nine cases out of a hundred, made so by ill-usage and not by nature. None but those who will take the trouble to make the experiment are aware how absolute a command the due admixture of firmness and kindness will soon give us over any horse.

THE ART OF HORSE-TAMING, AS PRACTICED BY WILLIAM AND JOHN S. RAREY.

The great success which has attended the system of training horses, as practiced by the Rarey brothers, induces us to publish their system; and to illustrate it with appropriate engravings.* Their success is certainly wonderful. The system which they follow is, at once humane, rational and philosophical; and we earnestly commend its adoption to all who manage horses not only, but all the other domestic animals.

As evidence of Mr. Rarey's success in England, we copy the following instances from the *London Review*.

---

*For the illustrations of the "Rarey system," we are under obligations to the *Rural New-Yorker*, and which it gives us pleasure to commend to the attention of our readers, as one of the most valuable family and agricultural journals published in this country. It has a wide circulation and well deserves it.

"Cruiser has been vicious from a foal, always troublesome to handle (we are using his owner's language), and showing temper on every opportunity. He would kneel in the street, and tear the ground with his teeth in his paroxysms of rage.—He would lean against the wall of his box, and kick and scream for ten minutes together; and he was returned from stables in which he had been placed, because his savage propensities rendered the care of him too dangerous an office for any man. For days, he would allow no one to enter his box; and on one occasion, tore an iron bar, one inch thick, in two with his teeth. Such an animal was not a very promising subject to operate upon; but Mr. Rarey undertook his cure. He first subjugated a two-year-old filley perfectly unbroken, in half an hour—riding her—opening an umbrella, beating a drum upon her, &c. He then took Cruiser in hand, and, says Lord Dorchester, 'in three hours, Mr. Rarey and myself mounted him.' He had not been ridden for nearly three years, and was so vicious that it was impossible even to dress him; and it was necessary to keep him muzzled constantly. The following morning Mr. Rarey led him behind an open carriage, on his way to London."

Twice the creature flew at the tamer with a fierce cry, but he kept out of his reach behind a half-door; at last he grew a little kinder, and Mr. Rarey succeeded in tying his head to the rack. This sense of restraint, which he had not known for three years, maddened the horse, the blood-vessels of the head dilated, and his frenzy for nearly twenty minutes was such, that Lord Dorchester begged Mr. Rarey not to peril his life, and to think no more of the £100 bond, which he had given, to return him cured in three months. However, America was not daunted; and when the horse was slightly exhausted, he made his first effort, and by the end of three hours the evil spirit seemed to have departed. On the Monday following, Mr. Rarey opened his school. The "incurably savage" horse was there, and was gentle as a dove, before an audience of full three hundred; all of whom had heard of his vicious propensities. You could have heard a pin drop, when the American horse-tamer asked his four-legged pupil to *shake hands* with him, at the termination of a lecture, listened to with intense interest, by an exalted and delighted assembly of the noblest and fairest in the land. The Wednesday after Mr. Rarey rode the horse about London.

PRINCIPLES OF THE RAREY SYSTEM.—"*First*—That the horse is so constituted by nature that he will not offer resistance to any demand made of him which he fully comprehends, if made in a way consistent with the laws of his nature. *Second*—That he has no consciousness of his strength beyond his experience, and can be handled according to our will without force. *Third*—That we can, in compliance with the laws of his nature, by which he examines all things new to him, take any object, however frightful, around, over, or on him, that does not inflict pain, without causing him to fear."

The affectionate enthusiasm with which the horse is spoken of by Mr. Rarey in the paragraph annexed, copied from his work, would also seem to indicate that any thing but harsh means are used in his subjection. Mr. Rarey says:

"The horse, according to the best accounts we can gather, has been

FIG. 1. FIRST POSITION.

the constant servant of man for nearly four thousand years, ever rewarding him with his labor, and adding to his comfort in proportion to his skill and manner of using him; but being to those who govern him by brute force, and know nothing of the beauty and delight to be gained from the cultivation of his finer nature, a fretful, vicious, and often dangerous servant; while to the Arab, whose horse is the pride of his life, and who governs him by the law of kindness, we find him to be quite a different animal. The manner in which he is treated from a foal gives him an affection and attachment for his master not known in any other country. The Arab and his children, the mare and her foal, inhabit the tent together; and, although the colt and the mare's neck are often pillows for the children to roll upon, no accident ever occurs, the mare being as careful of the children as of the colt. Such is the mutual attachment between the horse and his master, that he will leave his companions at his master's call, ever glad to obey his voice. And when the Arab falls from his horse, and is unable to rise again, he will stand by him and neigh for assistance; and if he lies down to sleep, as fatigue sometimes compels him to do in the midst of the desert, his faithful steed will watch over him, and neigh to arouse him if man or beast approaches. The Arabs frequently teach their horses secret signs or signals, which they make use of on urgent occasions to call forth their utmost exertions."

Mr. Rarey places much stress upon the kindly tones of the human voice, manner of speaking, the words used, and finishes his philosophizing upon the subject by detailing a short sketch of an "Arab and his steed," in which he endeavors to show the entire comprehension possessed by the horse of the language addressed to him. We quote it entire: " A Bedouin named Jabal possessed a mare of great celebrity. Hassan Pasha, then governor of Damascus, wished to buy the animal, and repeatedly made the owner the most liberal offers, which Jabal steadily refused. The Pasha then had recourse to threats, but with no better success. At length, one Gafar, a Bedouin of another tribe, presented himself to the Pasha, and asked him what he would give the man who should make him master of Jabal's mare. 'I will fill his horse's

THE HORSE.

FIG. 2. TEACHING THE HORSE TO KNEEL.

nose-bag with gold,' replied Hassan. The result of this interview having gone abroad, Jabal became more watchful than ever, and always secured his mare at night with an iron chain, one end of which was fastened to his hind fetlock, whilst the other, after passing through the tent-cloth, was attached to a picket driven in the ground under the felt that served himself and his wife for a bed. But one midnight Gafar crept silently into the tent, and succeeded in loosening the chain. Just before starting off with his prize, he caught up Jabal's lance, and, poking him with the butt end, cried out, 'I am Gafar; I have stolen your noble mare, and will give you notice in time.' This warning was in accordance with the customs of the desert, for to rob a hostile tribe is considered an honorable exploit, and the man who accomplishes it is desirous of all the glory that may flow from the deed. Poor Jabal, when he heard the words, rushed out of the tent, and gave the alarm; then, mounting his brother's mare, accompanied by some of his tribe, he pursued the robber for four hours. The brother's mare was of the same stock as Jabal's, but was not equal to her; nevertheless, he outstripped those of all the other pursuers, and was even on the point of overtaking the robber, when Jabal shouted to him, 'Pinch her right ear, and give her a touch of the heel.' Gafar did so, and away went the mare like lightning, speedily rendering further pursuit hopeless.

"The pinch in the ear and the touch with the heel were the secret signs by which Jabal had been used to urge his mare to her utmost speed. Jabal's companions were amazed and indignant at his strange conduct. 'O, thou father of a jackass!' they cried, 'thou hast enabled the thief to rob thee of thy jewel.' But he silenced their upbraidings by saying, 'I would rather lose her than sully her reputation. Would you have me suffer it to be said among the tribe, that another mare had proved fleeter than mine? I have at least this comfort left me, that I can say she never met with her match.'"

When you enter the stable, in which is the horse to be experimented upon, stand still for a short time and let the horse observe you, and as soon as he stands quiet advance slowly, upon the left or near side, on a line with the shoulder, your right hand hanging by your side—

DOMESTIC ANIMALS.

FIG. 3. THE HORSE IN A KNEELING POSTURE PREPARATORY TO LYING DOWN.

the left bent at the elbow, with the hand projecting. As you move forward go not too much toward his head or croup, so as not to make him move either forward or backward, thus keeping your horse stationary; if he does move a little either forward or backward, step a little to the right or left very cautiously; this will keep him in the right place. When almost in contact stand motionless for a second or two, giving the animal another opportunity to survey you, then, speaking in a soothing tone, place the hand lightly upon the shoulder, working up toward the neck, stroking in the direction in which the hair lies, down the side and front of the face to the nostrils. When the nose is reached suffer the hand to remain, that the horse may smell of it two or three times, and then as Mr. Rarey facetiously remarked, "you've got the animal." Now halter securely. Next in order, pass down the neck to the shoulder and onward to the fore-arm, when you must prevail upon the horse to lift the leg which is fastened in the manner described in our illustration, No. 1. A looped strap that can be slipped over the knee is the most expeditious. We will here remark that the floor should be liberally covered with straw (tan-bark or saw-dust is better), to prevent any injury resulting to the knees, and it would be well to apply knee-caps. While in this position, after letting him stand for a short period, buckle a strong surcingle around the horse, the surcingle having a loop upon it, (see fig. 2,) then fasten a strap around the fetlock of the off leg, passing the other extremity of the strap through the loop. When this portion of the business is completed you are ready for active operations.

The object now is, to back the horse about the stable until he is tired and evidently wishes to lie down, then compel him to move forward, and when the animal lifts the off foot for that purpose, draw upon the strap fastened around that leg, thus elevating it to a like position with its mate. The procedure is portrayed in our second engraving. Just as soon as this strap is drawn tightly, seize the halter close to the head and let the animal down easily upon his knees, as seen in fig. 3. This is a critical period, and the operator must possess coolness and energy to prevent disaster to himself or the animal. When the horse attempts to rise, pull his head around toward the shoulder and his demonstrations will prove futile. Bear your weight against his hips, and by voice and action endeavor to give him an idea of your wishes, continuing the movements as long as it is necessary, when he will

Fig. 4. LYING DOWN AND SUBDUED.

finally lie down. As soon as he is down (see fig. 4) and his struggling has ceased, caress his face and neck; handle every part of his body, making yourself familiar as possible. When in this position a short time, remove the straps, straighten out the limbs, fondle with him as much as you choose, and in fifteen or twenty minutes let him rise again to his feet. Repeat this operation, removing the straps as soon as he lies down, and in from two to five trials he is completely subdued—he will follow you like a dog, and you may take any liberties with him without a fear as to the result. If a thorough course of instruction is given—*and he must be educated; no boy's play about it*—he will seek the floor if you simply raise the fore-leg and give the command, " Lie down, sir."

We give the following rules for the guidance of any who may wish to practice, simply remarking that their *strict observance is imperative:*

First. The horse must not be forced down by violence, but must be tired out until he has a strong desire to lie down.

Second. He must be kept quiet on the ground until the expression of the eye shows that he is tranquilized, which invariably takes place by patiently waiting and gently patting the horse.

Third. Care must be taken not to throw the horse upon his neck when bent, as it may easily be broken.

Fourth. In backing him no violence must be used, or he may be forced on his haunches and his back broken.

Fifth. The halter and off rein are held in the left hand, so as to keep the head away from the latter; while, if the horse attempts to plunge, the halter is drawn tight, when, the off-leg being raised, the animal is brought on his knees, and rendered powerless for offensive purposes.

Catching the Colt.—If the colt is in the pasture, approach kindly and quietly, extending but one arm, and as you move toward him speak soothingly. If any difficulty is caused by his movements to avoid contact, keep the temper cool and persist in the effort to its completion, which cannot exceed a few minutes. If you rush after him with arms swinging, and hallooing, he fears bodily harm, and will exert his utmost strength to escape. This should not be—from first to last the presence of man should never be connected with the fear of injury.

Stabling the Colt.—Mr. Rarey calls stabling the most wary colt a ten minutes' job. Hitch a gentle horse by the stable door, and when all obstructions are removed, approach the colt on the opposite side quietly and slowly. To avoid you, he will move toward the horse and unsuspiciously enter the stable. The doorway is a novel thing to him—he possesses not the least idea of its purpose—he sees an opening and passes in to get away from those coming too near him, and the proximity of the trained horse insures his safety. Should he escape, patiently repeat the process. When secured, lead away the horse and give the colt a handful of grain.

General Rules.—As general rules for the various operations, Mr. Rarey recommends that the shed or stable used should be light, and high enough to admit of a man's riding around without danger to his head; that chickens, swine, and other animals be excluded, as serving to attract the attention of the horse; that on no account shall any person accompany the tamer, or be present at his operations, in order that the attention of the horse be not divided between two or more objects; that before entering the stable the tamer shall know accurately all the processes he intends to go through with the horse; and that sufficient time must be given the animal, at each stage of the proceedings, to fully comprehend what is being done, and what is wanted of him.

Putting on the Halter.—After your introduction to the colt, and by familiarity he has become at ease in your presence, you may proceed to halter him. A rope halter should never be used—one made of leather and properly fitted is the article needed. Approach him, and, after a few caresses, smoothing his head and neck without moving, fasten the end of the halter-strap about his neck. You stand at the left side of the colt. Laying your right arm across his neck, put, with your left hand, the long or buckle end of the upper part of your halter under his neck; hold it loosely with your right hand, and then loose your strap. Now you can lower the upper part; slip his nose into the appropriate place, and buckling the upper part, you have haltered your colt without in the least frightening him. Let him run around you, taking care never to check him roughly or draw him violently in any direction. Gradually approach him by shortening your hold upon the halter, until you can lay your hand upon his neck and again caress. When you have repeated this operation a few times, he will suffer you to reach his side without flying back or running away, and he is now ready for taking an advance step in his education.

Leading the Colt.—Up to this period the colt is ignorant of his strength, and it behooves the instructor to keep him so. If violence is resorted to—if the attempt to make him follow is instituted by pulling—he resists, and a battle commences. Stand a little on the near side, rub the nose and forehead, pull gently upon the strap, touching at the same time the hind-legs lightly with a whip, and he will start and advance a few steps. Repeat the operation several times, and he will soon learn to follow by gently pulling upon the halter.

Saddling and Bridling.—During the manipulations heretofore described, the mouth of the young colt should be frequently handled. Put a snaffle between his teeth, holding it with one hand while you caress him with the other. After a short time he will permit the bridle being placed upon him. The process of saddling is minutely described by Mr. Rarey, and we quote his remarks thereupon from the London papers. Mr. Rarey says:

"The first thing will be to tie each stirrup-strap into a loose knot, to make them short and prevent the stirrups from flying about and hitting him. Then double up the skirts and take the saddle under your right arm, so as not to frighten him with it as you approach. When you get to him, rub him gently a few times with your hand, and then raise the saddle very slowly, until he can see it, and smell and feel it with his nose. Then let the skirt loose, and rub it very gently against his neck the way the hair lies, letting him hear the rattle of the skirts as he feels them against him; each time getting a little further backward, and finally slipping it over his shoulders on his back. Shake it a little with your hand, and in less than five minutes you can rattle it about over his back as much as you please, and pull it off and throw it on again, without his paying much attention to it.

"As soon as you have accustomed him to the saddle, fasten the girth. Be careful how you do this. It often frightens the colt when he feels the girth binding him, and making the saddle fit tight on his back. You should bring up the girth very gently, and not draw it too tight at first, just enough to hold the saddle on. Move him a little, and then girth it as tight as you choose, and he will not mind it. You should see that the pad of your saddle is all right before you put it on, and that there is nothing to make it hurt him, or feel unpleasant to his back. It should not have any loose straps on the back part, to flap about and scare him.

"After you have saddled him in this way, take a switch in your right hand to tap him with, and walk about in the stable a few times with your right arm over your saddle, taking hold of the reins on each side of his neck with your right and left hands, thus marching him about in the stable until you teach him the use of the bridle, and can turn him in any direction, and stop him by a gentle pull of the rein. Always caress him, and loose the reins a little every time you stop him."

Mounting the Colt.—The weight of the arm in the saddle has accustomed him to a slight burden. Now get a block, or mounting-stool, about eighteen inches high, and place it at his side. Raise yourself very quietly upon the block, and when you have done so, loosen the stirrup-strap upon the rear side, place your foot in the stirrup, seize the off side of the saddle with the right hand, and cautiously bear your weight upon the stirrup and hand. After repeating this operation several times the colt learns there is nothing hurtful, and you must now lift yourself *very quietly* into the saddle. Once upon his back, speak gently to him, and if he does not move, pull the near rein a little and he will start. Repeat all the operations of getting on and off, and riding round, for a couple of hours.

The True Way to Bit a Colt.—The practice of placing a bitting harness upon a colt the first thing done with him, and buckling the bitting rein as tight as it can be drawn, as is frequently the case, meets the severe and just condemnation of Mr. Rarey. This is one of the most cruel punishments that can be inflicted upon a colt, and to one that is in the habit of carrying the head low, cannot fail of proving injurious. A horse should be well accustomed to the bit before you put on the bitting harness, and when you first bit him you should only rein his head up to that point where he naturally holds it, let that be high or low; he will soon learn that he cannot lower his head, and that raising it a little will loosen the bit in his mouth. This will give him the idea of raising his head to loosen the bit, and then you can draw the bitting a little tighter every time you put it on, and he will still raise his head to loosen it. By this means you will gradually get his head and neck in the position you wish him to carry it, and give him a graceful carriage without hurting him, making him angry, or causing his mouth to get sore.

Putting on the Harness.—The first requisite is a harness that will fit, and a little attention to this will facilitate matters very much. The collar needs special care, as hundreds of horses have been spoiled by those the chief features of which were defects. Take the harness into the stable, and go through the same process as with the saddle, letting the colt examine it as much as he desires; then put it on with care. When the operation is completed, put on the lines, using them gently, as the touch, if he is skittish, will startle him. Lead him back and forth until the fitting of the harness causes no disquietude, then take hold of the end of the traces, pulling slightly at first, and finally hitch him to whatever you wish him to pull.

To Hitch up the Colt.—As the colt has never paid any particular attention to a buggy or carriage, and does not know its uses, great caution must be observed on his introduction. Lead him gently to it; let him examine it in his own way—by sight, smell, and the exercise of the sense of feeling—and lead him all around it. Presently he will cease to notice it. Now draw the shafts to the left, and place him before the buggy. One man stands at his head. The other, at his right side, gently lifts the shafts, keeping one hand the while upon the colt's back, and drops the shafts on either side. They must not touch him as they are brought down. It is a nice job, and must be performed very deliberately. When you once have him between the shafts, shake them, so that he may not only hear but feel them against him. At first he is a little touchy. When he no longer minds them, you can fasten him up; and while the man at his head slowly leads him along, you work behind, get the lines over his back (which must be carefully done), and get in. Then you must not let him go faster than a walk. This Mr. Rarey insists upon, saying that the horse cannot at first comprehend the multifarious arrangements to which he is hitched, and if hurried is confused. If the horse is very wild, or attempts to kick, Mr. Rarey ties up one foot as seen in our illustration (fig. 1).

We have thus gone through the mode of training an unbroken colt to the saddle and harness, and to perfect docility, and shall now briefly treat of some other matters pertinent to the subject under consideration.

Blinkers on Horses.—Though not directly connected with the process of horse-taming, we cannot refrain from giving the opinions of Mr. Rarey upon the use of "blinkers." These we have long considered not only a useless appendage to the harness, but, in a greater or less degree, deleterious—affecting the sight—and have hailed, with gratified feelings, the slight movement that has been made in this country to dispose of them. Mr. Rarey says:

"I take great pleasure in stating that all my experience with and observation of horses proves clearly to me that blinkers should not be used, and that the sight of the horse, for many reasons, should not be interfered with in any way. Horses are only fearful of objects which they do not understand, or are not familiar with, and the eye is one of the principal mediums by which this understanding and this familiarity are brought about.

"The horse, on account of his very amiable nature, can be made, in the course of time, to bear almost any thing in any shape; but there is a quicker process of reaching his intelligence than that of wearing it into him through his skin and bones; and he, however wild or nervous, can be taught in a very short time to understand and not to fear any object, however frightful in appearance. Horses can be broken in less time and better without blinkers; but horses that have always worn them will notice the sudden change, and must be treated carefully the first drive. After that, they will drive better without the blinkers than with them.

"I have proved, by my own experiments, that a horse broken without blinkers can be driven past any omnibus, cab, or carriage, on a parallel line as close as it is possible for him to go, without ever wavering or showing any disposition to dodge. I have not in the last eight or ten years, constantly handling horses both wild and nervous, ever put blinkers on any of them, and in no case have I ever had one that was afraid of the carriage he drew behind him or of those he passed in the streets.

"The horse's eye is the life and beauty of the animal, as well as the index of all his emotions. It tells the driver, in the most impressive characters, what the horse's feelings are. By it he can tell the first approach of fear in time to meet any difficulty; he can tell if he is happy or sad, hungry or weary. The horse, too, when permitted to see, uses his eyes with great judgment. He sees better than we do. He can measure distances with his eyes better than we can, and, if allowed free use of them, would often save himself, by the quickness of his sight, from collisions, when the driver would fail to do so by a timely pull of the reins. It would also save many accidents to pedestrians in the streets, as no horse will run on to any person that he can see. * * * I have yet to find the man who, having once left them off, could ever be persuaded to put them on again. They are an unnecessary and injurious incumbrance to the horse, and I feel confident, if the cabmen of London will leave them off for one year, that blinkers on cab-horses will never be seen again in the streets, and will only be a thing to be read of as one of the follies happily reformed in the nineteenth century."

To Drive a Kicking Horse.—Bend up the near fore-foot (see fig. 1, first position), then draw a loop over the knee and up to the pastern joint, and secure it there. The horse cannot kick while standing on three legs, and there is this further advantage, handling in this plight conquers immediately. Sometimes he gets very angry, strikes the knee on the ground, and otherwise endeavors to get the knee loose. You can sit down and look at him at your ease till he gives up. When this takes place, let down the horse's foot, rub his leg, and caress him; let him rest a little, and then put the foot up again. Repeat this several times, till the horse has learned to walk on three legs. You then put the horse into a sulky. Having his foot hitched up, he cannot kick, howsoever much he may desire to; nor can he run away, if ever so much inclined. Mr. Rarey's theory is, that a horse kicks because he is afraid of something behind him, or of the man or other object approaching him. And he first incapacitates him from kicking, and then accustoms him to whatever he was before in fear of, be this a rattling vehicle, or a man's hand on his heels. A very few hours' time suffices to accomplish this taming of the most vicious brute.

About Balky Horses.—Mr. Rarey asserts that the horse knows nothing naturally about balking—and that the animal which practices any of the various freaks known under this name, does so either because bad management has led him into bad habits, or because, though willing to obey, he does not comprehend what his master desires of him. In all these cases, therefore, he maintains that the whip and the loud angry voice are entirely out of place, and only make bad worse. If the horse balks he is excited. The first thing, therefore, is to go to his head, speak to him kindly, pat and smooth him, and thus get him quieted down. The whip must not be shown at all. When he is calmed you can start your team. It is not a sudden jerk against the collar which moves the load, but a steady pressure. All kinds of violence, therefore, tend to the wrong course. The object is to start the horses even; and as the balky horse generally plunges first, you are to keep him back gently till they can both take the strain together. A quick way to accomplish this—but not the surest way, Mr. Rarey says—"is one I have myself seen practiced in Ohio. This is, to lift one fore-foot of the balky horse, and start the team. As he presses forward, you let him have his foot, when he will almost always take the strain with his mate." A better way, according to Mr. Rarey, is to let the lines hang quite slack, get the horses calmed down, and then stand in front of them, and turn them gently to the right without letting them bring a strain upon the traces. From this turn them as gently to the left. By this time they will be moving in unison, and, as you turn them again to the right, steady them in the collar, and they will go off together easily. If you are patient and careful, you can make any horse pull true by this management.

STABLE MANAGEMENT.—The first thing of importance in the treatment of a horse is the building which is provided for him, or his stable. Perhaps the best way of treating the subject is to show what his stable ought not to be, and that, unfortunately both for the animal and his owner, will be to show what it too generally is.

In the first place, it ought not to be dark; and in this respect there are but too many proprietors of horses who will, in their practice at any rate, be at issue with us, though the total or partial blindness of their horses should have taught them better; for from this cause in general springs the blindness of the animal, which, by nature, is no more predisposed to blindness than is his owner. And not only does a dark stable affect the sight of a horse, but his general health also, especially, as is often the case, if he be immured in his stable for days together. Light is just as essential to a healthy condition as food itself, and an animal can no more thrive without the one than the other. The man who invented dark stables was no doubt the progenitor of him who invented the barbarous practice of docking and nicking horses' tails.

The next thing to be considered is ventilation; and this—as stables are commonly ventilated, or rather not ventilated—is believed to be of no moment whatever. In many old country stables we find the door made of two portions, the upper one opening whilst the lower one is made fast. This is very well for farm stables; but this construction is not adapted for those where horses of the higher class are kept. With a door of this description, open at the top, and a lofty window at the other end, open at the top also, a draught takes place which is above the horse's back, and will ventilate the stable thoroughly, especially if the stable be lofty, as it always should be, though it is in general constructed so as to have a hay-loft over it—a great convenience, no doubt —but one which should not be permitted to reduce the height of the stable itself to some seven or eight feet; in which circumscribed space a team of horses are often confined for the night, under the necessity of breathing the same air as they have expired. To expect horses to be healthy or sound under such a condition is to expect an impossibility.

Ventilation.—A little consideration will show the importance of perfect ventilation. The air which the horse expires is as totally different a substance from that which he inhales as wood is from iron. He inhales atmospheric air, and the constituents of this pass through his lungs, and into his blood; he expires carbonic acid gas, one of the gases most inimical to animal life, as any man may convince himself who will go down into an old unused well. If this deadly gas be not carried off by proper ventilation, it becomes mixed with the atmospheric air of the stable, and is again inhaled, to the great injury of the animal's health. The greatest care is also requisite that it should be thoroughly carried off, and this can only be done as it comes out from the animal's body; when cold, it is heavier than atmospheric air, and sinks to the floor of the stable, in which case it is not so easily got rid of, but may lay the foundation of diseases innumerable, and will certainly shorten the usefulness, if not the life, of the animal. From this, as much as from any other cause, horses may truly be said not to live out half their days.

A thorough ventilation is as necessary in the winter as the summer, and there is infinitely less risk of injuring the horse by cold than by allowing him to breathe expired air over again. If accustomed to proper ventilation, he will never take cold from any judicious means adopted to promote his health and comfort. Pure air in winter is as necessary as in summer; whilst in the summer the more that can be admitted to cool the stable the better. The building should, then, be so constructed, as in summer to admit the greatest possible quantity of cool air, and in winter to admit sufficient for the preservation of the purity of the atmosphere, without running any risk from cold draughts. Care must also be taken not to admit draughts of air near the horse's heels, or diseased legs will be the result. Draughts cannot be too carefully guarded against, nor is it requisite that such should occur, if a little forethought only be exercised. Some writers on the subject advocate a chimney-shaft to be erected in the stable, by which the foul air can best escape, and also the admission of fresh air over the animal's head by means of perforated zinc.

Cleanliness.—The next consideration, and it is not less important than either of the preceding, is that of cleanliness. Too many persons believe, or they act as so believing, that the more a horse stands and sleeps among the filth of his own litter, the more he thrives. This is an error of ignorance or of idleness, perhaps both combined. The effect of it at any rate is to make the animal, in addition to breathing his own breath again, inhale the fetid ammoniacal steams which arise from his own ordure and urine. We have even heard farmers defend this mode, on the ground that the manure is better, as though the manure were worth any thing in comparison with the horse.

The Stable Floor.—A brick or stone stable floor is the best; if the latter, the stone should be roughened with small furrows, and in either case a deep drain sunk outside of the stable is necessary for keeping it perfectly dry, without which either brick or stone floors will be prejudicial from damp. This is of the utmost importance. Neither should such drains be used to carry off the urine. The floor should slope an inch to a yard, but only to the gutter which carries off the urine. Indeed, if this is carried off by an iron pipe with suitable openings, so much the better. A tub sunk outside the stable as a receptacle for the urine, will soon amply repay the farmer for his trouble; it is too valuable to be permitted to diffuse itself over the dung-heap in the yard, to be washed away by the first shower of rain.

Litter should always be allowed for a horse to stale upon, as it is easily removed, and a little gypsum thrown down occasionally will keep the stable free from smells. Nothing can be more offensive to either horse or man than the smell of putrid urine, whilst if this be permitted to run into a proper receptacle, and a little sulphuric acid added occasionally, nothing can exceed its value as a manure, which the farmer should be as careful to preserve as he is the corn which it fertilizes.

Within reason, the more room a horse has in his stall the less liable will he be to swollen legs. In no instance ought he to have less room than six feet, and if ten can be afforded him, so much the more will he thrive, the comfort being especially felt after a hard day's work. Loose boxes are indispensable to horses of value.

A perfect stable should never have a hay-loft over it. This of course will give a little more trouble to the stable-man, but where the comfort of a horse is concerned, that is of no consequence whatever. A deep manger with two or three iron bars across is far preferable to a rack or well for the reception of hay, and will more effectually prevent waste. An arrangement for water should also be provided. The front must of-course be boarded up, with the exception of the part from which the horse eats. The advantage of this arrangement would be, that all the hay would be eaten, and not pulled down, as is generally the case, and trodden underfoot amongst the litter. Much hay will be saved by the use of a deep manger as a substitute for a rack; and an equal saving would take place in grain if the manger were made to slope slightly inward instead of outward, as is usually the case. It would exceedingly puzzle a wasteful or mischievous horse to throw his corn out of such a manger if deep enough; but for this the manger as usually constructed affords him every facility.

Dung never ought to be allowed to be swept up in a corner, as is frequently the case, and all wet litter should be removed. In short, the more pains that are taken relative to a horse's comfort in a stable, the more will he repay those pains; and the farmer especially can have no better assurance that the more the horses thrive, the more will he himself thrive. The very fact of his attention to his horses independently of the more effective work arising therefrom, will beget a similar habit of attention to every thing else.

THE HORSE'S FOOD.—This should be oats and hay of the best quality; beans for hard-working horses occasionally varied with carrots or Swedes, bran mashes, and under some circumstances linseed gruel. Many persons are not aware that the price of musty grain and bad hay is vastly dearer than that of the same commodities of good quality, and that the worse the quality the higher the cost. It is so nevertheless, for whether the purchaser of inferior articles bargain for it or not, he always purchases with them indigestion, foulness of blood, looseness of the bowels, general debility, and glanders, all of these being too costly to be purchased into any stable. We once knew a farmer whose practice it was to sell all his best articles and keep the refuse of the farm for his own horses; the consequence was, that he never was without glanders or some other disease in his stable; and there was not a carter in the parish who did not give his team a wide berth wherever he met it with his own horses. It was the man's system, nevertheless, and he either could not see its banefulness or he would not alter it; so he died at last from it, having caught a glanderous infection from his own stable. Mr. Spooner, in speaking of this subject, thus testifies his own experience : " I have known a serious loss sustained by a proprietor of post and coach horses, from keeping a considerable stock of oats and neglecting to turn them; many horses became glandered and farcied, apparently in consequence of this circumstance."

Whole or Bruised Grain.—Much has been said of late respecting the advantage of bruising oats, and various machines are much in vogue for the purpose. Mr. Spooner says of them, "they are apt to produce diarrhœa, especially if the animal is worked hard." It is further alleged that many horses will not eat them with an appetite, and the opponents to the system go further, urging that unbruised oats excite a flow of saliva necessary to perfect digestion, which is not the case with those which are bruised. The explanation to the first of these questions supplies a very strong recommendation. The stomach having derived a sufficient quantity of nourishment from a moderate portion does not require more. With reference to the flow of the saliva, without entering upon the question how far it is necessary to assist digestion, no animal can swallow its food without a sufficiency of saliva to assist the act of deglutition; and it is not recommended to reduce the oats to flour, but merely to bruise them. Many persons fancy that by giving oats in small quantities and spreading them thinly over the manger the horses will be induced to masticate them. Those who have watched their operations will find that a greedy-feeding horse will drive his corn up into a heap, and collect with his lips as much as he thinks proper for a mouthful.

Little if any advantage arises from cutting hay into chaff, especially for the most valuable kind of horses. It is done in cart stables to prevent waste, which is often enormous in those departments where horses are permitted to pull the hay out of their racks and tread it underfoot.

The state of perfection to which the higher classes of the horse have been brought in this country, is attributable to the great attention devoted during a long period of time to the selection of the best descriptions for the purpose of perpetuating the species; the treatment they have received under the influence of a propitious climate, and the nature of the food with which they have been supplied; greater improvements are capable of being realized by judicious management.

Value of Different Kinds of Food.—Professor Playfair, who has made experiments on the quantity of nutritious matter contained in different kinds of food supplied to animals, found that in one hundred lbs. of oats, eleven lbs. represent the quantity of gluten wherewith flesh is formed, and that an equal weight of hay affords eight lbs. of similar substance. Both hay and oats contain about sixty-eight per cent. of unazotized matter identical with fat, of which it must be observed a vast portion passes off from the animal without being deposited. By this calculation, it appears that if a horse consumes daily four feeds of oats and ten lbs. of hay, the nutriment which he derives will be equivalent to about one lb. eleven oz. of muscle, and thirteen and a half lbs. of superfluous matter, which, exclusively of water, nearly approximates the exhaustion of the system by perspiration and the various evacuations.

Oats have been selected as that portion of the food which is to afford the principal nourishment. They contain seven hundred and forty-three parts out of a thousand of the nutritive matter. They should be about or somewhat less than a year old—heavy, dry and sweet. New oats will weigh ten or fifteen per cent. more than old ones, but the difference consists principally in watery matter, which is gradually evaporated. New oats are not so readily ground down by the teeth as old ones. They form a more glutinous mass, difficult to digest, and when eaten in considerable quantities are apt to occasion colic, or even staggers.

Barley is a common food of the horse on various parts of the Continent, and, until the introduction of the oat, seems to have constituted almost his only food. It is more nutritious than oats, containing nine hundred and twenty parts of nutritive matter in every thousand. There seems, however, to be something necessary besides a great proportion of nutritive matter, in order to render any substance strengthening, wholesome, or fattening; therefore it is that in many horses that are hardly worked, and indeed, in horses generally, barley does not agree with them so well as oats. They are occasionally subject to inflammatory complaints, and particularly to surfeit and mange.

When barley is given, the quantity should not exceed a peck daily. It should always be bruised, and the chaff should consist of equal quantities of hay and barley-straw, and not cut too short. If the farmer has a quantity of spotted or unsalable barley that he wishes thus to get rid of, he must very gradually accustom his horses to it, or he will probably produce serious illness among them. For horses that are recovering from illness, barley in the form of malt is often serviceable as tempting the appetite and recruiting the strength. It is best given in mashes—water considerably below the boiling heat being poured upon it, and the vessel or pail kept covered for half an hour.

The Swedish Turnip is an article of food the value of which has not been sufficiently appreciated, and particularly for agricultural horses. Although it is far from containing the quantity of nutritive matter which has been supposed, that which it has seems to be capable of easy and complete digestion. It should be sliced with chopped straw, and without hay. It quickly fattens the horse and produces a smooth glossy coat and a loose skin. It will be a good practice to give it once a day, and that at night when the work is done.

Carrots.—The virtues of this root are not sufficiently known, whether as contributing to the strength and endurance of the sound horse, or the rapid recovery of the sick one. To the healthy horse they should be given sliced in his chaff. Half a bushel will be a fair daily allowance. There is little provender of which the horse is fonder. The following account of the value of the carrot is not exaggerated: "This root is held in much esteem. There is none better, nor perhaps so good. When first given, it is slightly diuretic and laxative; but as the horse becomes accustomed to it, these effects cease to be produced. They also improve the state of the skin."

Potatoes have been given, and with advantage, in their raw state sliced with chaff; but where it has been convenient to boil or steam them, the benefit has been far more evident. Purging has then rarely ensued. Some have given boiled potatoes alone; and horses, instead of rejecting them, have soon preferred them even to the oat; but it is better to mix them with the usual manger feed, in the proportion of one pound of potatoes to two and a half pounds of the other ingredients. The use of the potato must depend on its cheapness and the facility for boiling it. Half a dozen horses would soon repay the expense of a steaming boiler in the saving of provender, without taking into the account their improved condition and capability for work.* A horse fed on potatoes should have his quantity of water materially curtailed.

---

* Professor Low says that fifteen pounds of potatoes yield as much nourishment as four pounds and a half of oats. You Thayer asserts that three bushels are equal to one hundred and twelve pounds of hay; and Curwen, who tried potatoes extensively in the feeding of horses, says that an acre goes as far as four acres of hay.

Effect on the Offspring.—It is now generally known that the embryo offspring partakes of the health or condition of the dam, therefore the food with which the mother is supplied must affect the foal. This is a subject too commonly disregarded by breeders, although it is constantly demonstrated after the foal comes into life. If a mare be supplied with food which produces relaxation, her foal will be in the same state; and constipation is recognized in a similar manner. The propriety of supplying a brood-mare with the best and most suitable kinds of food during pregnancy cannot be too strongly impressed. In the management of young stock every effort should be made, by giving them food which is adapted to the purpose, to bring them to maturity as early as possible; by these means the texture and development of the bones, the sinews, and the muscles is greatly accelerated. The constitution of each animal must be consulted, and it is highly important, if the acme of condition is to be attained by animals when they arrive at an age of maturity, that the growth and gradual development of their frames should be composed of those healthy and invigorating materials, upon which the structure of condition can be raised. To accomplish this, hay, oats, and occasionally beans, must form the principal items of food, and grass should be provided only in limited supplies during the summer months.

Grass, it may be observed, loses two-thirds of its weight, and a still greater proportion of bulk, when converted into hay; but that extraneous matter consists of moisture, possessing no portion of fibrine, consequently it contains none of those elements which increase muscular development. If a horse be supported upon grass alone, he must eat a vast quantity—equal to more than three times the proportion of hay—to derive an equivalent amount of nourishment; being very full of sap and moisture, it is quickly digested; consequently, the animal must be continually devouring it. This distends the stomach and bowels, and impairs the faculty of digestion; for the digestive powers require rest, as well as the other organs of the body, if they are to be preserved in a healthy state. The muscular system is debilitated, and fat accumulates; flatulent colic or gripes is produced, which not unfrequently becomes constitutional. Nothing can be more erroneous than the antiquated impression, that the purgative properties of young grass in the spring are conducive to the healthy state of the horse. When the *modus operandi* of that description of food is explained, the supposition of its being calculated to produce beneficial effects must vanish. The young green herbage is extensively overcharged with sap and moisture, of a crude, acrimonious nature, and it exists so abundantly, that a considerable portion of it cannot be taken up by the organs destined for the secretion of urine, or by the absorbent vessels of the body; a great quantity of this superfluous fluid, therefore, passes into the intestines, and is thus discharged in a watery state. But the mischief does not terminate immediately on the subsiding of the purgative action; the absorbent vessels, having been overloaded, become distended and relaxed, and some time intervenes before they resume their healthy tone, under the most judicious treatment. This is clearly exemplified by the habitual tendency which many horses exhibit of having swelled legs. When this evil exists, any persons who entertain a doubt as to the primary cause may readily convince themselves, by investigating the course of treatment to which the animal has been subjected. Horses which are reared on wet, marshy land are invariably afflicted with this relaxed condition of the absorbent vessels of the legs. Constant supplies of green succulent food render the defects constitutional, and the most scientific stable management is often frustrated when such animals are required to perform ordinary labor; their legs fail, not from anatomical defects, but from the cause explained, which operates injuriously upon a structure which is naturally perfect.

Superficial judges of horses do not mark the difference between the appearances of a fat and a muscular-formed animal. If the bones are covered, the points filled out, and the general contour looks pleasing to the eye, they conceive that every requisite is accomplished. A more fallacious impression cannot exist. A horse of very moderate pretensions, if in perfect condition, will prove himself infinitely superior in the quality of endurance or capability to perform work, than one of a higher character which is not in condition. If two horses are ridden side by side, at the moderate pace of seven or eight miles in the hour, on a warm day, in the summer, one of which has been taken out of a grass field, and the other fed on hay and grain, the difference will be very soon detected. The grass-fed horse will perspire profusely, yet the other will be cool and dry. This propensity to perspire likewise proves that the system of the former is replete with adipose deposit, and fluids destined to produce that substance ; an unnecessary encumbrance, and in such quantities opposed to freedom of action.

Under an impression that an abundance of luxuriant grass will increase the flow of milk, it is frequently given to brood mares, but if it has the effect of producing relaxation, it is exceedingly prejudicial. A moderate portion of good milk is far preferable to that which is weak and poor. Thorough-bred mares are not unfrequently deficient in their lacteal secretions, more so than those of a common description. It is obviously necessary that either class should be supplied with good and nutritious food for the purpose of augmenting it when insufficient, but the nature of the food requires to be regulated by the constitution of the individual.

A mistaken notion of economy frequently induces persons to turn their horses into the grass fields during the summer months. A few words may serve to dispel that delusion. Twenty-two bushels of oats, allowing one bushel per week, which is sufficient for young stock or horses not in work, from the 15th of May to the 16th of October, may be estimated as the produce of a trifle more than half an acre of land. From ten to twelve hundred weight of hay may be estimated as the produce of another half-acre, although a ton and a half per acre, is not more than an average crop on land in good condition. It will require an acre of grass land, capable of producing a ton and a half of hay, to support a horse during the above-named period. When the relative value of a horse which has been kept on hay and grain, is compared with that of one which has been grazed, the verdict will be considerably against the latter.

A simple but invaluable appendage to the cart-stable is *the nose-bag*. In order that the lungs of the horse may have their full play, and especially that the speed of the horse may not be impeded, an exceedingly small stomach was given to him. It is, consequently, soon emptied of food, and hunger, and languor, and indisposition, and inability to work, speedily succeed. At length food is set before him; he falls ravenously upon it; he swallows it faster than his contracted stomach can digest it; the stomach becomes overloaded; he cannot, from the peculiar construction of that organ, get rid of the load by vomiting, and the stomach, or some of the vessels of the brain, becomes ruptured, and the animal dies. The farmer attributes this to an unknown or accidental cause, and dreams not that it is, in the great majority of cases, to be traced to voracious feeding after hard work and long fasting. The nose-bag is a simple but a kind contrivance, and an effectual preventive. No cart-horse on a journey of more than four or five hours, should be suffered to leave the farmer's yard without it.

A very slight inspection of the animal will always enable the owner to determine whether he is too well fed or not sufficiently fed. The size of the horse, and the nature of the work, and the season of the year, will make considerable difference in the quantity and the quality of the food. The following accounts will sufficiently elucidate the general custom:—"Mr. Harper, of Bank Hall, Lancashire, plows seven acres per week, the year through, on strong land, with a team of three horses, and allows to each weekly two bushels of oats, with hay, during the winter six months, and, during the remainder of the year, one bushel of oats per week. Mr. Ellman, of Glynde, in Sussex, allows two bushels of oats, with pease-haulm or straw, with but very little hay, during the winter months. He gives one bushel of oats with green food during the summer." There is very little difference in the management of these two gentlemen, and that probably arising from circumstances peculiar to their respective farms. The grand principles of feeding, with reference to agricultural horses, are, to keep the animal rather above his work, to give him good and wholesome food, and, by the use of the nose-bag or other means, never to let him work longer than the time already mentioned without being baited.

The horse of quick work should be allowed as much as he will eat, care being taken that no more is put into the manger than he will readily dispose of; and that the grain be consumed before the hay is given; if the former be not eaten up with an appetite, it must be removed before the stable is shut up. The quantity actually eaten will depend on the degree of work and the natural appetite of the horse; but it may be averaged at about sixty-six pounds of chaff, seventeen pounds and a half of beans, and seventy-seven pounds of oats per week.

The *watering* of the horse is a very important but disregarded portion of his general management. The kind of water has not been sufficiently considered. The difference between what is termed *hard* and *soft* water is a circumstance of general observation. The former contains certain saline principles which decompose some bodies, as appears in the curdling of soap, and prevent the decomposition of others, as in the making of tea, the boiling of vegetables, and the process of brewing. It is natural to suppose that these different kinds of water would produce somewhat different effects on the animal frame; and such is the fact. Hard water, freshly drawn from the well, will frequently roughen the coat of the horse unaccustomed to it, or cause griping pains, or materially lessen the animal's power of exertion. The racing and the hunting groom are perfectly aware of this; and so is the horse, for he will refuse the purest water from the well, if he can obtain access to the running stream, or even the turbid pool. Where there is the power of choice, the softer water should undoubtedly be preferred.

The temperature of the water is of far more consequence than its hardness. It will rarely harm, if taken from the pond or the running stream, but its coldness when recently drawn from the well has often been injurious; it has produced colic, spasm, and even death.

There is often considerable prejudice against the horse being fairly supplied with water. It is supposed to chill him, to injure his wind, or to incapacitate him for hard work. It certainly would do so if, immediately after drinking his fill, he were galloped hard, but not if he were suffered to quench his thirst more frequently when at rest in the stable. The horse that has free access to water will not drink so much in the course of a day as another, who, in order to cool his parched mouth, swallows as fast as he can, and knows not when to stop.

A horse may with perfect safety be far more liberally supplied with water than he generally is. An hour before his work commences, he should be permitted to drink a couple of quarts. A greater quantity might probably be objected to. He will perform his task far more pleasantly and effectively than with a parched mouth and tormenting thirst. The prejudice both of the hunting and the training groom on this point is cruel, as well as injurious. The task or the journey being accomplished, and the horse having had his head and neck dressed, his legs and feet washed, before his body is cleaned he should have his water. When dressed, his grain may be offered to him, which he will readily take; but water should never be given immediately before or after the grain.

GROOMING.—Of this little need be said to the agriculturist, since custom, and apparently without ill effect, has allotted so little of the comb and brush to the farmer's horse. The animal that is worked all day and turned out at night, requires little more to be done to him than to have the dirt brushed off his limbs. Regular grooming, by rendering his skin more sensible to the alteration of temperature, and the inclemency of the weather, would be prejudicial. The horse that is altogether turned out, needs no grooming. The dandriff, or scurf, which accumulates at the roots of the hair, is a provision of nature to defend him from the wind and the cold.

It is to the stabled horse, highly fed, and little or irregularly worked, that grooming is of so much consequence. Good rubbing with the brush, or the curry-comb, opens the pores of the skin, circulates the blood to the extremities of the body, produces free and healthy perspiration, and stands in the room of exercise. No horse will carry a fine coat without either unnatural heat or dressing. They both effect the same purpose; they both increase the insensible persiration; but the first does it at the expense of health and strength, while the second, at the same time that it produces a glow on the skin, and a determination of blood to it, rouses all the energies of the frame. It would be well for the proprietor of the horse if he were to insist—and to see that his orders are really obeyed—that the fine coat in which he and his groom so much delight, is produced by honest rubbing, and not by a heated stable and thick clothing, and most of all, not by stimulating or injurious spices. The horse should be regularly dressed every day, in addition to the grooming that is necessary after work.

When the weather will permit the horse to be taken out, he should never be groomed in the stable, unless he is an animal of peculiar value, or placed for a time under peculiar circumstances. Without dwelling on the want of cleanliness, when the scurf and dust that are brushed from the horse lodge in his manger, and mingle with his food, experience teaches, that if the cold is not too great, the animal is braced and invigorated to a degree that cannot be attained in the stable, from being dressed in the open air. There is no necessity, however, for half the punishment which many a groom inflicts upon the horse in the act of dressing; and particularly on one whose skin is thin and sensible. The curry-comb should at all times be lightly applied. With many horses, its use may be almost dispensed with; and even the brush needs not to be so hard, nor the points of the bristles so irregular, as they often are. A soft brush, with a little more weight of the hand, will be equally effectual, and a great deal more pleasant to the horse. A hair-cloth, while it will seldom irritate and tease, will be almost sufficient with horses that have a thin skin, and that have not been neglected. After all, it is no slight task to dress a horse as it ought to be done. It occupies no little time, and demands considerable patience, as well as dexterity.

Exercise.—Our observations on this important branch of stable management must have only a slight reference to the agricultural horse. His work is usually regular, and not exhausting. He is neither predisposed to disease by idleness nor worn out by excessive exertion. He, like his master, has enough to do to keep him in health, and not enough to distress or injure him; on the contrary, the regularity of his work prolongs life to an extent rarely witnessed in the stable of the gentleman. Our remarks on exercise, then, must have a general bearing, or have principal reference to those persons who are in the middle stations of life, and who contrive to keep a horse for business or pleasure, but cannot afford to maintain a servant for the express purpose of looking after it. The first rule we would lay down is, that every horse should have daily exercise. The animal that, with the usual stable feeding, stands idle for three or four days, as is the case in many establishments, must suffer. He is predisposed to fever, or to grease, or most of all, diseases of the foot; and if, after three or four days of inactivity, he is ridden far and fast, he is almost sure to have inflammation of the lungs or of the feet.

A gentleman's or a tradesman's horse suffers a great deal more from idleness than he does from work. A stable-fed horse should have two hours' exercise every day, if he is to be kept free from disease. Nothing of extraordinary, or even of ordinary labor, can be effected on the road or in the field without sufficient and regular exercise. It is this alone which can give energy to the system, or develop the powers of any animal.

The exercised horse will discharge his task, and sometimes a severe one, with ease and pleasure; while the idle and neglected one will be fatigued ere half his labor is accomplished; and, if he is pushed a little too far, dangerous inflammation will ensue. How often, nevertheless, does it happen, that the horse which has stood inactive in the stable three or four days, is ridden or driven thirty or forty miles in the course of a single day! This rest is often purposely given to prepare for extra exertion—to lay in a stock of strength for the performance of the task required of him; and then the owner is surprised and dissatisfied if the animal is fairly knocked up, or possibly becomes seriously ill. Nothing is so common and so preposterous as for a person to buy a horse from a dealer's stable, where he has been idly fattened for sale for many a day, and immediately to give him a long run after the hounds, and then to complain bitterly, and think that he has been imposed upon, if the animal is exhausted before the end of the chase, or is compelled to be led home suffering from violent inflammation. Regular and gradually-increasing exercise would have made the same horse appear a treasure to his owner.

Exercise should be somewhat proportioned to the age of the horse. A young horse requires more than an old one. Nature has given to young animals of every kind a disposition to activity; but the exercise must not be violent. A great deal depends upon the manner in which it is given. To preserve the temper, and to promote health, it should be moderate, at least at the beginning and the termination. The rapid trot, or even the gallop, may be resorted to in the middle of the exercise, but the horse should be brought in cool.

Management of the Feet.—This is the only division of stable management that remains to be considered, and one sadly neglected by the carter and groom. The feet should be carefully examined every morning, for the shoes may be loose, and the horse would have been stopped in the middle of his work; or the clenches may be raised, and endanger the wounding of his legs; or the shoe may begin to press upon the sole or the heel, and bruises of the sole or corn may be the result; and, the horse having stood so long in the stable, every little increase of heat in the foot, or lameness, will be more readily detected, and serious disease may often be prevented.

When the horse comes in at night, and after the harness has been taken off and stowed away, the heels should be well brushed out. Hand-rubbing will be preferable to washing, especially in the agricultural horse, whose heels, covered with long hair, can scarcely be dried again. If the dirt is suffered to accumulate in that long hair, the heels will become sore, and grease will follow; and if the heels are washed, and particularly during the winter, grease will result from the coldness occasioned by the slow evaporation of the moisture. The feet should be stopped—even the feet of the farmer's horse—if he remains in the stable. Very little clay should be used in the stopping, for it will get hard and press upon the sole. Cow-dung is the best stopping to preserve the feet cool and elastic; but before the stopping is applied, the picker should be run round the whole of the foot, between the shoe and the sole, in order to detect any stone that may have insinuated itself there, or a wound on any other part of the sole.

SHOEING, etc.—Far more than is generally imagined, do the comfort and health of the horse, and the safety of his rider, depend upon shoeing.

In taking off the old shoe, the clenches of the nails should always be carefully raised or filed off; and, where the foot is tender, or the horse is to be examined for lameness, each nail should be partly punched out.

The edges of the crust are then to be rasped to detect whether any stubs remain in the nail-holes, and to remove the crust, into which dust and gravel have insinuated themselves.

Next comes the important process of paring out, with regard to which it is almost impossible to lay down any specific rules. This, however, is undoubted, that far more injury has been done by the neglect of paring, than by carrying it to too great an extent. The act of paring is a work of much more labor than the proprietor of the horse often imagines. The smith, except he is overlooked, will frequently give himself as little trouble about it as he can; and that portion of horn which, in the unshod foot, would be worn away by contact with the ground, is suffered to accumulate month after month, until the elasticity of the sole is destroyed, and it can no longer descend, and its other functions are impeded, and foundation is laid for corn, and contraction, and navicular disease, and inflammation. That portion of horn should be left on the foot which will defend the internal parts from being bruised, and yet suffer the external sole to descend. How is this to be ascertained? The strong pressure of the thumb of the smith will be the best guide. The buttress, that most destructive of all instruments, being, except on very particular occasions, banished from every respectable forge, the smith sets to work with his drawing knife, and removes the growth of horn, until the sole will yield, although in the slightest possible degree, to the strong pressure of his thumb. The proper thickness of horn will then remain.

The quantity of horn to be removed, in order to leave the proper degree of thickness, will vary with different feet. From the strong foot a great deal must be taken. From the concave foot the horn may be removed until the sole will yield to a moderate pressure. From the flat foot little needs be pared; while the pumiced foot should be deprived of nothing but the ragged parts.

The crust should be reduced to a perfect level all round, but left a little higher than the sole, or the sole will be bruised by its pressure on the edge of the seating.

The heels will require considerable attention. From the stress which is thrown on the inner heel, and from the weakness of the quarter there, the horn usually wears away considerably faster than it would on the outer one, and if an equal portion of horn were pared from it, it would be left lower than the outer heel. The smith should therefore accommodate his paring to the comparative wear of the heels, and be exceedingly careful to leave them precisely level.

The portion of the heels between the inflection of the bar and the frog should scarcely be touched—at least, the ragged and detached parts alone should be cut away. The foot may not look so fair and open, but it will last longer without contraction.

The bar, likewise, should be left fully prominent, not only at its first inflection, but as it runs down the side of the frog. The heel of the shoe is designed to rest partly on the heel of the foot and partly on the bar, for reasons that have been already stated. If the bar is weak, the growth of it should be encouraged; and it should be scarcely touched when the horse is shod, unless it has attained a level with the crust.

It will also be apparent, that the horn between the crust and the bar should be carefully pared out. Every horseman has observed the relief which is given to the animal lame with corns, when this angle is well thinned.

The degree of paring to which the frog must be subjected, will depend on its prominence, and on the shape of the foot. The principle has already been stated, that it must be left so far projecting and prominent, that it shall be just within and above the lower surface of the shoe; it will then descend with the sole sufficiently to discharge the functions that have been attributed to it. If it is lower, it will be bruised and injured; if it is higher, it cannot come in contact with the ground, and thus be enabled to do its duty. The ragged parts must be removed, and especially those occasioned by thrush, but the degree of paring must depend entirely on the principle just stated.

Putting on the Shoe.—The shoe should accurately fit the size of the foot; if too small, and the foot is rasped down to fit the shoe, the crust is thinned where it receives the nail, and the danger of puncture, and of pressure upon the sole, is increased; and a foot so artificially diminished in size, will soon grow over the shoe, to the hazard of considerable or permanent lameness.

The shoe should be properly beveled off, that the dirt, gravel, etc., which gets between it and the foot may be shaken out.

The web of the shoe is likewise of that thickness, that when the foot is properly pared, the prominent part of the frog shall lie just within and above its ground surface, so that in the descent of the sole, the frog shall come sufficiently on the ground to enable it to act as a wedge and to expand the quarters, while it is defended from the wear and injury it would receive, if it came on the ground with the first and full shock of the weight.

The nail-holes are, on the ground side, placed as near the outer edge of the shoe as they can safely be, and brought out near the inner edge of the seating. The nails thus take a direction inward, resembling that of the crust itself, and have firmer hold, and the weight of the horse being thrown on a flat surface, contraction is not so likely to be produced.

It is expedient not only that the foot and ground surface of the shoe should be most accurately level, but that the crust should be exactly smoothed and fitted to the shoe. Much skill and time are necessary to do this perfectly with the drawing-knife. The smith has adopted a method of more quickly and more accurately adapting the shoe to the foot. He pares the crust as level as he can, and then he brings the shoe to a heat somewhat below a red heat, and applies it to the foot, and detects any little elevations by the deeper color of the burned horn. This practice has been much inveighed against; but it is the abuse, and not the use of the thing which is to be condemned. If the shoe is not too hot, nor held too long on the foot, an accuracy of adjustment is thus obtained, which the knife would be long in producing, or would not produce at all. If, however, the shoe is made to burn its way to its seat, with little or no previous preparation of the foot, the heat must be injurious both to the sensible and insensible parts of the foot.

The heels of the shoe should be examined as to their proper width. Whatever is the custom of shoeing the horses of dealers, and the too prevalent practice in the metropolis of giving the foot an open appearance, although the posterior part of it is thereby exposed to injury, nothing is more certain than that, in the horse destined for road work, the heels, and particularly the seat of corn, can scarcely be too well covered. Part of the shoe projecting externally can be of no possible good, but will prove an occasional source of mischief, and especially in a heavy country. A shoe, the web of which projects inward as far as it can without touching the frog, affords protection to the angle between the bars and the crust.

Of the manner of attaching the shoe to the foot the owner can scarcely be a competent judge; he can only take care that the shoe itself shall not be heavier than the work requires—that, for work a little hard the shoe shall still be light, with a bit of steel welded into the toe—that the nails shall be as small, and as few, and as far from the heels as may be consistent with the security of the shoe; and that, for light work at least, the shoe shall not be driven on so closely and firmly as is often done, nor the points of the nails be brought out so high up as is generally practiced.

Calkins.*—There are few cases in which the use of calkins (a turning up or elevation of the heel) can be admissible in the fore-feet, except in frosty weather, when it may in some degree prevent unpleasant or dangerous slipping. If, however, calkins are used, they should be placed on both sides. If the outer heel only is raised with the calkin, as is too often the case, the weight cannot be thrown evenly on the foot, and undue straining and injury of some part of the foot or of the leg must be the necessary consequence.

Clips.—These are portions of the upper edge of the shoe, hammered out, and turned up so as to embrace the lower part of the crust and which is usually pared out a little, in order to receive the clip. They are very useful, as more securely attaching the shoe to the foot, and relieving the crust from that stress upon the nails which would otherwise be injurious. A clip at the toe is almost necessary in every draught-horse, and absolutely so in the horse of heavy draught, in order to prevent the shoe from being loosened or torn off by the pressure which is thrown upon the toe in the act of drawing. A clip on the outside of

---

* Vulgarly "corks."

each shoe, at the beginning of the quarters, will give security to it. Clips are likewise necessary on the shoes of all heavy horses, and of all others who are disposed to stamp, or violently paw with their feet, and thus incur the danger of displacing the shoe; but they are evils, inasmuch as they press upon the crust as it grows down, and they should only be used when circumstances absolutely require them. In the hunter's shoe they are not required at the sides. One at the toe is sufficient.

The Hinder Shoe.—In forming the hinder shoes, it should be remembered that the hind limbs are the principal instruments in progression, and that in every act of progression, except the walk, the toe is the point on which the whole frame of the animal turns, and from which it is propelled. This part, then, should be strengthened as much as possible; and therefore the hinder shoes are made broader at the toe than the fore ones. Another good effect is produced by this—that, the hinder foot being shortened, there is less danger of overreaching, forging, or clinking, and especially if the shoe is wider on the foot surface than on the ground one. The shoe is thus made to slope inward, and is a little within the toe of the crust.

The shape of the hinder foot is somewhat different from that of the fore foot. It is straighter in the quarters, and the shoe must have the same form. For carriage and draught-horses generally, calkins may be put on the heels, because the animal will be thus enabled to dig his toe more firmly into the ground, and urge himself forward, and throw his weight into the collar with greater advantage; but the calkins must not be too high, and they must be of an equal height on each heel, otherwise, as has been stated with regard to the fore feet, the weight will not be fairly distributed over the foot, and some part of the foot or the leg will materially suffer. The nails in the hinder shoe may be placed nearer to the heel than in the fore shoe, because, from the comparatively little weight and concussion thrown on the hinder feet, there is not so much danger of contraction.

Different Kinds of Shoes.—The shoe must vary in substance and weight with the kind of foot, and the nature of the work. A weak foot should never wear a heavy shoe, nor any foot a shoe that will last longer than a month. Here, perhaps, we may be permitted to caution the horse-proprietor against having his cattle shod by contract, unless he binds his farrier or veterinary surgeon to remove the shoes once at least in every month; for, if the contractor, by a heavy shoe, and a little steel, can cause five or six weeks to intervene between the shoeings, he will do so, although the feet of the horse must necessarily suffer. The shoe should never be heavier than the work requires, for an ounce or two in the weight of the shoe will sadly tell at the end of a hard day's work. This is acknowledged in the hunting-shoe, which is narrower and lighter than that of the hackney, although the foot of the hackney is smaller than that of the hunter. It is more decidedly acknowledged in the racer, who wears a shoe only sufficiently thick to prevent it from bending when it is used.

The Concave-Seated Shoe.—An illustration is subjoined of a shoe which is useful and valuable for general purposes. It is employed in many of

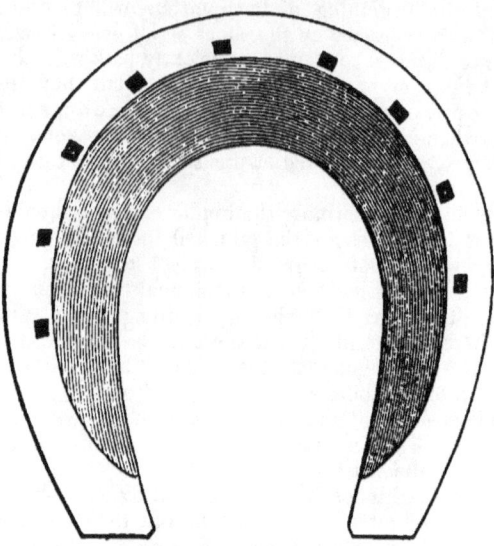

THE CONCAVE-SEATED SHOE.

our best forges, and promises gradually to supersede the flat and the simple concave shoe, although it must, in many respects, yield to the unilateral shoe.

It presents a perfectly flat surface to the ground, in order to give as many points of bearing as possible, except that, on the outer edge, there is a groove or fuller, in which the nail-holes are punched, so that, sinking into the fuller, their heads project but a little way, and are soon worn down level with the shoe.

The web of this shoe is of the same thickness throughout, from the toe to the heel; and it is sufficiently wide to guard the sole from bruises, and, as much so as the frog will permit, to cover the seat of corn.

On the foot side it is seated. The outer part of it is accurately flat, and of the width of the crust, and designed to support the crust, for by it the whole weight of the horse is sustained.

Toward the heel this flattened part is wider, and occupies the whole breadth of the web, in order to support the heel of the crust and its reflected part, the bar; thus, while it defends the horn included within this angle from injury, it gives that equal pressure from the bar and the crust which is the best preventive against corns, and a powerful obstacle to contraction.

It is fastened to the foot by nine nails—five on the outside, and four on the inner side of the shoe; those on the outside extending a little farther down toward the heel, because the outside heel is thicker and stronger, and there is more nail-hold; the last nail on the inner quarter being farther from the heel, on account of the weakness of that quarter. For feet not too large, and where moderate work only is required from the horse, four nails on the outside and three on the inside will be sufficient; and the last nail, being far from the heels, will allow more expansion there.

The inside part of the web is beveled off, or rendered concave, that it may not press upon the sole. Notwithstanding the shoe, the sole does, although to a very inconsiderable extent, descend when the foot of the horse is put on the ground. It is unable to bear constant or even occasional pressure, and if it came in contact with the shoe, the sensible sole between it and the coffin-bone would be bruised, and lameness would ensue. Many of our horses, from too early and undue work, have the natural concave sole flattened, and the disposition to descend, and the degree of descent, are thereby increased. The concave shoe prevents, even in this case, the possibility of much injury, because the sole can never descend in the degree in which the shoe is or may be beveled. A shoe beveled still farther is necessary to protect the projecting or pumiced foot.

THE UNILATERAL SHOE.

The Unilateral or One-Side Nailed Shoe.—This is a material improvement in the art of shoeing, for which we are indebted to Mr. Turner.

What was the state of the foot of the horse a few years ago? An unyielding iron hoof was attached to it by four nails in each quarter, and the consequence was, that in nine cases out of ten the foot underwent a very considerable alteration in its form and in its usefulness. Before it had attained its full development—before the animal was five years old, there was, in a great many cases, an evident contraction of the hoof. There was an alteration in the manner of going. The step was shortened, the sole was hollowed, the frog was diseased, the general elasticity of the foot was destroyed—there was a disorganization of the whole horny cavity, and the value of the horse was materially diminished. What was the grand cause of this? It was the restraint of the shoe. The firm attachment of it to the foot by nails in each quarter, and the consequent strain to which the quarters and every part of the foot were exposed, produced a necessary tendency to contraction, from which sprang almost all the maladies to which the foot of the horse is subject.

The unilateral shoe has this great advantage: it is identified with the grand principle of the expansibility of the horse's foot, and of removing or preventing the worst ailments to which the foot of the horse is liable. It can be truly stated of this shoe, that while it affords to the whole organ an iron defense equal to the common shoe, it permits, what the common shoe never did or can do, the perfect liberty of the foot. We are enabled to present our readers with the last improvement of the unilateral shoe.

The preceding cut gives a view of the outer side of the off or right unilateral shoe. The respective situations of the five nails will be observed; the distance of the last from the heel, and the proper situations at which they emerge from the crust. The two clips will likewise be seen—one in the front of the foot, and the other on the side between the last and second nail.

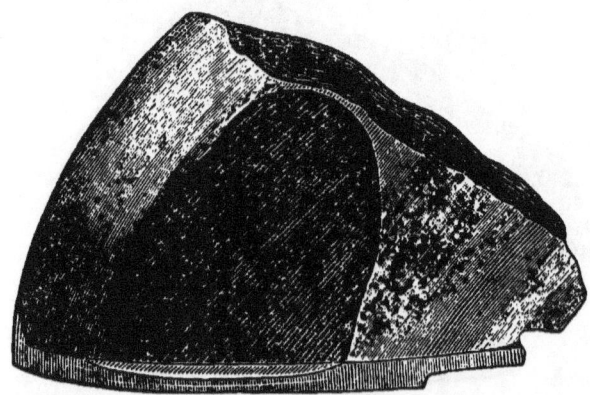

INNER SIDE OF UNILATERAL SHOE.

This cut gives a view of the inner side of the unilateral shoe. The two nails near the toe are in the situation in which Mr. Turner directs that they should be placed, and behind them is no other attachment, between the shoe and the crust. The portion of the crust which is rasped off from the inner surface of the shoe, is now, we believe, not often removed from the side of the foot; it has an unpleasant appearance, and the rasping is somewhat unnecessary. The heel of this shoe exhibits the method which Mr. Turner has adopted, and with considerable success, for the cure of corns; he cuts away a portion of the ground surface at the heel, and injurious compression or concussion is rendered in a manner impossible.

There can be no doubt that this one-sided nailing has been exceedingly useful. It has, in many a case that threatened a serious termination, restored the elasticity of the foot, and enabled it to discharge its natural functions. It has also restored to the foot, even in bad cases, a great deal of its natural formation, and enabled the horse to discharge his duty with more ease and pleasure to himself, and greater security to his rider.

The Bar-Shoe.—A bar-shoe is often exceedingly useful. It is the continuation of the common shoe round the heels, and by means of it the pressure may be taken off from some tender part of the foot, and thrown on another which is better able to bear it, or more widely and equally diffused over the whole foot. It is principally resorted to in cases of corn, the seat of which it perfectly covers—in pumiced feet, the soles of which may be thus elevated above the ground and secured from pressure—in sand-crack, when the pressure may be removed from the fissure, and thrown on either side of it, and in thrushes, when the frog is tender, or is become cankered, and requires to be frequently dressed, and the dressing can by this means alone be retained. In these cases the bar-shoe is an excellent contrivance, if worn only for one or two shoeings, or as long as the disease requires it to be worn; but it must be left off as soon as it can be dispensed with. If it is used for the protection of a diseased foot, however it may be chambered and laid off the frog, it will soon become flattened upon it; or if the pressure of it is thrown on the frog in order to relieve the sand-crack or the corn, that frog must be very strong and healthy which can long bear the great and continued pressure. More mischief is often produced in the frog than previously existed in the part that was relieved. It will be plain that in the use of the bar-shoe for corn or sand-crack, the crust and the frog should be precisely on a level; the bar also should be the widest part of the shoe, in order to afford as extended bearing as possible on the frog, and therefore less likely to be injurious. Bar-shoes are evidently not safe in frosty weather. They are never safe when much speed is required from the horse, and they are apt to be wrenched off in a heavy, clayey country.

Tips.—Tips are short shoes reaching only half round the foot, and worn while the horse is at grass, in order to prevent the crust being torn by the occasional hardness of the ground or the pawing of the animal. The quarters at the same time being free, the foot disposed to contract has a chance of expanding and regaining its natural shape.

The Expanding Shoe.—Our subject would not be complete if we did not describe the supposed expanding shoe, although it is now almost entirely out of use. It is either seated or concave like the common shoe, with a joint at the toe, by which the natural expansion of the foot is said to be permitted, and the injurious consequences of shoeing prevented. There is, however, this radical defect in the jointed shoe, that the nails occupy the same situation as in the common shoe, and prevent as they do the gradual expansion of the sides and quarters, and allow only of the hinge-like motion at the toe. It is a most imperfect accommodation of the expansion of the foot to the action of its internal parts, and even this accommodation is afforded in the slightest possible degree, if it is afforded at all. Either the nails fix the sides and quarters as in the common shoe, and then the joint at the toe is useless; or if that joint merely opens like a hinge, the nail-holes near the toe can no longer correspond with those in the quarters, which are unequally expanding at every point. There will be more stress on the crust at these holes, which will not only enlarge them and destroy the fixed attachment of the shoe to the hoof, but often tear away portions of the crust. This shoe, in order to answer the intended purpose, should consist of many joints, running along the sides and quarters, which would make it too complicated and expensive and frail for general use.

While the shoe is to be attached to the foot by nails, we must be content with the concave-seated or unilateral one, taking care to place the nail-holes as far from the heels, and particularly from the inner heel, as the state of the foot and the nature of the work will admit; and where the country is not too heavy nor the work too severe, omitting all but two on the inner side of the foot.

Felt or Leather Soles.—When the foot is bruised or inflamed, the concussion or shock produced by the hard contact of the elastic iron with the ground gives the animal much pain, and aggravates the injury or disease. A strip of felt or leather is therefore sometimes placed between the seating of the shoe and the crust, which, from its want of elasticity, deadens or materially lessens the vibration or shock, and the horse treads more freely and is evidently relieved. This is a good contrivance while the inflammation or tenderness of the foot continues, but a very bad practice if constantly adopted. The nails cannot be driven so surely or securely when this substance is interposed between the shoe and the foot. The contraction and swelling of the felt or leather from the effect of moisture or dryness will soon render the attachment of the shoe less firm, there will be too much play upon the nails, the nail-holes will enlarge, and the crust will be broken away.

After wounds or extensive bruises of the sole, or where the sole is thin and flat and tender, it is sometimes covered with a piece of leather, fitted to the sole and nailed on with the shoe. This may be allowed as a temporary defense of the foot; but there is the same objection to its permanent use for the insecurity of fastening, and the strain on the crust and the frequent chipping of it. There are also these additional inconveniences, that if the hollow between the sole and the leather is filled with stopping and tow, it is exceedingly difficult to introduce them so evenly and accurately as not to produce partial or injurious pressure. A few days' work will almost invariably so derange the padding as to cause unequal pressure. The long contact of the sole with stopping of almost every kind, will produce not a healthy elastic horn, but that of a scaly, spongy nature, and if the hollow is not thus filled, gravel and dirt will insinuate themselves and eat into and injure the foot.

Stopping the Feet.—The general habit of stopping the feet requires some consideration. It is a very good or very bad practice, according to circumstances. When the sole is flat and thin it should be omitted, except on the evening before shoeing, and then the application of a little moisture may render the paring of the foot safer and more easy. If it were oftener used it would soften the foot, and not only increase the tendency to descent, but the occasional occurrence of lameness from pebbles or irregularities of the road.

Professor Stewart gives a valuable account of the proper application of stopping: "Farm horses seldom require any stopping. Their feet receive sufficient moisture in the fields, or if they do not get much they do not need much. Cart-horses used in the town should be stopped once a week or oftener during winter, and every second night in the hot weeks of summer. Groggy horses and all those with high heels, concave shoes, or hot and tender feet or an exuberance of horn, require stopping almost every night. When neglected, especially in dry weather, the sole becomes hard and rigid, and the horse goes lame or becomes lame if he were not so before."

One of two substances or a mixture of both is generally used for stopping the feet—clay and cow-dung. The clay used alone is too hard and dries too rapidly. Many horses have been lamed by it. If it is used in the stable, it should always be removed before the horse goes to work. It may perhaps be applied to the feet of heavy draught-horses, for it will work out before much mischief is done.

Cow dung is softer than the clay, and it has this good property, that it rarely or never becomes too hard or dry. For ordinary work, a mixture of equal parts of clay and cow-dung will be the best application; either of them, however, must be applied with a great deal of caution, where there is any disposition to thrush. Tow used alone or with a small quantity of tar will often be serviceable.

In the better kind of stables a felt pad is frequently used. It keeps the foot cool and moist, and is very useful when the sole has a tendency to become flat. For the concave sole tow would be preferable.

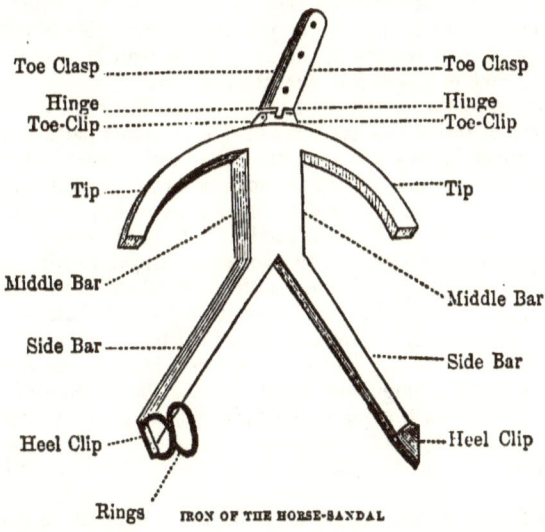

IRON OF THE HORSE-SANDAL

The Sandal.—The shoe is sometimes displaced when the horse is going at an ordinary pace, and more frequently during hunting; and no person who is a sportsman needs to be told in what a vexatious predicament every one feels himself who happens to loose a shoe in the middle of a chase.

3*

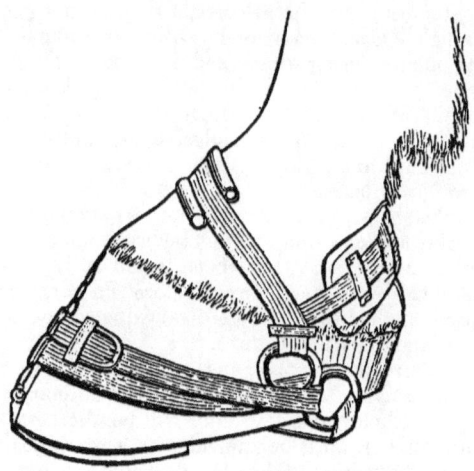

THE SANDAL.

Mr. Percivall has invented a sandal which occupies a very small space in the pocket, can be buckled on the foot in less than two minutes, and will serve as a perfect substitute for the lost one on the road or in the field, or may be used by the race-horse when traveling from one course to another; or may be truly serviceable in cases of diseased feet, that may require at the same time exercise and daily dressing. The above is a sketch of the horse sandal.

From an inspection of the cut on the preceding page it will be seen that the iron of the sandal consists of three principal parts, to which the others are appendages—which are the tip, so called from its resemblance to the horse-shoe of that name; the middle bar, the broad part proceeding backward from the tip; and the side bars, or branches of the middle bar, extending to the heels of the hoof. The appendages are, the toe-clasp, the part projecting from the front of the tip, and which moves by a hinge upon the toe-clip, which toe-clasp is furnished with two iron loops. The heel-clips are two clips at the heels of the side bars which correspond to the toe-clip, the latter embracing the toe of the crust whilst the former embrace its heels. Through the heel-clips run the rings, which move and act like a hinge, and are double for the purpose of admitting both the straps. In the plate, the right ring only is represented; the left being omitted, the better to show the heel-clip. The straps, which are composed of web, consist of a hoof-strap and a heel and coronet-strap.

The hoof-strap is furnished with a buckle, whose office it is to bind the shoe to the hoof; for which purpose it is passed through the lower rings, and both loops of the shoe, and is made to encircle the hoof twice.

The heel and coronet-strap are furnished with two pads and two sliding loops; one, a movable pad, reposes on the heel, to defend that part from the pressure and friction of the strap; the other, a pad attached to the strap near the buckle affords a similar defense, to the coronet in front. The heel-strap runs through the upper rings, crosses the heel, and encircles the coronet; and its office is to keep the heels of the shoe closely applied to the hoof, and to prevent them from sliding forward.

In the application of the sandal, the foot is taken up with one hand, and the shoe slipped upon it with the other. With the same hand, the shoe is retained in its place, while the foot is gradually let down to rest on the ground. As soon as this is done, the straps are drawn as tight as possible, and buckled.

The preceding engraving represents an accurate delineation of the sandal, when properly fastened to the foot.

TO MANAGE A FALLEN HORSE.—Horses occasionally fall from bad riding, or bad shoeing, or overreaching, or an awkward way of setting on the saddle. The head, the neck, the knees, the back, or the legs will oftenest suffer. It is often difficult to get the animal on his legs again, especially if he is old and exhausted, or injured by the fall. The principal object is, to support the head, and to render it a fixed point from which the muscles may act in supporting the body.

If the horse is in harness, it is seldom that he can rise until he is freed from the shafts and traces. The first thing is to secure the head, and to keep it down, that he may not beat himself against the ground. Next, the parts of the harness connected with the carriage must be unbuckled—the carriage must then be backed a little way, so that he may have room to rise. If necessary, the traces must be taken off; and after the horse gets up, he must be steadied a little, until he collects himself.

THE VICES AND DISAGREEABLE OR DANGEROUS HABITS OF THE HORSE.—The horse has many excellent qualities, but he has likewise defects, and these occasionally amounting to vices. Some of them may be attributed to natural temper, for the human being scarcely discovers more peculiarities of habit and disposition than does the horse. The majority of them, however, as perhaps in the human being, are the consequences of a faulty education. Their early instructor has been ignorant and brutal, and they have become obstinate and vicious.

Restiveness.—At the head of all the vices of the horse is restiveness, the most annoying and the most dangerous of all. It is the produce of bad temper and worse education; and, like all other habits founded on nature and stamped by education, it is inveterate. Whether it appears in the form of kicking, or rearing, plunging, or bolting, or in any way that threatens danger to the rider or the horse, it rarely admits of cure.

A determined rider may to a certain extent subjugate the animal; or the horse may have his favorites, or form his attachments, and with some particular person he may be comparatively or perfectly manageable; but others cannot long depend upon him, and even his master is not always sure of him. It is a rule, that admits of very few exceptions, that he neither displays his wisdom nor consults his safety, who attempts to conquer a restive horse.

Balking.—Some horses have the habit of balking at first starting, but more from playfulness than desire of mischief. A moderate application of the whip will usually be effectual. Others, even after starting, exhibit considerable obstinacy and viciousness. This is frequently the effect of bad breaking. Either the shoulder of the horse had been wrung when he was first put to the collar, or he had been foolishly accustomed to be started in the break up-hill, and, therefore, all his work coming upon him at once, he gradually acquired this dangerous habit.

A hasty and passionate breaker will often make a really good-tempered young horse an inveterate balker. Every young horse is at first shy of the collar. If he is too quickly forced to throw his weight into it, he will possibly take a dislike to it, that will occasionally show itself in the form of balking as long as he lives. The judicious horse-breaker will resort to no severity, even if the colt should go out several times without even touching the collar. The example of his companion will ultimately induce him to take it voluntarily and effectually.

A large and heavy stone should be put behind the wheel before starting, when the horse, finding it more difficult to back than to go forward, will gradually forget this unpleasant trick. It will likewise be of advantage, as often as it can be managed, so to start that the horse will have to back up-hill. The difficulty of accomplishing this will soon make him readily go forward. A little coaxing, or leading, or moderate flagellation will assist in accomplishing the cure.

When, however, a horse, thinking he has had enough of work, or has been improperly checked or corrected, or beginning to feel the painful pressure of the collar, swerves, and balks, and backs, it is a more serious matter. Persuasion should first be tried; and, afterward, reasonable coercion, but no cruelty: for the brutality which is often exercised to compel a balking horse to throw himself habitually into the collar, never yet accomplished the purpose. The horse may, perhaps, be whipped into motion; but if he has once begun to balk, he will have recourse to it again whenever any circumstance displeases or annoys him, and the habit will be so rapidly and completely formed, that he will become insensible to all severity.

Sometimes a horse not often accustomed to balk betrays a reluctance to move, or a determination not to move. Before resorting to severity, the cause, if practicable, should be ascertained. The horse may be over-taxed, his withers may be wrung, or he may be insupportably galled or pained by the harness. These things should be examined into, and, if possible, rectified; for, under such circumstances, cruelty may produce obstinacy and vice, but not willing obedience.

They who are accustomed to horses know what seemingly trivial circumstances occasionally produce this vice. A horse whose shoulders are raw, or have frequently been so, will not start with a cold collar. When the collar has acquired the warmth of the parts on which it presses, the animal will go without reluctance. Some determined balkers have been reformed by constantly wearing a false collar, or strip of cloth round the shoulders, so that the coldness of the usual collar should never be felt; and others have been cured of the habit by keeping the collar on night and day, for the animal is not able to lie down completely at full length, which the tired horse is always glad to do. When a horse balks, not at starting, but while doing his work, it has sometimes been useful to line the collar with cloth instead of leather; the perspiration is readily absorbed, the substance which presses on the shoulder is softer, and it may be far more accurately eased off at a tender place.

Biting.—This is either the consequence of natural ferocity, or a habit acquired from the foolish and teasing play of grooms and stable-boys. When a horse is tickled and pinched by thoughtless and mischievous youths, he will first pretend to bite his tormentors; by degrees he will proceed farther, and actually bite them, and very soon after that, he will be the first to challenge to the combat, and without, provocation, seize some opportunity to gripe the incautious tormentor. At length, as the love of mischief is a propensity too easily acquired, this war, half playful and half in earnest, becomes habitual to him, and degenerates into absolute viciousness.

It is seldom that any thing can be done in the way of cure. Kindness will aggravate the evil, and no degree of severity will correct it. "I have seen," says Professor Stewart, "biters punished until they trembled in every joint, and were ready to drop, but have never in any case known them cured by this treatment, or by any other. The lash is forgotten in an hour, and the horse is as ready and determined to repeat the offense as before. He appears unable to resist the temptation, and in its worst form biting is a species of insanity."

Prevention, however is in the power of every proprietor of horses. While he insists on gentle and humane treatment of his cattle, he should systematically forbid this horse-play.

Getting the Cheek of the Bit into the Mouth.—Some horses that are disposed to be mischievous try to do this and are very expert at it. They soon find what advantage it gives them over their driver, who by this maneuver loses almost all command. Harsh treatment is here completely out of the question. All that can be done, is, by some mechanical contrivance to render the thing difficult or impossible, and this may be managed by fastening a round piece of leather on the inside of the cheek of the bit.

Kicking.—This, as a *vice*, is another consequence of the culpable habit of grooms and stable-boys of teasing the horse. That which is at first an indication of annoyance at the pinching and tickling of the groom, and without any design to injure, gradually becomes the expression of anger and the effort to do mischief. The horse, likewise, too soon recognizes the least appearance of timidity, and takes advantage of the discovery, and he cannot be justified who keeps a kicking horse in his stable.

Some horses acquire, from mere irritability and fidgetiness, a habit of kicking at the stall or the bail, and particularly at night. The neighboring horses are disturbed, and the kicker gets swelled hocks, or some more serious injury. This is also a habit very difficult to correct if suffered to become established. Mares are far more subject to it than horses.

Before the habit is inveterately established, a thorn bush or a piece of furze fastened against the partition or post will sometimes effect a cure. When the horse finds that he is pretty severely pricked, he will not long continue to punish himself. In confirmed cases it may be necessary to have recourse to the log, but the legs are often not a little bruised by it. A rather long and heavy piece of wood attached to a chain has been buckled above the hock, so as to reach about half-way down the leg. When the horse attempts to kick violently, his leg will receive a severe blow: this, and the repetition of it may, after a time, teach him to be quiet.

A much more serious vice is kicking in harness. From the least annoyance about the rump or quarters, some horses will kick at a most violent rate, and destroy the bottom of the chaise, and endanger the limbs of the driver. Those that are fidgety in the stable are most apt to do this. If the reins should perchance get under the tail, the violence of the kicker will often be most outrageous; and while the animal presses down his tail so tightly that it is almost impossible to extricate the reins, he continues to plunge until he has demolished every thing behind him.

This is a vice standing foremost in point of danger, and which no treatment will always conquer. It will be altogether in vain to try coercion. If the shafts are very strong and without flaw, or if they are plated with iron underneath, and a stout kicking-strap resorted to which will barely allow the horse the proper use of his hind limbs in progression, but not permit him to raise them sufficiently for the purpose of kicking, he may be prevented from doing mischief; or, if he is harnessed to a heavy cart, and thus confined, his efforts to lash out will be restrained: but it is frequently a very unpleasant thing to witness these attempts, though ineffectual, to demolish the vehicle, for the shafts or the kicking-strap may possibly break, and extreme danger may ensue. A horse that has once begun to kick, whatever may have been the original cause of it, can never be depended upon again, and he will be very unwise who ventures behind him. The man, however, who must come within reach of a kicker should come as close to him as possible. The blow may thus become a push, and seldom is injurious.*

Unsteadiness while being Mounted.—When this merely amounts to eagerness to start—very unpleasant, indeed, at times, for many a rider has been thrown from his seat before he was fairly fixed in it—it may be remedied by an active and good horseman. We have known many instances in which, while the elderly, and inactive and fearful man has been making more than one ineffectual attempt to vault into the saddle, the horse has been dancing about to his annoyance and danger; but the animal had no sooner been transferred to the management of a younger and more agile rider than he became perfectly subdued. Severity will here, more decidedly than in any other case, do harm. The rider should be fearless—he should carelessly and confidently approach the horse, mount at the first effort, and then restrain him for a while; patting him, and not suffering him to proceed until he becomes perfectly quiet.

---

* See Rarey's Method of correcting this and other vices, at page 35.

Horses of this kind should not be too highly fed, and should have sufficient daily exercise.

When the difficulty of mounting arises, not from eagerness to start, but unwillingness to be ridden, the sooner that horse is disposed of the better. He may be conquered by a skillful and determined horseman; but even he will not succeed without frequent and dangerous contests that will mar all the pleasure of the ride.

Rearing.—This sometimes results from playfulness, carried indeed to an unpleasant and dangerous extent; but it is oftener a desperate and occasionally successful effort to unhorse the rider, and consequently a vice. The horse that has twice decidedly and dangerously reared, should never be trusted again, unless, indeed, it was the fault of the rider, who had been using a deep curb and a sharp bit. Some of the best horses will contend against these, and then rearing may be immediately and permanently cured by using a snaffle-bridle alone.

The horse-breaker's remedy, that of pulling the horse backward on a soft piece of ground, should be practiced by reckless and brutal fellows alone. Many horses have been injured in the spine, and others have broken their necks, by being thus suddenly pulled over; while even the fellow who fears no danger, is not always able to extricate himself from the falling horse. If rearing proceeds from vice, and is unprovoked by the bruising and laceration of the mouth, it fully partakes of the inveteracy which attends the other divisions of restiveness.

Running Away.—Some headstrong horses will occasionally endeavor to bolt with the best rider. Others with their wonted sagacity endeavor thus to dislodge the timid or unskillful one. Some are hard to hold, or bolt only during the excitement of the chase; others will run away, prompted by a vicious propensity alone. There is no certain cure here. The method which affords any probability of success is, to ride such a horse with a strong curb and sharp bit; to have him always firmly in hand; and, if he will run away, and the place will admit of it, to give him (sparing neither curb, whip, nor spur) a great deal more running than he likes.

Vicious to Clean.—It would scarcely be credited to what an extent this exists in some horses that are otherwise perfectly quiet. It is only at great hazard that they can be cleansed at all. The origin of this is probably some maltreatment. There is, however, a great difference in the sensibility of the skin in different horses. Some seem as if they could scarcely be made to feel the whip, while others cannot bear a fly to light on them without an expression of annoyance. In young horses the skin is peculiarly delicate. If they have been curried with a broken comb, or hardly rubbed with an uneven brush, the recollection of the torture they have felt makes them impatient, and even vicious, during every succeeding operation of the kind. Many grooms, likewise, seem to delight in producing these exhibitions of uneasiness and vice; although, when they are carried a little too far, and at the hazard of the limbs of the groom, the animals that have been almost tutored into these expressions of irritation are brutally kicked and punished.

This, however, is a vice that may be conquered. If the horse is dressed with a lighter hand, and wisped rather than brushed, and the places where the skin is most sensitive are avoided as much as thorough cleanliness will allow, he will gradually lose the recollection of former ill-treatment, and become tractable and quiet.

Vicious to Shoe.—The correction of this is more peculiarly the business of the smith; yet the master should diligently concern himself with it, for it is oftener the consequence of injudicious or bad usage than of natural vice. It may be expected that there will be some difficulty in shoeing a horse for the first few times. It is an operation that gives him a little uneasiness. The man to whom he is most accustomed should go with him to the forge; and if another and steady horse is shod before him, he may be induced more readily to submit. It cannot be denied that, after the habit of resisting this necessary operation is formed, force may be sometimes necessary to reduce our rebellious servant to obedience; but we unhesitatingly affirm that the majority of horses *vicious to shoe* are rendered so by harsh usage, and by the pain of correction being added to the uneasiness of shoeing. It should be a rule in every forge that no smith should be permitted to strike a horse, much less to twitch or to gag him, without the master-farrier's order; and that a young horse should never be twitched or struck. There are few horses that may not be gradually rendered manageable for this purpose by mildness and firmness in the operator. They will soon understand that no harm is meant, and they will not forget their usual habit of obedience; but if the remembrance of corporal punishment is connected with shoeing, they will always be fidgety, and occasionally dangerous.

Swallowing Without Grinding.—Horses have many unpleasant habits in the stable and on the road, which cannot be said to amount to vice, but which materially lessen their value.

Some greedy horses habitually swallow their grain without properly grinding it, and the power of digestion not being adequate to the dissolving of the husk, no nutriment is extracted, and the oats are voided whole. This is particularly the case when horses of unequal appetite feed from the same manger. The greedy one, in his eagerness to get more than his share, bolts a portion of his grain whole. If the farmer, without considerable inconvenience, could contrive that every horse shall have his separate division of the manger, the one of smaller appetite and slower feed would have the opportunity of grinding at his leisure, without the fear of the greater share being stolen by his neighbor.

Some horses, however, are naturally greedy feeders, and will not, even when alone, allow themselves time to chew or grind their grain. In consequence of this they carry but little flesh, and are not equal to severe work. If the rack was supplied with hay when the grain was put into the manger, they will continue to eat on, and their stomachs will become distended with half-chewed and indigestible food. In consequence of this they will be incapable of considerable exertion for a long time after feeding, and, occasionally, dangerous symptoms of staggers will occur.

The remedy is, not to let such horses fast too long. The nosebag should be the companion of every considerable journey. The food should likewise be of such a nature that it cannot be rapidly bolted. Chaff should be plentifully mixed with the grain, and, in some cases, and especially in horses of slow work, it should, with the grain, constitute the whole of the food. This will be treated on more at large under the article "Feeding."

In every case of this kind the teeth should be carefully examined. Some of them may be unduly lengthened, particularly the first of the grinders; or they may be ragged at the edges, and may abrade and wound the cheek. In the first place the horse cannot properly masticate his food; in the latter he will not; for these animals, as too often happens in sore-throat, would rather starve than put themselves to much pain.

Crib-Biting.—This is a very unpleasant habit, and a considerable defect, although not so serious a one as some have represented. The horse lays hold of the manger with his teeth, violently extends his neck, and then, after some convulsive action of the throat, a slight grunting is heard, accompanied by a sucking or drawing in of air. It is not an effort at simple eructation, arising from indigestion. It is the inhalation of air. It is that which takes place with all kinds of diet, and when the stomach is empty as well as when it is full.

The effects of crib-biting are plain enough. The teeth are injured and worn away, and that, in an old horse, to a very serious degree. A considerable quantity of grain is often lost, for the horse will frequently crib with his mouth full of it, and the greater part will fall over the edge of the manger. Much saliva escapes while the manger is thus forcibly held, the loss of which must be of serious detriment in impairing the digestion. The crib-biting horse is notoriously more subject to colic than other horses, and to a species difficult of treatment and frequently dangerous. Although many a crib-biter is stout and strong, and capable of all ordinary work, these horses do not generally carry so much flesh as others, and have not their endurance. On these accounts crib-biting has very properly been decided to be unsoundness. We must not look to the state of the disease at the time of purchase. The question is, does it exist at all? A case was tried before Lord Tenterden, and thus decided: "a horse with crib-biting is unsound."

It is one of those tricks which are exceedingly contagious. Every companion of a crib-biter in the same stables is likely to acquire the habit, and it is the most inveterate of all habits. The edge of the manger will in vain be lined with iron, or with sheep-skin, or with sheep-skin covered with tar or aloes, or any other unpleasant substance. In defiance of the annoyance which these may occasion, the horse will persist in the attack on his manger. A strap buckled tightly round the neck, by compressing the wind-pipe, is the best means of preventing the possibility of this trick; but the strap must be constantly worn, and its pressure is too apt to produce a worse affection, viz., an irritation in the wind-pipe, which terminates in roaring.

Some have recommended turning out for five or six months; but this has never succeeded except with a young horse, and then rarely. The old crib-biter will employ the gate for the same purpose as the edge of his manger, and we have often seen him galloping across a field for the mere object of having a gripe at a rail. Medicine will be altogether thrown away in this case.

The only remedy is a muzzle, with bars across the bottom; sufficiently wide to enable the animal to pick up his corn and to pull his hay, but not to grasp the edge of the manger. If this is worn for a considerable period, the horse may be tired of attempting that which he cannot accomplish, and for a while forget the habit, but in a majority of cases, the desire of crib-biting will return with the power of gratifying it.

The causes of crib-biting are various, and some of them beyond the control of the proprietor of the horse. It is often the result of imitation; but it is more frequently the consequence of idleness. The high fed and spirited horse must be in mischief if he is not usefully employed. Sometimes, but we believe not often, it is produced by partial starvation, whether in a bad straw-yard, or from unpalatable food. An occasional cause of crib-biting is the frequent custom of grooms, even when the weather is not severe, of dressing them in the stable. The horse either catches at the edge of the manger, or at that of the partition on each side, if he has been turned, and thus he forms the habit of laying hold of these substances on every occasion.

Wind-Sucking.—This bears a close analogy to crib-biting. It arises from the same causes; the same purpose is accomplished; and the same results follow. The horse stands with his neck bent; his head drawn inward; his lips alternately a little opened and then closed, and a noise is heard as if he were sucking. If we may judge from the same comparative want of condition and the flatulence which we have described under the last head, either some portion of wind enters the stomach, or there is an injurious loss of saliva. This diminishes the value of the horse almost as much as crib-biting; it is as contagious, and it is as inveterate. The only remedies, and they will seldom avail, are tying the head up, except when the horse is feeding, or putting on a muzzle with sharp spikes toward the neck, and which will prick him whenever he attempts to rein his head in for the purpose of wind-sucking.

Not Lying Down.—It not uncommonly happens that a horse will seldom or never lie down in the stable. He sometimes continues in apparent good health, and feeds and works well; but generally his legs swell, or he becomes fatigued sooner than another horse. If it is impossible to let him loose in the saddle, or to put him into a spare box, we know not what is to be done. No means, gentle or cruel, will force him to lie down. The secret is that he is tied up, and either has never dared to lie down through fear of the confinement of the halter, or he has been cast in the night and severely injured. If he can be suffered to range the stable, or have a comfortable box in which he may be loose, he will usually lie down the first night. Some few horses, however, will lie down in the stable, and not in a loose box. A fresh, well-made bed, will generally tempt the tired-out horse to refresh himself with sleep.

Overreach.—This unpleasant noise, known also by the term "clicking," arises from the toe of the hind-foot knocking against the shoe of the fore-foot.

If the animal is young, the action of the horse may be materially improved; otherwise nothing can be done, except to keep the toe of the hind foot as short and as round as it can safely be, and to bevel off and round the toe of the shoe, like that which has been worn off by a stumbling horse, and perhaps, to lower the heel of the fore-foot a little.

Pawing.—Some hot and irritable horses are restless even in the stable, and paw frequently and violently. Their litter is destroyed, the floor of the stable broken up, the shoes worn out, the feet bruised, and the legs sometimes sprained. If this habit does not exist to any great extent, yet the stable never looks well. Shackles are the only remedy, with a chain sufficiently long to enable the horse to shift his posture, or move in his stall; but these must be taken off at night, otherwise the animal will seldom lie down. Except, however, the horse possesses peculiar value, it will be better to dispose of him at once, than to submit to the danger and inconvenience that he may occasion.

Quidding.—A horse will sometimes partly chew his hay and suffer it to drop from his mouth. If this does not proceed from irregular teeth, which it will be the business of the veterinary surgeon to rasp down, it will be found to be connected with sore-throat, and then the horse will exhibit some other symptoms of indisposition, and particularly the swallowing of water will be accompanied by a peculiar gulping effort. In this case the disease (catarrh with sore-throat) must be attacked, and the quidding will cease.

Rolling.—This is a very pleasant and perfectly safe amusement for a horse at grass, but cannot be indulged in the stable without the chance of his being dangerously entangled with the collar-rein (halter) and being cast. Yet, although the horse is cast and bruised, and half-strangled, he will roll again on the following night and continue to do so as long as he lives. The only remedy is not a very pleasant one for the horse, nor always quite safe; yet it must be had recourse to, if the habit of rolling is inveterate. "The horse," says Mr. Castley, "should be tied with length enough of halter to lie down, but not to allow of his head resting on the ground; because, in order to roll over, a horse is obliged to place his head quite down upon the ground."

Shying.—We have before briefly treated of the cause of this vice, and observed that while it is often the result of cowardice or playfulness, or want of work, it is at other times the consequence of a defect of sight. It has been remarked, and we believe very truly, that shying is oftener a vice of half or quarter bred horses, than of those who have in them more of the genuine racing blood.

In the treatment of shying, it is of great importance to distinguish between that which is the consequence of defective sight, and what results from fear or newness of objects, or mere affectation or skittishness. For the first, the nature of which we have explained before, every allowance must be made, and care must be taken that the fear of correction is not associated with the imagined existence of some terrifying object. The severe use of the whip and the spur cannot do good here, and are likely to aggravate the vice tenfold. A word half encouraging and half scolding with a slight pressure of the heel or a slight touch of the spur, will tell the horse that there is nothing to fear, and will give him confidence in his rider on a future occasion.

The shying from skittishness or affectation is quite a different affair, and must be conquered—but how? Severity is altogether out of place. If he is forced into contact with the object by dint of correction, the dread of punishment will afterward be associated with that object, and on the next occasion his startings will be more frequent and more dangerous. The way to cure him is to go on, turning as little as possible out of the road, giving a harsh word or two and a gentle touch with the spur, and then taking no more notice of the matter. After a few times, whatever may have been the object which he chose to select as the pretended cause of affright, he will pass it almost without notice.

Under the head *Breaking-in* we described how the colt may be cured of the habit of shying from fear or newness of objects; and if he then is accustomed as much as possible to the objects among which his services will be required, he will not possess this annoying vice when he grows to maturer age.

It is now generally admitted by all riding-masters and colt-breakers, that a great deal more is to be effected by lenient than by harsh treatment. Rewards are found to operate more beneficially than punishments, and therefore the most scientific and practiced riding-masters adopt methods based upon the former.

Let us not be understood to mean that the animal is to receive any encouragement to shy; for by no other expression can be characterized that erroneous and foolish practice of patting the horse or "making much of him," either just before or during the time he evinces shyness. The former is bad, because it draws the attention of the animal to the object he dreads; the latter is worse, because it fills him with the impression either that the object itself is really terrific, or that he has acted right in shying at it, and ought to do so again.

Whether we are approaching the frightful object or the horse is actually shying, "we should let him alone," "we should take no notice whatever of him," neither letting him perceive that we are aware that we are advancing toward any thing he dislikes, nor do more with him while in the act of shying than is necessary for due restraint with a steady hand upon the rein. We may depend upon it, that battling on our part will only serve to augment affright and arouse resistance on his, and that the most judicious course we can pursue is to persevere in mild forbearant usage.

Shying on coming out of the stable is a habit that can rarely or never be cured. It proceeds from the remembrance of some ill-usage or hurt which the animal has received in the act of proceeding from the stable, such as striking his head against a low doorway or entangling the harness.

When the cure, however, is early attempted, it may be so far overcome that it will be unattended with danger or difficulty. The horse should be bridled when led out or in. He should be held short and tight by the head, that he may feel he has not liberty to make a leap, and this of itself is often sufficient to restrain him. Punishment, or a threat of punishment, will be highly improper. It is only timid or high-spirited horses that acquire this habit, and rough usage invariably increases their agitation and terror.

Slipping the Collar or Halter.—This is a trick at which many horses are so clever, that scarcely a night passes without their getting loose. It is a very serious habit, for it enables the horse sometimes to gorge himself with food, to the imminent danger of staggers; or it exposes him, as he wanders about, to be kicked and injured by the other horses, while his restlessness will often keep the whole team awake. If the web of the halter, being first accurately fitted to his neck, is suffered to slip only one way, or a strap is attached to the halter and buckled round the neck, but not sufficiently tight to be of serious inconvenience, the power of slipping the collar will be taken away.

Tripping.—He must be a skillful practitioner or a mere pretender who promises to remedy this habit. If it arises from a heavy forehand, and the fore-legs being too much under the horse, no one can alter the natural frame of the animal; if it proceeds from tenderness of the foot, grogginess, or old lameness, these ailments are seldom cured. Also if it is to be traced to habitual carelessness and idleness, no whipping will rouse the drone. A known stumbler should never be ridden or driven by any one who values his safety or his life. A tight hand or a strong bearing rein are precautions that should not be neglected, although they are generally of little avail; for the inveterate stumbler will rarely be able to save himself, and this tight rein may sooner and farther precipitate the rider. If after a trip the horse suddenly starts forward, and endeavors to break into a short trot or canter, the rider or driver may be assured that others before him have fruitlessly endeavored to remedy the nuisance.

If the stumbler has the foot kept as short, and the toe pared as close as safety will permit, and the shoe is rounded at the toe or has that shape given to it which it naturally acquires in a fortnight, from the peculiar action of such a horse, the animal may not stumble quite so much; or if the disease which produced the habit can be alleviated, some trifling good may be done, but in almost every case a stumbler should be got rid of, or put to slow and heavy work. If the latter alternative is adopted, he may trip as much as he pleases, for the weight of the load and the motion of the other horses will keep him upon his legs.

Weaving.—This consists in a motion of the head, neck, and body from side to side, like the shuttle of a weaver passing through the web, and hence the name which is given to this peculiar and incessant and unpleasant action. It indicates an impatient, irritable temper and a dislike to the confinement of the stable. A horse that is thus incessantly on the fret will seldom carry flesh, or be safe to ride or drive. There is no cure for it but the close tying up of the animal, or at least allowing him but one loose rein, except at feeding-time.

SOUNDNESS, AND THE PURCHASE AND SALE OF HORSES.—There are few sources of greater annoyance, both to the purchaser and the seller of the horse, than disputes with regard to the soundness of the animal.

That horse is sound in whom there is no disease, and no alteration of structure that impairs, or is likely to impair, his natural usefulness. The horse is unsound that labors under disease, or has some alteration of structure which does interfere, or is likely to interfere, with his natural usefulness. The term "*natural usefulness*" must be borne in mind. One horse may possess great speed, but is soon knocked up; another will work all day, but cannot be got beyond a snail's pace : a third with a heavy forehand is liable to stumble, and is continually putting to hazard the neck of his rider; another, with an irritable constitution and a loose, washy form, loses his appetite and begins to scour if a little extra work is exacted from him. The term unsoundness must not be applied to either of these; it would be opening far too widely a door to disputation and endless wrangling. The buyer can discern, or ought to know, whether the form of the horse is that which will render him likely to suit his purpose, and he should try him sufficiently to ascertain his natural strength, endurance, and manner of going. Unsoundness, we repeat, has reference only to disease, or to that alteration of structure which is connected with, or will produce disease, and lessen the usefulness of the animal.

These principles will be best illustrated by a brief consideration of the usually supposed appearances or causes of unsoundness.

Broken Knees certainly do not constitute unsoundness, after the wounds are healed, unless they interfere with the action of the joint; for the horse may have fallen from mere accident, or through the fault of the rider, without the slightest damage more than the blemish. No person, however, would buy a horse with broken knees, until he has thoroughly tried him, and satisfied himself as to his form and action.

Capped Hocks may be produced by lying on an unevenly paved stable, with a scanty supply of litter, or by kicking generally, in neither of which cases would they constitute unsoundness, although in the latter they would be an indication of vice; but, in the majority of instances, they are the consequence of sprain, or of latent injury of the hock, and accompanied by enlargement of it, and would constitute unsoundness. A special warranty should always be taken against capped hocks.

Contraction is a considerable deviation from the natural form of the foot, but not necessarily constituting unsoundness. It requires, however, a most careful examination on the part of the purchaser or veterinary surgeon, in order to ascertain that there is no heat about the quarter, or ossification of the cartilage—that the frog, although diminished in size, is not diseased—that the horse does not step short and go as if the foot were tender, and that there is not the slightest trace of lameness. Unless these circumstances, or some of them, are detected, a horse must not be pronounced to be unsound because his feet are contracted; for many horses with strangely contracted feet do not suffer at all in their action. A special warranty, however, should be required where the feet are at all contracted.

Corns manifestly constitute unsoundness. The portion of the foot in which bad corns are situated, will not bear the ordinary pressure of the shoe; and accidental additional pressure from the growing down of the horn, or the introduction of dirt or gravel, will cause serious lameness.

They render it necessary to wear a thick and heavy shoe, or a bar-shoe, in order to protect the weakened and diseased part; and they are very seldom radically cured. There may be, however, and frequently is, a difference of opinion as to the actual existence or character of the corn. They are sometimes, too, so slight that they do not diminish the value of the horse, and will disappear on the horse being shod with ordinary skill and care, even without any alteration in the shoe.

Cough.—This is a disease, and consequently unsoundness. However slight may be its degree, and of whatever short standing it may be, although it may sometimes scarcely seem to interfere with the usefulness of the horse, yet a change of stabling or slight exposure to wet and cold, or the least over-exertion, may, at other times, cause it to degenerate into many dangerous complaints. A horse, therefore, should never be purchased with a cough upon him, without a special warranty; or if—the cough not being observed—he is purchased under a general warranty, that warranty is thereby broken. It is not law, that a horse may be returned on breach of the warranty. The seller is not bound to take him back, unless he has contracted so to do; but he is liable to damages. Lord Ellenborough has completely decided this matter. "I have always held," said he, "that a warranty of soundness is broken, if the animal, at the time of sale, had any infirmity upon him that rendered him less fit for present service. It is not necessary that the disorder should be permanent or incurable. While he has a cough, he is unsound, although that may either be temporary or prove mortal."

In deciding on another case, the same judge said, " I have always held it that a cough is a breach of the warranty. On that understanding I have always acted, and think it quite clear." It was argued on the other hand that two-thirds of the horses in London had coughs, yet still the judge maintained that the cough was a breach of warranty. When it was farther argued that the horse had been hunted the day after the purchase, and the cough might have been increased by this, the reply was singular, but, decisive. "There is no proof that he would have got well if he had not been hunted."

Roaring, Wheezing, Whistling, High-blowing, and Grunting, being the result of alteration of structure, or disease in some of the air-passages, and interfering with the perfect freedom of breathing, especially when the horse is put on his speed, without doubt constitute unsoundness. There are decisions to the contrary, which are now universally admitted to be erroneous. Broken-wind is decidedly still more unsoundness.

Crib-Biting.—Although some learned judges have asserted that crib-biting is simply a trick or bad habit, it must be regarded as unsoundness. This unnatural sucking in of the air must, to a certain degree, injure digestion. It must dispose to colic, and so interfere with the strength, usefulness, and health of the horse. Some crib-biters are good goers, but they probably would have possessed more endurance had they not acquired this habit; and it is a fact well established that, as soon as a horse becomes a crib-biter, he, in nine cases out of ten, loses condition. In its very early stage it may be a mere trick—confirmed, it must have produced morbid deterioration. The wear of the front teeth, and the occasional breaking of them, make a horse old before his time, and sometimes render it difficult or impossible for him to graze, when the state of the animal or the convenience of the owner requires that he should be turned out.

Curb constitutes unsoundness while it lasts, and perhaps while the swelling remains, although the inflammation may have subsided; for a horse that has once thrown out a curb is, for a while at least, very liable to do so again, to get lame in the same place on the slightest extra exertion; or, at all events, he would there first fail on extraordinary exertion. A horse, however, is not returnable, although he should spring a curb five minutes after the purchase; for it is done in a moment, and does not necessarily indicate any previous unsoundness or weakness of the part.

Cutting, as rendering a horse liable to serious injury of the legs, and indicating that he is either weak, or has an awkwardness of gait inconsistent with safety, produces, rather than this, unsoundness. Many horses go lame for a considerable period after cutting themselves severely; and others have dropped from the sudden agony, and endangered themselves and their riders. As some doubt, however, exists on this subject, and as it is a very material objection to a horse, cutting, when evident, should have its serious consequences provided against by a special warranty.

Enlarged Glands.—The enlargement of the glands under the jaw has not been so much considered as it ought to have been in our estimate of the soundness of the horse. Simple catarrh will occasionally, and severe affection of the chest will generally, be accompanied by swelling of these glands, which does not subside for a considerable time after the cold or fever has apparently been cured. To slight enlargements of the glands under the jaw much attention need not be paid; but if they are of considerable size, and especially if they are tender, and the glands at the root of the ear partake of the enlargement, and the membrane of the nose is redder than it should be, we should hesitate in pronouncing that horse to be sound. We must consider the swelling as a symptom of disease.

Enlarged Hock.—A horse with enlarged hock is unsound, the structure of this complicated joint being so materially affected that, although the horse may appear for a considerable time to be capable of ordinary work, he will occasionally fail even in that, and a few days' hard work will always lame him.

The Eyes.—That inflammation of the eye of the horse which usually terminates in blindness of one or both eyes, has the peculiar character of receding or disappearing for a time, once or twice, or thrice, before it fully runs its course. The eye, after an attack of inflammation, regains so nearly its former natural brilliancy, that a person even well acquainted with horses will not always recognize the traces of former disease. After a time, however, the inflammation returns, and the result is inevitable. A horse that has had one attack of this complaint is long afterward unsound, however perfect the eye may seem to be, because he carries about with him a disease that will probably again break out, and eventually destroy the sight. Whether, therefore, he may be rejected or not depends on the possibility of proving an attack of inflammation of the eye prior to the purchase. Next to direct evidence of this are appearances about the eye, of which the veterinary surgeon at least ought not to be ignorant. They consist chiefly of a puckering of the lids toward the inner corner of one or both eyes—a difference in the size of the eyes, although perhaps only a slight one, and not discovered except it be looked for—a gloominess of the eye—a dullness of the iris—a little dullness of the transparent part of the eye generally—a minute, faint, dusky spot deep in the eye, and generally with little radiations of white lines proceeding from it. If these symptoms, or the majority of them, existed at the time of purchase, the animal had assuredly been diseased before, and was unsound. Starting has been considered as unequivocal proof. It is usually an indication of defective sight, but it is occasionally a trick. Connected, however, with the appearances just described, it is a very strong corroborative proof.

Lameness, from whatever cause arising, is unsoundness. However temporary it may be, or however obscure, there must be disease which lessens the utility of the horse, and renders him unsound for the time. So says common sense, but there are contradictory decisions on the case. "A horse laboring under a temporary injury or hurt, which is capable of being speedily cured or removed, is not, according to Chief Justice Eyre, an unsound horse; and where a warranty is made that such a horse is sound, it is made without any view to such an injury; nor is a horse so circumstanced within the meaning of the warranty. To vitiate the warranty, the injury the horse had sustained, or the malady under which he labored, ought to be of a permanent nature, and not such as may arise from a temporary injury or accident."

On the contrary, Lord Ellenborough says: "I have always held, and now hold, that a warranty of soundness is broken, if the animal at the time of sale has any infirmity upon him which renders him less fit for present service. It is not necessary that the disorder should be permanent or incurable. While a horse has a cough he is unsound, although it may either be temporary or may prove mortal. The horse in question having been lame at the time of sale, when he was warranted to be sound, his condition subsequently is no defense to the action.* The decision of Mr. Baron Parke, already referred to, confirms this doctrine.

Neurotomy.—A question has arisen how far a horse that has undergone the operation of the division of the nerve of the leg and has recovered from the lameness with which he was before affected, and stands his work well, may be considered to be sound. Chief Justice Best held such a horse to be unsound, and in our opinion there cannot be a doubt about the matter. The operation of neurotomy does not remove the disease causing the lameness, but only the sensation of pain. A horse on whom this operation has been performed may be improved by it—may cease to be lame—may go well for many years; but there is no certainty of this, and he is unsound, within our definition, unless nature gave the nerve for no useful purpose.

Ossification of the Lateral Cartilages constitutes unsoundness, as inter-

---

* 4 CAMPBELL. 251, Elton vs. Brogden.

fering with the natural expansion of the foot, and, in horses of quick work, almost universally producing lameness.

Pumiced-Foot.—When the union between the horny and sensible laminæ, or little plates of the foot is weakened, and the coffin-bone is let down, and presses upon the sole, and the sole yields to this unnatural weight, and becomes rounded, and is brought in contact with the ground, and is bruised and injured, that horse must be unsound, and unsound forever, because there are no means by which we can raise the coffin-bone again into its place.

Quidding.—If the mastication of the food gives pain to the animal, in consequence of soreness of the mouth or throat, he will drop it before it is perfectly chewed. This, as an indication of disease, constitutes unsoundness. Quidding sometimes arises from irregularity in the teeth, which wound the cheek with their sharp edges; or a protruding tooth renders it impossible for the horse to close his jaws so as to chew his food thoroughly. Quidding is unsoundness for the time; but the unsoundness will cease when the teeth are properly filed, or the soreness or other cause of the imperfect chewing removed.

Quitter is manifestly unsoundness.

Ring-Bone.—Although when the bony tumor is small, and on one side only, there is little or no lameness—and there are a few instances in which a horse with ring-bone has worked for many years without its return—yet from the action of the foot, and the stress upon the part, the inflammation and the formation of bone may acquire a tendency to spread so rapidly, that we must pronounce the slightest enlargement of the pasterns, or around the coronet, to be a cause of unsoundness.

Sand-Crack is manifestly unsoundness. It may, however, occur without the slightest warning, and no horse can be rejected on account of a sand-crack that has sprung after purchase. Its usual cause is too great brittleness of the crust of the hoof; but there is no infallible method of detecting this, or the degree in which it must exist in order to constitute unsoundness. When the horn round the bottom of the foot has chipped off so much that only a skillful smith can fasten the shoe without pricking the horse, or even when there is a tendency in the horn to chip and break in a much less degree than this, the horse is unsound, for the brittleness of the crust is a disease of the part, or it is such an altered structure of it as to interfere materially with the usefulness of the animal.

Spavin.—Bone spavin, comprehending in its largest sense every bony tumor on the hock, is not necessarily unsoundness. If the tumor affects in the slightest degree the action of the horse, it is unsoundness;—even if it does not, it is seldom safe to pronounce it otherwise than unsoundness. But it may possibly be (like splint in the fore-leg) so situated as to have no tendency to affect the action. A veterinary surgeon consulted on the purchase will not always reject a horse because of such a tumor. His evidence on a question of soundness will depend on the facts. The situation and history of the tumor may be such as to enable him to give a decisive opinion in a horse going sound, but not often.

Bog or Blood Spavin is unsoundness, because, although it may not be productive of lameness at slow work, the rapid and powerful action of the hock in quicker motion will produce permanent, yet perhaps not considerable lameness, which can scarcely ever be with certainty removed.

Splint.—It depends entirely on the situation of the bony tumor on the shank-bone, whether it is to be considered as unsoundness. If it is not in the neighborhood of any joint, so as to interfere with its action, and if it does not press upon any ligament or tendon, it may be no cause of unsoundness, although it is often very unsightly. In many cases, it may not lessen the capability and value of the animal.

Stringhalt.—This singular and very unpleasant action of the hind-leg is decidedly an unsoundness. It is an irregular communication of nervous energy to some muscle of the thigh, observable when the horse first comes from the stable, and gradually ceasing on exercise. It has usually been accompanied by a more than common degree of strength and endurance. It must, however, be traced to some morbid alteration of structure or function; and it rarely or never fails to deteriorate and gradually wear out the animal.

Thickening of the Back Sinews.—Sufficient attention is not always paid to the fineness of the legs of the horse. If the flexor tendons have been sprained, so as to produce considerable thickening of the cellular substance in which their sheaths are enveloped, they will long afterward, or perhaps always, be liable to sprain, from causes by which they would otherwise be scarcely affected. The continuance of any considerable thickness around the sheaths of the tendons indicates previous violent sprain. This very thickening will fetter the action of the tendons, and, after much quick work, will occasionally renew the inflammation and the lameness; therefore such a horse cannot be sound. It requires, however, a little discrimination to distinguish this from the *gumminess* or roundness of leg peculiar to some breeds. There should be an evident difference between the injured leg and the other.

Thoroughpin, except it is of great size, is rarely productive of lameness, and therefore cannot be termed unsoundness; but as it is the consequence of hard work, and now and then does produce lameness, the hock should be most carefully examined, and there should be a special warranty against it.

Thrush.—There are various cases on record of actions on account of thrush in horses, and the decisions have been much at variance, or perfectly contradictory. Thrush has not been always considered by legal men as unsoundness. We, however, decidedly so consider it; as being a disease interfering and likely to interfere with the usefulness of the horse. Thrush is inflammation of the lower surface of the inner or sensible frog—and the secretion or throwing out of pus—almost invariably accompanied by a slight degree of tenderness of the frog itself, or of the heel a little above it, and, if neglected, leading to diminution of the substance of the frog, and separation of the horn from parts beneath and underrunning, and the production of fungus and canker, and ultimately a diseased state of the foot, destructive of the present and dangerous to the future usefulness of the horse.

Windgalls.—There are few horses perfectly free from windgalls, but they do not interfere with the action of the fetlock, or cause lameness, except when they are numerous or large. They constitute unsoundness only when they cause lameness, or are so large and numerous as to render it likely that they will cause it.

In the purchase of a horse, the buyer usually receives, embodied in the receipt, what is termed a warranty. It should be thus expressed:

"Received of A B two hundred dollars for a gray mare, warranted only five years old, sound, free from vice, and quiet to ride or drive.
"$200. "C D."

A receipt including merely the word "warranted" extends only to soundness; "warranted sound" goes no farther; the age, freedom from vice, and quietness to ride and drive, should be especially named. This warranty comprises every cause of unsoundness that can be detected, or that lurks in the constitution at the time of sale, and to every vicious habit that the animal has hitherto shown. To establish a breach of warranty, and to be enabled to tender a return of the horse and recover the difference of price, the purchaser must prove that it was unsound or viciously disposed at the time of sale. In case of cough, the horse must have been heard to cough immediately after the purchase, or as he was led home, or as soon as he had entered the stable of the purchaser. Coughing, even on the following morning, will not be sufficient; for it is possible that he might have caught cold by change of stabling. If he is lame, it must be proved to arise from a cause that existed before the animal was in the purchaser's possession. No price will imply a warranty, or be equivalent to one; there must be an express warranty. A fraud must be proved in the seller, in order that the buyer may be enabled to return the horse or maintain an action for the price. The warranty should be given at the time of sale. A warranty, or a promise to warrant the horse given at any period antecedent to the sale, is invalid, for horse-flesh is a very perishable commodity, and the constitution and usefulness of the animal may undergo a considerable change in the space of a few days. A warranty after the sale is invalid, for it is given without any legal consideration. In order to complete the purchase, there must be a transfer of the animal, or a memorandum of agreement, or the payment of the earnest-money. The least sum will suffice for earnest. No verbal promise to buy or to sell is binding without one of these. The moment either of these is effected, the legal transfer of property or delivery is made, and, whatever may happen to the horse, the seller retains, or is entitled to the money. If the purchaser exercises any act of ownership, by using the animal without leave of the vender, or by having any operation performed, or any medicine given to him, he makes him his own. The warranty of a servant is considered to be binding on the master.

If the horse should be afterward discovered to have been unsound at the time of warranty, the buyer may tender a return of it, and, if it be not taken back, may bring his action for the price; but the seller is not bound to rescind the contract, unless he has agreed so to do.

Although there is no legal compulsion to give immediate notice to the seller of the discovered unsoundness, it will be better to have it done.

The animal should then be tendered at the house or stable of the vendor. If he refuses to receive him, the animal may be sent to a livery-stable and sold, and an action for the difference in price may be brought. The keep, however, can be recovered only for the time that necessarily intervened between the tender and the determination of the action. It is not legally necessary to tender a return of the horse as soon as the unsoundness is discovered. The animal may be kept for a reasonable time afterward, and even proper medical means used to remove the unsoundness; but courtesy, and indeed justice, will require that the notice should be given as soon as possible. Although it is stated, on the authority of Lord Loughborough, that "no length of time elapsed after the sale will alter the nature of a contract originally false," yet it seems to have been once thought it was necessary to the action to give notice of the unsoundness in a reasonable time. The cause of action is certainly complete on breach of the warranty.

It used to be supposed that the buyer had no right to have the horse medically treated, and that he would waive the warranty by doing so. The question, however, would be, has he injured or diminished the value of the horse by this treatment? It will generally be prudent for him to refrain from all medical treatment, because the means adopted, however skillfully employed, may have an unfortunate effect, or may be misrepresented by ignorant or interested observers.

The purchaser possibly may like the horse, notwithstanding his discovered defect, and he may retain, and bring his action for the depreciation in value on account of the unsoundness. Few, however, will do this, because his retaining the horse will cause a suspicion that the defect was of no great consequence, and will give rise to much cavil about the quantum of damages, and, after all, very slight damages will probably be obtained. "I take it to be clear law," says Lord Eldon, "that if a person purchases a horse that is warranted, and it afterward turns out that the horse was unsound at the time of warranty, the buyer may, if he pleases, keep the horse, and bring an action on the warranty; in which he will have a right to recover the difference between the value of a sound horse and one with such defects as existed at the time of warranty; or he may return the horse, and bring an action to recover the full money; but, in the latter case, the seller has a right to expect that the horse shall be returned to him in the same state he was when sold, and not by any means diminished in value; for if a person keep a warranted article for any length of time after discovering its defects, and when he returns it, it is in a worse state than it would have been if returned immediately after such discovery, I think the party can have no defense to an action for the price of the article on the ground of non-compliance with the warranty, but must be left to his action on the warranty to recover the difference in the value of the article warranted, and its value when sold.*

Where there is no warranty, an action may be brought on the ground of fraud; but this is very difficult to be maintained, and not often hazarded. It will be necessary to prove that the dealer knew the defect,

---

* Curtis *vs.* Hannay, 3 Esp. 83.

and that the purchaser was imposed upon by his false representation, or other fraudulent means. If the defect was evident to every eye, the purchaser has no remedy—he should have taken more care; but if a warranty was given, that extends to all unsoundness, palpable or concealed. Although a person should ignorantly or carelessly buy a blind horse, warranted sound, he may reject it—the warranty is his guard, and prevents him from so closely examining the horse as he otherwise would have done; but if he buys a blind horse, thinking him to be sound, and without a warranty, he has no remedy. Every one ought to exercise common circumspection and common sense.

A man should have a more perfect knowledge of horses than falls to the lot of most, and a perfect knowledge of the vender too, who ventures to buy a horse without a warranty.

If a person buys a horse warranted sound, and discovering no defect in him, and, relying on the warranty, resells him, and the unsoundness is discovered by the second purchaser, and the horse returned to the first purchaser, or an action commenced against him, he has his claim on the first seller, and may demand of him not only the price of the horse, or the difference in value, but every expense that may have been incurred.

Absolute exchanges, of one horse for another, or a sum of money being paid in addition by one of the parties, stand on the same ground as simple sales. If there is a warranty on either side, and that is broken, an action may be maintained: if there be no warranty, deceit must be proved.

The trial of horses on sale often leads to disputes. The law is perfectly clear, but the application of it, as in other matters connected with horse-flesh, attended with glorious uncertainty. The intended purchaser is only liable for damage done to the horse through his own misconduct. The seller may put what restriction he chooses on the trial, and takes the risks of all accidents in the fair use of the horse within such restrictions.

If a horse from a dealer's stable is galloped far and fast, it is probable that he will soon show distress; and if he is pushed farther, inflammation and death may ensue. The dealer rarely gets recompensed for this; nor ought he, as he knows the unfitness of his horse, and may thank himself for permitting such a trial; and if it should occur soon after the sale, he runs the risk of having the horse returned, or of an action for its price.

It is proper, however, to put a limit to what has been too frequently asserted from the bench, that a horse warranted sound must be taken as fit for immediate use, and capable of being immediately put to any fair work the owner chooses. A hunter honestly warranted sound is certainly warranted to be in immediate condition to follow the hounds. The mysteries of condition, as has been shown in a former part of the work, are not sufficiently unraveled.

One of the regulations of the Bazaar in King Street was exceedingly fair, both with regard to the previous owner and the purchaser, viz.—

" When a horse, having been warranted sound, shall be returned within the prescribed period, on account of unsoundness, a certificate from a veterinary surgeon, particularly describing the unsoundness, must accompany the horse so returned; when, if it be agreed to by the veterinary surgeon of the establishment, the amount received for the horse shall be immediately paid back; but if the veterinary surgeon of the establishment should not confirm the certificate, then, in order to avoid further dispute, one of the veterinary surgeons of the college shall be called in, and his decision shall be final, and the expense of such umpire shall be borne by the party in error."

DISEASES OF THE HORSE AND THEIR TREATMENT.—This work, not being prepared for the veterinary practitioner, but for all horse owners, our aim, therefore, in arranging this part of it will be to make them acquainted with the causes, nature, and remedies of the diseases of the horse, so that they may avoid the causes, detect the existence of disease, and themselves apply the remedies, or secure their application by experienced persons.

It may be readily supposed that the animal doomed to the manner of living which every variety of the horse experiences, will be peculiarly exposed to numerous forms of suffering; every natural evil will be aggravated, and many new and formidable sources of pain and death will be superadded.

The principal diseases of the horse are connected with the circulatory system. From the state of habitual excitement in which the animal is kept, in order to enable him to execute his task, the heart and bloodvessels will often act too impetuously; the vital fluid will be hurried along too rapidly, either through the frame generally, or some particular part of it, and there will be *congestion,* accumulation of blood in that part, or *inflammation,* either local or general, disturbing the functions of some organ, or of the whole frame.

Congestion.—Take a young horse on his first entrance into the stables; feed him somewhat highly, and what is the consequence? He has swellings of the legs, or inflammation of the joints, or perhaps of the lungs. Take a horse that has lived somewhat above his work, and gallop him to the top of his speed: his nervous system becomes excited—the heart beats with fearful rapidity—the blood is pumped into the lungs faster than they can discharge it—the pulmonary vessels become gorged, fatigued, and utterly powerless—the blood, arrested in in its course, becomes viscid, and death speedily ensues. We have but one chance of saving our patient—the instantaneous and copious extraction of blood; and only one means of preventing the recurrence of this dangerous state; namely, not suffering too great an accumulation of the sanguineous fluid by over-feeding, and by regular and systematic exercise, which will inure the circulatory vessels to prompt and efficient action when they are suddenly called upon to exert themselves. This is an extreme case, but the cause and the remedy are sufficiently plain.

Again, the brain has functions of the most important nature to discharge, and more blood flows through it than through any other portion of the frame of equal bulk. In order to prevent this organ from being oppressed by a too great determination of blood to it, the vessels although numerous, are small, and pursue a very circuitous and winding course. If a horse highly fed and full of blood is suddenly and sharply exercised, the course of the blood is accelerated in every direction, and to the brain among other parts. The vessels that ramify on its surface, or penetrate its substance, are completely distended and gorged with it; perhaps they are ruptured, and the effused blood presses upon the brain; it presses upon the origins of the nerves, on which sensation and motion depend, and the animal suddenly drops powerless. A prompt and copious abstraction of blood; or, in other words, a diminution of this pressure, can alone save the patient. Here is the nature, the cause, and the treatment of *apoplexy*.

Sometimes this disease assumes a different form. The horse has not been performing more than his ordinary work, or perhaps he may not have been out of the stable. He is found with his head drooping and his vision impaired. He is staggering about. He falls, and lies half unconscious, or he struggles violently and dangerously. There is the same congestion of blood in the head, the same pressure on the nervous organs, but produced by a different cause. He has been accustomed habitually to overload his stomach, or he was, on the previous day, kept too long without his food, and then he fell ravenously upon it, and ate until his stomach was completely distended and unable to propel forward its accumulated contents. Thus distended, its blood-vessels are compressed, and the circulation through them is impeded or altogether suspended. The blood is still forced on by the heart, and driven in accumulated quantity to other organs, and to the brain among the rest, and there congestion takes place, as just described, and the animal becomes sleepy, unconscious, and if he is not speedily relieved, he dies. This, too, is apoplexy: the horseman calls it *stomach staggers*. Its cause is improper feeding. The division of the hours of labor, and the introduction of the *nose-bag*, have much diminished the frequency of its occurrence. The remedies are plain: bleeding, physicking, and the removal of the contents of the stomach by means of a pump contrived for that purpose.

Congestions of other kinds occasionally present themselves. It is no uncommon thing for the blood to loiter in the complicated vessels of the *liver*, until the covering of that viscus has burst, and an accumulation of coagulated black blood has presented itself. This congestion constitutes the *swelled legs* to which so many horses are subject when they stand too long idle in the stable; and it is a source of many of the accumulations of serous fluid in various parts of the body, and particularly in the chest, the abdomen, and the brain.

Inflammation is opposed to *congestion*, as consisting in an active state of the capillary arterial vessels; the blood rushes through them with far greater rapidity than in health, from the excited state of the nervous system by which they are supplied.

Inflammation is either *local* or *diffused*. It may be confined to one organ, or a particular portion of that organ; it may involve many neighboring ones, or it may be spread over the whole frame. In the latter case it assumes the name of *fever*. Fever is general or constitutional inflammation, and it is said to be *sympathetic* or *symptomatic* when it can be traced to some local affection or cause, and *idiopathic* when we cannot so trace it. The truth probably is, that every fever has its local cause; but we have not a sufficient knowledge of the animal economy to discover that cause.

Inflammation may be considered with reference to the membranes which it attacks.

The *mucous membranes* line all the cavities that communicate with the external surface of the body. There is frequent inflammation of the membrane of the mouth. *Blain*, or *Glysynthrax*, is a vesicular enlargement which runs along the side of the tongue. Its cause is unknown. It should be lanced freely and deeply, and some aperient medicine administered. *Barbs*, or *paps*, are smaller enlargements, found more in the neighborhood of the bridle of the tongue. They should never be touched with any instrument: a little cooling medicine will generally remove them. *Lampas* is inflammation of the palate, or enlargement of the bars of the palate. The roof of the mouth may be slightly lanced, or a little aperient medicine administered; but the sensibility of the mouth should never be destroyed by the application of the heated iron. *Canker and wounds in the mouth*, from various causes, will be best remedied by diluted tincture of myrrh, or a weak solution of alum.

Foreign Bodies in the Gullet may be generally removed by means of the probang used in the hove of cattle; or the œsophagus may be opened, and the obstructing body taken out.

It is on the mucous membranes that *poisons* principally exert their influence. The *yew* is the most frequent vegetable poison. The horse may be saved by timely recourse to equal parts of vinegar and water ejected into the stomach, after the poison has been as much as possible removed by means of the stomach-pump. For arsenic or corrosive sublimate there is rarely any antidote.

Spasmodic Colic is too frequently produced by exposure to cold, the drinking of cold water, or the use of too much green food. The horse should be walked about, strong friction used to the belly, and spirit of turpentine given in doses of two ounces, with an ounce each of laudanum and spirit of nitrous ether, in warm water, ale, or gruel. If the spasm is not soon relieved, the animal should be bled, and injections of warm water with a solution of aloes thrown up, if constipation exists. This spasmodic action of the bowels, when long continued, is liable to produce *introsusception*, or *entanglement*, of them; and the case is then hopeless.

Superpurgation often follows the administration of a too strong or improper dose of physic. The torture which it produces will be evident by the agonized expression of the countenance, and the frequent looking at the flanks. Plenty of thin starch or arrowroot should be given both by the mouth and by injection; and, twelve hours having passed without relief being experienced, chalk, catechu, and opium should be added to the gruel.

Worms in the intestines are not often productive of much mischief, except they exist in very great quantities. Small doses of emetic tartar or calomel, with a little ginger, may be given to the horse half an hour before his first meal, in order to expel the round white worm; it must be worked off with linseed-oil or aloes, and injections of linseed-oil or aloes will usually remove the ascarides, or needle-worms.

4*

The **Respiratory Passages** are all lined by the mucous membrane. *Catarrh*, or *cold*, inflammation of the upper air-passages, should never be long neglected. A few mashes or a little medicine will usually remove it. If it is neglected, and occasionally in defiance of all treatment, it will degenerate into other diseases. The larynx may become the principal seat of inflammation. *Laryngitis* will be shown by extreme difficulty of breathing, accompanied by a strange roaring noise, and an evident enlargement and great tenderness of the larynx when felt externally. The windpipe must be opened in such case, and the best advice will be necessary. Sometimes the subdivisions of the trachea, before or when it first enters the lungs, will be the part affected, and we have *bronchitis*. This is characterized by a quick and hard breathing, and a peculiar wheezing sound, with the coughing up of mucus. Here, too, decisive measures must be adopted, and a skillful practitioner employed. His assistance is equally necessary in *distemper*, *influenza*, and *epidemic catarrh*, names indicating varieties of the same disease, and the product of atmospheric influence; differing to a certain degree in every season, but in all characterized by intense inflammation of the mucous surfaces, and rapid and utter prostration of strength, and in all demanding the abatement of that inflammation, and yet little expenditure of vital power.

Cough may degenerate into *inflammation of the lungs;* or this fearful malady may be developed without a single premonitory symptom, and prove fatal in twenty-four or even in twelve hours. It is mostly characterized by deathly coldness of the extremities, expansion of the nostril, redness of its lining membrane, singularly anxious countenance, constant gazing at the flank, and an unwillingness to move. A successful treatment of such a case can be founded only on the most prompt and fearless and decisive measures; the lancet should be freely used. Counter-irritants should follow as soon as the violence of the disease is in the slightest degree abated; sedatives must succeed to them; and fortunate will he be who often saves his patient after all the decisive symptoms of pneumonia are once developed.

The diseases of the lungs have been recently carefully investigated, and we are enabled to detect three important varieties in the inflammatory affections of the lungs and chest, viz., congestive inflammation of the lungs, or *pulmonary apoplexy—pneumonia*, or true inflammation of the lungs—and *pleurisy*, or pleuritis. The first consists in the distention of the small vessels of the lungs with dark venous blood, and is generally produced by over-exertion, particularly if the animal, when attacked, is not in proper condition for work. The symptoms are rapid breathing, cold extremities, and short duration of the disease, ending either in death or recovery. When death supervenes, the lungs are black. With regard to treatment, bleeding should be adopted if the pulse is distinct as well as rapid; if not, a diffusible stimulant should first be given and bleeding should follow.

True pneumonia is longer in its duration, but the symptoms are often obscure at first. There is considerable distress, but there does not appear to be any active pain; and in this respect it may generally be distinguished from *pleurisy*. The pulse is full, strong, and rapid—pain, sometimes acute, but varying from time to time, and the blood presenting a considerable quantity of buff, or fibrine. The tendencies of the disease are either the deposition of water in the chest, or else fibrous flakes, and sometimes both conjoined.

Sometimes pneumonia and pleurisy are combined together, causing *pleuropneumonia*, and then the danger is increased at the same time, as the symptoms are rendered more obscure.

Blood-letting is one of the first of our remedial measures for these diseases, but is called for in a more marked degree in pleurisy than in pneumonia. The pulse, however, in both cases must be our guide as to the quantity to be taken; and, as stated in the text, a decided effect should be obtained. Repetition of bleeding, too, may be had recourse to with greater freedom, in pleurisy than in pneumonia. In the latter disease, we must take care that we do not shipwreck the vital powers by repeated and too copious bleeding, or mistake the effects produced by bleeding for the symptoms of the disease itself. It is only by the conjoint aids of science and experience that these nice discriminations can be made; it is therefore the height of folly for the inexperienced owner to attempt to treat such cases himself.

When pleurisy and pneumonia are combined, the symptoms, though extremely severe, are yet very obscure, and the chances of successful treatment are much diminished. The water in the chest spoken of in the text, is the termination of pleurisy, and becomes fatal in a majority of cases (particularly if, in addition to this serous fluid, flakes of lymph are also thrown out.) In some cases where water in the chest has supervened early, and the inflammation has otherwise subsided, relief has been obtained by tapping.

We have little to add with regard to the treatment of these inflammatory diseases, except that we do not approve of many repeated bleedings. It is rarely the case that more than one bleeding is desirable, but this in general should be very copious. The best guide as to the propriety of bleeding is the strength of the pulse and not its frequency. If some hours after the first bleeding the pulse is still strong and full, as well as quick, then bleeding is most probably called for again, and more particularly if the blood has exhibited a thick buffy coat. If the first bleeding has exhibited no buff on the surface, then a repetition of bleeding is rarely demanded. Aloes should be always eschewed, and diuretics should not be continued after twelve drachms, or two ounces of nitre or resin have been taken. We have also found very good effects from the administration of small doses of calomel and opium, twice a day, two scruples of the former, and one of the latter, being sufficient for a dose; and we have also found an ounce or two of the spirit of nitrous ether very serviceable in the early stage of the disease, particularly if the legs and ears are cold.

Among the consequences of these severe affections of the lungs, are *chronic cough*, not always much diminishing the usefulness of the horse, but strangely aggravated at times by any fresh accession of catarrh, and too often degenerating into *thick wind*, which always materially interferes with the speed of the horse, and in a great proportion of cases terminates in broken wind. It is rare, indeed, that either of these diseases admits of cure. That obstruction in some part of the respiratory canal, which varies in almost every horse, and produces the peculiar sound termed *roaring*, is also rarely removed. There are as many degrees or intonations of roaring, as there are notes on the gamut; and those notes ascend from piano to forte. This renders it difficult in some slight cases to decide positively whether a horse is a roarer or not; and good judges may be mistaken. The state of the animal very frequently occasions an impediment to an accurate decision; if he be in very plethoric condition, he will not unfrequently give slight indications of roaring; but when he is divested of that superabundance of fat, all the disagreeable symptoms disappear. The usual test of startling the animal, is by no means an infallible criterion, neither is the stethoscope in all cases to be relied upon. There is but one positive mode of determining the question; the animal being in a proper condition, he must be ridden and tried in all his paces. With stallions this proof is not often practicable; and unless they are badly affected, it is often impossible to prove that they are roarers.

Glanders, the most destructive of all the diseases to which the horse is exposed, is *the consequence of breathing the atmosphere of foul and vitiated stables*. It is the winding up of almost every other disease, and in every stage it is most contagious. Its most prominent symptoms are a small but constant discharge of sticky matter from the nose; an enlargement and induration of the glands beneath and within the lower jaw, on one or both sides, and, before the termination of the disease, chancrous inflammation of the nostril on the same side with the enlarged gland. Its contagiousness should never be forgotten, for if a glandered horse is once introduced into a stable, almost every inhabitant of that stable will sooner or later become infected and die.

If some persons underrate the danger, it is because the disease may remain unrecognized in the infected horse for some months, or even years, and therefore, when it appears, it is attributed to other causes, or to after-inoculation. No glandered horse should be employed on any farm, nor should a glandered horse be permitted to work on any road, or even to pasture on any field. He should be destroyed.

In a well settled case of glanders it is not worth while, except by way of experiment at a veterinary school, to attempt any remedies. The chances of cure are too remote, and the danger of infection too great.

The contagious nature of glanders is very well known, and not only is it so with regard to the horse, but it is capable of being communicated to the human being; and, indeed, there have been very many deaths from this cause, and most horrible deaths they are. It is generally by means of some cut or abrasion which comes in contact with the glandered matter that the infection is communicated. The utmost caution should therefore be exercised by the attendants; and it is most unpardonable to keep glandered horses any length of time for the sake of their work; and we are scarcely justified in tampering long with them under the idea of effecting a cure, when the cases are decidedly glandered.

The urinary and genital organs are also lined by mucous membranes. The horse is subject to inflammation of the kidneys from eating musty oats or mow-burnt hay, from exposure to cold, injuries of the loins, and the imprudent use of diuretics. Bleeding, physic and counter-irritants over the region of the loins should be had recourse to. Diabetes or profuse staling is difficult to treat. The inflammation that may exist should first be subdued, and then opium, catechu, and the *Uva ursi* administered. Inflammation of the bladder will be best alleviated by mucilaginous drinks of almost any kind, linseed-gruel taking precedence of all others. Inflammation of the neck of the bladder, evinced by the frequent and painful discharge of small quantities of urine will yield only to the abstraction of blood and the exhibition of opium. A catheter may be easily passed into the bladder of the mare and urine evacuated; but it will require a skillful veterinary surgeon to effect this in the horse. A stone in the bladder is readily detected by the practitioner, and may be extracted with comparative ease. The sheath of the penis is often diseased from the presence of corrosive mucous matter. This may easily be removed with warm soap and water.

To the mucous membranes belong the conjunctival tunic of the eye; and the diseases of the eye generally may be here considered. A scabby itchiness on the edge of the eyelid may be cured by a diluted nitrated ointment of mercury. Warts should be cut off with the scissors and the roots touched with lunar caustic. Inflammation of the haw should be abated by the employment of cooling lotions, but that useful defense of the eye should never if possible be removed. Common ophthalmia will yield as readily to cooling applications as inflammation of the same organ in any other animal; but there is another species of inflammation, commencing in the same way as the first, and for a while apparently yielding to treatment, but which changes from eye to eye, and returns again and again, until blindness is produced in one or both organs of vision. The most frequent cause is hereditary predisposition. The reader cannot be too often reminded that the qualities of the sire, good or bad, descend, and scarcely changed, to his offspring. How moon blindness was first produced no one knows; but its continuance in our stables is to be traced to this cause principally, or almost alone; and it pursues its course until cataract is produced for which there is no remedy. *Gutta serena* (palsy of the optic nerve) is sometimes observed, and many have been deceived, for the eye retains its perfect transparency. Here also medical treatment is of no avail.

The serous membranes are of great importance. The brain and spinal marrow with the origins of the nerves are surrounded by them; so are the heart, the lungs, the intestinal canal, and the organs whose office it is to prepare the generative fluid.

Inflammation of the Brain.—Mad-staggers falls under this division. It is inflammation of the meninges or envelopes of the brain, produced by over-exertion or by any of the causes of general fever, and it is characterized by the wildest delirium. Nothing but the most profuse bloodletting, active purgation and blistering the head will afford the slightest hope of success. Tetanus, or *locked jaw*, is a constant spasm of all the voluntary muscles, and particularly those of the neck, the spine and the head, arising from the injury of some nervous fibril—that injury spreading to the origin of the nerve—the brain becoming affected, and universal and unbroken spasmodic action being the result. Bleeding, physicking, blistering the course of the spine, and the administration of opium in enormous doses, will alone give any chance of cure. *Epilepsy* is not a frequent disease in the horse, but it seldom admits of cure. It is also very apt to return at the most distant and uncertain intervals. *Palsy* is the suspension of nervous power. It is usually confined to the hinder limbs and sometimes to one limb only. Bleeding, physicking, antimonial medicines, and blistering of the spine are most likely to produce a cure; but they too often utterly fail of success. *Rabies*, or madness, is evidently a disease of the nervous system, and once being developed, is altogether without remedy. The utter destruction of the bitten part with the lunar caustic soon after the infliction of the wound, will, however, in a great majority of cases, prevent that development.

Founder.—Founder, when acute, requires a treatment like that of other inflammations, with such differences as the situation of the disease may suggest.

Bleeding is indispensable, and that to its fullest extent. If the disease is confined to the fore-feet, four quarts of blood should be taken as soon as possible from the toe of each; care being taken to open the artery as well as the vein. The feet may likewise be put into warm water, to quicken the flow of the blood, and increase the quantity abstracted. Poultices of linseed meal, made very soft, should cover the whole of the foot and pastern, and be frequently renewed, which will promote evaporation from the neighboring parts, and possibly through the pores of the hoof, and by softening and rendering supple the hoof, will relieve its painful pressure on the swelled and tender parts beneath. More fully to accomplish this last purpose, the shoe should be removed, the sole pared as thin as possible, and the crust, and particularly the quarters, well rasped. All this must be done gently, and with a great deal of patience, for the poor animal can scarcely bear his feet to be meddled with. There used to be occasional doubt as to the administration of physic, from fear of metastasis (shifting) of inflammation which has sometimes occurred, and been generally fatal. When, however, there is so much danger of losing the patient from the original attack, we must run the risk of the other. Sedative and cooling medicines should be diligently administered, consisting of digitalis, nitre, and emetic tartar.

Chronic Founder.—This is a species of founder insidious in its attack, and destructive to the horse. It is a milder form of the preceding disease. There is lameness, but it is not so severe as in the former case. The horse stands as usual. The crust is warm, and that warmth is constant, but it is not often probably greater than in a state of health. The surest symptom is the action of the animal. It is diametrically opposite to that in the navicular disease. The horse throws as much of his weight as he can on the posterior parts of his feet.

The treatment should be similar to that recommended for the acute disease—blood letting, poultices, fomentations, and blisters, and the last much sooner and much more frequently than in the former disease.

Bog and Blood-Spavin.—Attached to the extremities of most of the tendons, and between the tendons and other parts, are little bags containing a mucous substance to enable the tendons to slide over each other without friction, and to move easily on the neighboring parts. From violent exercise these vessels are liable to enlarge. Windgalls and thoroughpins are instances of this. There is one of them on the inside of the hock at its bending. This sometimes becomes considerably increased in size, and the enlargement is called a *bog-spavin*. A vein passes over the bag, which is pressed between the enlargement and the skin, and the passage of the blood through it is impeded; the vein is consequently distended by the accumulated blood, and the distension reaches from this bag as low down as the next valve. This is called *blood-spavin*. Blood-spavin, then, is the consequence of bog-spavin. It very rarely occurs, and is, in the majority of instances, confounded with bog-spavin.

Blood-spavin does not always cause lameness, except the horse is very hard-worked; but this, as well as bog-spavin, constitutes unsoundness, and materially lessens the value of the horse. The proper treatment is, to endeavor to promote the absorption of the contents of the bag. This may be attempted by pressure long applied. A bandage may be contrived to take in the whole of the hock, except its point; and a compress made of folded linen being placed on the bog-spavin, may confine the principal pressure to that part. It is, however, very difficult to adapt a bandage to a joint which admits of such extensive motion; therefore most practitioners apply two or three successive blisters over the enlargement, when it usually disappears. Unfortunately, however, it returns if any extraordinary exertion is required from the horse.

Strangles.*—This is a disease principally incident to young horses—usually appearing between the fourth and fifth year, and oftener in the spring than in any other part of the year. It is preceded by cough, and can at first scarcely be distinguished from common cough, except that there is more discharge from the nostril, of a yellowish color, mixed with pus, and generally without smell. There is likewise a considerable discharge of ropy fluid from the mouth, and greater swelling than usual under the throat. This swelling increases with uncertain rapidity, accompanied by some fever and disinclination to eat, partly arising from the fever, but more from the pain which the animal feels in the act of mastication. There is considerable thirst, but after a gulp or two the horse ceases to drink, yet is evidently desirous of continuing his draught. In the attempt to swallow, and sometimes when not drinking, a convulsive cough comes on, which almost threatens to suffocate the animal—and thence, probably the name of the disease.

The tumor is under the jaw, and about the center of the channel. It soon fills the whole of the space, and is evidently one uniform body, and may thus be distinguished from glanders, or the enlarged glands of catarrh. In a few days it becomes more prominent and soft, and evidently contains a fluid. This rapidly increases; the tumor bursts, and a great quantity of pus is discharged. As soon as the tumor has broken the cough subsides, and the horse speedily mends, although some degree

---

* Usually termed "*Horse distemper*" in the United States.

of weakness may hang about him for a considerable time. Few horses, possibly none, escape its attack; but the disease having passed over, the animal is free from it for the remainder of his life. Catarrh may precede, or may predispose to, the attack, and, undoubtedly, the state of the atmosphere has much to do with it, for both its prevalence and its severity are connected with certain seasons of the year and changes of the weather. There is no preventive for the disease, nor is there any thing contagious about it. Many strange stories are told with regard to this; but the explanation of the matter is, that when several horses in the same form, or in the same neighborhood, have had strangles at the same time, they have been exposed to the same powerful but unknown exciting cause.

As soon as the tumor under the jaw is decidedly apparent, the part should be actively blistered. From the thickness of skin, poultices, fomentations, etc., are of little avail. The blister will also abate the internal inflammation and soreness of the throat, and thus lessen the cough and wheezing.

As soon as the swelling is soft on its summit, and evidently contains matter, it should be freely and deeply lanced. It is a bad, although frequent practice, to suffer the tumor to burst naturally, for a ragged ulcer is formed, very slow to heal and difficult of treatment. If the incision is deep and large enough, no second collection of matter will be formed: and that which is already there may be allowed to run out slowly, all pressure with the fingers being avoided. The part should be kept clean, and a little friar's balsam injected daily into the wound.

The remainder of the treatment will depend on the symptoms. If there is much fever, and evident affection of the chest, and which should carefully be distinguished from the oppression and choking occasioned by the pressure of the tumor, it will be proper to bleed. In the majority of cases, however, bleeding will not only be unnecessary, but injurious. It will delay the suppuration of the tumor, and increase the subsequent debility. A few cooling medicines, as nitre, emetic tartar, and perhaps digitalis, may be given, as the case requires. The appetite, or rather the ability to eat, will return with the opening of the abscess. Bran-mashes, or fresh-cut grass or tares, should be liberally supplied, which will not only afford sufficient nourishment to recruit the strength of the animal, but keep the bowels gently open. If the weakness is not great, no further medicine will be wanted, except a dose of mild physic in order to prevent the swellings or eruptions which sometimes succeed to strangles. In cases of debility, a small quantity of tonic medicine, as chamomile, gentian, or ginger, may be administered.

Poll-Evil.—From the horse rubbing and sometimes striking his poll against the lower end of the manger, or hanging back in the stall and bruising the part with the halter—or from the frequent and painful stretching of the ligaments and muscles by unnecessary tight reining, and, occasionally, from a violent blow on the poll, inflammation ensues, and a swelling appears, hot, tender, and painful. It used to be a disease of frequent occurrence, but it is now, from better treatment of the animal, of comparatively rare occurrence.

It has been stated that the ligament of the neck passes over the atlas, or first bone, without being attached to it, and the seat of inflammation is between the ligament and the bone beneath; and being thus deeply situated, it is serious in its nature and difficult of treatment.

The first thing to be attempted is to abate the inflammation by bleeding, physic, and the application of cold lotions to the part. In a very early period of the case a blister might have considerable effect. Strong purgatives should also be employed. By these means the tumor will sometimes be dispersed. This system, however, must not be pursued too far. If the swelling increases, and the heat and tenderness likewise increase, matter will form in the tumor; and then our object should be to hasten its formation by warm fomentations, poultices, or stimulating embrocations. As soon as the matter is formed, which may be known by the softness of the tumor, and before it has time to spread around and eat into the neighboring parts, it should be evacuated. Now comes the whole art of treating poll-evil; *the opening into the tumor must be so contrived that all the matter shall run out*, and continue afterward to run out as quickly as it is formed, and not collect at the bottom of the ulcer, irritating and corroding it. This can be effected by a seton alone. The needle should enter at the top of the tumor, penetrate through its bottom, and be brought out at the side of the neck, a little below the abscess. Without any thing more than this, except frequent fomentation with warm water, in order to keep the part clean, and to obviate inflammation, poll-evil in its early stage will frequently be cured.

If the ulcer has deepened and spread, and threatens to eat into the ligaments of the joints of the neck, it may be necessary to stimulate its surface, and perhaps painfully so, in order to bring it to a healthy state, and dispose it to fill up. In extreme cases, some highly stimulating application may be employed. All measures, however, will be ineffectual unless the pus or matter is, by the use of setons, perfectly evacuated. The application of these setons will require the skill and anatomical knowledge of the veterinary surgeon. In desperate cases, the wound cannot be fairly exposed to the action of the caustic without the division of the ligament of the neck. This may be effected with perfect safety; for, although the ligament is carried on to the occipital bone, and some strength is gained by this prolongation of it, the main stress is on the second bone; and the head will continue to be supported. The divided ligament, also, will soon unite again, and its former usefulness will be restored when the wound is healed.*

---

* All cooling applications to the poll-evil are useless, for when once the swelling which constitutes the disease has appeared, we have never known it dispersed, but sooner or later it suppurates. It often takes many months before the matter reaches the surface; but the more complete the suppuration is, the easier it is to effect a cure. The injury, which generally arises from striking the poll against a low doorway, is deep-seated, and the surface of the bone is often diseased from the beginning.

It must be confessed that the poll-evil is very difficult to cure, a difficulty arising not from the character of the injury, but rather from its situation, and the nature of the surrounding parts. When matter forms in any situation, it has a tendency to pass downward, and to seek an exit where the least obstacles are offered to its passage. It consequently forms passages or sinuses (pipes) amongst the muscles, and when these are filled the matter points to the surface. This tendency con-

DOMESTIC ANIMALS.

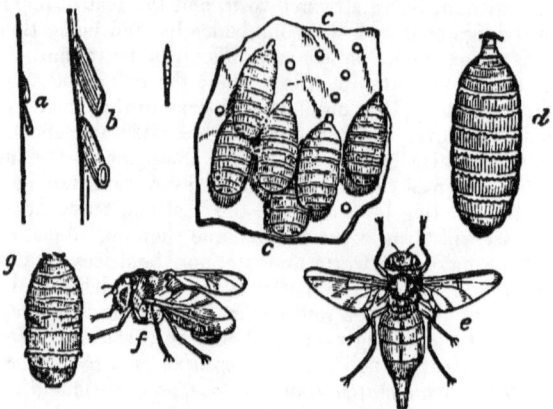

a and *b*, the eggs of the gad-fly adhering to the hair of the horse; *c*, the appearance of the bots on the stomach, firmly adhering by their hooked mouths. The marks or depressions are seen which are left on the coat of the stomach when the bots are detached from their hold; *d*, the bot detached; *e*, the female of the gad-fly of the horse, prepared to deposit her eggs; *f*, the gad-fly by which the red bots are produced; *g*, the smaller, or red bot.

Bots.—In the spring and early part of the summer, horses are much troubled by a grub or caterpillar, which crawls out of the anus, fastens itself under the tail, and seems to cause a great deal of itching or uneasiness. Grooms are sometimes alarmed at the appearance of these insects. Their history is curious, and will dispel every fear with regard to them. We are indebted to Mr. Bracy Clark for almost all we know of the bot.

A species of gad-fly, *e*, the *œtrus equi*, is in the latter part of the summer exceedingly busy about the horse. It is observed to be darting with great rapidity toward the knees and sides of the animal. The females are depositing their eggs on the hair, and which adhere to it by means of a glutinous fluid with which they are surrounded (*a* and *b*). In a few days the eggs are ready to be hatched, and the slightest application of warmth and moisture will liberate the little animals which they contain. The horse in licking himself touches the egg; it bursts,

---

tinues after an external opening is made, and deep sinuses are formed in various directions, rendering it almost impossible to get a depending opening.

The abscess should not be opened till the matter is thoroughly formed, and then a depending opening should be made, through which a seton may be passed. The great error frequently made in the treatment of poll-evil is, that these openings are not made half large enough, so that much of the pus flows in another direction, and there forms sinuses. Now, the chief art in the treatment of this disease is to use the bistoury freely, to lay all the sinuses open as much as possible, and to throw them together; then to make the lower opening extremely large, and as low down as possible—large enough, indeed, for two fingers to be inserted. If the bone is injured, it will be necessary to apply some caustic application, in order to cause a healthy slough. Pressure is found very useful in keeping the sides of the wound together, and preserving the formation of sinuses. With this view, it has been recommended to apply a tight compress, by means of bandages, round the part, but it is extremely inconvenient to apply them, in consequence of the windpipe interfering.—*Spooner.*

and a small worm escapes, which adheres to the tongue, and is conveyed with the food into the stomach. There it clings to the cuticular portion of the stomach, c, by means of a hook on either side of its mouth; and its hold is so firm and so obstinate, that it must be broken before it can be detached. It remains there feeding on the mucus of the stomach during the whole of the winter, and until the end of the ensuing spring; when, having attained a considerable size, d, and being destined to undergo a certain transformation, it disengages itself from the cuticular coat, is carried into the villous portion of the stomach with the food, passes out of it with the chyme, and is evacuated with the dung.

The *larva*, or maggot, seeks shelter in the ground, and buries itself there; it contracts in size, and becomes then a chrysalis, or grub, in which state it lies inactive for a few weeks, and then, bursting from its confinement, assumes the form of a fly. The female, becoming impregnated, quickly deposits her eggs on those parts of the horse which he is most accustomed to lick, and thus the species is perpetuated.

There are several plain conclusions to be drawn from this history. The bots cannot, while they inhabit the stomach of the horse, give the animal any pain, for they have fastened on the cuticular and insensible coat. They cannot be injurious to the horse, for he enjoys the most perfect health when the cuticular part of his stomach is filled with them, and their presence is not even suspected until they appear at the anus. They cannot be removed by medicine, because they are not in that part of the stomach to which medicine is usually conveyed; and if they were, their mouths are too deeply buried in the mucus for any medicine, that can be safely administered, to affect them; and, last of all, in due course of time they detach themselves, and come away. Therefore the wise man will leave them to themselves, or content himself with picking them off when they collect under the tail and annoy the animal.

The smaller bot, *f* and *g*, is not so frequently found.

Wind-Galls.—In the neighborhood of the fetlock there are occasionally found considerable enlargements, oftener on the hind leg than the fore one, which are denominated wind-galls. Between the tendons and other parts, and wherever the tendons are exposed to pressure or friction, and particularly about their extremities, little bags or sacs are placed, containing, and suffering to ooze slowly from them, a mucous fluid to lubricate (make slippery) the parts. From undue pressure, and that most frequently caused by violent action and straining of the tendons, or often from some predisposition about the horse, these little sacs are injured. They take on inflammation and sometimes become large and hardened. There are few horses perfectly free from them. When they first appear, and until the inflammation subsides, they may be accompanied by some degree of lameness; but otherwise, except when they attain a great size, they do not interfere with the action of the animal, or cause any considerable unsoundness. The farriers used to suppose that they contained wind—hence their name, wind-galls; and hence the practice of opening them, by which dreadful inflammation was often produced, and many a valuable horse destroyed. It is not uncommon for wind-galls entirely to disappear in aged horses.

A slight wind-gall will scarcely be subjected to treatment; but if these tumors are numerous and large, and seem to impede the motion of the limb, they may be attacked first by bandage. The rollers should be of flannel, and soft pads should be placed on each of the enlargements, and bound down tightly upon them. The bandage should also be wetted with the lotion recommended for sprain of the back sinews. The wind-gall will often diminish or disappear by this treatment, but will too frequently return when the horse is again hardly worked. A blister is a more effectual but too often temporary remedy. Wind-galls will return with the renewal of work. Firing is still more certain, if the tumors are sufficiently large and annoying to justify our having recourse to measures so severe; for it will not only effect the immediate absorption of the fluid and the reduction of the swelling, but by contracting the skin will act as a permanent bandage, and therefore prevent the reappearance of the tumor. The iodine and mercurial ointments have occasionally been used with advantage in the proportion of three parts of the former to two of the latter.

The following formulæ may be said to contain most of the remedies necessary for the use of the amateur; when disease prevails, the safest plan is to call in the assistance of a veterinary practitioner.

When calomel or emetic tartar is given for the expulsion of worms, it should be mixed in a small portion of bran mash, after fasting the animal five or six hours; two doses given at similar intervals will be most effective. They must be worked off with linseed oil or aloes, after an equivalent lapse of time; and as alkalies neutralize the effects of either of those medicines, soap must be excluded if the form of ball is preferred.

As an external stimulating application for the throat in cases of inflammation arising from cold or other causes, common mustard, mixed with water as for the table is an excellent remedy, and is equal if not superior to any of the more complicated nostrums.

When cooling remedies are required to the legs, cold water is the best. The introduction of nitre and sal-ammoniac will increase the evaporation; but great care is requisite to renew such medicated lotions very frequently; because when the refrigerating process is over, they become stimulants; thus on ordinary occasions cold water constantly applied with very loose linen bandages is to be preferred.

TABLE SHOWING THE PROPORTIONS OF MEDICINES TO BE GIVEN TO HORSES AT VARIOUS AGES.

	Calomel or Tartarized Antimony. Grains.		Linseed Oil. Ounces.		Aloes. Drachms.	
To foals............	10		4	to 6	¼	to ¾
Yearlings..........	15	to 20	6	8	1	1½
Two years old......	20	25	8	12	2	2½
Three years old....	25	30	12	15	2½	3½
Four years old and upward	30	60	1	2 pts.	4	6

Common Aloetic Purgative.—Aloes finely powdered, four drachms; hard soap and ginger, each two drachms. Mix and form a ball, varying the proportions according to the age and constitution of the horse.

Aloetic Purgative without Soap.—Aloes broken in pieces, four drachms; olive oil or lard, one drachm; ginger in powder, two drachms; treacle, one and a half drachms. The aloes and oil, or lard, must be melted in a jar placed in a saucepan over the fire, and when melted, the ginger and treacle are added. The aloes must not be boiled longer than to effect their solution.

Aloetic Alteratives.—Aloes in fine powders, two drachms; nitre, two drachms; soap, two drachms. Mix and form one ball. To be given daily till a slight action of the bowels is produced.

Antimonial Alterative.—Sulphur and sulphuret of antimony, each two to three drachms. Treacle to form a ball. One of which may be given four, five, or six days in succession.

The preparation necessary before giving aloetic purges should be very scrupulously attended to. Bran mashes must be liberally substituted for hay during the twenty-four hours previous to giving the ball; and the horse requires to be walked out during its operation.

MEDICINES FOR THE HORSE—THEIR ACTION AND DOSES.

NAMES.	ACTION.	DOSE.
Muriatic acid,	Tonic,	1 to 2 drachms
Nitric acid,	Tonic,	1 to 2 drachms.
Sulphuric acid,	Tonic,	1 to 2 drachms.
Gentian,	Tonic,	2 to 4 drachms.
Peruvian bark,	Tonic,	2 to 4 drachms.
Sulphate of iron,	Tonic,	2 to 4 drachms.
Myrrh,	Tonic,	2 to 4 drachms.
Sulphate of zinc,	Tonic astringent,	1 to 2 drachms.
Oxide of zinc,	Tonic,	1 to 2 drachms.
Strychnine,	Tonic for nerves,	1 to 3 grains.
Iodide of iron,	Alterative and tonic,	½ to 1 drachm.
Alum,	Astringent,	2 to 4 drachms.
Nut-galls,	Astringent,	2 to 4 drachms.
Sugar of lead,	Astringent,	½ to 1 drachm.
Iodine,	Alterative,	5 to 10 grains.
Corrosive sublimate,	Alterative,	4 to 6 grains.
Hydriodate of potash,	Alterative,	1 drachm.
Calomel,	Alterative,	10 to 20 grains.
Epsom salts,	Purgative,	½ lb. to 1 lb.
Glauber salts,	Purgative,	½ lb. to 1 lb.
Aloes,	Purgative,	½ to 2 drachms.
Calomel,	Purgative,	½ to 2 drachms.
Croton oil,	Purgative,	20 to 30 drops.
Nitrate of potash,	Diuretic,	2 to 4 drachms.
Carbonate of potash,	Diuretic and sedative,	2 to 4 drachms.
Tincture digitalis,	Diuretic and narcotic,	1 to 2 drachms.
Tincture colchicum,	Diuretic and laxative,	1 to 2 drachms.
Cream of tartar,	Diuretic,	1 to 2 ounces.
Spirits of nitre,	Diuretic,	1 to 2 ounces
Resin,	Diuretic,	½ to 1 ounce.
Spirits of turpentine,	Diuretic,	½ to 1 ounce.
Emetic tartar,	Nauseant and diaphoretic,	½ to 1 drachm.
Opium,	Narcotic,	1 to 2 drachms.
Laudanum,	Narcotic,	½ to 2 ounces.
Extract hyoscyamus,	Narcotic,	1 to 2 drachms.
Caraway seeds,	Carminative,	½ to 1 ounce.
Sulphur,	Laxative and alterative,	1 to 2 ounces.
Camphor,	Narcotic,	1 to 2 drachms.
Tinc. veratrum viride,	Sedative,	20 to 30 drops
Belladonna,	Sedative and narcotic,	1 to 2 drachms.

Used externally, muriatic acid, nitric acid, sulphuric acid, and corrosive sublimate are caustic, iodine is alterative; and sugar of lead is sedative.

CATTLE:

THE DAIRY AND FAT-PRODUCING BREEDS,

AND

THEIR MANAGEMENT

IN

HEALTH AND DISEASE.

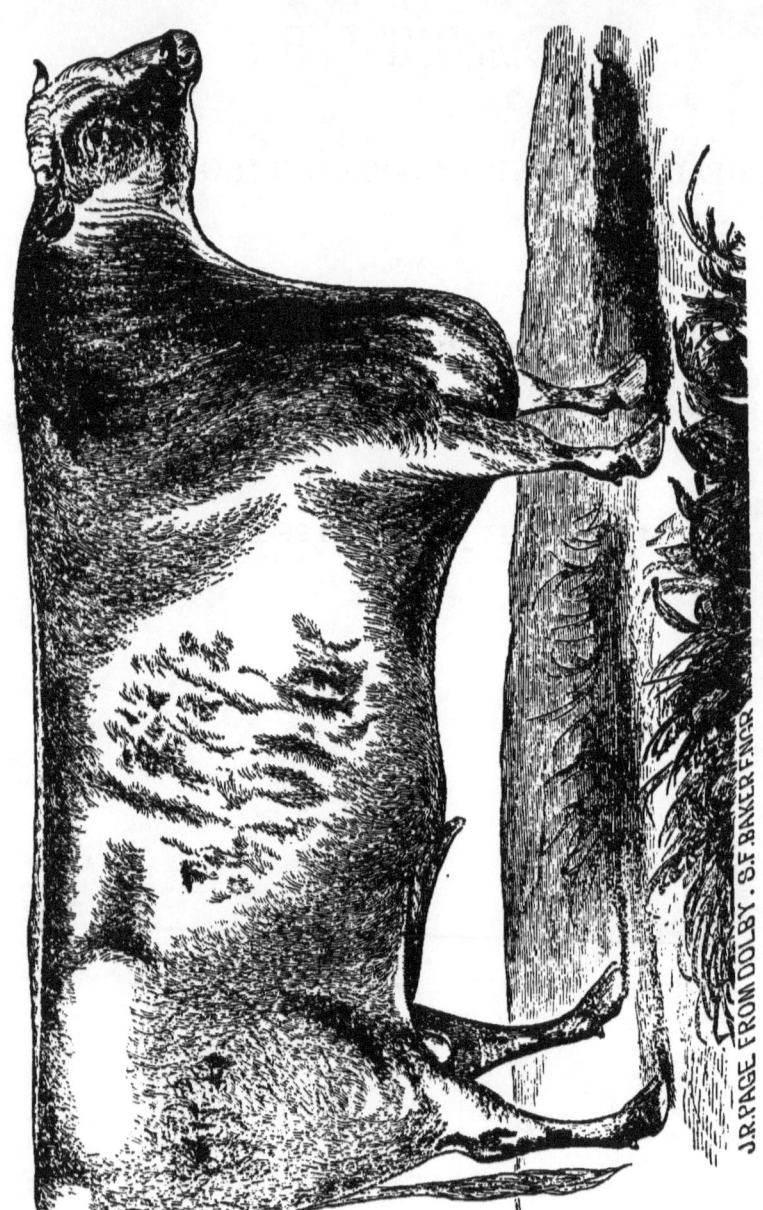

SHORT HORN BULL "COUNT."

CATTLE:

THEIR BREEDS, MANAGEMENT, ETC.

CATTLE, THEIR VALUE.—There is not a race of animals to which the community is on the whole more indebted, than to cattle. They not only cultivate the land, but afford food of various kinds, in different circumstances of their existence; and also, at death, supply very important articles of clothing and utility, and are amongst those animals to which we owe by far the most of the comforts and conveniences of life. Not to mention the use of cattle in many districts of country for the purposes of labor; they supply, during life, those most important of necessaries, milk and cream; they afford the luxuries of cheese and of butter; and at their death they are the sources of supply of the food which has become associated with national peculiarities even, and which is one of the most nutritious of the necessaries of life. Nor in death does their utility cease. Their hide provides the protection to our feet and the trappings to our horses—their horns, combs and ornaments—their hoofs even, and their waste, supply glue and gelatine; while their bones afford the handles for our knives and many useful articles in manufactures; and the refuse again, of these, returns to our soils as a most valuable manure.

THE DAIRY BREEDS OF CATTLE.—The great object for which cattle are kept by the farmer is either to grow beef for the market, or to produce milk, which shall be converted into butter or cheese, or sold as milk, to supply the great towns. Hence the former selects the fat-producing, and the latter the milk-producing class of animals. Nature, as a general thing, has provided that different races of animals, and different individuals of these races, are, more than others, adapted to the secretion of one or the other of these necessary products. The objects of the two secretions are essentially different, and the tendencies and qualities necessary for both are never active in the same animal at the same time. For while the former is a reservoir of the carbonaceous matter of the food, laid by for subsequent use in the respiratory system, the latter is the secretion of a substance necessary to support the young progeny until it is able to sustain itself, and to procure from the green pastures the food there provided for it. Hence, to produce milk is, more or less, the natural quality of all kinds and races of cattle; but some will produce large quantities, but thin and poor in quality; some smaller quantities, and rich in oily matter, while others will afford a small quantity, but abundant in solid matter; and the first class would be selected by the milk-man near the populous city, the second by the dairy-man whose product was intended to be butter, and the third by the maker of cheese. There are some tribes of cattle that are both good fatteners and good milkers, but never at the same time.

The milk-producing breeds are more widely diffused than any other, because they are capable of being kept to advantage on qualities of

5

herbage which are inadequate profitably to sustain the fat-secreting breeds. Grass-land on the clay soils on the sides of the uplands, and even on the poorer sands, is quite adequate to supply the means of making butter or cheese; but it will very ill repay the person who attempts to feed cattle on herbage so inferior; while the rich alluvial feeding pastures which generally skirt the rivers, are far more profitably employed in raising summer beef than in the production of milk, of cheese, or of butter. Some races of long-horns, of short-horns, or of middle horns, or even of polled animals, are to be placed amongst the one class we have alluded to, and some amongst the other, and we prefer arranging the breeds most celebrated for the quantity or quality of their milk under the first head, and reserve the second to the races with special aptitude for fattening.

The question arises very naturally how far it is possible, by external conformations of the individual animal, to detect its capabilities for the secretion of milk. There are instances in every breed where it is evident nature has been more bountiful, or more niggardly, in bestowing the qualities calculated to produce the secretion for which the race may be celebrated; and there are, doubtless, marks, well known to the dairyman, which seldom fail to indicate the power of the animal in the range of qualities peculiar to his race. On the continent of Europe this has been professed to be carried to a very minute extent. François Guénon, a Frenchman, professed to have found, by close observation, a mode of deciding authoritatively, not only the quantity and quality of milk which would be given by any particular cow, but also the period for which she would retain her milk after calving, and this he proposed to do by external appearances alone, and these of a somewhat arbitrary kind.

It is not within the compass of this work to give any thing like a description of the mode he adopted, now made public,* but the foundation of it is, his classification of all kinds of cattle into eight classes, or families; each family is divided into three sections, according to size only, and each section is again subdivided into eight orders.

The distinguishing marks by which he divides these are: 1. The Gravure, commencing at the udder, and extending to the bearing; 2. The Epis, a soft brush of hair upon the animal; and 3, Contrepoil, or hair growing the contrary way. The peculiarities of these marks constitute the distinction between the families and orders. Thus, if the gravure be large, the reservoir of milk will be large, and the product abundant; if it be formed of fine hair, if the skin be yellowish, and if a kind of bran powder which comes off the skin be of that color, they are all signs of a good

CLASS I. FLANDRINES OF GUENON'S SYSTEM

---

* This work, with the original figures and a full elucidation of the system, can be procured of C. M. Saxton, 25 Park Row, New York. It is an ingenious and plausible system, and well worthy the attention of dairymen.—ED.

milker. The rationale of this is, that this gravure is but a continuation of, and corresponds with the lactiferous vessels under the belly of the animal. These "epis," he states, correspond with the reservoir of milk, and are tufts of hair growing the wrong way on the right or left of the bearing. The largest epis indicates the most rapid loss of milk. The contrepoil, or hair growing the wrong way on the gravure amidst that which grows upward, shows a default in the production of milk, even if the gravure be large. We give a fac-simile of his class 1. FLANDRINES So far is a very general description of a system which he invests with minutiæ of no ordinary kind, and it is so precise and prolix that it requires a series of some score of plates to show the variations of family, class, and order.

Without definitively pronouncing that there is no merit in his observations, it seems perfectly clear that many of his indications are of a character generally indicative of quality, but are pushed far beyond their legitimate objects; for while a wide capacity of upper udder—a fine hair—a yellow scurf, are somewhat too indefinite to classify very precisely, they are just the points which may indicate the fineness of quality, and a large lactiferous capacity which may add to the physiological signs by which a milking-cow is judged by the practical grazier. Beauty of form is about the last qualification in a good dairy cow. Symmetry to a breeder is no criterion of milking qualities. The parallelogram is the beau ideal of a fattened ox in section, and a cylinder is that of his superficies—thus exhibiting an essence of roundness, whereas the very converse is the perfection of a milker, *i. e.* "flatness." The following are the best-settled marks or characteristics of a milking cow. Head small and fine, eye bright and full, but with a quiet and placid expression, neck thin and deep, which gives it an appearance of hollowness; shoulder and breast narrow, but projecting; ribs flat; rumps broad, and tapering down to the knee-joint, owing to the thighs being thin; tail small; udder large and round, with teats well formed, tapering to the end, and at a moderate distance from each other; thin in its skin, and with plenty of skin above; its fore-teats round and full, and with a large subcutaneous or milk vein.

The Ayrshire Cow.—In Ayrshire and the adjacent portion of the Lowlands there is an admirable breed of milch cattle, independently of those that are grazed there for the butcher, which, from whatever source they originated, owe much to the care and selection of judicious breeders. At some period or other there has evidently been a cross of the Durham or Holderness, and perhaps also of the Alderney. This breed, which became established from the middle to the close of the eighteenth century, has found its way not only into England, but also into Ireland and Wales, recommended by the excellency of the cows as milkers, although they are under the middle size. It has been estimated that a good Ayrshire cow will yield, for two or three months after calving, five gallons of milk daily; for the next three months three gallons daily, and a gallon and a half for the following three months. This milk is calculated to return about two hundred and fifty pounds of butter annually, or five hundred pounds of cheese. The foregoing estimate is, however, somewhat exaggerated; and perhaps during the best of the season four

AYRSHIRE COW, FANNY.—Property of G. W. Penny, Newark, Ohio.

or four and a half gallons of milk is the average product daily of a good cow, kept in fair condition. Every thirty-two gallons of unskimmed milk will yield about twenty-four pounds of cheese, and ninety gallons twenty-four pounds of butter. We are supposing a good farm and a first-rate stock of Ayrshire cows; and considering the size of the cattle, this return from each cow is very considerable. The mode in which the cows are treated by an enterprising and successful farmer of Kirkum is thus detailed: "He keeps his cows constantly in the byre (or shed) till the grass has risen so as to afford them a full bite. Many put them out every good day through the winter and spring, but they poach the ground with their feet, and nip up the young grass as it begins to spring, which, as they have not a full meal, injures the cattle. Whenever the weather becomes dry and hot, he feeds his cows on cut grass in the byre, from six o'clock in the morning to six at night, and turns them out to pasture the other twelve hours. When rain comes, the house feeding is discontinued. Whenever the pasture grass begins to fail in harvest, the cows receive a supply of the second growth of clover, and afterward of turnips strewed over the pasture-ground. When the weather becomes stormy, in the months of October and November, the cows are kept in the byre during the night, and in a short time afterward during both night and day; they are then fed on oat-straw and turnips, and continue to yield a considerable quantity of milk for some time. Part of the turnip crop is eaten at the end of harvest and beginning of winter, to protract the milk, and part is stored up for green food during the winter. After this store is exhausted, the Swedish turnip and potatoes are used along with dry fodder, till the grass can support the cows. Chaff, oats, and potatoes are boiled for the cows after calving, and they are generally fed on rye-grass during the latter part of the spring."

The improved Ayrshire cow of the present day has the head small, but rather long, and narrow at the muzzle, though the space between the roots of the horns is considerable; the horns are small and crooked, the eye is clear and lively, the neck long and slender, and almost destitute of a dewlap; the shoulders are thin, and the fore-quarters generally light; the back is straight and broad behind, especially across the hips, which are roomy; the tail is long and thin. The carcass is deep, the udder capacious and square, the milk-vein large and prominent; the limbs are small and short, but well knit; the thighs are thin; the skin is rather thin, but loose and soft, and covered with soft hair. The general figure, though small, is well proportioned. The color is varied with mingled white and sandy red.

Whether the Ayrshires are judged by their actual produce, or by the external points which by experience and observation are acknowledged to denote dairy qualities, it must be admitted that they take a high rank. From a fair consideration of their merits, it is believed that their adoption for the dairy would secure the following advantages over the stock commonly kept for that purpose in this country:

1. A greater quantity of milk, butter and cheese for the food consumed. 2. Greater uniformity in the general character of the stock from its inherent or hereditary qualities. 3. Better symmetry and constitution, and greater tendency to gain flesh when not giving milk.

AYRSHIRE BULL, DUKE.—Property of G. M. Perry, Newark, Ohio.

At the present time there are several breeders in the State of New York who are turning their attention to the Ayrshires. The principal stocks known to the writer are those of E. P. Prentice, near Albany; L. G. Morris, Fordham, Westchester county; and J. C. Tiffany, Coxsackie. Of these Mr. Prentice's comprises the largest number, over twenty head. They have been derived from the imported cow *Ayr*, the importations of Mr. Ward, Captain Randall, Mr. Lawson, and Mr. Shurtleff, of Massachusetts, and one or two other imported animals.

The Alderneys or Jerseys.—The Jersey cow is a singularly docile and gentle animal; the male, on the contrary, is apt to become fierce after two years of age. In those bred on the heights of St. Ouen, St. Brelade, and St. Mary, there is a hardiness and sound constitution that enables them to meet even a Scotch winter without injury; those bred in the low grounds and rich pastures are of larger carcass, but are more delicate in constitution.

Of the ancient race it was stated, perhaps with truth, that it had no tendency to fatten; indeed some cows of the old breed were so ungainly, high-boned, and ragged in form—Meg Merrilies of cows—that no attempt to fatten them might succeed, the great quantities of milk and cream which they produced probably absorbing all their fattening properties.

Yet careful attention to crossing has greatly remedied this defect. By having studied the habits of a good cow with a little more tendency to fatten than others, and crossing her with a fleshy, well-conditioned bull, of a race that was also known to produce quality and quantity of butter—the next generation has proved of a rounder form, with a tendency to make fat, without having lost the butyraceous nature.

Some of these improved animals have fattened so rapidly while being stall-fed, from the month of December to March, as to suffer in parturition, when both cow and calf have been lost; to prevent which it is indispensable to lower the condition of the cow, or bleed, in good time. Such animals will fatten rapidly. Their beef is excellent; the only defect being in the color of the fat, which is sometimes too yellow. It is now a fair question, whether the improved breed may not fatten as rapidly as any breed known.

It was anciently thought that the cream from the Jersey cow was too rich for making cheese. Mr. Le Feuvre, of La Houge, who has a fine breed of cows, tried the experiment two years since, and succeeded to admiration. It was made from the pure milk, cream and all, as it comes from the cow. It was found that the quantity of milk that would have produced a pound of butter, afforded one pound and a half of cheese.

From the quantity of milk which produced a cheese of twenty pounds' weight, the *drainings* of the curds and whey, on being churned, yielded four pounds of butter. This butter was of an inferior quality when eaten with bread, but was superior to any other for the making of pastry; it was peculiarly hard, and of excellent texture for such use in the hot weather. The writer has tasted cheeses from Mr. Le Feuvre's farm quite equal in quality to the richest double-Glo'ster.

On one or two farms, besides General Fouzel's, butter is made from

ALDERNEY COW, SYLPH.—Property of James O. Sheldon, Geneva, N. Y.

clouted cream in the Devonshire mode; but as this is not peculiar to Jersey, it is not noticed further than that ten pounds of butter are usually made in five minutes by this process. The usual way of procuring the cream is by placing the milk in pans about six inches deep, the glazed shallow earthenware having taken the place of the unglazed deep vessels.

It is admitted that the richest milk and cream are produced by cows whose ears have a yellow or orange color within. Some of the best cows give twenty-six quarts of milk in twenty-four hours, and fourteen pounds of butter from such milk in one week. Such are rare. Good cows afford twenty quarts of milk daily, and ten pounds of butter weekly, in the spring and summer months. Butter is made every second or third day.

Lactometers indicate the degrees of richness of cream which the milk of any cow affords, with great nicety. This varies with different food. The mode is to fill the lactometer up to zero with the first milk that is drawn from the cow in the morning; then, when the udder is nearly emptied, to fill a second lactometer with the residue of the milk, throwing a little out of the lactometer, to refill it to zero with the very last drops which can be drawn from the cow: these will be nearly all cream. The lactometer filled with the first milking may only indicate four degrees of cream, while that filled with the last milking may indicate forty degrees of cream. Then, by dividing the sum total, forty-four by two, we have twenty-two degrees of cream, which a very good cow will produce; others so little as ten or fifteen.

Jersey butter made when the cows are partially fed on parsnips, or white carrots and grass in September and October, when salted and potted will keep till the following spring, preserving as well as Irish butter, with a much less rank flavor.

The foregoing, from Colonel J. Le Couteur, of the Island of Jersey, one of the most intelligent breeders and judges of this breed of cattle, and the accompanying illustrations of the improved animals, show that they are not now the angular, ill-shapen animals they once were; but that, like the Ayrshires, they are worthy the attention of our dairymen.

The Yorkshire Cow.—Having given instances of milk-producing cows from the middle-horn and crumpled-horn breeds, we place next one of the short-horn class; not, indeed, the high bred Durham short-horn, but a large capacious animal, possessing several of its qualities, and giving a large quantity of milk, with as much aptitude to fatten as is consistent with the production of milk, and hence is selected by the dairymen of large towns, and especially of London, for the supply of milk for a given period, and then to be fatted on distillers' refuse, and other waste matters which a town will afford, and thus give a double pay to the dairyman.

The Yorkshire cow is of much larger size than either of those we have been considering; and, when fat, will weigh from eight to eleven hundred pounds. Her head is fine, and somewhat small; there is a serene placidity of eye, which shows a mild and gentle disposition, tending alike to produce fat and milk. The horns are small and white, the muzzle without black spots; the breast deep and prominent, but that and the shoulders thin; the neck somewhat narrow, but full below the

ALDERNEY BULL, IVANHOE.—Property of James O. Sheldon, Geneva, N. Y

shoulders, and without any loose skin; the barrel somewhat round; the belly capacious; milk-vein large; back perfectly straight; rump wide, and flat as a table; tail small, and set on so that there is almost a straight line from the tail to the head. The prevailing color is roan, or red or white; and sometimes white, with the tips of the ears red. The thighs are thin; but the legs are straight and somewhat short. The udder is very large and muscular, projecting forward, well filled up behind, and so broad as to give the cow the appearance of a waddle in her walking. Indeed, her qualities are not inappropriately described in some doggerel lines often quoted; and two of the verses we shall venture to give, as most aptly descriptive of the Yorkshire cow·

> "She's broad in her ribs, and long in her rump,
> A straight and flat back without ever a hump;
> She's wide in her hips, and calm in her eyes;
> She's fine in her shoulders, and thin in her thighs
>
> "She's light in her neck, and small in her tail,
> She's wide in her breast, and good at the pail;
> She's fine in her bone, and silky of skin;
> She's a grazier's without, and a butcher's within."

The quantity of milk given by these cows by far exceeds that of any others, though less perhaps than that of some others in proportion to her size. The writer has had instances where as much as thirty quarts per day, in summer, have been given. The distended udder has so swollen before calving, that she was obliged to be milked several days before she calved; and, after calving, had to be milked three times a day, for fear of the consequences of an over-distended udder. She, moreover, gave a large quantity of butter as well as milk, and soon after calving she has given fifteen pounds per week.

All these things being considered, and taking into account the carcass value of the cow after she has yielded her milk, it is not too much to say that there is no breed of cows so highly gifted with milk-secreting qualities who are also otherwise so profitable as the Yorkshire.

The Leicestershire Breed.—The old breed of England has had a more successful struggle for existence than the native breed of Gloucestershire. It was here that Bakewell exerted his talents to improve the long-horned breed of cattle, and, though he succeeded in removing the coarseness from these animals, and increased their tendency to fatten, it appears he did not attain the object of either establishing or improving their dairying qualities; and hence his breed is but little prized by the Leicestershire dairymen, who prefer the coarser and larger animals, which give large quantities of good milk, to those which have less milk-giving capabilities, but are more suitable for the grazier.

The yield of cheese, rather than that of milk, is the object of the dairymen of Leicestershire. A good cow will give some four hundred pounds of cheese, and produce as many gallons of milk in the year, allowing for the seven weeks when she is supposed to be dry. In some districts the cows are kept for six, or seven, and even more years, especially when they are good cheese producers; for it is of more consequence to the farmer to have a cow which, fo. six years, gives him an annual supply of the stock-in-trade of his farm—his cheese—than to get a few pounds more or less when she is sold. Indeed a smaller difference really takes place than may be at first imagined. The rich Leicestershire grass enables the farmer, on a large scale at least, to sell off his cattle fat, which would have been disposed of for the dairy. Hence as old cows of any kind are not expected to be very valuable grazers, he does not expect her to do wonders; and if he succeeds in getting her moderately fat, he is satisfied to take a smaller price per stone for her beef than is received for a primer animal.

The Cheshire Breed is, like that of Gloucestershire, or even more so, becoming rapidly extinct. The old breed of the county was, like that of most dairy districts, a long-horned variety; but the vicinity of the large-town dairy system, introduced into the country by the springing up of large towns, has brought here, as elsewhere, the short-horn cow of Yorkshire into competition with the native breed; the extra quantity of milk they produce has been regarded somewhat more than its quality, and, in consequence, the character of the Cheshire cheese has somewhat deteriorated in the markets.

The Dorsetshire Breed.—In this, as in most dairy districts, the milk is rather an object than either form or fat, and hence a somewhat coarse, ill-shapen class of cattle prevails. The cattle are of a long-horn breed, large, and coarse, principally of a red color, with flat chests and buttocks. Attempts have been made to cross this also with the Devon, Hereford, and Ayrshire breeds, but this does not appear to have succeeded; and the only advance the dairymen have been enabled to make in this county has been to introduce one Alderney cow to a dairy for every ten or twelve of the native breed; this is found to have a very beneficial tendency, to increase the quantity of cream, and to improve much the quality of the butter.

The Kerry Breed.—Crossing the Irish Channel, there is a hardy small-sized cow celebrated as a cottier's dairy-cow—the neat pet-like cow of Kerry. Her placid countenance, patient, meek deportment, fine head and legs, her small tail, fine shoulders, breast, and quarters, and her skinny udder and large milk-vein, bespeak the characteristics of the milker, and well they may, for she is a treasure to the cottage farmer! —so hardy, that she will live where other cattle will starve; she will yield milk at the expense of her own muscles, nay, will yield it abundantly when they seem all but gone; and will give it also of quality so rich, that she is a perfect machine for converting the hardest and coarsest cattle-food into rich and nutritious milk and butter.

FAT-PRODUCING BREEDS OF CATTLE.—Whatever theoretical objections may be raised against overfed cattle, and great as may be the attempts to disparage the "mountains of fat," as highly-fed cattle are sometimes designated, there is no doubt of the practical fact, that the best butcher cannot sell any thing but the best-fatted beef; and of whatever age, size, or shape, a half-fatted ox may be, he is never selected by judges as fit for human food. Hence a well-fatted animal always commands a better price per pound than one imperfectly fed, and the parts selected as the primest beef are just the parts where there are the largest deposits of fat. The rump, the crop, and the sirloin, the very favorite cuts, which always command from twenty to twenty-five per cent. more than any other part of the ox, are just those parts on which the largest quantities of fat are found; so that instead of the taste and fashion of the age being against the excessive fattening of animals, it is, practically, exactly the reverse. Where there is most fat there is the best lean; where there is the greatest amount of muscle without its share of fat, that part is accounted inferior, and used for a different purpose; in fact, so far from fat being a disease, it is a condition of muscle, necessary to its utility as food—a source of luxury to the rich, and of comfort to the poor, furnishing a nourishing and healthy diet for their families.

Fattening is a secretive power which grazing animals possess, enabling them to lay by a store of the superfluous food they take for seasons of cold or scarcity. It collects round the angular bones of the animal, and gives the appearance of rotundity; hence the tendency to deposit fat is indicated, as we have stated, by a roundness of form, as opposed to the flatness of a milk-secreting animal. But its greatest use is, that it is a store of heat-producing aliment, laid up for seasons of scarcity and want. The food of animals for the most part may be said to consist of a saccharine, an oleaginous, and an albuminous principle. To the first belong all the starchy, saccharine, and gummy parts of the plants, which undergo changes in the digestive organs similar to fermentation before they can be assimilated in the system; by them also animal heat is sustained. In indolent animals the only parts of plants are deposited and laid up as fat; and, when vigor and strength fail, it is taken up, and also used in breathing to supply the place of the consumed saccharine matter. The albuminous, or gelatinous principle of plants, is mainly useful in forming muscle, while the ashes of plants, the unconsumable parts, are for the supply, mainly, of bone, hair, and horn, but also of muscle and of blood, and to supply the waste, which continually goes on. Now, there are several qualities which are essentially characteristic of a disposition to fatten. There have not, as yet, been any book-rules laid down, as in the case of Mr. Guénon's indications of milking cows; but there are marks so definite and well understood, that they are comprehended and acted upon by every grazier, although they are by no means easy to describe. It is by skillful acumen that the grazier acquires his knowledge, and not by theoretical rules; observation, judgment, and experience, powerful perceptive faculties and a keen and minute discrimination and comparison, are essential to his success.

The first indication he relies on is the touch. It is the absolute criterion of quality, which is supposed to be the keystone of perfection in all animals, whether for the pail or the butcher. The skin is so intimately connected with the internal organs, in all animals, that it is questionable whether even the schools of medicine might not make more use of it, in a diagnosis of disease. Of physiological tendencies in cattle, however, it is of the last and most vital importance. It must neither be thick, nor hard, nor adhere firmly to the muscles. If it is so, the animal is a hard grazer, a difficult and obstinate feeder—no skillful man will purchase her—she must go to a novice, and even to him at a price so low as to tempt him to be a purchaser. On the other hand, the skin must not be thin, like paper, nor flaccid, nor loose in the hand, nor flabby. This is the opposite extreme, and is indicative of delicateness, bad, flabby flesh, and possibly of inaptitude to retain the fat. It must be elastic and velvety, soft and pliable, presenting to the touch a gentle resistance, but so delicate as to give pleasure to the sensitive hand—a skin, in short, which seems at first to give an indentation from the pressure of the fingers, but which again rises to its place by a gentle elasticity. The hair is of nearly as much importance as the skin. A hard skin will have straight and stiff hair; it will not have a curl, but be thinly and lankly distributed equally over the surface. A proper grazing animal will have a mossy coat, not absolutely curled, but having a disposition to a graceful curl, a semifold, which presents a waving inequality, but as different from a close and straightly-laid coat, as it is from one standing off the animal at right angles, a strong symptom of disease. It will also, in a thriving animal, be licked here and there with its tongue, a proof that the skin is duly performing its functions. There must be also the full and goggle eye, bright and pressed outward by the fatty bed below, because, as this is a part where nature always provides fat, an animal capable of developing it to any considerable extent will have its indications here, at least when it exists in excess.

So much for feeding qualities in the animal, and their conformations indicative of this kindly disposition. Next come such formations of the animal itself as are favorable to the growth of fat, other things being equal. There must be size where large weights are expected. Christmas-beef, for instance, is expected to be large as well as fat. The symbol of festivity should be capacious as well as prime in quality. But it is so much a matter of choice and circumstance with the grazier that profit alone will be his guide. The axiom will be, however, as a general rule, that the better the grazing soil the larger the animal may be; the poorer the soil the smaller the animal. Small animals are unquestionably much more easily fed, and they are well known by experienced men to be those best adapted to second-rate feeding pastures. But beyond this there must be breadth of carcass. This is indicative of fattening perhaps beyond all other qualifications. If rumps are favorite joints, and produce the best price, it is best to have the animal which will grow the longest, the broadest, and the best rump; the same of crop, and the same of sirloin; and not only so, but breadth is essential to the consumption of that quantity of food which is necessary to the development of a large amount of fat in the animal. Thus a deep wide chest, favorable for the respiratory and circulating functions, enables it to consume a large amount of food, to burn up the sugary matter, and to deposit the fatty matter—as then useless for respiration, but hereafter to be prized. A full level crop will be of the same physiological utility, while a broad and open framework at the hips will afford scope for the action of the liver and kidneys.

There are other points also of much importance; the head must be small and fine; its special use is indicative of the quick fattening of the animal so constructed, and also it is indicative of the bones being small and the legs short. For constitutional powers, the beast should have his ribs extended well toward the thigh-bones or hips, so as to leave as little unprotected space as possible. There must be no angular or abrupt points; all must be round, and broad, and parallel. Any depression in the lean animal, will give a deficient deposit of flesh and fat at that point, when sold to the butcher, and thus deteriorate its value; and hence the animal must be round and full. But either fancy, or accident, or skill—we will not pretend to say which—has associated symmetry with quality and conformation, as a point of great importance in animals calculated for fattening; and there is no doubt that, to a certain extent, this is so. The beast must be a system of mathematical lines. To the advocate of symmetry the setting on of a tail will be a condemning fault; indeed, the ridge of the back, like a straight line, with the outline of the belly exactly parallel, viewed from the side, and a depth and squareness when viewed from behind, which remind us of a geometrical cube rather than a vital economy, may be said to be the indications of excellence in a fat ox. These qualities are inherent in some breeds; there may be cases and instances in all the superior breeds, and in most there may be failures.

By far the first in the list for feeding excellence are—

The Short-Horn or Durham Breed.—The origin of the breed is involved in great obscurity. They are supposed by some to be traced into Holderness; and to have been imported from Holstein, according to others; from continental Europe they certainly seem to have come; and, being successively improved by a variety of breeders, they have ended in that distinct race of animals, extraordinary beyond all others for their astonishing propensities to feed. Others, again, refer their origin to a native race of cattle called the Teeswater, because they have from time immemorial inhabited the valley which the Tees has formed by its washings down of the mountain limestone rocks, in which it has its origin; these, it is said, being crossed by the Holderness importations, gradually became a new race.

The late Mr. Bates traces back the short-horns to a breed in the possession of the Aslabies of Studley, and the Rev. H. Berry to an improvement in the East Riding of Yorkshire, by the importation of a breed from Holland by Sir W. St. Quintin of Scampston. Of these early ages of the short-horns, however, it is hardly necessary to say more than this—that a breed from time immemorial inhabited the valley of the Tees, and, trained and bred to feed, for a vast succession of generations, on its fertile deposits, acquired the habits of speedy fat-forming; for in these valleys, where hay alone will feed the largest ox, the production of fat would be so far an object that breeders would always select the best and easiest feeding animals; and thus the character of the district, through a number of centuries, might easily lay the groundwork of that improvement which the Milbanks, the Greys, the Booths, the Coates, and, above all, the Collings, have effected.

We will give the latest description of the qualities of the modern short-horn from the most recent authority, Mr. Dickson. After referring to the general symmetry of the frame and its delicate color, either deep-red cream-colored, white, or delicate roan—the latter the most fashion-

112 DOMESTIC ANIMALS.

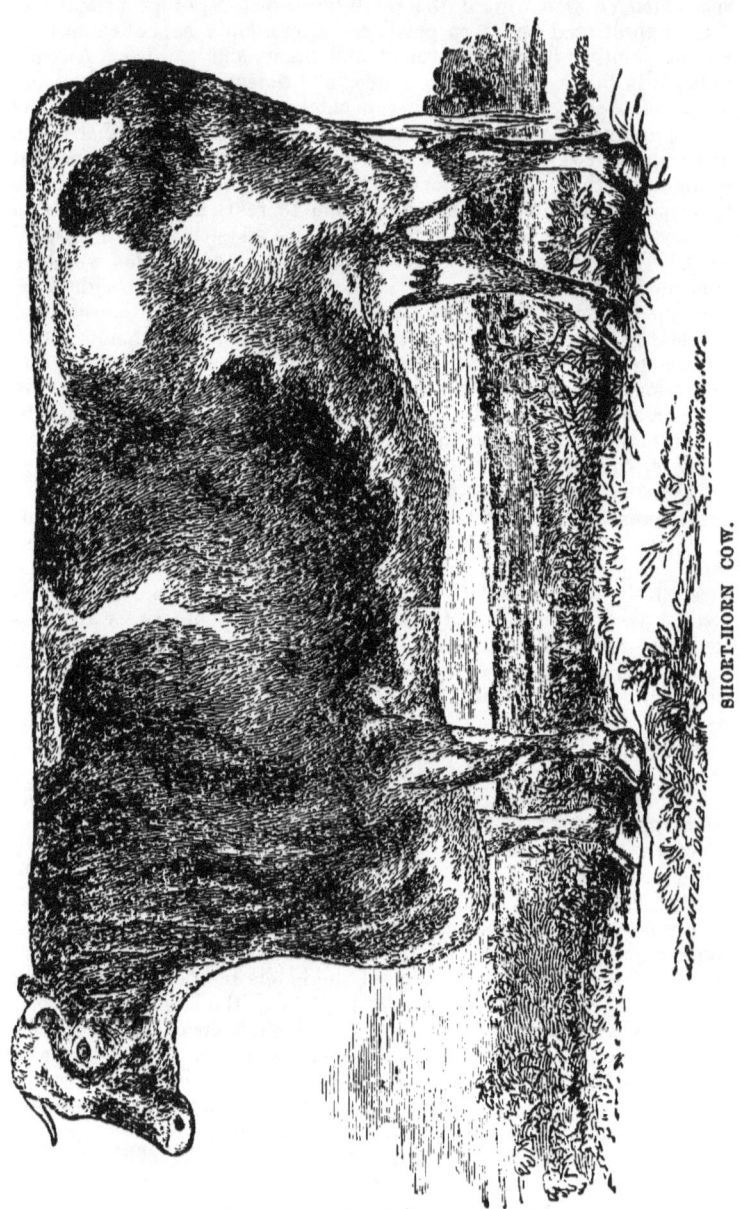

SHORT-HORN COW.

able and indeed prevailing color—he speaks of it as possessing "the mellowest touch, supported on small clean limbs, showing, like those of the greyhound and the race-horse, the union of strength with fineness, and ornamented with a small, lengthy, tapering head, neatly set on a broad, firm, deep neck; furnished with a small muzzle, wide nostrils, prominent mildly-beaming eyes; thin, large, veiny ears, set near the crown of the head, and protected in front with semicircularly-bent white or waxy-colored short, smooth, pointed horns; all these several parts combine to form a symmetrical harmony which has never been surpassed in beauty and sweetness by any other species of the domesticated ox."

Keeping in mind what was said to be the perfection of a fat animal, the same authority, speaking of the short-horn, says: "We have a straight level back from behind the horns to the top of the tail, full buttocks, and a projecting brisket; we have, in short, the rectangular form; we have also the level line across the hook-bones (hip), and the level top of the shoulder across the ox, and perpendicular lines down the hind and fore legs on both sides; these constituting the square form when the ox is viewed before and behind; and we have straight parallel lines from the sides of the shoulders along the utmost parts of the ribs and the sides of the hind quarters; and we have these lines connected at their ends by others of shorter and equal length across the end of the rump and the top of the shoulder; thus constituting the rectangular form of the ox when viewed from above down the back."

It will be very wide from our purpose to show either the immense amount of fat which has at one time or another accumulated on the backs of these wonderful animals, or the speed with which this has been done. Neither would it tend much to elucidate the principles of breeding or grazing to detail at any length the prices which short-horns have commanded and do command.

Nor is it in their rapid fattening alone that this race of cattle excels. They are, beyond all question, the most remarkable for early maturity. Fat deposits are generally the result of a mature state of the animal. There are few animals who will lay it on, to any degree, at least, until they are fully formed. The short-horn is an exception. They commence the fat-forming process as calves. This seems to increase with their growth, and at a year old they have all the semblance of cows.

The feeders of short-horns, instead of keeping them to three, four, or five years of age, fatten them and sell them off at from two to two and a half years; they can thus turn off one-half more at least, if not a greater proportion, of beef, from their farms or their stalls, than could possibly be done with any other breed. Hence they have quick returns and large amounts of beef for the food-consumer. We will not deny that the short-horn requires good keep, and shelter, and care. She needs nourishing diet; but she pays for all, for she is a cow when another is a calf—the ox is fat when the other is growing. Hence the short-horn stands the very first on the list of the fat-producing breeds of cattle.

The Hereford Breed.—This is a middle-horn breed of cattle, upon which a good deal of pains has lately been taken. The success of short-horn breeders,—of the Booths, the Bates, the Wileys, the Hoppers, and a score more of short-horn patrons, have caused a healthy emulation, and the difference between the Hereford cattle now exhibited, and those shown some ten or twelve years ago, shows not only that these breeders have judgment and skill, but it must also be confessed, that the breed have fattening capabilities. The old Hereford was a deep-brown animal, sometimes with an ochery cast, free from white, like the Devons; but an improved breed now possess the county, in which the invariable fashion is a dark red, with a white face, white belly, and not unfrequently a white back. The skin is thicker and less mellow than that of the short-horn, nor has the hair the mossy softness or graceful curl of the latter. The eye is full and lively; the chest deep and broad, the loin also broad, and the hips well-expanded; a level broad rump, a round barrel, and full crop, full, deep flank, well-ribbed home; small bones, clean and perpendicular thighs, belly almost parallel with back, head small. Indeed, color and symmetry are perhaps the predominant qualifications which secure the high favor of the breeder.

From the above description it will be seen that the Hereford, possessing many essentials in form, is destitute of the quality producing early maturity and speedy disposition to fatten. He lays on his flesh, soft and mottled, on the best parts; he has full sirloins, rumps, and crop, but he shows his beef on the outside; and he requires much more time to develop his qualities than the short-horn. In milking qualities the cow is even behind the ox in feeding, and it must in general be three and a half to four years old before it can be fatted with any very marked success. They require a rich pasture, though a hardy animal, and the average weight when fat does not exceed eight to ten hundred pounds. Herefordshire being more a breeding than a feeding county, the cattle are reared there, and sold off at three years old to graze in the counties of Leicester, Northampton, and the rich grass districts; but, with all its good qualities, it must be admitted that it requires from ten to twelve months more to feed than its more favored compeer, the short-horn. We give a sketch of first-rate specimens. Much controversy has gone on lately as to the merits of the two breeds—the short-horn and the Hereford; but it must be conceded, that while the short-horn is penetrating into the heart of Scotland, into the south of England, and into the county of Gloucester, on the one hand, and into Norfolk on the other, the Hereford is hardly keeping his ground, he is making no inroads into any one important new grazing district; and unless the gigantic efforts now made to amend the characteristics of the breed effect something more, they will dwindle still further away.

The West Highland Scot.—Next to the Hereford in the ranks of fattening animals, we place this breed of cattle; and they well deserve it,—for they will fatten in places and on food on which both the short-horn and the Hereford, too, would perish. This West Highland breed is somewhat wild in its nature, and will not bear the least confinement, tying, or control. It is eminently gregarious, and if kept alone will generally fret and pine. The peculiarity of the breed is, that it is a small animal, generally deep jet-black, pale red, or dun, seldom any white spots on any part of the body; its horns are long, and turned

HEREFORD COW, GRACE.—Property of Erastus Corning, Jr., Albany, N. Y.

upward and outward. The coat is peculiar, soft, long, and absolutely curled, so as to form a sort of fleece. Another peculiarity is, that they form their beef almost entirely on the back, which is therefore straight; the body is round; and they lay on fat rapidly under circumstances in which another animal would literally starve.

He can assimilate, from a soil so barren as to be sterile for others, as much food as will enable him to feed—for to grow is out of the question, that process is performed on his native hills; if indulged, however, he will pay for it in the rapidity of his fattening, and the excellence of his beef. They will weigh, with amazingly little care, from seven hundred to one thousand pounds. The exceptions to this rule, however, are very important in special cases. The Duke of Northumberland having a very promising Argylshire "stot"—bullocks, as they are called more generally in England—kept him as long as he saw him improve, to see what he would weigh. He was five and a half years old, and weighed exclusive of offal, one thousand four hundred and four pounds. Though, perhaps, one of the heaviest of the breed ever slaughtered, he was neither the fattest nor the most inactive, but seemed in that state to possess all the activity which he had on his native hills. To give an idea of his keeping, and of the hardihood of his race, it is only necessary to give an account of his food. In the first winter he was turned out to a poor pasture, with a little bad hay; in the summer he had again a poor land pasture; in the next winter he had again a poor pasture, but a few turnips; in the following summer he had a fair pasture, and the same pasture in winter, with a more liberal allowance of turnips; in the third summer he was tolerably well grazed; in the fourth winter, he had as many turnips as he could eat in the sheltered straw fold, and in the summer in which he was fatted, he had all the indulgence of a feeding animal, viz., cut clover, hay, mangel-wurzel, turnips, bean-meal, and a little oil-cake; the latter of which he always disliked. Mr. Quarl says his "fat was distributed in an uncommonly equable manner, of a color resembling the finest grass butter, and as firm as wax; the muscle was in ample proportion, bright in color, of fine texture, and beautifully marbled by admixture of his excellent fat."

The Devon Breed.—If this had been a treatise on drawing cattle, we should have placed this middle-horned description of animals first in our list, instead of almost last. They are physiologically well formed animals; they are a very old and carefully-kept distinct breed of animals. They are docile and tractable, patient and gentle; hardy, notwithstanding their warm and humid climate; but they are not first-rate milkers, although very good feeders. They will grow to a considerable size; and they produce a class of beef at all periods of their growth of capital quality. The red color—all red, and nothing but red—is a *sine qua non* in a Devonshire ox; he has a moderately straight top, a fine serene countenance, and small head; a somewhat thin skin, covered with curly hair. The rump is narrower than in the short-horns and the chine lighter and flatter; but the brisket is large and full, the legs fine, the shoulder slanting, the neck long and thin. He is a beast of draught, and for this he is unequaled.

CATTLE. 117

DEVON COW, FAIRY.—THE PROPERTY OF LINSLEY BROTHERS, WEST MERIDEN, CONN.

Mr. Parkinson, in his invaluable Treatise on Live Stock, gives the weight of some specimens of six years' old cattle, which weighed some eight hundred pounds, but the cows much less. He says of them: "On the whole, they must be allowed to be good cattle for their soils, and particularly where oxen are worked at the plow. When slaughtered, they are a sort of beef that suits the consumption of many customers."

Among the most successful breeders of Devonshire cattle may be mentioned Mr. Turner, of Barton, near Exeter, Mr. Quartly of Motland, (who is the most distinguished winner,) Mr. Merson of Brinsworthy, and Mr. Davy of Moulton.

Galloway Breed.—The Galloways are prominent fat-producing animals of Scotland, and are bred in great numbers in Galloway and Dumfriesshire. They are hornless, mostly black, are small in size, compact, short-legged, hardy, have thick mossy coats, and are good feeders. As milkers they are very indifferent, although, like all small milkers, the quality is rich. They are mostly driven south and fed off on the good pastures in England, and like the Highlanders, bring the highest price in the London markets. The joints are of a good size for family roasts, and the meat is of the best description; thus making it the most desirable.

The Angus Breed.—We shall close our remarks on the fat-producing class of oxen by shortly describing a hornless or polled race of animals—the Angus "Doddies," as they are called. Being bad milkers, they are generally used for grazing, and very much fatted in their native country; they are also preferred for feeding by the graziers of Leicestershire and Norfolk. Their color is generally black, but occasionally red; the head fine; the breast deep; the back not quite straight, being a little depressed at the loin and somewhat narrow; the eye full and clear; the touch generally good, and the hair thick and curly. The tendency of the flesh, as in all the hardy Scottish cattle, is to form on the back; but they will weigh from a thousand to fourteen hundred pounds.

Qualities are so co-existent with conformation that, as a general rule, it may be received as an axiom. And as dairy and butcher qualities are generally combined only to a very limited extent, and as both qualities are rarely high in the same breed, it becomes the agriculturist to make his selection according to the object he has in view.

THE PRINCIPLES OF CATTLE-BREEDING.—We may offer a few remarks on the principles by which the breeder ought to be guided in the successful management or improvement of his stock, in whatever points he wishes it to excel, whether in those required by the grazier or the dairy-farmer. Every man, whether grazier or dairy-farmer, is desirous of turning his cattle to the most advantage; nor can this be done, unless the size of the farm, soil, climate, the produce, and the nature and extent of the pasturage, be well considered; for the cattle that the farm is best adapted for maintaining will be the most profitable. It is, however, essential, whatever the cattle be, whether for the purpose of the dairy, or for the immediate supply of the markets with their flesh,

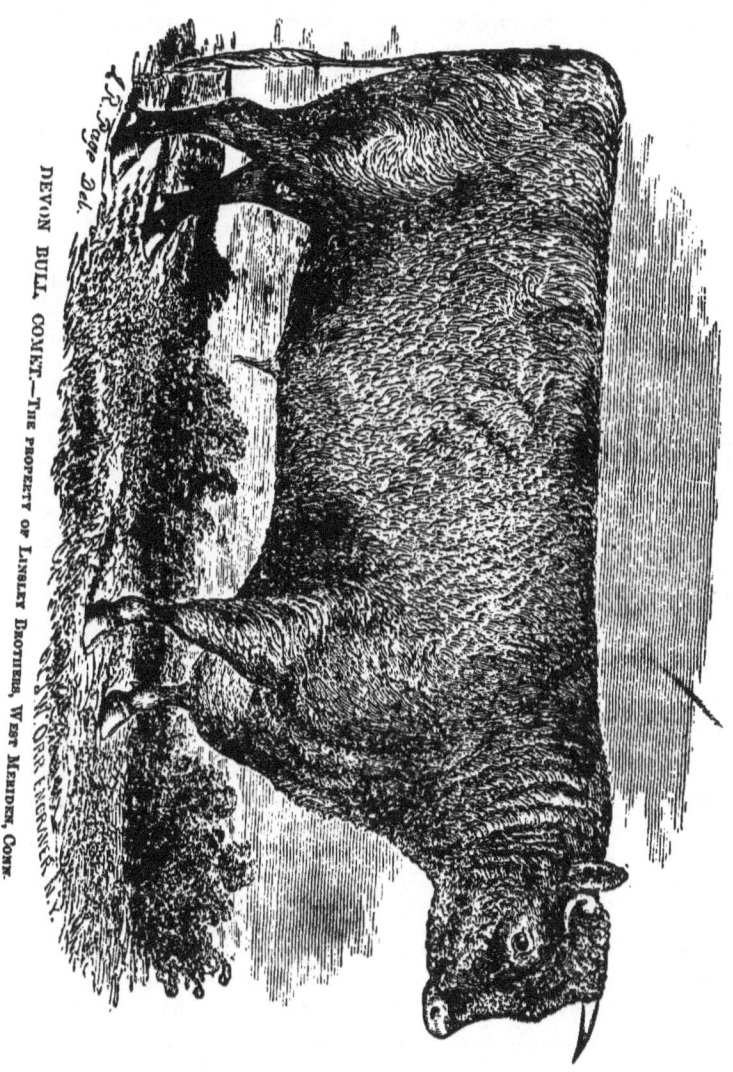

DEVON BULL, COMET.—THE PROPERTY OF LINSLEY BROTHERS, WEST MERIDEN, CONN.

that they be well bred, and excellent of their kind. To the dairy farmer, the most important points are, the quantity of milk yielded, its quality, its value for the production of butter, or of cheese, a freedom in the cows from vicious habits and ill temper, their character as good and healthy breeders, the ease with which, when useless as milkers, they become fattened for the market, and the nature and quantity of food requisite for this purpose. To the grazier, the quickness of becoming fat, and at as little expense as possible, the fineness of the grain of the meat, or of the muscular fibers, the mode of laying on the fat, the smallness of bone, soundness of constitution, and congeniality with the soil and the climate, are the chief points which he takes into consideration. If he is wise, he will never stint keep, nor transfer his stock from a good to an indifferent soil; and this is true also with respect to the dairy-farmer.

Contour, or beauty of form, is desirable; indeed, it is more or less connected with what may be termed utility of form, that is, a preponderance of those parts in the beast which are most delicate for the table, and bear the highest price, over the parts of inferior quality, or offal. This is connected with smallness of bone, but not a preternatural smallness, and with a tendency to depositions of fat, which, however, should not be carried to an extreme, otherwise the quantity of flesh is disproportionate, and its fiber is dry and insipid; nor is the weight of the beast proportionate to its admeasurement. Previously to the time of Mr. Bakewell,* the cattle in general were large, long-bodied, big-boned, flat-sided, slow to fatten, great consumers of food, and often black, or foul-fleshed, or, as it is called in Yorkshire, "lyery." This truly patriotic breeder, acting upon true principles, energetically set to work upon the improvement of cattle, and in defiance of opposition and a thousand difficulties, lived to see the success of his long-continued efforts. Experience and a close and acute observation had taught him that "like produces like;" in other words, that the qualities of the parents, such as beauty, or utility of form, disposition to fatness, goodness of flesh, abundance of milk, and even temper, were inherited by their offspring; and that by careful selections on the side both of the sire and dam, a breed might be ultimately established to which the title *blood* could be distinctly applied. This, of course supposes a primary selection, then a selection of such of the offspring as exhibited the properties which constituted their perfection, in the highest degree; and again of the offspring of these, and so on progressively.† At first Mr. Bakewell was necessitated to breed in and in, but as his stock increased, he was enabled to interpose more or less remote removes between the members of the same family; and ultimately he established the Dishley, or New Leicester long-horns, a breed remarkable for smallness of bone, roundness of form, aptitude to fatten upon a moderate allowance, and fineness of flesh.

---

* Born at Dishley, in Leicestershire, 1725. His father and grandfather resided on the estate before him.

† Bates' rule was, "Breed in and in from a oan stock, and you commit ruin and devastation; *but if a good stock be selected, you may breed in and in as much as you please;*" and he followed this practice for fifty years, and yet had one of the finest herds ever known.

But while he accomplished this, rendering the animals admirably suited for the grazier, it was found that their qualities as milkers were much deteriorated; the dairy-farmers consequently retained their old breed, noted for the richness, though perhaps not the great abundance of the milk. We are not here speaking about the differences or the distinguished excellences of the various breeds of cattle, but of the principles upon which excellences, it matters not of what sort, may be obtained. "Like produces like," and both parents must present the same excellencies, the same characteristics. It was by following out these rules that Mr. Bakewell arrived at perfection in his breed; indeed by some he is thought to have pushed his principles too far, and the following remarks have perhaps some justice in them:—" It was his grand maxim, that the bones of an animal intended for food could not be too small; and that the fat, being the most valuable part of the carcass, could not, consequently be too abundant. In pursuance of this leading theory, by inducing a preternatural smallness of bone and rotundity of carcass, he sought to cover the bones of all his animals externally with masses of fat. Thus the entirely new Leicester breed, from their excessive tendency to fatten, produce too small a quantity of eatable meat, and that, too, necessarily of inferior flavor and quality. They are, in general, found defective in weight, proportionally to their bulk; and if not thoroughly fattened, their flesh is crude and without flavor; while, if they be so, their carcasses produce little else but fat, a very considerable part of which must be sold at an inferior price, to make candles instead of food; not to forget the very great waste that must ever attend the consumption of over-fattened meat.

"This great and sagacious improver (Mr. Bakewell), very justly disgusted at the sight of those huge, gaunt, leggy, and misshapen animals with which his vicinity abounded, and which scarcely any length of time, or quantity of food, would thoroughly fatten, patriotically determined upon raising a more sightly and profitable breed; yet, rather unfortunately, his zeal impelled him to the opposite extreme. Having painfully, and at much cost, raised a variety of cattle, the chief merit of which is to make fat, he has apparently laid his disciples and successors under the necessity of substituting another that will make lean."— *Illustrations of Natural History*, p. 5.

Granting the truth of these strictures, which we scarcely can to the full extent, what is the inference as it respects the system of breeding? Namely, this: that by pursuing the proper mode, by proper selections, and by joining like excellencies and properties in the sire and dam, and not by rashly crossing distinct breeds, but by making one breed the great foundation, and working upon it, remembering that "like produces like," not only will the point aimed at be attained, but it may even be overshot, thus demonstrating the power which the judicious breeder possesses.

Since Mr. Bakewell's time the New Leicester breed has become degenerated; by some the stock has been bred in and in too closely, and by others very injudiciously crossed. In the mean time the short-horned breeds of cattle have been gaining an ascendancy, so that few really excellent long-horns are now to be seen. This, however, has nothing to do with the great principles we have endeavored to illustrate; they apply alike to all breeds of cattle. Every breeder, then, should well consider the properties of the stock from which he breeds, investigate their good qualities and their bad qualities, and while he endeavors to keep up or improve the former, he should study to remove the latter. His selection must be strict; the heifer or cow should have as few of the bad points as possible, every excellence in perfection, and be in good health; the bull should be of the same kind, and if related, only in a remote degree; nor should he have been brought up on a pasturage differing from that of the cow, or under the influences of a different local climate; he should not only possess the good points *desired*, in all their perfection, but he should also have the points which the farmer considers to be the excellences of his own stock, as admirably developed. Thus acting with judgment he may expect improvement; and if he fail, there is some concealed fault which has been overlooked, either on the one side or the other, or some defect in their parents, and which (in accordance with the tendency there is in families to exhibit, from time to time, certain peculiarities, latent perhaps for a generation) has again made itself manifest; consequently, on both sides there ought to be what is termed "good *blood*." But this is to suppose a stock already improved to a great extent; and here we may repeat the injunctions laid down by the Rev. H. Berry, which more particularly apply to the farmer commencing *de novo*: "A person selecting a stock from which to breed, notwithstanding he has set up for himself a standard of perfection, will obtain them with qualifications of different descriptions, and in different degrees. In breeding from such he will exercise his judgment, and decide what are indispensable or desirable qualities, and will cross with animals with a view to establish them. His proceeding will be of the '*give and take kind*.' He will submit to the introduction of a trifling defect, in order that he may profit by a great excellence; and between excellences perhaps somewhat incompatible, he will decide on which is the greatest, and give it the preference.*

"To a person commencing improvement, the best advice is to get as good a bull as he can, and if he be a good one of his kind, to use him indiscriminately with all his cows; and when by this proceeding, which ought to be persisted in, his stock has, with an occasional change of bull, become sufficiently stamped with desirable excellences, his selection of males should then be made to eradicate defects which he thinks desirable to be got rid of.

"He will not fail to keep in view the necessity of good blood in the bulls resorted to, for that will give the only assurance that they will

---

* "A person would often be puzzled; he would find different individuals possessing different perfections in different degrees:—one, good flesh and a tendency to fatten, with a bad form: another, with fine form, but bad flesh, and little disposition to acquire fat. What rule should he lay down, by the observance of which good might be generally produced, and as little evil as possible effected? UTILITY. The truly good form is that which secures constitution, health, and vigor: a disposition to lay on flesh with the greatest possible reduction of offal. Having obtained this, other things are of minor, though perhaps sometimes of considerable importance."
—*PrizeEssay*, by the Rev. H. Berry.

transmit their own valuable properties to their offspring; but he must not trust to this alone, or he will soon run the risk of degeneracy. In animals evincing an extraordinary degree of perfection, where the constitution is decidedly good, and there is no prominent defect, a little close breeding may be allowed; but this must not be injudiciously adopted, or carried too far; for, although it may increase and confirm valuable properties, it will also increase and confirm defects; and no breeder need be long in discovering that, in an improved state, animals have a greater tendency to defect than to perfection. Close breeding from affinities impairs the constitution and affects the procreative powers, and therefore a strong cross is occasionally necessary."

The dairy-farmer, however, is less concerned in this high breeding than the grazier; yet he is not by any means indifferent in the matter; for his aim ought to be, to obtain a breed no less valuable as milkers than for their disposition to fatten when the milk is dried. These two qualifications are not to be attained very easily; yet they may be, and, indeed, have been attained, and especially among the improved short-horn breeds, as those of Durham and Yorkshire, or the cross-breeds between the old Shropshire, and the Holderness. The breeds most valued in the great dairies around the metropolis are mixed between the Yorkshire, Holderness, and Durham. For quality and quantity of milk they are eminent; they yield, on the average, each cow, two gallons of milk at a time, and often nine quarts; and when dry, they are in general readily fattened for the butcher.

With respect to the points of symmetry in cattle, of which the various breeds exhibit several degrees of modification, there are certain rules which are generally acknowledged as applicable to good cattle of all kinds.

The Bull.—The forehead of the bull should be broad and short, the lower part, that is, the nasal part and jaws, tapering; and the muzzle fine; the ears moderate; the neck gently arched from the head to the shoulders, small and fine where it joins the head, but boldly thickening as it sweeps down to the chest, which should be deep, almost to a level with the knees, with the briskets well developed. The shoulders should be well set, the shoulder-blades oblique, with the humeral joint advancing forward to the neck. The barrel of the chest should be round, without hollowness between it and the shoulders. The sides should be ribbed home, with little space between them and the hips; the whole body being barrel-shaped, and not flat-sided. The belly should not hang down, being well supported by the oblique abdominal muscles, and the flanks should be round and deep. The hips should be wide and round, the loins broad, and the back straight and flat. The tail should be broad and well-haired, and set on high, and fall abruptly. The breast should be broad; the forearms short and muscular, tapering to the knee; the legs straight, clean, and fine-boned. The thighs should be full and long, and close together when viewed from behind. The hide should be moderately thin, with a mellow feel, and movable, but not lax; and it should be well covered with fine soft hair. The nostrils should be large and open; the eyes animated and prominent; the horns clean and white.

The Ox.—In the ox, the masculine characters, so prominent in the bull, are softened; the neck is carried nearly straight from the top of the shoulders, without an arch; and the general frame is lighter, but the points of excellence are the same.

The Cow.—Cows of a coarse, angular, gaunt figure may give good milk, and that in abundance, as, indeed, was the case with some of the old unimproved breeds; but it is desirable, and moreover it is possible, to unite qualities as a milker with such an aptitude to fatten as will render her valuable when dry, and profitable to the butcher. In a cow thus constituted, the head must be long, rather small and fine; the neck thin and delicate at its junction with the head, but thickening as it approaches the shoulder and descends to the chest; the breast should be at least moderately broad and prominent, with a small dewlap; the chine should be full and fleshy; the ribs well arched, and the chest barrelled; the back straight, the shoulders fine, the loins wide, the hips well formed and rounded, the rump long; the udder should be moderate, with a fine skin, and of equal size both before and behind; the teats should not be too large or lax, and they should be equi-distant from each other. If the vascular system be well developed, the milk-vein, as it is termed, is generally large; and though this vein is not connected with the udder, but carries the blood from the foreparts to the inguinal vein, still it has been taken, and with some justice, as the criterion of a good milker. The eyes should be clear, calm, and tranquil, indicative of a gentle temper; the skin thin, but mellow; and the hair soft. Cows thus admirably formed will often yield from twenty to twenty-four quarts of milk daily, and some, in the spring time, in good pasturage, even thirty, or more. The milk may, perhaps, yield less butter in proportion than that of some other breeds of cattle; but it would appear that, as the cow advances in age to her sixth and seventh year the milk becomes richer; and it is well known that the extensive dairymen of London prefer a cow which has had a third or fourth calf, and is five or six years old, to a younger animal.

We are perfectly aware that Mr. Culley ("Observations on Live Stock,") considers it as an impossibility to unite good milkers with good feeders; for, he says, whenever we attempt both, we are sure to get neither in perfection:—"In proportion as we gain the one, in the same proportion we lose the other; the more milk, the less beef; and the more we pursue beef, the less milk we get. In truth, they seem to be two different varieties of the same kind, for very different uses; and if so, they ought most certainly to be differently pursued by those who employ them. If the dairyman wants milk, let him pursue the milking tribe; let him have both bull and cows of the best and greatest milking family he can find; on the contrary, he that wants feeding or grazing cattle, let him procure a bull and cows of that sort which feed the quickest, wherever they are to be found. By pursuing too many objects at once, we are apt to lose sight of the principle; and, by aiming at too much, we often lose all. Let us only keep to distinct sorts, and we shall obtain the prize in due time. I apprehend it has been much owing to the mixing of breeds and improper crossings that has kept us so long from distinguishing the most valuable kinds." Mr. Culley wrote in 1807, and since his day many improvements have taken place in the breeds of cattle; and experience has proved, that the improved Yorkshire cow, in which the characters of the Durham and Holderness are mingled, unites the two qualities in high perfection.

Reproduction, Rearing and Fattening.—The heifer ought not to be permitted to breed until over two years old; the reason is obvious. Her own system before this period is not sufficiently matured for the tax upon it—a tax which will be paid not only by the dam, but also by her progeny, for both will suffer from a deficiency in nutriment, the whole of which is necessary for the growth of the former, which during the second year is rapid. If the bull be kept separate from the herd of cows, the farmer may regulate the succession of calves almost at pleasure, so as to suit his pasture or his arrangements. The best time as it respects the mother, the calf, and the free supply of milk, is when the spring grass is beginning to shoot luxuriantly, affording a good and sufficient store of nutriment. It is true that veal and butter yield a better profit at an earlier period, but the breeder must judge in points of this nature from circumstances. The period of gestation in the cow is generally stated as nine calendar months, or 270 days; but there is often considerable variation of time. M. Tessier observes (in a memoir read to the Royal Academy of Sciences in Paris), that the shortest period, as far as his opportunities of observation enabled him to ascertain, was 240 days, the longest 321; the difference being eighty-one days.* This range of time is very extraordinary, and appears to depend on the care paid to the animal, and on its state of health; by which the development of the calf is influenced through the sanguiferous system of the mother. With respect to the bull, he does not attain to a due degree of strength till two years old, and is in higher vigor at three; but how long the breeder may keep him after that age must depend upon his own judgment, and a variety of circumstances. The cow seldom produces more than a single calf, sometimes, however, twins, and very rarely three. In the case of twins, if they be respectively male and female, the female is generally, but not always, unproductive.

It is sometimes desirable that the farmer should possess the power of *controlling the ratio of the sexes in the animals he breeds*. The wonderful ratio in which they are produced in nature, is one proof of the all-wise provisions of the Almighty in making them subject to certain laws. Many investigations have been made to show how far this is within the control of man. A dairy-man is particularly interested in the production of heifer calves, wherewith to increase his dairy stock; a grazier may be equally desirous of producing bullocks for large weights and summer grazing; while a breeder for sale may be anxious to see a goodly proportion of bulls. How far he can control this production is a question of interest and importance. Hofkener, a German, made some calculations as regards the human species, which tended to show that where the father was younger than the mother, the proportion of male

---

* In the *Bulletin des Sciences*, by the Soc. Philomatique, Paris, 1797, M. Tessier says, that out of 160 cows, some calved in 241 days, and five in 308; giving a latitude of 67 days.—See Sir E. Home's Paper on Phil. Trans. Part 1, for 1822.

births to females was 90.6 per cent.; when of equal age, 90 per cent.; but when the age of the father was greater than the mother, nine to eighteen years, it was 143 per cent.

Similar in principle was the experience of M. C. C. de Buzareurgnes, who professed to have the power of controlling the sexes in sheep; his principle being the same as the above, viz, that vigor was favorable to female, and the converse to male births. For females he proposed to select young rams, and place them in a good pasture; for males, three to five shear animals, and to place them in an inferior pasture. His experiment was successful. In his female trial there were seventy-six female lambs produced against thirty-five males; and, in his male trial, there were produced eighty males against fifty-five females. Another trial was made by M. Cournuejouls. One section was put to young male lambs, and on a good pasture; the other on a poorer pasture, and with old rams. The result was, that in the first experiment there were fifteen males and twenty-five females, and, in the second, there were twenty-six males and fourteen females.

Buzareurgnes also showed that in several lots the approximations to male or female births, were also in the ratio of the ages of the animals on both sides. Thus, of the young ewes put to the young rams, the two-year old ewes produced fourteen males and twenty-six females, the three-year old gave sixteen males and twenty-nine females; whereas the four-year old ewes, to the aged rams, and on the poor pasture, produced thirty-three males and fourteen females.

More than this is not known; but there is quite sufficient to indicate that the breeder possesses at least considerable power in controlling the proportion of the sexes, and that the more vigor he has of frame and food, the greater will be the proportion of females; and that the converse of this will hold equally good. There is enough in the principle to deserve a trial.

We now proceed with details descriptive of the management of cattle, under the heads of rearing and fattening. The first object being to secure a suitable breeding stock, and a provision for proper buildings for their accommodation and shelter.

Rearing.—It is most advantageous to have the calves drop in the early part of the year, that the young grass may be ready for them about the time of weaning. New milk is best for the young calf for the first fortnight, when it may be trained to feed upon other food, such as linseed-cake, or sweet hay; and when it will eat these freely, its allowance of milk may be gradually reduced, and sliced Swedes or carrots added to its food. The cribs should be kept clean, the food regularly supplied, and the calves themselves should always receive kind and gentle treatment. Perseverance in such management will greatly aid the growth of the young animals; when kindly treated, there will be no restless excitement on the approach of strangers, and they are easily managed when surgical operations become necessary from disease or accident. All graziers are fully alive to the importance of docility in all fatting animals.

After three or four weeks the male calves may be castrated, an operation attended with less risk and pain when done at an early age. It is advisable to keep the calves in separate cribs until five or six weeks old, after which they may be turned together into a comfortable house, with sufficient room for exercise. And when the pasturage permits, and fine weather is well established, they may be turned out, at first for a few hours only in the middle of the day, to inure them to the change. As winter approaches, they must again have the shelter of a comfortable yard and be supplied with roots mixed with straw-chaff. An addition of one pound of oil-cake in summer, and two pounds to their ordinary food during winter, will greatly assist their condition and early maturity. The yards should, of course, be well sheltered and littered, and cattle of the same age and size have separate inclosures, otherwise the weaker beasts will be driven about by the master ones. In the spring the young cattle are again turned to grass, and the treatment continues in a similar manner until the cattle are fattened off at home, or are sold off for that purpose into other districts. By liberal feeding whilst in a young state, the cattle are kept in good condition and rapid growth.

We believe that food for calves may be prepared of a much more nutritious nature, and much more likely to be of advantage to the producers; some of these, on which we have successfully reared calves for several years, we shall place before the reader:—

1. **Wheatmeal Porridge.**—This is made in the following manner: boil two gallons of water, and mix a pint of fine flour with cold water, sufficient to make it into the consistency of a thick cream. This should be thoroughly mixed, and put into a bowl capable of holding half a gallon; a small quantity of the hot water is added to the mixture, and stirred so as gradually to raise the temperature of the flour and water in the bowl, and prevent it from running into lumps. This is plunged into boiling water, and stirred until the whole boils again. This coagulates the mass, and forms a thick nutritious porridge. It is a great improvement to the mixture if one-sixth part of old skimmed milk is mixed with it; which not only gets scalded itself, but very materially improves it. Two gallons of the mixture per day will be found sufficient.

2. **Linseed Jelly** combined with the milk, is a very valuable auxiliary. We ourselves have scarcely tried the seed by itself sufficiently to be able to give a very decided opinion upon it; and we much prefer the pressed seed, in the shape of cake, crushed to a powder; and, for this reason, if we wanted to lay on the fat, we should give them the crushed seed, because its fatty matter would, when cooked, be easily assimilated into animal fat; but when bone and muscle are to be formed, every pound of fattening matter in the food displaces other substances calculated to build up the animal structure; for this reason we most approve of the jelly produced by the crushed cake. The proportions of the crushed cake to the water should be as follows:—to two gallons of water take two pounds of oil-cake bruised or crushed nearly to a powder, sprinkle it in the water, stir, and allow it to boil ten minutes. Cool with skim-milk, if convenient. A rich jelly-like mass, of the most nourishing kind, is produced, which should be given in a lukewarm state.

3. **Broth Porridge.**—This is a somewhat unnatural mixture; but it is often used very successfully, combined with other mixtures, for feeding calves. The water in which bacon has been boiled is carefully preserved,

and diluted with perhaps one-half of its quantity in water. It may be expected that a substance like bacon, from which nitrogenized and phosphoric matter may be expected to be dissolved by the action of boiling, will be of use; but, to make it alimentary, it is necessary to mix it with a considerable proportion of milk. However unnatural this mixture may appear; how contrary soever to all theories of natural history it may be to give carnivorous matter to herbivorous animals, we may find in it an analogy by no means unimportant, in the disposition evinced by mature animals of this description to select and chew, for hours together, a piece of bone, which they will search for with instinctive pertinacity, and relinquish with reluctance. Is it not because she finds in it the nitrogen or the phosphates denied her in the food upon which she is confined? And if this be so—if she is guided by her instinct to select and choose animal matter, why may not a decoction of animal substance be useful to the calves, in their younger stages, as an auxiliary, and, to a certain extent, a substitute for the beverage which nature has given them, but which man denies them.

Solid Food for calves will soon, however, displace much of the liquid. At five or six weeks old they ought to be trained to eat sliced roots. To do this it is only necessary to supply them in convenient forms in a trough within their reach. Their moments of leisure will be employed in playing with and sucking these pieces, until they begin to masticate them. The roots should, for this purpose, be cut into oblong pieces, one inch broad, half an inch deep, and two inches long; these shapes are better than either slices or squares, being more adapted to their conformation, and better calculated to make them learn to eat of their own accord. Calves should be reared from the months of September to March. We do not approve of late-bred calves; if they are reared late, they become tender and require nursing the following winter. In the months we have named, however, turnips are always plentiful; or, if mangel-wurzel is cultivated, it will be found a very successful substitute; although we prefer Swedes. These appear not only to agree with the palate of the animal and to make it thrive, but they exercise a very beneficial influence on its subsequent development. Is it because they contain a large share of the phosphates? Sprengel makes the relative proportions of the phosphates in the Swedes to be nearly six times as great as in the common turnips, and sulphate ten times.

	Phos. acid.	Sulph. acid.	
Common turnips	73	41	} per 1000 lbs.
Swedes	408	890	

Other auxiliaries are sometimes adopted, such as bean-meal, pea-meal, oatmeal, cattle sago, and Indian meal; all these being very material aids in rearing calves.

CATTLE-FEEDING.—This question is one of economy simply: *how can the largest number of pounds of beef be produced at the least possible cost?* This is the real question still unsettled, and on this we will proceed to show the present extent of our knowledge.

First. The grazier must select such animals as will lay on fat rapidly; and, by a physiological law, as we have seen, there are those which will soonest attain maturity so as to be fit for feeding. We stop not now to examine whether or not the two principles of taking on fat early as well as rapidly are necessarily connected—though it is very probable they are—and that a tendency to lay on fat will show itself at a very early period of the animal's history; though it may possibly be a mere result of the breeder's skill to obtain the two qualities combined.

Now, every good grazier knows an animal which will thrive, that being a simple matter of judgment. A skillful man will select out of a drove, five, or ten, or twenty animals, and nineteen of the twenty will be the best grazers for his particular farm. The eye guides him partially—the signs we have described in our remarks on the breeds of cattle also—but more than all he is directed by the touch.

Having selected the animal, the mode of feeding him is to turn him out into a grass field skirting a river—if such be within the grazier's power—where alluvium of ages has been washed into the soil so deep that the roots of the herbage cannot find its bottom, and so firmly comminuted as to admit of the minutest filaments of the radicles of the plants to penetrate it with facility, so porous as to admit the air to enter, and the water to filter gently through, and containing its elements in a state of solution so delicate that they are ready for food to the plants which consume them; but last, though of greater importance than all, having the elements of vegetation in plentiful abundance. Now, all men know that on such a soil, in five, six, or even in four months, a lean animal will become fat. He has all he requires—a little attention to see that he is well is all that is needed, from the time of his being placed in the pasture to being taken out to the butcher. There is neither labor, pains, or expense incurred. He is worth twenty-five dollars more when he is taken out than when he was put in, and that is all the grazier knows or cares for. Now, we shall find out the requisites here for feeding, strictly laid down. There is plenty of fresh and highly nutritive food; there is scarcely any labor in searching for and obtaining it; with water, and shelter, and warmth; and also plenty of air, and freedom from constraint.

Now, this is what the feeder must aim at in his winter-fed cattle. They cannot feed in the open air; the cold and wet would deprive him of the flesh as fast as the food laid it on. Here he must provide shelter. Now, one of the controversies of cattle-feeding in winter is, which is the best mode of providing this. The Scotch farmer loudly contends for full and perfect liberty to the animal. If he is too warm he will sweat, and if too closely confined he will fret and murmur; and he declares that practice has decided that they should be fatted in open places; a sheltered shed they may have, but nothing beyond it. The midland counties man says this exposure is dreadful. It wastes their beef, and renders them subject to disease, and involves long feeding. Another class again insist on the tying up of the animals as injurious to their health; that a little exercise, but absolute confinement, are equally necessary; and that they should have shelter with freedom—these two classes are controverting the merits of box and stall-feeding.

And both of them are right. Take a Highland Scot, consider his wild habits, his long stray of mountain and glen, his wide-spread pasture

6*

of peat and heather, from which he could in his native fastness smell afar off his friend or his enemy man! Tie him by the head and he becomes fretful or furious; he will pine, and fret, and worry himself, while, in his gregarious state, with a herd of his fellows in open yards, or sheds, he will thrive. Nay, he has a nature which will lay on fat despite the cold and wet, as the rye among plants can assimilate food from the barrenest soil; so he has a natural shelter in his hair and constitution, for which the owner of more delicate and tender animals will not give him credit, forgetting that the Scotchman has a different animal to deal with in his shed-feeding from the short-horn.

The short-horn feeder, on the contrary, possesses a tame, quiet, gentle, lethargic animal, which shows that universal mark of good breeding in men and animals—he is always quiet. He will neither pine at never beholding the light, nor feel the want of exercise if he never leaves his stall, provided he has food and comfort in plenty. Nay, he will hardly take the exercise necessary to keep his limbs in healthy action. But keep him from the cold and wet; prevent the blast from passing over him; he likes protection, and thrives best in boxes.

Take a Devon, or, if you like, a Sussex ox. He is large and cumbrous; but he is active. Give him liberty, and he will roam and harass himself; but he is tame enough to keep to his stall without pain or fretting. He requires a stall.

The **Temperature** at which it is desirable to keep feeding animals is a matter of more importance than might be inferred from the apparently small amount of investigation bestowed upon it. The question is, are we to run the risk of a wasting expenditure of food by perspiration under excessive heat? or are we to induce them to waste it, to keep up animal heat, by exposure to too much cold? Nay, will not different classes of feeding animals be subject to different consequences, from the same degree of heat? In the same cow-house there may be some too hot, and others too cold, from their different constitutions. Oxen generally sweat at a temperature in which heifers thrive admirably; this happens at any rate till Christmas, after which they seem to be able to bear the same degree of heat as female animals.

H. S. Thompson, Esq., tied up two sets of feeding bullocks, eight into a warmer shed than the rest. They had the same quantity and kind of food; but those in the warmer shed made more beef than those in the colder, showing that warm air, as well as warm food, was highly favorable to fattening short-horns; which breed, we believe, he invariably fattens. The temperature he aims at is about 55° to 60° of Fahrenheit; an increase of this caused them to get off their food, and lose their tone and appetite.

Stillness, with the limitations given in our remarks on shelter, is necessary to successful feeding. This is well known to geese feeders, who even nail them to the boards; and it was shown very strikingly by Mr. Childers, M. P., in his experiments on shed-feeding, and by Lord Bathurst, on stall-feeding sheep. An animal in the very effort of searching and securing his food, expends the principle necessary to make fat; hence it is necessary that his turnips be brought to him instead of driving him to the turnips. They are cut and placed before him, that he may have as little effort as possible in the operation of chewing, and he has ample allowance of room, so that when he has fed, he may lie down and sleep.

It is a question whether animals feed fastest in the dark or not. There can be no doubt whatever that any thing which distracts their attention, which excites action, or which produces nervous irritation, is opposed to fattening; and, as darkness will induce sleep, inaction, and promote quietness, it is so far favorable; but it is not so easy to have darkness and sufficiency of fresh air at the same time, and therefore the best possible state, perhaps, is to have the feeding-houses rather in a state of shady gloom than in absolute darkness. A certain amount of nervous energy is necessary to give tone to the vital powers, and, beyond this, repose and quietness are easily attained by a simple gloom, while shelter from flies and heat in summer, and from blasts, wet, and extreme cold in winter, should be carefully provided.

Abundance of Good Food and Regularity of Feeding, are essentials in all kinds of fattening. Though it is not desirable to allow the animals to have food standing before them when they are filled, they should never, on the other hand, experience a single feeling of want. The usual hours of feeding should be strictly adhered to, for the two-fold purpose of inducing regular periods of sleep and for supplying the system with food at the first call of appetite.

Variety of Food is a most essential element of rapid fattening; and it is not far from the truth to say that all kinds of food are *equally* fattening, if they are given in sufficient variety. If roots, grain and hay be changed every few days, the appetite is never cloyed; and the whole are devoured with a relish which develops fat in the most rapid manner.

The Formation of Fat is the work of the grazier. His animals are generally full grown, or nearly so, and, though there may be a small increase of muscle, still the bulk of the material of increased weight is *fat* and not *flesh*. In this country, food to be palatable—to be consumable—must be fat; unless it has this recommendation it is absolutely unsalable. The appetites of the higher and the necessities of the lower class, urge on the demand for fatted beef, mutton and pork; and any brought to market in a state other than fat, is looked upon as carrion. Hence the grazier must supply the whole of his animals in a fat state to the consumer; and therefore it is not the number of animals, nor their weight he has to consider, but he has to provide for them the means of fattening before they can be brought to the consumer.

The saccharine matter of vegetables, and their starch, will supply the means of fuel-food; the fatty matter will produce ready-formed fat to deposit; and the albuminous matter will afford the flesh which waste is continually throwing into the excretory system, and for the small additions which may be necessary to carry the requisite amount of fat.

It is not our intention to enter into the dispute between the two schools of physiologists, as to whether the fat was formed by transmutation of the sugar and starch of the food, or whether it consisted of the ready formed fat of the food on which the animals fed. Without for a moment pretending to settle this point, it is at least desirable so far to supply both saccharine and fatty matters, as to give the system the choice of selection.

Preparation of Food for the animal's stomach, or a system of cooking, is a very important question. Steaming hay, potatoes and turnips, has been tried very carefully in Scotland, and failed. For *cattle*, at least, it is useless; how valuable soever it may be for pigs. It is pretty certain, however, that, with certain combinations, all that a feeder can desire is attained by the *cooking of flax-seed*.

The fat of animals is strictly analogous to vegetable oil; its elements are much of the same character as sugar, starch and gum, and no doubt is entertained, by physiologists and chemists, that the fatty matter (vegetable oil) in plants, is assimilated into animal fat, with but little change. The elements of those compounds severally are:—

	Sugar.	Starch.	Gum.	Mucilage.	Animal fat (stearine).
Carbon	12	12	12	24	71
Hydrogen	11	10	10	19	69
Oxygen	11	10	10	19	7

The oil contained in many seeds is given by Professor Johnston—

	Oil per cent.		Oil per cent.
Flax-seed	11 to 22 say 17	White mustard	36 to 38 say 37
Hemp-seed	14 " 25 " 19	Sweet almond	40 " 54 " 47
Rape-seed	40 " 70 " 55	Bitter do	28 " 46 " 37

This would naturally indicate that any of these seeds would, so far as they were palatable, be useful; and when linseed contains as much as seven per cent. of mucilage, ten per cent. of sugar, and fifteen of soluble albumen, it is clearly indicated as being a seed most valuable for feeding and nourishing purposes.

Various attempts have been made to adapt it to the feeding of cattle. There was some difficulty in grinding it by ordinary mills, as it clogged up the teeth; and when given to animals either alone, or combined with considerable quantities of corn, meal, or other feeding matter, the effect on the animals was purgative, and but few breeders persevered in the use of the seed alone. The demand for the oil, however, induced the crushing of the seeds to obtain it, and the refuse left was found to be very valuable as feeding material; while the portability of oil-cake, its cleanliness, and capability of being long kept, made it a general and desirable food, both for growing and feeding stock. The oil abstracted, the cake contains, according to the same authority:—

Water	10.05
Mucilage	39.10
Albumen and gluten	22.14
Oil	11.93
Husks	9.53
Saline matter and sand	7.25
	1.00

We do not see exactly how the cake can contain so large a proportion of oil relatively with the seed; but it is probable that the seed had originally contained a large proportion of oil, and that it had been but indifferently crushed. Good English-made cake, however, has been thoroughly established as one of the best of fattening products; and the extensive farmers of Lincolnshire and other places expend upon a single farm, in one year, as much as £400 to £500, for this article of food; and so well understood is its fertilizing character, that many land-owners are willing to make themselves and their incoming tenants, chargeable with proportions of the money so expended, at the rate of one-half to one-third. It is the opinion of some of the best farmers, that when cake can be purchased at the same price per ton, in pounds, that beef and mutton can be sold at per stone in shillings, it will be paid for in the cattle and animals fed, without reference to the manure.* The price of cake, however, depends on no such element of calculation; the demand for it has increased far beyond that of the oil, and in some seasons it has been so great, that the former became an object of commerce rather than the latter.

Attempts have been occasionally made to render the uncrushed seed available by a cooking process, but it has been generally found more adapted for calves than for store stock or for fattening; where used at all for the latter purpose, it has only been to supply a deficiency in turnips.

The most decisive step, however, in the use of cooked linseed, was taken by Mr. Warnes, of Trimmingham, near North Walsham, in Norfolk, in 1841, when a discussion was appointed by the Farmers' Club there, on feeding cattle with linseed cake. Mr. Warnes commenced by inquiring into the nature of cake. He immediately commenced a series of experiments with flax-seed in various forms—both crushed, steeped, boiled, and cooked in various ways. He also tried the boiling of barley and other food on various animals. He ultimately adopted a mode of feeding, on what was called by him flax-seed compound. He carried out, in connection with his experiments, growing, dressing and preparing the flax, the feeding of cattle with the prepared seed in boxes as antagonist to tying up, and the summer grazing of cattle by soiling.

His cooking apparatus is so simple, that it is managed by a blind man, whose happy countenance bespeaks neither over-weening anxiety, nor unremunerated toil. The apparatus consists of two cast-metal boilers, fixed in brick, and having a fire-place beneath them; the water is made to boil before the flax-seed is put in. The seed is crushed by a very powerful implement, consisting of two cylinders, one of them being of large diameter; they are made to press upon each other in their revolutions by two lunar springs, and two men will thoroughly grind two bushels in ten minutes; at this rate the men are able to work the whole day. The mill is, however, capable of being reduced to the capacity of one man. The crushed flax-seed is sprinkled upon the boiling water at the rate of one gallon of seed to eight gallons of water; great stress is laid on sprinkling the seed very gradually, otherwise it is apt to adhere in lumps, and cleave to the sides or bottom of the boiler. With this precaution, however, Mr. Warnes assures us he has had no instance, for several years, of this occurrence. This mixture is boiled six minutes, and for that period is slightly stirred; at the end of that

---

* The pound sterling is $4.85; the shilling is 24 cents; the stone weight 14 lbs.

time it is found to be a thick gelatinous mass. In one minute after this the mass became more mucilaginous, and was improved. Nine bushels of cut pea straw were then placed very gradually, and by one bushel at a time, in a tub twenty-eight inches high; the liquid jelly was now taken out in a scoop, poured upon it, and as each addition was made the whole was rammed down by a kind of beater, more for the purpose of mixing the mass, and confining the heat, than for any other object. The present cost of the animals in flax-seed is 3s. per head per week. In addition to this, they have also about one bushel of cut Swedes per day.

Mr. Warnes occasionally mixes his compound with meal. This, when used, is also sprinkled over the boiling mucilage. So soon as the first boiling was nearly emptied from the boiler, it was again filled with water, and was ready for another boil, when required.

As a test of its value, Mr. Warnes furnished the following remarks and experiments illustrative of the effects of his system: "Flax-seed," he says, "has five essential properties, namely, mucilage, oil, albumen, gluten and sugar. The shell, or external crust, is the hardest of all seeds, and the most difficult to break in pieces; but not too hard for the miller, who has every particle ground almost to powder, in order that all the oil may be expressed, which it could not be if coarsely crushed. This is demonstrated by the cake, in which the presence of seed is scarcely apparent. To a similar state seed for the cattle compounds ought to be reduced; otherwise some, at least, of the properties above described will pass off without benefit to the fattening animals. This the scientific grazier will discover by the excrements, in which he will find sufficient cause for grinding, not only flax-seed, but all grain or pulse, if possible, into flour. From researches like these the profitable returns for grazing upon my premises, may be dated." The expenses of this copper, with the whole working apparatus for eighty or one hundred head of stock, will not be more than four pounds.

A part of Mr. Warnes's system is the feeding in boxes, the growth of flax-seed, the manufacture of the fiber into flax, and the soiling of cattle with green food and compound in summer. It would swell this article much beyond its legitimate limits, if the box system were more fully described. It may suffice to say, that the boxes at Mr. Warnes's have been put up very cheaply—they form two sides of what has formerly been a fold-yard. The sides have had a roof put along the wall, supported by pillars of wood, and divided by rails of any ordinary wood; the front next the yard being inclosed by two gates. The box is eight feet six inches square; and adjoining the wall is a passage from which the food is given in troughs, which are made to slide up or down as the manure accumulates. The manure is never carted out until it is taken to the fields; and, as the boxes are walled for one foot from the bottom, there is not the slightest escape of the liquid manure or of the ammonia, and therefore it is peculiarly rich, from this circumstance and from the stimulating food supplied to the fattening animals.

Much has been said as to the dirt and filth, and unnatural state of the animals; but their condition is precisely the reverse, in every respect; they are quiet, have exercise sufficient for healthy secretion, can feed at leisure, and, whenever we observed them, they were clean and free from smell, and every thing objectionable. The fact of the treading, and thorough consolidation by the animals' feet, prevents fermentation, and the consequent evolution of gases which would take place if mere stall-feeding were practiced. On the whole, we think there are many more valid reasons in favor of than against box-feeding.

The direction given to men's minds by the experiments of Mr. Warnes, induced trials with all kinds of modifications of flax-seed cooking; but the one which has obtained the greatest amount of favor is that adopted by Mr. Marshall, near Thirsk. The great difference between Mr. Marshall's plan and that of Mr. Warnes, is, that the material cooked has not the heat applied to it directly, but to the outside of the boiler in which it is to be cooked, so that no direct application of the fire shall take place to burn the mucilaginous matter. Mr. Marshall insists that, to cook the material properly, it must be boiled at least two hours.

His mode is this:—one pound of flax-seed is boiled for two or three hours in about one and a half gallons of water. Five pounds of straw are chopped, say one inch long, and mixed with two and a half pounds of ground oats or barley meal very intimately, which is then placed on a floor of flags of bricks, and the boiled seed poured upon the mass, and turned, and then allowed to cool one or two hours, when it is given to the cattle.

The cost of the apparatus or fitting will be about £50 (or $250.) On the whole we think it very desirable to adopt one or the other process in all situations where an increased quantity, and better quality of manure is a desideratum, not to mention the more profitable return, as exhibited in both the systems described.

Mr. Warnes, altogether unprejudiced in favor of his own peculiar system, has been experimenting on the mode recommended by some graziers, of steeping the linseed-meal in cold water for some twelve or fourteen hours,—when a slight mucilaginous deposit was the result. The experiment will no doubt be carefully and accurately made under his directions; but, we confess, our prepossessions are in favor of the cooked materials.

The following is a plan of Mr Warnes's shed boxes for cattle-feeding:

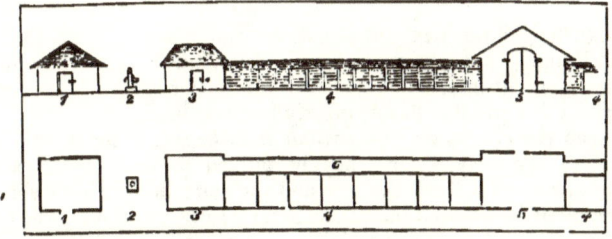

1. Cooking-house, 20 by 16 feet.
2. Pump.
3. Storehouse, for roots, &c.
4, 4. Boxes averaging 90 square feet each.
5. Fodder-house, with tank under the floor.
6. Passage, 4 feet.

Mr. Thompson, of Moat Hall, Yorkshire, a most skillful and accurate investigator, made some very important experiments as to the relative value of *hot and cold preparation* of flax-seed. He took two animals, and fed the one on hot and the other on cold food. He had both weighed before he started, and both again weighed at the expiration of six weeks. The animal fed on cold food weighed, when put up, 107 stone 11 lbs. (1,509 lbs.); that fed on hot, 108 stone 7 lbs. (1,533 lbs.) At the end of six weeks the first had gained 40 lbs.; while the last, the one fed on hot food, had gained 71 lbs. To guard against the one having any special aptitude to fatten which the other did not possess, he reversed the order; and then it turned out that the animal now fed on cold food, and before on hot, gained 53 lbs., while the other, now fed on hot food, gained 71 lbs.

But not only on the animals did the results of cooked food show itself in this striking manner; for, while one fed on hot food had only 80 lbs. of Swedish turnips per day, the one fed on cold food was not satisfied till his feed was increased to 87 lbs. of turnips in the same time, showing a greater consumption of other food to make up for the want of heat!

Food as Affecting the Quality and Quantity of Milk.—Messrs. Dumas and Boussingault tried a number of very careful and interesting experiments on the quantity of milk and its products which would be given by cows fed on different kinds of food. They tried nearly all the combinations usually given, except perhaps bean meal, and the result was, that the greatest quantity of milk was given when the cow had green clover, in every case, *i. e.*, that in each instance this yielded the greatest quantity of butter, and, with one exception, the greatest produce also of cheese; and that exception was when the cow had been but one day calved, which would account for the abundance of cheesy matter in the milk. The table is so instructive, that we will quote one or two of the items:—

Food.	Days after calving.	Milk.	Butter.	Cheese.
Potatoes and hay	176	9.3	4.8	3.3
Hay and green clover	182	8.9	4.5	4.0
Green clover	193	9.8	2.2	4.0
Clover in flower	204	7.8	3.5	3.7
Potatoes	229	5.0	4.0	3.4
Turnips	207	6.0	4.2	3.0
Red beet	215	5.6	4.0	3.4

Into their philosophical investigations and reasonings we shall not enter. Mangel-wurzel, bean meal, and grains, much increase the milk.* Good hay and oat mash much increase the butter, and turnips, though they give a disagreeable flavor, greatly increase both.

To keep the cow as *long as possible in milk* is sometimes an object. Some cows dry early,—some may be milked through, though always with disadvantage to both the cow and the calf; both being feeble and impaired, if it is persisted in. In summer weather, however, when cows are very deep milkers, and in high condition, it is not only sometimes

---

* Indian meal fed in cool weather, while it is a highly nutritious food, also adds greatly to the quantity and quality of the milk. The erroneous prejudice against its use for milch cows has been fully refuted by careful experiments.

advisable but absolutely necessary. A cow not put to the bull will hold to her milk much longer than one which is regularly breeding.

THE DAIRY—BUTTER AND CHEESE MAKING.—In all dairy establishments ventilation and cleanliness are indispensable; and if butter is made, the dairy proper, or butter-room, should be as near the cow-house as possible, as the milk suffers more or less considerably from being agitated, or too much cooled, before it is set for the cream to rise. The milk should be brought from the cows without being exposed to the outer air, before it is set to cream; which should be in vessels arranged on a stone slab, below the level of the ground; the apartment being sunk to the depth of three or four feet, and kept perfectly dry. The air may be admitted through perforated zinc plates, or woven-wire windows, placed opposite to each other, having shutters which may be opened or closed according to the temperature and state of the weather. Glazed windows may be added, and should be open, excepting in very hot or very cold weather. The situation should be dry, and well shielded from the north, east, and south.

The Dairy-House is, perhaps, of all other appliances, the one on which success most depends. It should be apart from all household operations, from open grates, and from dung-heaps, and should have as much as possible the means of an equable temperature. As, however, it is much easier to keep a cold building warm, than to cool a hot one, it is desirable that it should be as much as possible shielded from the sun's rays. It should have its side to the north, its end to the east, and should, if possible, be let into the earth a few feet, but not so deep as to interfere with the drainage. If covered by a large tree it would be all the better. Around it should be either a hollow wall, or peat earth should be walled round its exterior; or, as another alternative, and possibly the best but most expensive, it should be surrounded by a veranda. It should also have a double roof, and abundant top and side ventilation—either of which should admit of being closed. It is necessary to have in it a pump, the floor sloping, and on the highest part a perforated pipe should be connected with the pump, to allow of the cleansing of the floor with cold spring water when necessary. The bowls should either be earthen-ware or glass dishes, placed upon wooden tables—fir, maple, or sycamore are the best; or leaden bowls may be used, placed on frames, and surrounding the dairy. Stones are the best for the floors, and a lining for the walls of white pottery is not only elegant but useful; a pipe connected with the boiler attached to the kitchen fire is a great advantage, with a stop-cock, so as to regulate the heat of the room in winter. The scalding and churning rooms should be distinct from the milk-house, and the latter should be kept as free as possible from all kinds of foreign matter. An outer veranda is useful for drying the dishes and pails, and therefore desirable, when the dairy is sufficiently extensive to render the expense of its erection judicious.

Butter is the fat or oleaginous part of the milk of various animals, principally of the domestic cow. The milk of the cow is composed of three distinct ingredients—the curd, the whey, and the butter; the two first form the largest portion, and the last the most valuable. The comparative value of the milk of different cows, or of the same cows fed on different pastures, is estimated chiefly by the quantity of butter contained in it; and in this respect some breeds of cows are far superior to others. The union of the component parts of milk is chiefly mechanical, as they separate by subsidence according to their specific gravities, the cream being the lightest, and the curd the heaviest; the curd, however, requires a slight chemical change for its separation from the whey, which at the same time produces a peculiar acid, called the lactic acid. From the moment that milk is drawn from the cow, it begins to be affected by the air and changes of temperature, and circumstances almost imperceptible to our senses will materially affect its quality; hence the importance of extreme care in every step of the process of the dairy, especially in making butter.

The cows should be milked in the cool of the morning and evening; they should not be much driven immediately before milking, and it is best to bring them to the place of milking some time before the operation begins. In some situations it is better to milk them in the pastures and carry the milk home; in others to drive the cows gently to the cow-stalls. In mountainous countries the first mode is generally adopted, because the cows are apt to leap down steep places, and shake the milk in their udder more than is done by carrying it in the pail. The same practice holds good in Holland from another cause, which is the distance of the pastures from the home-stalls, and the facility of transporting the milk in small boats, all the best pastures being surrounded by small canals communicating with the greater; thus the milk may be carried several miles without the least agitation.

As soon as the milk is brought into the dairy, it is strained through a fine sieve or cloth, and it is then poured into shallow pans or troughs lined with lead. The best pans are of metal, either of iron, carefully tinned, or of brass. Such pans are cool in summer, and in winter allow of the application of heat, which is often very useful to make the cream rise. When leaden troughs are used, they are generally fixed to the wall, and have a slight inclination toward one end, where there is a hole with a plug in it, by drawing which the thin milk is allowed to run off slowly, leaving the cream behind, which runs last through the hole into the pan placed under to receive it. The milk in the pans or troughs is generally four or five inches in depth, which is found most conducive to the separation of the cream. The place where the milk is set should have a thorough draught of air by means of opposite wire windows. The sun should be carefully excluded by high buildings or trees, and the floor, which should always be of brick or stone, should be continually kept moist in summer, that the evaporation may produce an equal, cool temperature. A small stove in winter is a great advantage, provided smoke or smell be most carefully avoided, and the temperature be carefully regulated by a thermometer. In Switzerland men are chiefly employed to milk the cows, and in all the process of the preparation of butter and cheese. The women only clean the utensils, and carry green food to the cows when they are kept in the stable. When the milk has stood twelve hours, the finest parts of the cream have risen to the surface, and if they are then taken off by a skimming-dish, and immediately churned, a very delicate butter is obtained; but in general it is left twenty-four hours, when the cream is collected by skimming, or the thin milk is let off by taking out the plug in the troughs. All the cream is put into a deep earthen jar, which should be glazed, but not with lead; stone-ware is the best. More cream is added every day, till there is a sufficient quantity to churn, which in moderate dairies is every two days. It is usual to stir the cream often, to encourage a slight acidity, by which the process of churning is accelerated. This acidity is sometimes produced by the addition of vinegar or lemon-juice; but however this may facilitate the conversion of the cream into butter, the quality is decidedly injured by it, especially butter which is to be salted. It has been asserted by some authors that butter will not separate from the buttermilk until acidity is produced, and, no doubt, there is more or less of lactic acid in all buttermilk; but perfectly fresh cream, which has stood only one night and is churned early next morning, will generally produce excellent butter in a quarter of an hour or twenty minutes in summer, and no acid taste can be discovered in the buttermilk. The change by which the butter is separated in a solid form is accompanied by the development of heat in churning.

TABLE CHURN.

Churn.—As to the form of churn there may be a variety of opinions. The ultimate object is to secure that form which will facilitate a rapid, steady, and shaking pressure of the contents; and this is effected either by a flapper, driven through the cream, at a considerable rate, by means of a piston with a perforated base; by a perpendicular motion, raised up and down in a cylindrical or similarly formed vessel; or, what is more common, and by no means the worst form of churn, a cylinder studded with perforated beaters, fastened to its inner surface, and revolving round its two axles, admitting of one handle or two, according to the quantity of the cream. By this means the specific gravity of the cream, as well as the force and impetus of the machine, are both brought into play to excite the heat, the pressure, and the agitation necessary to the proper and speedy development of the butter. To this horse or steam power may be easily attached, and though there have been many forms of churn in use, we are not certain that any very great improvement on the above form has so far been discovered. Plans have been adopted to diminish the labor, but this has often ended in defective operation. The American and the table churns, available for the extemporaneous manufacture of butter every morning for the tables of the rich, are so far a step in advance, and a luxury; but for the large operations of the dairy-farmer, a better application than the churn of his forefathers has not yet been discovered.

Some experienced dairy-men pretend that the butter is deteriorated by much washing, and therefore they express the buttermilk by simply beating the butter with the hand, kept cool by frequently dipping it in cold water, or with a moist cloth wrapped in the form of a ball, which soaks up all the buttermilk, and leaves the butter quite dry. This operation requires the greatest attention, especially in warm weather, and no person should work the butter who has not a cool hand. The less it is handled the better, and therefore a wooden spoon or spatula is much to be preferred.

When it is entirely freed from the buttermilk, and of a proper consistency, it is divided into portions of the weight required, if it is intended to be sold fresh. But the greatest part of the butter that is made, especially at a distance from large towns, is immediately salted and put into casks, which usually contain fifty-six pounds, and are called firkins. The quality of the salt used is of great importance; if it be pure, the butter will keep its flavor a long time; but when it is impure, and contains bitter and deliquescent salts, the butter soon becomes rancid. The Dutch are very particular on this point. They use a kind of salt which is made by slow evaporation, and perfectly crystallized. The salt is intimately mixed with the butter. From three pounds to five pounds is sufficient for a firkin of fifty-six pounds.* The casks are made of clean white wood. They are carefully washed inside with strong brine made hot, and rubbed over with salt. The butter, being quite dry, is pressed close into the cask, a small layer of salt having been first put on the bottom. Every addition is carefully incorporated with the preceding portion. If there is not a sufficient quantity to fill the cask at once, the surface is made smooth, some salt is put over it, and a cloth is pressed close upon it to exclude the air. When the remainder is added, at the next churning, the cloth is taken off, and the salt, which had been put on the surface, is carefully removed with a spoon. The surface is dug into with a small wooden spade, and laid rough, and the newly-salted butter is added and incorporated completely. This prevents a streak, which would otherwise appear at the place where the two portions joined. When the cask is full, some salt is put over it, and the head is put in. If the butter was well freed from all the buttermilk, and the salt mixed with it was quite dry, it will not shrink in the cask, and it will keep its flavor for a long time. Should

---

* The following mixture has been found superior to salt alone in curing butter—half an ounce of dry salt pounded fine, two drachms of sugar, and two drachms of saltpetre, for every pound of butter.

there be an appearance of shrinking, the cask must be opened, and melted butter poured round it so as to fill up the interstices between the butter and the cask. There is a mode of preserving butter for domestic use without salt, in the following manner: the butter is set in a clean pan over the fire, and melted very gently; it is not allowed to boil, but is heated very nearly to the boiling point. Experience has shown this heat to be attained when the reflection of the white of the eye is distinctly seen on the surface of the butter on looking down into the pan. All the watery particles are then evaporated, and the curd, of which a portion always remains in the butter, and which is one cause of its becoming rancid, falls to the bottom. The clear butter is poured into an earthen vessel and covered over with paper, and a bladder or a piece of leather is tied over the jar to exclude the air. When it is cooled, it much resembles hogs' lard. It has lost some of its flavor, but it is much superior to salt butter for culinary purposes, and especially for pastry.

The Devonshire method of making butter is peculiar to that county. The milk, instead of being set for the cream to rise, is placed in tin or earthen pans, holding about eleven or twelve quarts each. Twelve hours after milking, these pans are placed on a broad iron plate, heated by a small furnace. The milk is not allowed to boil, but a thick scum rises to the surface. As soon as small bubbles begin to appear, where a portion of this scum is removed with a spoon, the milk is taken off and allowed to cool. The thick part is taken off the surface, and this is called clouted cream; it is a sweet, pleasant substance, more solid than cream, but not so solid as butter, and is generally considered a dainty. A very slight agitation converts it into real butter, after which it is treated exactly as we have before described.

Another method of making butter, which is more generally adopted, is to churn the milk and cream together. This method is pursued in parts of Holland, Scotland and Ireland, and is said to produce a greater abundance of butter from the same quantity of milk. In the Dutch method the milk is put into deep jars in a cool place, and each meal, or portion milked at one time, is kept separate. As soon as there is a slight appearance of acidity, the whole is churned in an upright churn, which, from the quantity of milk, is of very large dimensions. The plunger is worked by machinery moved by a horse, or sometimes by a dog walking in a wheel, which he turns by his weight. When the butter begins to form into small kernels, the contents of the churn are emptied on a sieve, which lets the buttermilk pass through. The butter is then formed into a mass, as described before.

It is an acknowledged fact, that such are the niceties of the dairy that great experience alone can insure a produce of superior quality, and this experience would be more readily acquired if the circumstances were accurately observed and noted. We would recommend to those who have extensive dairies, to mark by the thermometer the temperature of the milk and cream in the different stages of the process; occasionally to test the acidity of the buttermilk by means of alkalis; and to note any peculiarity in the atmosphere by an electrometer. A few observations, carefully noted, repeated, and compared, would throw more light on the true causes which favor or oppose the production of good butter, than all the guesses that have hitherto been made.

The quality of the butter depends materially on the nature of the pasture. The best is made from cows fed in rich natural meadows. Certain plants, which grow in poor and marshy soils, give a disagreeable taste to the butter. The common notion that the yellow flower called the buttercup gives color and flavor to butter is a mistake; cows never crop the flower if they can avoid it, and the whole plant is acrid and unpalatable. When cows are fed with cut grass in the stable, the butter is inferior, except in the case of some artificial grasses, such as lucern. Turnips and other roots given to cows in winter communicate more or less of a bad taste to butter, which is corrected in some degree by means of a small quantity of water and saltpetre added to the milk; and also, it is said, by giving salt to the cows with their food. But there is no butter made in winter equal to that which is made when the cows are fed entirely with good meadow hay, especially of the second crop, called after-math hay, which contains few seed stalks.

The yellow color of May butter is frequently imitated artificially, by mixing some ground anatto root, or the juice of carrots, with the cream. This is easily detected by the taste of the butter, which is not improved by it, and has not the peculiar flavor of fine grass butter; but in other respects it is a harmless addition. Some cows give a much yellower cream than others, especially the Alderney cows; and the butter made from it is of a peculiarly fine flavor. When a cow has lately calved, the milk is also much yellower, but this soon goes off, if it be not the natural color; and the butter made by mixing this with other milk, although of a deeper color, is not improved by it.

According to the accounts of the produce of butter from different countries and various breeds of cows, we may state that, on an average, four gallons of milk produce sixteen ounces of butter; and to make the feeding of cows for the dairy a profitable employment, a good cow should produce six pounds of butter per week in summer, and half that quantity in winter, allowing from six weeks to two months for her being dry before calving; that is one hundred and twenty pounds in twenty weeks after calving, and eighty pounds in the remainder of the time till she goes dry—in all, about two hundred pounds in the year. If she produces more, she may be considered as a superior cow; if less, she is below par.

The quality of the butter produced in England and in Holland is considered the best. A considerable quantity of Dutch butter is exported, but all that is produced in England is consumed at home, in addition to large quantities imported from Ireland and the continent of Europe. The quantity imported has been for some time progressively increasing.

Premium Butter-Making.—The following, read at the last meeting of the American Institute Farmers' Club, details the practice of one of the best butter-makers in the State of New York, Mr. Jesse Carpenter, of Elmira, in that state. It was communicated by Mr. H. E. Lowman. We invite the special attention of all our dairy readers to the views here propounded, as they come from a source entitling them to the highest confidence. Mr. Carpenter has long been known in the butter making region, and in the market, as one of the most intelligent and successful dairymen and farmers in the county, and as a manufacturer of the veritable " *Orange county butter :*"

" The basis for a good and profitable butter-dairy is, a stock fulfilling as nearly as practicable all those constitutional and structural conditions which combine in the animal high milking qualities, with good size, robust health, and longevity. The next step is a prompt and thorough practice of the best method of treatment of the same by which the largest yield of the best quality of milk is secured. The next and best step in the achievement of a first-class dairy of butter is the application to its manufacture of an intimate and critical knowledge of the true process—from the expressing of the milk to the final touch the butter receives preparatory to the transit of the package to market.

" How to take the first step? *i. e.,* lay in the stock, or near it, Mr. Carpenter thinks can be known much more satisfactorily by reference to and study of popular authorities on the subject—writers who have made the rearing of stock with that view a speciality, and yet it is practical, common sense, and close and accurate observation which must be the main dependence at last. The next branch of inquiry, which is none the less important, is not so easily pursued to satisfactory results by an appeal to the same sources of information. Long and close experience has confirmed Mr. Carpenter in the accuracy of the following system or mode of treatment: the best summer food for the dairy stock, that which yields the largest quantity and best quality of milk, is a mixture of the finer grasses, such as red and white clover, timothy, and blue grass, all of which thrive well in desirable combination in the pasture fields of the Chemung Valley. All coarse, rank, and strongly-flavored weeds, of whatever description, must be banished from the feeding range of the dairy stock, otherwise butter of the finest quality cannot be made. Neither should they be fed during the milking season on any description of roots or coarse pungent vegetables, such as cabbage, if the butter is to be packed in firkins or any other vessel with the purpose of keeping.

" Even pumpkins are not desirable, though they may be used without material detriment. In the spring the season roots are most commonly used and advised. A small allowance of grain is much more beneficial. It accomplishes just what is needed, without contributing to undesirable results. It gives additional strength of muscle—the main thing desired—while, if judiciously given, it does not materially increase the deposit of fat. It also increases the quantity, and improves the quality of the milk, while roots and vegetables increase the quantity, but rather deteriorate the quality.

" During the milking season the cows must be moved from the pasture-field with great caution to prevent overheat of the system. That cannot take place in any degree without the milk being unfavorably affected in a corresponding ratio. And when they are in the heat of the sexual or copulating fever, the milk should not be used in the dairy, or with that from which butter for packing is to be made. For at such periods nature has provided for a medical interruption of the secretion of the animal, and the milk is greatly reduced in quantity, and in like measure improved in quality. Indeed the abnormal heat produced in the udder is of itself sufficient cause for rejecting the milk for butter-making. In the fall, where the grass begins to fail, and loses its nutritive or milk-producing elements, there is nothing that can equal cornstalks as a substitute. The corn should be sown for the purpose.

"During the winter months the stock should be stabled or otherwise sheltered from the severities of the weather for the night, and while they feed. And the care, and amount and kind of food must be so appointed that they rather improve in condition and vigor than otherwise; at least they must not be allowed to run down to poor flesh and weakness; for then no amount of attention and good nursing through the summer will restore them to full milking capacities. The loss is irreparable for the season.

"A very thorough and practical understanding of the next and last branches, i. e., the treatment of the milk, and the process of butter making, is much more difficult to obtain, because the knowledge is much more difficult to impart. With all the rules that may be given, there must be superadded, as conditions for their successful application, the necessity for close and critical observation. For there are constantly arising circumstances to modify the most of such which may be laid down in a general system.

"For depositing the milk when strained, the tin pail of the capacity of about twelve quarts is preferable to any other kind of vessel. It is sufficiently large to fulfill all the requirements in that particular; while its superiority over the shallow pan—which is considerably used—is too palpable to admit of doubt. The following propositions in point, are sustained by facts, the application or pertinency of which, all who have ever made butter, or who have been in a dairy with their eyes open to the every day phenomena therein, will readily apprehend, viz.: that milk, in order to realize from it the largest quantity and best quality of butter, must stand in an atmosphere of a given temperature a specific length of time, in all cases, in order to perfect it for the churn; that natural or artificial causes, either accelerating or retarding the processes of change in its elements from that fixed standard, have their like certain results of deterioration, both in the quality and the quantity of the butter produced; that a given quantity of milk, with the greatest surface exposure to the action of the atmosphere, in a given temperature, will change more rapidly than a like quantity in a like temperature, with a less surface exposure. The facts in proof, it need scarcely be intimated, condemn the use of the shallow pan.

"Every dairy-woman has observed the effects of a close, muggy and humid atmosphere such as often precedes rain-storms in the summer— upon the milk; also, of a thunder-storm, also of only partly filling a vessel. In all cases named, the change in the milk is much more rapid than when the temperature of the atmosphere is even, and the equilibrium of its vital elements more perfectly sustained; and then in pails filled to their capacity. In all these instances too, the milk must be churned sooner. But there is no method that will prevent a loss of product in quantity and quality.

"It is difficult to reach fully the truth of the first proposition. But we can approximate to it, and then adapt our practice as nearly to such standard or rule as it is possible to do. The temperature of the room where the milk is set must never exceed 65° F., and must be as steady and even as possible. The atmosphere of the same must be kept perfectly pure; for any odor peculiar to the decomposition of vegetable or organic substances mingling therewith, will inevitably leave its taint upon the milk and its product.

When the casein is precipitated or the milk coagulated, it is ready to churn. It must not stand until the second change takes place in the lacteal or the sugar of milk; that is, until the lactic acid becomes butyric acid, the latter stage of which may be known from the discolored spots of mould gathered on the surface of the cream. The thick milk should always be emptied with the cream into the churn. There are two important reasons in support of this method. First, the cream never all rises to the surface, and there must always remain with the coagulated part quite a fraction of the fatty matter, which is lost if not churned. Second, there is a virtue in the casein and lactic acid which is essential in the process of churning to import to the product the element of preservation. It is a fact which should be known by all dairy-men and dealers, that the product of cream exclusively, however skillfully manipulated, will not, if packed for keeping, preserve for any length of time the finer qualities of good butter.

"The milk in the churn, when fit for churning, should indicate 64° Fah., and should be agitated with a movement of the dash at not less than fifty strokes to the minute. Less motion will fail to divide properly the butter from the milk. When done, the butter should be taken from the churn and thrown into a tub or a small churn partly filled with water 42° to 44° Fah., and the buttermilk forced out with a small dash. It should then be put into trays and washed until the water used ceases to be the least discolored with buttermilk. It is then ready for salting, which should be done and the trays immediately carried to the cellar. The proper amount is $1\frac{1}{4}$ oz. to the pound of butter after working—*i. e.*, the butter should retain that amount when ready for packing. When it has stood three or four hours after the first salting, it should be stirred with a ladle and left in the form of a honey-comb, in order to give it the greatest possible surface exposure to the air, which gives color and fixes the high flavor.

"Butter when well manufactured, while standing preparatory to packing, is composed of granulated particles, between which are myriads of infinitesimal cells filled with brine, which is its life. At this period it should be touched with a light hand, as too much and too careless working will destroy its granular and cellular character, and reduce the whole to a compact and lifeless mass, with an immediate loss of flavor, and a certain and reliable prospect, if packed, of a rapid change of its character from indifferently good to miserably poor butter. It should never be worked in the tray while in a dry state, or all the ill results just alluded to will be realized. As a general rule, after the butter has stood in the trays twenty-four hours, and has been worked three or four times, as directed, it is ready for packing. After the firkin is filled, it should stand a short time, and then should be covered with a clean piece of muslin, and the whole covered with brine.

"It will not be out of place for the writer to state from his own knowledge, and upon his own responsibility, a few facts in connection with the above, referring solely to Mr. Carpenter's success as a dairyman. For the last twenty years, besides fattening the calves to the customary age of four weeks, he has averaged a fraction over two firkins to the cow per year. He has had butter stand in packages in his cellar for one year and a half, and open them with a flavor so fresh and sweet that the very best and most critical judges and buyers were deceived one year in its age—none even suspecting it to be the product of a former year. He never has, during that period, failed to reach in New-York market the highest figure representing the maximum market for Orange county butter; and latterly, he has very often overreached the very highest market half a cent to two and a half cents per lb."—*Tribune.*

Messrs. Charles R. Huntington & Co., produce commission merchants in New-York, give the following directions to their consignors for the shipment of butter to them, &c.

"The best butter is obtained at a temperature of fifty-one degrees, and the greatest quantity at a temperature of forty-six degrees, Fahr. During the process of churning the agitation will increase the heat to about five degrees more than it was when the cream was put into the churn. The operation of churning, whether it be of cream alone, or cream and milk, is performed in the same manner. The milk requires more time than cream to complete the process, from two to three hours being considered necessary; while cream alone may be effectually churned in an hour and a half. The operation should be slow in warm weather, for if done too hastily the butter will be soft and white. If the cream is at too high a temperature, the churn should be cooled with cold spring water, to reduce it to the proper degree of heat. In winter, again, the operation of churning should be done as quickly as possible, the action being regular, and the churn should be warmed to raise the temperature of the milk or cream. The air which is generated in the churn should be allowed to escape, or it will impede the progress by the froth which it creates.

"After the churning is performed, the butter should be washed in cold spring water, with a little salt in it, two or three times, to extract all the milk which may be lodging about the mass. The less milk which is in the butter, its quality is proportionably improved; after all the milk has been carefully extracted, the butter should be mixed with the finest ground rock-salt, in the proportion of five ounces to seven pounds. The butter and salt should be well mixed together with the hand or ladle. This superior salt for dairy purposes may always be obtained at the very lowest prices by addressing your orders to us.

"Firkins made of oak, with walnut hoops, to contain one hundred pounds of butter, net, are generally the most desirable; but many prefer Welsh tubs, either ash or oak. Packages should be made smooth, and should be got into market as bright and cleanly as possible. The demand is about equally divided between tubs and firkins.

"Butter, as it is received by merchants from small dairies, should be packed down solid, while it is fresh and sweet; and as there is usually a diversity of color, great pains should be taken to keep each shade by itself. To accomplish this, several packages may be filling at the same time, each one receiving its respective shade; so that when they are full, it will bore uniform in color upon the trier. A clean linen cloth, thoroughly saturated with strong brine, should be laid on the top, and a slight layer of moistened salt upon it. This not only preserves the butter, but gives to it a neat appearance.

"Nothing pleases commission merchants more than to receive a strictly fine dairy of butter—sweet, yellow, rosy to the smell, and delicious to the taste. It sells readily at a satisfactory price, and every body is pleased, from producer to consumer. Common and inferior butter *sticks*, notwithstanding its *greasiness*, at every stage, causing dissatisfaction and trouble from beginning to end. It is either over-salted, under-salted, colorless, milky, sticky, strong, rank or rancid, or all these combined—at any rate, it is not what it should be, and is consequently unsalable."

Cheese and Cheese Making.—In the making of cheese there are certain general principles which are essential, but slight variation in the process produces cheeses of very different qualities; and although the most important circumstance is the nature of the pasture on which the cows are fed, yet much depends on the mode in which the different stages of the fabrication are managed; and hence the great superiority of the cheeses of particular districts or dairies over those of others, without any apparent difference in the pasture. In those countries where the cows are chiefly kept tied up in stalls, and are fed with a variety of natural and artificial grasses, roots, and vegetables, superior cheese is often made.

The first process in making cheese is to separate the curd from the whey, which may be done by allowing the milk to become sour; but the cheese is inferior in quality, and it is difficult to stop the acid fermentation and prevent its running into the putrefactive. Various substances added to milk will soon separate the curd from the whey. All acids curdle milk. Muriatic acid is used with success for this purpose in Holland. Some vegetables contain acids which readily coagulate milk, such as the juice of the fig-tree, and the flowers of the Galium verum, or yellow lady's bed-straw, hence called *cheese-rennet*. Where better rennet cannot be procured, they may be substituted for the best curdler of milk, which is the gastric juice of the stomach of a sucking calf. This juice rapidly coagulates the milk as the calf sucks; and the only difficulty is in collecting and keeping it from putrefaction, which begins from the instant the stomach is taken from the calf. The preparation of the *rennet*, as it is called, is a most important part of the process of cheese-making. The following may be considered as the simplest, and perhaps the best. As soon as a sucking calf is killed, the stomach should be taken out, and if the calf has sucked lately, it is all the better. The outer skin should be well scraped, and all fat and useless membranes carefully removed. It is only the inner coat which must be preserved. The coagulated milk should be taken out and examined; and any substance besides curd found in it should be carefully removed. The scrum left in it should be pressed out with a cloth. It should then be replaced in the stomach with a large quantity of the best salt. Some add a little alum and sal prunella; others put various herbs and spices, with a view of giving the cheese a peculiar flavor; but the plain simple salting is sufficient. The skins or vells, as they are called, are then put into a pan, and covered with a saturated solution of salt, in which they are soaked for some hours; but there must be no more liquor than will well moisten the vells. They are afterward hung up to dry, a piece of flat wood being put crosswise into each to stretch them out. They should be perfectly dried and look like parchment. In this state they may be kept in a dry place for any length of time, and are always ready for use. In some places, at the time of making cheese, a piece of vell is cut off, and soaked for some hours in water or whey, and the whole is added to the warm milk. In other places, pieces of vell are put into a linen bag, and soaked in warm water, until the water has acquired sufficient strength, which is proved by trying a portion of it in warm milk. The method employed in Switzerland is as follows:—a dry vell is taken and examined; it is scraped with a knife, and where any veins or pieces of tough membrane appear, they are removed. The whole surface is examined and washed carefully, if any dust or dirt has adhered to it; but otherwise it is only wiped with a cloth. A handful of salt is then put into it, and the edges of the vell are folded over and secured with a wooden skewer stuck through it. In this state it forms a ball of about three inches diameter, and is laid to soak twenty-four hours in a dish containing about a quart of clear whey, which has been boiled, and all the curd taken out. The next day the vell is well squeezed, and put into fresh whey; the first infusion being put into a proper vessel, the second is afterward mixed with it, and bottled for use. Half a pint of this liquor, of a proper strength, is sufficient to curdle forty gallons of milk. Experience alone enables the dairyman to judge of the strength of his rennet; for this purpose he takes in a flat ladle some milk which has been heated to about ninety-five degrees of Fahr., and adds a small measure of rennet. By the rapidity with which it curdles, and by the form of the flakes produced, he knows its exact strength, and puts more or less into the caldron in which the milk is heated for curdling.

There are different kinds of cheese, according to the mode of preparing it: soft and rich cheeses are not intended to be kept long; hard and dry cheeses are adapted to be kept and stored for provisions. Of the first kind are all cream cheeses, and those soft cheeses, called Bath cheeses and Yorkshire cheeses, which are sold as soon as made, and if kept too long become soft and putrid. Stilton and Gruyère cheeses are intermediate; Parmesan, Dutch, Cheshire, Gloucestershire, and similar cheeses, are intended for longer keeping. The poorer the cheese is, the longer it will keep; and all cheese that is well cleared from whey, and sufficiently salted, will keep for years. The small Dutch cheeses, called Edam cheeses, are admirably adapted for keeping, and form an important article in the victualing of ships.

The Gruyère and Parmesan cheeses only differ in the nature of the milk, and in the degree of heat given to the curd in different parts of the process. Gruyère cheese is entirely made from new milk, and Parmesan from skimmed milk. In the first nothing is added to give flavor:

in the latter saffron gives both color and flavor; the process in both is exactly similar. A large caldron, in the shape of a bell, capable of holding from 60 to 120 gallons of milk, hangs from an iron crane over a hearth where a wood fire is made. The milk, having been strained, is put into this caldron, and heated to nearly blood-heat (95° to 100°). It is then turned off the fire, and some rennet, prepared as stated above, is intimately mixed with the warm milk by stirring it with the hand, in which is held a flat wooden skimming-dish, which is turned round in the milk while the hand and arm stir it. A cloth is then laid over the caldron, and in half an hour, more or less, the coagulum is formed. This is ascertained by pressing the skimming-dish on the surface, when the whey will appear on the part pressed. If it is longer than an hour in coagulating, the milk has been too cool, or the rennet not strong enough. When the curd is properly formed, it is cut horizontally in thin slices by the same skimming-ladle. Each slice, as it is taken off, is poured along the side of the caldron which is nearest to the operator; by this means every portion of the curd rises successively to the surface, and is sliced thin. The whole is then well stirred, and the caldron is replaced over the fire. A long staff, with a small knob of hard wood at the end, and which has smaller cross pieces or sticks passed through holes in it at right angles to each other near the end, is now used to stir and break the curd, and the heat is raised to about 135°, which is as hot as the arm can well bear, even when used to it. The caldron is again swung off the fire, and the curd is stirred with the staff, which is moved round with a regular rotatory motion, the knob running along the angle formed with the side by the bottom of the caldron, which is in the form of a bowl. After stirring in this manner nearly an hour, the curd is found divided into small dies about the size of a pea, which feel elastic and rather tough under the finger. Experience alone can teach the exact feel they should have. The whey, of which a portion is removed occasionally, now floats at top, and the curd is collected in the bottom by giving a very rapid rotatory motion to the contents of the caldron by means of the staff. A cloth is now introduced into the bottom, and all the curd collected over it; it is raised by the four corners, and laid on an instrument like a small ladder, which is placed across the mouth of the caldron. The whey runs out through the cloth, which is a common cheese-cloth, woven with wide interstices; and the curd in the cloth is placed in a shape or hoop, made of a slip of wood, four inches and a half wide, the two ends of which lie over each other, so that the diameter can be increased or lessened. A cord fixed to one end of the hoop is passed with a loop over hooks on the outer surface of the other end, and prevents the ring from opening more than is required. The curd is pressed into this ring with the hands, and the ends of the cloth are folded over it. A round board, two inches thick, and strengthened by cross pieces nailed on it, is placed over the curd, and the press let down upon it.

During the next six or eight weeks the cheeses are turned and wiped every day, and a small quantity of fine salt is sifted on the surface, and rubbed in with the hand until they will take no more. The cheese-room is always very cool, and little light is admitted. A free circulation of air is essential. The cheeses are in perfection in about six months, and will keep two years. A quantity of elastic fluid is disengaged in the ripening, and forms those round eyes which are a peculiar feature in these cheeses. The smaller and rounder the eyes, the better the cheese is reckoned. They should contain a clear salt liquor, which is called the tears; when these dry up, the cheese loses its flavor.

In Cheshire the making of cheese is carried on in great perfection, and the greatest pains are taken to extract every particle of whey. For this purpose, the curd is repeatedly broken and mixed, the cheeses are much pressed, and placed in wooden boxes, which have holes bored into them. Through these holes sharp skewers are stuck into the cheese in every direction, so that no particle of whey can remain in the curd. The elastic matter formed also escapes through these channels, and the whole cheese is a solid mass without holes, which in this cheese would be looked upon as a great defect. The salt is intimately mixed with the curd, and not merely rubbed on the outside. This checks internal fermentation, and prevents the formation of elastic matter.

Gloucester and Somersetshire cheeses are similarly made, with this difference, that the curd is not so often broken or the cheese skewered; and a portion of the cream is generally abstracted to make butter. After the curd has been separated from the whey, and is broken fine, warm water is poured over it, for the purpose of washing out any remaining whey, or perhaps to dissolve any portion of butter which may have separated before the rennet had coagulated the milk.

Stilton cheese is made by adding the cream of the preceding evening's milk to the morning's milking. The cream should be intimately incorporated with the new milk; great attention should be paid to the temperature of both, as much of the quality of the cheese depends on this part of the process. To make this cheese in perfection, as much depends on the management of the cheese after it is made as on the richness of the milk. Each dairy-woman has some peculiar method which she considers the best; and it is certain that there is the greatest difference between cheeses made in contiguous dairies. The rennet should be very pure and sweet. When the milk is coagulated, the whole curd is taken out, drained on a sieve, and very moderately pressed. It is then put into a shape in the form of a cylinder, eight or nine inches in diameter, the axis of which is longer than the diameter of the base. When it is sufficiently firm, a cloth or tape is wound round it to prevent its breaking, and it is set out on a shelf. It is occasionally powdered with flour, and plunged into hot water. This hardens the outer coat, and favors the internal fermentation which ripens it. Stilton cheese is generally preferred when a green mould appears in its texture. To accelerate this, pieces of a mouldy cheese are sometimes inserted into holes made for the purpose by the scoop, called a *taster*, and wine or ale is poured over for the same purpose; but the best cheeses do not require this, and are in perfection when the inside becomes soft like butter, without any appearance of mouldiness. In making very rich cheeses, the whey must be allowed to run off slowly, because, if it were forced rapidly, it might carry off a great portion of the fat of the cheese. This happens more or less in every mode of making cheese. To collect this superabundant butter, the whey is set in shallow pans, as is done with milk when butter is made; and an inferior kind of butter called whey-butter is made from the cream of fat skimmed off.

Cheeses are frequently colored—a practice which probably arose from the notion of making the cheese look richer; but now it deceives no one. Yet if some cheeses were not colored they would not be so marketable, owing to the association that subsists between the color and the quality of the cheese. The substance used for coloring is most commonly anatto. It is ground fine on a stone, and mixed with the milk at the time the rennet is put in. The juice of the orange carrot, and the flower of marigold, are also used for this purpose. Cheddar, a cheese made in Somersetshire, which is highly prized, Stilton, Derby, and some other cheeses, are never colored; Cheshire slightly; but Gloucester and North Wiltshire deeply. Foreign cheeses are only colored very slightly, if at all. The Dutch cheeses are made in a very similar manner to the Gloucester cheeses, but the milk is generally curdled by means of muriatic acid, or spirits of salt; and great care is taken to prevent fermentation, and to extract the whole of the whey. For this purpose the curd is repeatedly broken and pressed; and before it is made up into the round shape in which it is usually sold, the broken curd is well soaked in a strong solution of common salt in water. This diffuses the salt throughout the whole mass, and effectually checks fermentation. When the cheeses are finally pressed, all the whey which may remain is washed out with the brine; salt is likewise rubbed over the outside, and they are set to dry on shelves in a cool place. The flavor of the cheese is perhaps impaired by the stoppage of the fermentation; but it never heaves, and it acquires the valuable quality of keeping well even in warm climates. From the place where this cheese is commonly made, it is known by the name of Edam cheese. A finer cheese is made at Gouda and other places, by imitating the process in making Gruyère cheese; but this cheese is always full of small cavities, and will not keep so long as the Edam. The cheese most commonly met with in Holland is a large kind of skim-milk cheese, which is made very like Cheshire cheese. It grows hard and dry, and has not much flavor. To supply this defect, cummin seeds are mixed with the curd, which those who are accustomed to it consider a great improvement. On the whole, it is a better cheese than our Suffolk skim-milk cheese, and forms an important part of the provisions usually stored for a Dutch family. In France, the Roquefort cheese is compared to our Stilton, but is much inferior, although a good cheese. The little cheeses made from cream and folded in paper, called Neufchâtel cheeses, are imported from France as a delicacy. They can be easily imitated, being nothing more than cream thickened by heat, and pressed in a small mould. They undergo a rapid change, first becoming sour and then mellow, in which state they must be eaten.

The green Swiss cheese, commonly called *Schabzieger*, is produced in the Canton of Glarus. The curd is pressed in boxes, with holes to let the whey run out; and when a considerable quantity has been collected, and putrefaction begins, it is worked into a paste with a large proportion of a certain dried herb reduced to powder. This herb, called in the country dialect *Zieger kraut* (curd herb), is the *Melilotus officinalis*, which is very common in most countries, and has a peculiar aromatic flavor in the mountains of Switzerland. The paste thus produced is pressed into moulds of the shape of a common flower-pot, and the putrefaction being stopped by the aromatic herb, it dries into a solid mass, which keeps unchanged for any length of time. When used, it is rasped or scraped, and the powder, mixed with fresh butter, is spread upon bread. It is either much relished or much disliked, like all those substances which have a peculiar taste and smell.

When a cheese which has been much salted and kept very dry is washed several times in soft water, and then laid in a cloth moistened with wine or vinegar, it gradually loses its saltness, and from being hard and dry, becomes soft and mellow, provided it be a rich cheese. This simple method of improving cheese is worth knowing. It is generally practiced in Switzerland, where cheeses are kept stored for many years, and if they were not very salt and dry they would soon be the prey of worms and mites. A dry Stilton cheese may thus be much improved.

The Lactometer.—This instrument is designed to test the cream qualities of milk. Pour the milk into the tubes, and the cream, when risen, will show how rich the milk is. The depth of cream will be shown by the figures on the tubes. By the lactometer the difference in the quality of the milk of different cows may be readily ascertained.

The qualities of cream vary much in the different breeds, depending on the modes of management, as well as the food. Thus, in some experiments made, it required twelve quarts from a short-horn cow to produce one pound of butter—something like a day's supply of milk; while nine and a half quarts of an Ayrshire cow's would give the same quantity; but it is often very variable in the same animal at different periods, and different animals of the same breed will produce very different results both in cream and butter.

Profits of the Cow.—Our first illustration is from Mr. Thomas Tufts, of Le Roy, Genesee county, N. Y. On the 1st of November, 1838, he says: "I have a cow six years old last spring. On the 29th of May she brought a calf; and on the 27th of June I took from her at three milkings, morning, noon, and night, of one day, thirty-one and a half quarts of good rich measured milk, which was not more than an average for the whole month. The last week in July, I found that her milk failed a little, and being some trouble, I stopped milking her three times a day. On the last day of July, at two milkings, twenty-four quarts; on the last day of August, twenty-one and a half quarts; on the last day of September, eighteen quarts; and on the 31st day of October, I took from her fifteen quarts. She had no feed but that of common pasture, in which, however, was plenty of good water and shade, from the first of June till the last of September, and lodged at night in the barn-yard. On the 1st of October she was turned into a mowing-field; and during the last week in that month was fed once a day on hay, and twice a day on ruta-baga tops."

In July, 1845, a writer in the *Agriculturist* says: "I have a cow that calved about the middle of January, and is now eleven years old. The calf I fattened in the following manner: the first week I gave it one teat; the second week, two; afterward, three. The calf was sold for nearly six dollars; and in the mean time, milk to the amount of $1.75. Since that time I have realized for milk sold between fourteen and fifteen dollars; making the profit of the cow thus far, the present year, nearly twenty-three dollars, besides what I used in my own family, consisting of eight persons." Dr. Woodward informed the editor of the same journal that he had a cow which, in the year 1844, gave one thousand and fifty gallons of milk, which, at four cents a quart, would amount to one hundred and sixty-eight dollars. He also had, on the Hospital Farm, Worcester, Massachusetts, several other cows nearly as good. And William Cushman, of New Braintree, in that state, says, July 14th, 1845: "I have a cow which has given, for ten days in June, from fifty-four and a half to sixty-three pounds of milk per day." She was one-fourth of the Durham breed.

Peter H. Schenck, formerly a merchant of New York, but having a country residence in Dutchess county, in October, 1843, says: "My cow Emma was nine years old last spring; and till the summer of 1842 I never kept her milk separate from that of three other cows I have. Then I made the experiment for one week, during which she gave eighteen quarts per day, and the milk made fifteen pounds of butter." On the 21st of the following May—that is, 1843—he renewed the experiment, and for the three weeks ensuing she made sixty-five and a half pounds of butter. On the 15th of June, that same year, the milk that came from her was churned by itself, and the butter weighed three pounds eight ounces. The next day her butter weighed three pounds four ounces.

In 1843, a gentleman in the neighborhood of Troy, New York, says: "George Vail, Esq., of that city, was the owner of two cows only, one a full-blooded Durham, seven or eight years old, and the other four years old, seven-eighths Durham. He kept an accurate account of their milk and butter for thirty days. The result was as follows: one hundred and eight pounds of butter, besides supplying a family of five persons with new milk and cream for ordinary family use, and nine quarts of new milk daily for a calf. The average weight of milk per day, from the oldest cow, was sixty-eight pounds, and from the other, sixty pounds, during the thirty days. In the same year, Judge Walbridge, of Ithaca, in that state, had a cow that gave in the seven days ending June 24th, three hundred and ninety-five pounds ten ounces of milk, being an average of fifty-six and a half pounds per day, or twenty-eight and a half quarts per day. She had made two pounds one ounce per day, when two quarts of the milk were taken for family use. And the Rev. William Wisner, in the same neighborhood, had a cow, that in May of the same year made forty-seven pounds of butter, and supplied two families with new milk daily, during the time."

Among the more recent statistics of the dairy, the two following are selected. The first is from the Exeter *News-Letter*, which says: "Mr. Abraham Rowe, of Kensington, N. H., has a cow he raised from an Eastern breed, six years old, from which was made, between the 20th of May and the 20th of October, 1849, one hundred and fifty-six pounds of butter, averaging over one pound a day from pasture feed

7*

only. It being his only cow, furnished his family with their cream and milk besides." The second is from the *Farmer and Mechanic*, which says: "The best cow now in the United States is probably owned near Geneva, N. Y., which through the month of June, 1849, gave forty-two quarts of milk per day; and for five days she gave forty-five quarts per day. The cow is half Durham and half of the native breed."

The *Somerset Messenger*, New Jersey, contains a communication from J. W. Van Arsdale, stating the profits of a half-blooded Durham cow owned by him, for ten months from the 1st of April, 1849, to the 1st of February following. He sold in that time to the retailer 3,022 quarts, at 2 and 2½ cents a quart, amounting to $70.51, besides reserving a sufficient quantity for the use of his family of eleven persons, and about two messes of milk twice a week for baking purposes. The 3,022 quarts were sold by the retailer at double the price he gave for it, that is, for $141.02. He calculates that this amount of milk would have made 302 pounds of butter, which, at 20 cents a pound, amounts to $60.40. The cow has not had extraordinary care—having had two quarts of oat and corn meal per day during the drought last summer, and three quarts last spring before grass and this winter. And a farmer in Essex county, in that state, realized during twelve months previous to February 1st, 1850, a net profit of $456.09 from three ordinary cows—animals of the common breed of the country—that in most other hands would not probably much more than have paid for their keeping. As it is, they have supplied the family with all their milk and cream, paid for their keeping in full, as appears by a minute daily account, and yielded the above-named profit of $456.09.

It is unnecessary to gather up more similar cases. Our agricultural journals are filled with them. Now, suppose a farmer resolve that he would keep no cow that did not hold out a good milker nine months in the year, and that did not give sixteen quarts of milk per day for two months after calving, twelve quarts per day for the next four months, six quarts per day for the next three months, and two quarts per day for the following month; such a cow would yield per annum 3,000 quarts of milk, which, at four cents a quart, would be $120. Considering the cases above given, is not this feasible? With such cows, what if it does cost five or ten dollars a year more to keep them than is ordinarily expended for the purpose? May not such cows be raised? No matter if they do cost fifty or sixty dollars each; they soon pay for themselves.

If the various modes of obtaining this object were resorted to at once throughout the country, there would be a vast improvement in a very short time. No young animal of promising appearance for milk would go to the butcher. More care would be taken of young stock. More young stock would be retained to insure a better selection for milk cows. Farmers would think more of the advantages of employing the improved breed. Heifers would be milked with great care and very thoroughly, to get them in the habit of holding out longer as milkers. If they once dry early, no care and keeping will afterward correct the fault. Heifers with the first calf, especially, should be well fed, and with some additional care, the last three months they are in milk, to make them hold out.

It is supposed that a milk cow of medium quality, in this part of the country, will give twelve quarts of milk for two months after calving, seven quarts per day on grass for the next four months, four quarts per day for the following two months, and perhaps two quarts per day for one month more; making altogether 1,500 quarts in the year.*

THE SPAYING OF COWS.†—A land-owner in the United States, Mr. Winn, seems to have had the first practice in spaying cows. The object of the operation was to maintain in the cow, without interruption, a supply of the same quantity of milk that she gave at the time of spaying. Notwithstanding the favorable results that Mr. Winn claimed to have obtained, the operation remained almost unknown in France until a veterinary surgeon of Lausanne (a Swiss), M. Levrat, made known the experiments practiced by him, and their effects. The treatise of M. Levrat ends with the following conclusions:

"The effect of spaying seems to me to be, to cause a more abundant and constant secretion of milk, which possesses also superior qualities, whence the following advantages result to the proprietor:

"1. An increase of one third in the quantity of milk.

"2. The certainty of having almost constantly the same quantity of milk.

"3. Exemption from accidents which may happen during the period of heat, when the cows mount each other, or are covered by too large bulls.

"4. Exemption from the risk of accidents which sometimes accompany or follow gestation and calving.

"5. Ease in fatting cows, when their milk begins to dry up.

"6. In fine, spaying is the only means of preventing onerous expenses, occasioned by cows becoming '*taurelières*,' which is so frequently the case in some countries, that it is rare to see cows kept more than two or three years without getting in this state; as, for example, in the environs of Lausanne and Lavaux, where they are obliged for this reason to change all their cows every two or three years, which is quite ruinous."

M. Levrat confirmed, after a year's observations, this fact, that the quantity of milk was constantly kept the same after the time of spaying.

M. Régère, veterinary surgeon at Bordeaux, inserted in the *Recueil de Médécine Vétérinaire*, a series of facts upon the spaying of cows, that had been acted upon by various proprietors.

It appears from these facts, which he recounts with many details, and whose authenticity is fixed, that the spayed cows have given, without interruption, after the operation, a quantity of milk at least double the average of what they gave during the preceding years. "After the researches that I have made since I commenced all these experiments, to the present time," says M. Régère, "this calculation is very exact, and if the cows continue to give milk during their whole life, in like manner,

---

* "Farmer's Evening Day-Book."
† Statement of M. P. A. Morin, Veterinary Surgeon at the Royal Depôt at Langonnet. Translated for the *Working Farmer*, from "*La Normandie Agricole Journal d'Agriculture Pratique.*"

the operation of spaying will furnish incontestable advantages, particularly in large cities, and their vicinity, where fodder is very dear, and where milk always sells well."

A remark made by MM. Levret and Régère is, that some cows, although they have been spayed, have had their heat, notwithstanding the removal of their ovarium, and the incapacity for their reproduction. These animals present, at the time of their heat, this difference from what we remark during the same period in cows not spayed, that their milk does not undergo any alteration in either quantity or quality.

We may add, that the school of Alfort has, recently, practiced this operation upon different cows, and that all the results obtained have reached the point we have above stated.

Leaving this, we arrive at the facts determined by M. Morin:

"Young cows ought to receive that nourishment which favors the secretion of milk, and which in consequence renders active their lactiferous vessels. The cow is not usually in full production until after the third or fourth calf; she continues to give the same return up to the seventh or eighth; from this time lactation diminishes after each new calving. On the other hand, from the moment that the cow has received the bull, and gradually as gestation advances, the quantity of milk progressively diminishes in most breeds, until three or four months before healthy parturition, the secretion of milk is almost nothing. It is to guard against this loss, and other inconveniences, that we lay down what we have obtained after some years' experience in spaying the cow, and the happy results that we meet with daily.

"*Of the Spaying of the Cow, and the Advantages of this Operation.*— The operation of spaying in the cow is productive of great advantages.

"1. The cow spayed a short time after calving, that is to say, thirty or forty days afterward, and at the time when she gives the largest quantity of milk, continues to give the like quantity, if not during her whole lifetime, at least during many years, and at the time when the milk begins to dry up the animal fattens. We are able to add, moreover, at this day, certain facts, the result of many years' experiment, that the milk of the spayed cow, although as abundant, and sometimes more so, than before the operation, is of a superior quality to that from a cow not spayed; that it is uniform in its character, that it is richer, consequently more buttery, and that the butter is always of a golden color.

"We believe that we ought to remark in passing, that if we feed the spayed cow too abundantly, lactation diminishes, and that the beast promptly fattens. It is therefore important that the feeding should not be more than sufficient to enable us to obtain the desired result.

"2. The spayed cow fattens more easily; its flesh, age considered, is better than that of the ox; it is more tender and more juicy.

"Indeed, no one is ignorant of the fact that all domestic animals, females as well as males, deprived of their procreative organs, fatten more quickly than those which retain them; that the flesh of the spayed females is more tender and more delicate than that of males. The same phenomena take place among spayed cows that occur among other females that have submitted to this operation; so, besides the advantage of furnishing a long-continued supply, before commencing a course of fattening, of abundant milk, and butter of a superior quality, the cow fattens easily and completely, and a certain benefit follows this course.

"3. In spaying decrepit cows, that is to say, of the age of from six to seven years, puny, small ones; those which, though fine in appearance, bear badly; those which are subject to miscarriage; those which frequently experience difficult calving, or delivery; those difficult to keep; and finally, all those that are *taurelières*—that is to say, constantly in heat—we have, in addition to an abundant production of milk and butter, and a facility of fattening, the advantage of preventing a degeneration of the species, and, moreover, of avoiding a crowd of accidents or maladies which frequently take place during or after gestation, and of diminishing those which happen during the period of heat, such as that of heavy cows mounting others, or being jumped upon by too heavy bulls.

"Except under peculiar circumstances, we should take care in spaying the cow that its teats have acquired their complete development, and that the milk has the proper qualities. The most suitable time is after the third or fourth calving.

"Many societies of agriculture, impressed with the important results that this operation effects, fix yearly at their agricultural meetings premiums for the encouragement of the spaying of old cows. We doubt not that other societies—who have not yet adopted this plan, not being convinced of its importance, when they are—will imitate their example. By this means they bestow upon the country a new source of products.

"We have been engaged for four years in researches upon this valuable discovery; we believe that it is incumbent upon us to state the results that we have obtained up to the present time. In the number of twenty-seven cows, aged from six to fifteen years, that we have actually spayed, we have had the following results: 1. Increase of milk in cows of six years; 2. Constant production in those that have passed that age; 3. Milk richer than that of the cow not spayed, consequently more buttery, and the butter both of a uniformly golden color, and having an aroma and taste far superior to that of a cow that has not undergone this operation.

"Early in July, 1842, we obtained, as a subject of experiment, a cow from Brittany, of the small kind, twelve years old, calved about two months before, and which gave, when we obtained her, about six quarts of milk daily. The next day after we performed the operation of spaying—indeed the first eight days after that—the secretion of milk sensibly diminished, in consequence of the light diet on which she had been put, but, on the ninth day, the time at which the cure was complete and the cow put on her ordinary food, the milk promptly returned, as to its former quantity, and she at the same time assumed a plumpness that she had not had previously. Customarily bringing together the yield of three days for butter-making, being eighteen quarts, it produced constantly two kilograms of butter of the best quality. From the month of December to the following March, the quantity of milk diminished about one-third, and the butter proportionally, the cow during that time having been put on dry fodder. But so soon as we were able to turn her into pasture—about the beginning of April—the milk, after eight days of this new food, resumed its former course, and the animal continued daily to furnish the same relative amounts of milk and butter as before.

"Three cows, two of which were fourteen years old, and the other fifteen, have dried up two years after the operation, and at the same time promptly fattened, without increase or change of food.

"One cow, eight years old, plentifully supplied with trefoil and cabbage, gave, a short time after the operation, a quantity of milk nearly double that which she gave before, although she was kept on the same kind of food. She has during a year continued to furnish the same amount, and has, in addition, fattened so rapidly, that the owner has been obliged, seeing her fatness, to sell her to the butcher, although she was still very good for milk.

"Another fact, no less worthy of remark, we must not pass over in silence; and which goes to prove the superior and unchanging quality of the milk of a spayed cow. It is, that a proprietor having spayed a cow five years old, recently calved, with the special intention of feeding with her milk a newly-born infant, the infant, on arriving at the age of six months, of a robust constitution, refused its pap when it was once accidentally prepared with milk different from that of the spayed cow.

"The other cows which had been spayed continued to give entire satisfaction to their owners, as well in respect to the quantity and quality of the milk, as also by their good condition.

"Six cows manifested, shortly after the operation, and on divers occasions, the desire for copulation; but we have not remarked this peculiarity except among the younger ones. In other respects, as my colleagues MM. Levrat and Régère have stated, the milk has not indicated the least alteration in quantity or quality.

"Indeed, the happy results that are daily attained from this important discovery are so conclusive, and so well known at this time in our part of the country, that, as we write, many proprietors bring us constantly good milch cows, since we have called upon them to do so, for us to practice the operation of spaying upon them. Every owner of cattle is aware that, from the time that the cow has received a bull, and in proportion as gestation advances, the milk changes and diminishes progressively, until at last, two or three months before a healthy parturition, the animal gives very little or no milk, whence ensues considerable loss; while at the same time, after the cows are subjected to the bull, the milk and butter are, for fifty days at least, of a bad quality, and improper to be exposed for sale; but, in addition to this, breeding cows are generally subjected to such loss in winter, and their keepers find themselves during a great part of the year entirely deprived of milk and butter, and at a time, too, when they most need them.

"By causing the cows to undergo this operation, as we have mentioned in the preceding remarks, the owner will never fail of having milk and butter of excellent quality; will fatten his animals easily when they dry up, and also will improve the race, an anxiety for which is perceived in many provinces of France.

"In general, the means employed by farmers to obtain the best possible price for old cows, beyond being useful, or, to use a commercial term, not merchantable, is to bring them to the bull, intending that gestation shall give them more suitable plumpness, so that they may be sold on more advantageous terms to the butcher; but does this state of fictitious *embonpoint* or fatness, render the flesh of these beasts better? Assuredly not. It is merely bloated, flabby flesh, livid, and which easily taints. Broth made from it is not rich, is without flavor, and without an agreeable smell; the lean and fat are in a measure infiltrated with water, and are consequently of bad quality and very difficult sale. These causes ought then to determine farmers to adopt the advice we give: they, as well as the butcher and the consumer, will derive very great advantage from it.

"As our method of operating may be slightly different from that pointed out by our colleague, M. Levrat, we will describe that which we practice.

"Having covered the eyes of the cow to be operated upon, we place her against a wall provided with five rings firmly fastened, and placed as follows: the first corresponds to the top of the withers; the second to the lower anterior part of the breast; the third is placed a little distance from the angle of the shoulder; the fourth is opposite to the anterior and superior part of the lower region, and the fifth, which is behind, answers to the under part of the buttocks. We place a strong assistant between the wall and the head of the animal, who firmly holds the left horn in his left hand, and with his right, the muzzle, which he elevates a little. This done, we pass through and fasten the end of a long and strong plaited cord in the ring which corresponds to the lower part of the breast; we bring the free end of the cord along the left flank, and pass it through the ring which is below and in front of the withers; we bring it down along the breast behind the shoulders and the angle of the fore-leg to pass it through the third ring; from there, we pass it through the ring which is at the top of the back; then it must be passed around against the outer angle of the left hip, and we fasten it, after having drawn it tightly to the posterior ring by a simple bow-knot.

"The cow being firmly fixed to the wall, we place a cord, fastened by a slip-noose around its hocks, to keep them together in such manner that the animal cannot kick the operator; the free end of the cord and the tail are held by an assistant. The cow, thus secured, cannot, during the operation, move forward, nor lie down, and the veterinary surgeon has all the ease desirable, and is protected from accident.

"M. Levrat advises that an assistant should hold a plank or bar of wood obliquely under the teats and before its limbs to ward off the kicks; but this method is not always without danger, both to the operator and the animal, because, at the commencement, that is, when the surgeon makes the incision through the hide and the muscles, the cow makes such sudden movements, and tries so frequently to strike with its left hind foot, that it may happen that upon every movement, the plank or the bar may be struck against the operator's legs. On the other hand, although the defense may be firmly held by the assistant, yet it may happen that, in spite of his exertions, he sometimes may be thrown against the operator by the movements she may attempt, and there may be an uncontrollable displacement of the plank or bar; and then it may happen that she becomes wounded, and at the same time prevents the operation, while, by the mode we point out, there is no fear of accident, either to the operator or the beast. In case of the want of a wall provided with rings, we may use a strong palisade, a solid fence, or two trees a suitable distance apart, across which we fix two strong bars of wood, separated from each other according to the size of the cow.

"There is another means of confining them that we have employed for some time past, where the cows were very strong and irritable, more simple than the preceding, less fatiguing for the animal, less troublesome to the operator, and which answers perfectly. It consists: *First.* In leaving the cow almost free, covering her eyes, holding her head by two strong assistants, one of whom seizes the nose with his hand and strongly pinches the nostrils, whenever the animal makes any violent movements during the operation. *Second.* To cause another assistant to hold the two hind legs, kept together by means of a cord passed above and beneath the hocks; this assistant also holds the tail and pulls it, whenever the animal seeks to change its place.

"The cow being conveniently disposed, and the instruments and appliances, such as curved scissors, upon a table, a convex-edged bistoury, a straight one, and one buttoned at the point, a suture needle filled with double thread of desired length, pledgets of lint of appropriate size and length, a mass of tow (in pledgets) being collected in a shallow basket, held by an intelligent assistant, we place ourselves opposite to the left flank, our back turned a little toward the head of the animal; we cut off the hair which covers the hide in the middle of the flanks, at an equal distance between the back and the hip, for the space of thirteen or fourteen centimetres in circumference; this done, we take the convex bistoury, and place it opened between our teeth, the edge out, the joint to the left; then, with both hands, we seize the hide in the middle of the flank and form of it a wrinkle of the requisite elevation, and running lengthwise of the body. We then direct an assistant to seize with his right hand the right side of this wrinkle; we then take the bistoury that we held in our teeth, and we cut the wrinkle at one stroke through the middle; the wrinkle having been suffered to go down, a separation of the hide is presented of sufficient length to enable us to introduce the hand; thereupon we separate the edges of the hide with the thumb and forefinger of the left hand, and in like manner, we cut through the abdominal muscles, the *iliax* (slightly obliquely) and the *lumbar* (across) for the distance of a centimetre from the lower extremity of the incision made in the hide; this done, armed with the straight bistoury, we make a puncture of the peritoneum at the upper extremity of the wound; we then introduce the buttoned bistoury, and move it obliquely from above to the lower part up to the termination of the incision made in the abdominal muscles. The flank being opened, we introduce the right hand into the abdomen and direct it along the right side of the cavity of the pelvis, behind the *cul de saurumen* (paunch) and underneath the rectum, where we find the *cornes de l'uterus* (matrix); after we have ascertained the position of these viscera, we search for the *ovaries* (organs of reproduction), which are at the extremity of the *cornes*, and when we have found them, we seize them between the thumb and forefinger, detach them completely from the ligaments that keep them in their place, pull lightly, separating the cord, and the vessels (uterine or fallopian tube) at their place of union with the ovarium, by means of the nail of the thumb of the forefinger, which presents itself at the point of touch; in fact, we break the cord and bring away the ovarium. We then introduce again the hand into the abdominal cavity, and we proceed in the same manner to extract the other ovaria. This operation terminated, we, by the assistance of the needle, place a suture of three or four double threads waxed at an equal distance, and at two centimetres or a little less, from the lips of the wound; passing it through the divided tissues, we move from the left hand with the piece of thread; having reached that point, we fasten with a double knot, we place the seam in the intervals of the thread from the right, and as we approach the lips of the wound, we fasten by a simple knot, with a bow, being careful not to close too tightly the lower part of the seam, so that the suppuration which may be established in the wound, may be able to escape. This operation effected, we cover up the wound with a pledget of lint kept in its place by three or four threads passed through the stitches, and all is completed, and the cow is then led back to the stable.

"It happens, sometimes, that in cutting the muscles, of which we have before spoken, we cut one or two of the arteries, which bleed so much that there is necessity for a ligature before opening the peritoneal sac, because, if this precaution be omitted, blood will escape into the abdomen, and may occasion the most serious consequences.

"**Care After the Operation.**—The regimen we prescribe during the first eight days following the operation, is a light diet, and a soothing lukewarm draught; if the weather should be cold, we cover the cow with a woolen covering. We must prevent the animal from licking the wound and from rubbing it against other bodies. The third day after the operation, we bathe morning and evening about the wound, with water of mallows, lukewarm, and in default of this, we anoint it with a salve of hogs' lard, and we administer an emollient glyster during three or four days.

"Eight days after the operation we take away the bandage, the lint, the fastenings and the threads; the wound is at that time completely cicatrized, as we have observed that a reunion takes place almost always by the first intention, as we have only observed suppuration in three cows, and then it was very slight. In this case we must use a slight pressure above the part where the suppuration is established, so as to cause the pus to leave it, and if it continues more than five or six days, we must supply emollients by alcoholized water, or chloridized, especially if it be in summer. We then bring the cow gradually back to her ordinary nourishment.

"We have remarked in some cows a swelling of the body a short time after being spayed, a state that we have attributed to the introduction of cold air into the abdomen during the operation; but this derangement has generally ceased within twenty-four hours. If the contrary should occur, we administer one or two sudorific draughts; such as wine, warm cider, or half a glass of brandy, in a quart of warm water; treatment which suffices in a short time to re-establish a healthy state of the belly, the animal at the same time being protected by two coverings of wool.

"The operation which we have been describing, ought to be performed as we have said before, thirty to forty days after calving, upon a cow which has had her third or fourth calf, so that we may have a greater abundance of milk. The only precaution to be observed before the operation, is, that on the preceding evening we should not give so copious a meal as usual, and to operate in the morning before the animal has fed, so that the operator shall not find any obstacle from the primary digestive organs, especially the paunch, which, during its state of ordinary fullness, might prevent operating with facility.

"Conclusion.—From what has preceded, it is fixed and irrefutable— 1. That spaying induces permanency of milk, increase of quantity, and improvement of quality; richer, more buttery, superior color, finer taste and flavor. 2. The most suitable age is six years, and after the third or fourth calf. 3. The spayed cow fattens more easily, and furnishes beef of a better quality. 4. Cows that are bad breeders may be kept as good milkers, and the quality of good cattle kept up."

DISEASES AND REMEDIES.—This is perhaps the most unsatisfactory division on which a writer on cattle can pretend to write. There are more cattle destroyed than cured by the strange quackery and drenching pursued by their over-officious owners; and to write any thing to encourage a system so ruinous is to perpetuate the evil. The first thing a dairyman or grazier does is to get a long list of "receipts" inserted in a book, classified or not, but all under the names of certain diseases. A cow falls ill. She has the yellows, or the staggers, or the worms, not because there are any clear and decided symptoms, but because the owner fancies it is so, and his specific is administered. He watches intently, and no good effect is produced; he runs for another medicine prescribed by another hand; the one opposing, and perhaps counteracting the other. One neighbor looks in, and perhaps another; each advises a medicine, as empirical as that of the owner, and all must be given, until the symptoms increase and get so bad that the village quack is sent for, who is more clever than the rest, because he has a larger range of "receipts," and he adds his quota of drugs, until the beast dies, poisoned by medicine!

Now, so long as unprofessional men will continue to prescribe and treat obstinate and complicated complaints; and so long as the public press will pander to the receipt-mania, there is no hope of any amendment. Certainly we shall lend no aid to the system.

But there are some simple and manifest ailments where the farmer may himself administer simple medicines; and there are some cases of emergency, too, when it may be necessary to do something, till scientific aid can be obtained. To these cases we will allude. We will take the complaints in the order of their frequency.

Felon.—This is a complaint common to all kinds of cattle. It proceeds from cold and exposure, and is accompanied by low fever. The beast is more or less off his food. His coat is staring, his eye dull, his nose dry, his *back sore*, he will flinch from the touch, and his teeth feel loose. It is an attack of felon. He requires rousing by cordials. Let him be housed and given a drink: one ounce of turmeric, one ounce of fenugreek, one ounce of liquorice, one ounce of aniseed powder, in a quart of ale; and he will generally recover; if not, repeat the dose. A very common and a very safe process is also to divide the nerve of the under side of the tail. This relieves the back, and is thus performed: Feel for a soft place in the under side of the tail. The knobs are the joints, the soft place is the bone. Cut the skin across at the soft part, and it will bleed for eight or ten minutes. Tie up the tail with a piece of linen cloth, and great relief will be afforded. This is not mentioned in any work we ever met with, but we have seen its efficacy in hundreds of instances.

Hoven, Blown, or "Over Full."—Sometimes a change of food, or a feed of wet clover or potatoes, greedily eaten, will induce fermentation in the stomach instead of digestion. The sides will be blown up, until the stomach presses on the skin, with a force which renders it hard to the fingers. For this the probang is by far the best remedy. Introduce this into the stomach by the throat, and the foul air will immediately escape. This instrument is not always at hand, and the beast will lie down, and the disease may continue until the walls of the stomach are ruptured. In these cases an ounce of ammonia will often give relief. A pint of vinegar we have known to effect it; but the safest remedy is a *pint of linseed oil*. It lubricates the mouth of the stomach, and assists the air to escape by both the orifices, otherwise closed up. Gentle exercise will be useful; but all violence, and, above all, such horrid drenches as tar and salt, with the idea of making them eject their saliva, can only do harm. It is sometimes necessary to cut into the stomach, an operation a veterinary surgeon alone can perform.

Choking.—A beast will often get a turnip or potato fast in its throat, which will resist all efforts to get it either up or down; and, what is worse, when once this has taken place, the beast will always after be liable to the same accident. The mouth should first be carefully examined, to see that the turnip cannot be extracted with the hand; if it can be, this is the best mode by far for effecting its extraction. If not, the probang, invented by Dr. Munro, is absolutely necessary. Let a little sweet oil be first given to the animal, and then let the probang be carefully and cautiously put down, the cup end downward; if the turnip offers much resistance it must again be withdrawn, and by this its position may be changed. Generally it will go down, with a very slight effort, and sometimes it may be got up by running the thumbs up each side of the neck, and gently pressing with the hand.

Calving.—This, though not a disease, is rightly classed amongst them, because it is strictly a subject of medical and surgical treatment; and, though a natural operation, is always accompanied by more or less danger. In old cows, or cows after their first and second calves, if the right presentation takes place, the animal will generally calve without mechanical help. It often happens, that cows which calve unobserved, do the best, and we know a very careful and successful grazier who makes a point of never interfering in ordinary cases. There is certainly more danger from premature assistance than from delay. Usually the waters are the first symptoms of decided labor. A thin filmy bag first breaks, and after this the cow will sometimes eat, and seem comfortable for an hour. The second is larger and thicker, and envelops the feet of the calf. When the feet are there, or one begins to protrude, the other may be sought for, and when both are brought forward, mechanical assistance may safely be rendered, if the head is found between and above them. A cow-tie may be strung round each foot, and certainty of the head being between them is a signal for a slow and gentle pull, avoiding any thing like force, and the pulling being downward towards the udder. But above all things, *give time*. The muscles relax and give way for the calf, if proper time is allowed. When calving is over, follow the directions formerly given in regard to the management of the mother and produce,—the latter should suck, and the mother lick the calf.

False Presentations will sometimes take place;—a single foot, or the head, or the hind legs. In either of these cases, the operator must wait for one of the throes being over, and then gently put back the calf, and introduce his hand, which has been previously oiled, and bring forward the legs which are wanting. If this cannot easily be done, a veterinary surgeon will be necessary. When the hind legs alone are presented, it is only necessary to proceed in the usual way. In cases of difficulty, of malformation in the mother, of water in the head, or monstrosity in the calf, it is always best to call in a veterinary surgeon.

Some parties have a practice of giving every cow a calving drink. We uniformly prefer, as we said, nature's medicine, the licking of the calf, to any and all others which can be given. If it has been a long and protracted labor, a drink of warm gruel will be useful. If the cow refuses to lick the calf, which heifers of their first calves will sometimes do, it is seldom necessary to do more than run the hand over the newly dropped calf, and then pass it across the mouth and lips of the mother.

Abortion is a habit with some individual cows, and is often the result of the presence of blood, or bad smells, arising from putrid matter decaying near the cow-houses or yards; and once introduced into a cow-house, it often so affects the imaginations of the rest, as to become epidemic. Let the cow and the remains of the calf be instantly removed from the rest, and kept alone and quiet. Chloride of lime should be plentifully sprinkled near the stall where she was, and the whole of the herd should have their noses besmeared with tar.

Retention of the Placenta, or failing to cleanse, after calving, sometime occurs; and it requires great care to prevent its retention, when the expulsion does not take place in a few hours after calving. It indicates weakness, and want of tone in the uterus. A mild stimulant may be given—nothing better than an infusion of chamomile flowers, say two handfuls in a quart of water, added to a quart of good boiled ale, and if necessary, an injection of soap-suds, to keep open the bowels and prevent inflammatory action. If it resists all efforts, and begins to putrefy, it will be necessary to consult a veterinary surgeon.

Red Water.—This is a complaint which frequently attacks cows in summer; and, on some pastures, it is a regular occurrence. If taken in an early stage, a dose of eight ounces of Epsom salts, dissolved in a pint of water, will almost invariably set the beast right. If not at hand, a pound of common salt may be given, and the dose repeated, in case of need.

Quarter Felon.—Inflammatory fever, or quarter-ill, is one of the most obstinate diseases with which cattle can be afflicted; and, though odd instances of a cure have been reported, they are extremely few, unless the disease has been attacked in a very early stage. It is also highly contagious, and will sometimes go through an entire herd of calves before they are a year old, for it seldom occurs after that period. The calf gets off its food, and becomes lame and stiff in one foot. The foot may be examined, and no cause of lameness discovered, but soon the disease has become general; air bubbles are formed between the skin and muscles, and there is a cracking sensation to the hand on passing it over the skin, especially in the legs. Inflammatory fever is disorganizing the body.

Preventives, as the seton in the dewlap, bleeding, in autumn, doses of dyer's madder, etc., are favorite remedies. The seton can do no harm, —it may be tried; but no specific, either remedy or prevention, has yet been discovered.

Foul in the Foot.—This is a tiresome, worrying disease, to which large heavy milk cows are specially subject; and is to the cow what foot-rot is to the sheep. There is inflammatory action between the claws; it begins to discharge fetid matter, and is a source of pain and irritation, which often dries up the milk, and is often a painful and annoying complaint to cure. Let the foot first be well cleaned and fomented with warm water, and all loose flesh be cut or clipped off. The foot may then be poulticed for one night with flaxseed-meal poultice, and then again fomented and anointed with tar; and, if it should smell very offensively, a little charcoal, or a few drops of chloride of lime may be added to the water. Next day the inflammation will be relieved and brought out externally by the tar, and the foot may be then dressed with the butter of antimony (chloride of antimony) night and morning, and the tar applied afterward. The foot should be confined in a boot or stocking, and kept free from dirt. A little salts or linseed-oil should be given to keep the bowels in a state of gentle activity.

Milk Fever.—This is a common complaint with cows which are deep milkers, at least in summer. Prevention is all the farmer has to do with, for the cure, if any, must be left in the hands of the veterinary surgeon. He must, if he see the udder distended, milk the cow before calving regularly three times a day; she must be kept as cool and quiet as possible, and have mashes of bran only, for a few days after calving. This is cooling and somewhat laxative, and if the udder should be hard, which it should not be after this treatment, let it be rubbed with marsh mallow ointment. A gentle dose of purgative medicine may be given if the cow is in very high condition, and she should be driven a few miles every day before calving. With these precautions there is little danger, at least of its being fatal.

The Yellows, or Jaundice.—This is easily distinguishable. White cattle are peculiarly subject to it, and it makes its firt appearance by a yellowness of the eyes and under the anus; the bowels become costive, the teeth loose, the appetite gone, and rapid weakness sets in. Give 4 oz. common salt, half oz. Barbadoes aloes, 1 dr. ginger, 1 quart home-brewed ale, made into gruel.

Loss of Cud.—All ruminating animals are sometimes subject to this. The stomach, with a sort of convulsive action, throws the half masticated food back into the mouth to be rechewed, and sometimes this healthy contractile tone of the stomach is lost. Give—6 dr. Barbadoes aloes, 6 oz. common salt, 3 dr. ginger, 1 oz. alspice, in a quart of gruel.

Inflammation.—This is a disease known by coldness of the horns and extremities, generally accompanied by much acute and constant pain. All home attempts to cure this disorder will be impotent; a veterinary surgeon should be at once consulted. The same may be said of *staggers*, *strangury*, and a variety of acute disorders.

Pleuro-Pneumonia is only mentioned to say that nothing like a specific has, so far, been discovered. The fearful medicine of a gill of spirits of turpentine and a gill of spirits of sweet nitre seems to be the most successful but desperate remedy. If the animal is fat, there is scarcely a chance of recovery. If the animal is lean, remedial measures may be tried, but they are more likely to fail than be successful.

The Epidemic, or Sore Mouth and Feet,—for so a disease which affects the mouth with blisters and the feet with pain and inflammation, is best known, has lost much of the virulence it possessed from 1839 to 1844, but still is sometimes troublesome. A dose of Glauber or Epsom salts, in the first stage, with shelter and bran mashes, will generally prevent evil consequences. Should the foot break out, the same treatment will be useful that we advised in the foul of the foot.

Diseases of Calves.—If well managed, calves are subject to few diseases; and if starved, neglected, or ill managed, they will be scarcely kept alive by medicine. The most fatal disease is the *scour* or *diarrhœa*. As it usually proceeds from some foreign, often acrid matter, in the bowels, a tablespoonful of sulphur in the milk will generally remove it in due time. If it should continue after this, give a teaspoonful of laudanum and a tablespoonful of tincture of rhubarb. We once had a calf nearly dead of diarrhœa; medicine seemed to have no impression upon the obstinate attack. It was dying. We gave it a bottle of port wine, expecting it would be dead in the morning. In the morning, however, it was well and crying for its breakfast. A pint of good old port will often work wonders when all other remedies have failed, both in man and beast.

Costiveness is sometimes a disease in calves, as well as the opposite extreme. Here it is undesirable to give medicine, unless it be very severe. A handful of onions, boiled with an ounce of fat bacon, is by far the best remedy, and it never does injury, but is nutritious to the animal even if well.

Gripes is a complaint to which young calves are subject, which have had sour milk given to them; and there is often acute pain exhibited, kicking of the belly with the hind legs, pawing, etc. A cure is generally effected, in a remarkably short time, by a cupful of peppermint water and a teaspoonful of laudanum.

The great secret of keeping all animals is to tend them carefully and keep them well. Let the land said to be subject to disease be well drained and better farmed; let the bad herbage and cold beds of the cattle be cured and they will be healthier and thrive better. It is better always to pay the cake-crusher or the miller, than to pay the veterinary surgeon, however skillful he may be.

In conclusion, treat the cow well, and she will be grateful. Let all your proceedings be dictated by humanity and kindness, and a more patient and grateful servant you cannot have.

THE
DOMESTIC SHEEP:

THEIR

BREEDS, MANAGEMENT,

AND

DISEASES.

SOUTH-DOWN SHEEP.

THE DOMESTIC SHEEP:

THEIR BREEDS, MANAGEMENT, ETC.

BREEDS OF SHEEP IN THE UNITED STATES.—The principal breeds of sheep in the United States are the *Native sheep*, the *Spanish* and *Saxon Merinos*, the *New Leicester*, or *Bakewell*, the *South-Down*, the *Cotswold*, the *Cheviot* and the *Lincoln*.

The **Native Sheep** are the variously mixed descendants of those originally introduced by the first colonists. They yielded wool suited only to the coarsest fabrics. They were slow in arriving at maturity, compared with the improved English breeds; and the weight of fleece, and quality and quantity of mutton, were inferior to the improved English breeds. They have now, however, become nearly extinct, by crosses with foreign breeds of later introduction.

American Merinos.—Of these there are three classes, or varieties. The *first* is a large, short-legged and hardy sheep, the wool ranging from medium to fine, and without hair when well fed—rarely exhibiting gum externally—their wool thick, and comparatively long on the back and belly, and whiter than that of the French sheep called the Rambouillets, and their skin has the rich rose-color of the latter. The *second* general class of American Merinos are smaller than the preceding—less hardy—wool as a general thing finer—covered with a black pitchy gum on its extremities—fleece about one-fourth lighter than in class first. The *third* class, which have been bred mostly South, are still smaller and less hardy—and carry still finer and lighter fleeces. The fleece is destitute of external gum. The sheep and wool bear a close resemblance to the Saxon; and if not actually mixed with that blood, they have been formed into a similar variety, by a similar course of breeding. Class *first* are a larger and stronger sheep than those originally imported from Spain, carry much heavier fleeces, and in well selected flocks, or individuals, the fleece is of a decidedly better quality.*

The Merino fleece is in Spain sorted into four parcels. The following cut, while it contains the portrait of a Merino ewe, points out the parts whence the different wools are generally procured. The division cannot always be accurate, and especially in sheep of an inferior quality, but it is more to be depended upon in the Merino sheep wherever found, for the fleece is more equally good, and the quantity of really bad wool is very small.

Both Lasteyrie and Livingston agree in this division. The *refina*, or the pick-lock wool begins at the withers, and extends along the back to the setting on of the tail. It reaches only a little way down at the quarters, but, dipping down at the flanks, takes in all the superior part of the chest, and the middle of the side of the neck to the angle of the lower jaw. The *fina*, a valuable wool, but not so deeply serrated, or

---
* Randall's "Sheep Husbandry."

DOMESTIC ANIMALS.

possessing so many curves as the *refina*, occupies the belly, and the quarters and thighs, down to the stifle joint. The *terceira*, or wool of the third quality, is found on the head, the throat, the lower part of the neck, and the shoulders, terminating at the elbow: the wool yielded by the legs, and reaching from the stifle to a little below the hock, forms a part of the same division. A small quantity of very inferior wool is procured from the tuft that grows on the forehead and cheeks—from the tail, and from the legs below the hock.

The Spanish wool continues to be highly valued by the manufacturer; and the Spanish breed of sheep will be regarded with interest as the improver of the best old short-wooled ones, and the parent of a new race, spreading through every quarter of the world, and with which, so far as the fleece is concerned, none of the old breeds can be for a moment compared.

Saxon Merinos.—This breed is the result of transferring, nearly a century ago, the best Spanish sheep into Saxony, where they appeared to thrive better than in their native region.

Very great care is taken by the Saxon sheep-master in the selection of the lambs which are destined to be saved in order to keep up the flock: there is no part of the globe in which such unremitting attention is paid to the flock. Mr. Charles Howard, in a letter with which he favored the author, says, that "when the lambs are weaned, each in his turn is placed upon a table, that his wool and form may be minutely observed." The finest are selected for breeding, and receive a *first* mark. When they are one year old, and prior to shearing them, another close examination of those previously marked takes place: those in which no defect can be found, receive a *second* mark, and the rest are condemned. A few months after, they in like manner receive a *third* mark, when the slightest blemish causes a rejection of the animal.

The utmost care is also taken in the housing and feeding of their flocks, evidently aiming rather at a fine staple of wool, than a hardy race of sheep. Mr. Carr, a large sheep-owner in Germany thus describes their management and its effects:

They are always housed at night, even in summer, except in the very finest weather, when they are sometimes folded in the distant fallows, but never taken to pasture until the dew is off the grass. In the winter they are kept within doors altogether, and are fed with a small quantity of sound hay, and every variety of straw, which has not suffered from wet, and which is varied at each feed; they pick it over carefully, eating the finer parts, and any grain that may have been left by the threshers. Abundance of good water to drink, and rock-salt in their cribs, are indispensables. . . . . They cannot thrive in a damp climate, and it is quite necessary that they should have a wide range of dry and hilly pasture of short and not over-nutritious herbage. If allowed to feed on swampy or marshy ground, even once or twice in autumn, they are sure to die of liver complaint in the following spring. If they are permitted to eat wet grass, or exposed frequently to rain, they disappear by hundreds with consumption. In these countries it is found the higher bred the sheep is, especially the Escurial, the more tender.

The American Saxon sheep have been so largely intermixed with

American Merinos, and other imported and native breeds, as to render it difficult to find one of pure breed; yet careful breeders have generally such good stocks, that it is questioned by good authority, whether the admixture, after all, has deteriorated the Saxons among us,—that crossing with Merinos has a tendency to increased hardiness in the animal, without in any important degree affecting the fineness of the wool staple.

The wool of the American Saxons is much finer than that of American Merinos, their fleeces average from two or two and a quarter to three pounds. They are relatively tender, requiring more protection and care than any other imported sheep. They are not as long-lived as the Merinos, do not fatten as well, nor consume as much food. Their lambs are less vigorous and require more care to rear them.

The New Leicester, or Bakewell.—It was about the middle of the last century that Mr. Bakewell, of Dishley in Leicestershire, first applied himself to the improvement of the old Leicesters. This old breed had many good points, yet it had its defects, and these of no trifling character; it was large, heavy, and coarse-grained, the mutton having l ttle flavor, and no delicacy; it was long in the carcass, flat-sided, large-boned, and clumsy; the ewes weighed eighteen or twenty pounds the quarter, the wethers from twenty to thirty pounds. The wool measured from ten to fifteen inches in the length of the staple, and was variable as to quality, but generally coarse. These sheep were slow feeders, and returned little profit.

Such was the stock common to Leicestershire and the adjacent counties, on which Mr. Bakewell began his course of experiments; in the prosecution of which he violated all the old axioms of his day, and proceeded upon principles totally at variance with those by which the breeders had previously regulated their practice. They aimed at size, irrespective of symmetry and aptitude to fatten; and at heavy fleeces, considering weight of wool as of primary importance. Mr. Bakewell on the contrary regarded symmetry and aptitude to fatten as first-rate qualities; he found these to be inherent in small, not in large heavy-boned sheep, which latter consumed an extravagant abundance of food without returning an adequate profit; whereas the smaller sheep he found to increase more rapidly in weight, proportionately, even upon a less consumption of diet. His experience had also taught him another point, viz., that sheep carrying a heavy fleece had always less aptitude to fatten, and were far slower in ripening, than those whose fleece was moderate; and he considered symmetry and early ripening to be of more importance than the loss of a few pounds in the fleece. In short, he considered that the value of the carcass was the first object to be attended to in breeding of sheep; and he looked upon the fleece as of secondary importance—not that the loss of two or three pounds in the fleece was not an object, but still he thought that if to preserve this the farmer not only lost ten or twelve pounds of mutton by it, but had to feed his sheep for twelve or eighteen months longer than he ought, he would pay dearly for his three pounds of wool extra. Mr. Bakewell was right; and on these principles he addressed himself to his task.

The improved Leicesters are not adapted for scanty pasturage, over which the sheep must travel all day in order to procure a sufficiency of food. They require a good, or at least moderate soil, and on this they fatten with incredible rapidity, and are consequently very profitable to the breeder. If in the establishment of this breed Mr. Bakewell erred, it was in the very little regard he paid to the wool, in which his immediate followers imitated him, some even going so far as to prefer sheep with bad fleeces to those with good, as if a fine and perfect carcass and good wool were incompatible with each other. But this false notion is now corrected, and the fleece obtains its due share of attention.

With respect to the quality of the mutton of the improved Leicesters, we do not estimate it so highly as that of some of the short-wooled breeds. When not over fat, it is tender and juicy, but destitute of high flavor; but when fattened to a high degree, the interstices of the fibers of the muscles are replete with fat in such a manner that the line of distinction between fat and lean is almost, as it were, lost; the carcass appears to be a mass of fat, and is any thing but attractive. Besides, such meat is not profitable to the purchaser, though it may be to the cook. We admit, however, that it is the grazier's fault if he carries the fattening process beyond the point at which he ought to stop, whether he regards his own profit or the interest of the consumer. It is the character of the breed to ripen early and quickly. As soon as the sheep are in a proper condition for the butcher, the grazier, instead of wasting more food upon them, should get rid of them, and commence the feeding of another lot, to be disposed of in their turn, as soon as ready.

It is for the accumulation of outside fat that the Leicesters are chiefly remarkable. They have comparatively little loose inside fat or tallow —a point of some consequence to the butcher, who deems this as adding to his profit. By way of a counterbalance, however, the smallness of the head, the thinness of the pelt, and the general greater weight of the carcass than the appearance of the animal would indicate, should be taken into consideration. Whatever it may be to the butcher, "this diminution of offal is advantageous to the grazier; for it shows a disposition to form fat outwardly, and is uniformly accompanied by a tendency to quickness of improvement." In this latter quality the new Leicesters, *cæteris paribus*, are unrivaled.

The new Leicesters, with all their good qualities, are not a hardy race, neither are they so prolific as many other breeds. The ewes seldom produce twins, nor indeed did the founders of this stock deem the production of twins desirable. They aimed at bringing forward the lamb as early as possible, and rightly considered that few ewes could produce two such lambs as would meet with their wishes and realize their object. The fact, moreover, is, that the exclusive attention paid to the establishment of a race, the vital energies of which were to be exhibited in the attainment of early maturity, and in the quick accumulation of fat, while productive of the results aimed at, necessarily entailed counterbalancing deficiencies. A tendency to rapid fattening and early ripeness is not coexistent, as a general rule, with great fertility. In this point, then, the new Leicesters are defective, but less so than formerly. Still the ewes do not yield any great abundance of milk, and the lambs are tender, delicate, and unfitted to endure any great inclemency of weather.

As a whole the *New Leicesters* have not succeeded so well in this country as in England, owing to the severity of our winters and to the heat and dryness of our summers. They do not find that luxuriance and abundance in our pastures so necessary to their highest thrift. Their flesh has not sufficient admixture of lean to be palatable to our people. The breed, however, succeeds well in rich lowland pastures, and yields a profitable return.

The South-Downs.—Formerly the South-Down sheep were very indifferent; it is true that they carried very fine wool, but then the carcass was ill-formed, a disadvantage which more than counterbalanced the excellence of the fleece. They were small, thin in the neck, high in the shoulders and in the loins, down on the rump, with the tail set very low; the back was sharp, the ribs flat, and the fore-quarters narrow; yet there were materials to work upon, and besides, these sheep had some excellent qualifications; they arrived at early maturity, were extremely hardy, thrived upon scanty keep and short feed on the natural pastures, and the mutton was fine-grained and of good flavor.

Attempts were first made to improve on South-Downs by crosses with the Leicesters, a long-wooled sheep, but these attempts ended in utter failure, nor were crosses between them and the Merinos ultimately advantageous. It was by careful selections, and the keeping in view of a definite purpose in the choice of breeding-stock, that the improvement of the South-Downs was achieved. It is to Mr. Ellman of Glynde that the elevation of this breed to its unrivaled position in its own line as a hill sheep is due.

Mr. Culley, in his "Live Stock," 1807, notices the exertions "of the ingenious Mr. Ellman, whose flock is already superior to that of most of his neighbors, both in carcass, quantity, and quality of wool." This enterprising and skillful breeder did not, however, content himself with mediocrity; and in the *Annals of Agriculture*, Mr. A. Young thus speaks of Mr. Ellman's South-Downs: "His flock, I must observe, is unquestionably the first in the country, the wool the finest, and the carcass the best proportioned. Both these valuable properties are united in the flock at Glynde. He has raised the merits of the breed by his unremitting attention, and it now stands unrivaled." Mr. Ellman's own description of them is very unpretending. He says: "They are now much improved both in shape and constitution; they are smaller in the bone, equally hardy, with a greater disposition to fatten, and much heavier in carcass when fat. They used seldom to fatten until they were four years old; but it would now be a rare sight to see a pen of South-Down wethers at market more than two years old, and many are killed before they reach that age." Doubtless the age is reckoned, as is usual with sheep, not from the time when lambed, but from the time of the first shearing.

The average dead weight of South-Down wethers, varies from 100 to 150 pounds. They are very healthy and hardy, seldom affected with the rot and the diseases common with other varieties.

THE SHEEP.

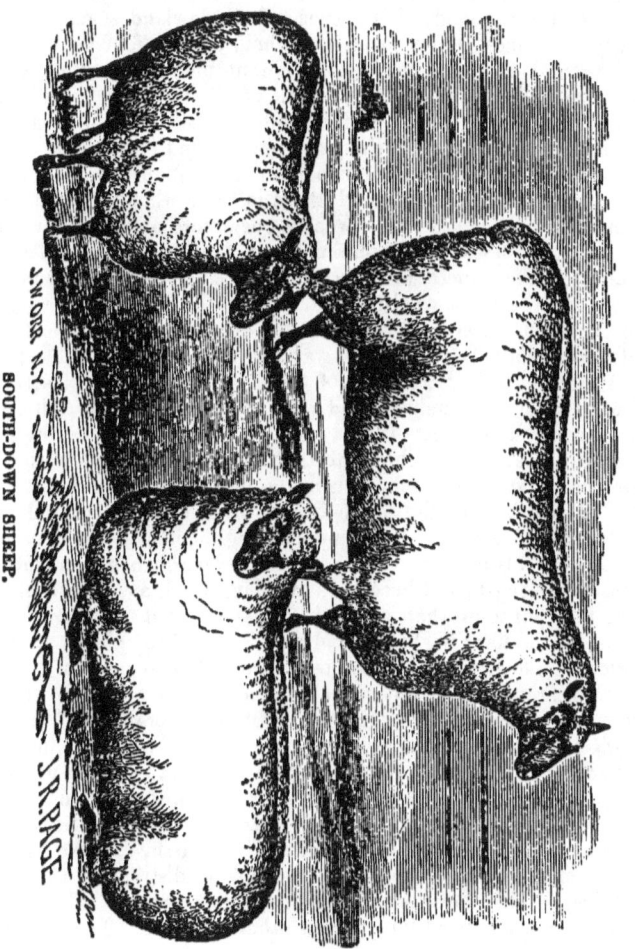

SOUTH-DOWN SHEEP.

This animal has a patience of occasional short keep, and an endurance of hard stocking scarcely surpassed by any other sheep, an early maturity not inferior to that of the Leicesters, the flesh finely grained, and the wool of the most useful quality.

The average weight of the fleece of a South-Down hill sheep was stated by Mr. Luccock, in 1800, to be two pounds; it has now increased to three pounds. The fleece of the lowland sheep, that used to be three pounds, is now three and a half, or even four pounds. This is the natural consequence of the different mode of feeding, and the larger size of the animal. The length of the staple in the hill sheep rarely exceeded two inches, and was oftener not more than one and a half inches: it is now more than two inches, and in some of the lowland sheep it has reached to four inches. The number of hill sheep had rather decreased since 1800, and those in the lowlands had materially so; but now that South-Down wool is once more obtaining a remunerating price, the flocks are becoming larger than they were. The color of the wool differs materially, according to the color of the soil. The shortest and the finest wool is produced on the chalky soil, where the sheep have to travel far for their food; but there is a hardness and a brittleness about this wool which was always seriously objected to.

The greater comparative bulk of the fiber, and paucity of serrations, will account for the harshness and want of felting property, which have been considered as defects in this wool. The brittleness of the pile is, perhaps, to be attributed chiefly to the soil. The clothiers were always careful not to use too much of it in the making of their finest cloths. When most in repute, the South-Down was principally devoted to the manufacture of servants' and army clothing, or it was sparingly mixed with other wools for finer cloth. Now, however, when it is materially increased in length, and become a combing wool, and applicable to so many more purposes than it was before—now that it enters into the composition of flannels, baizes, and worsted goods of almost every description—its fineness and its felting, compared with some of the other short wools, render it a truly valuable article. The South-Down sheepmaster justly repudiates the charge of its deterioration—*it has only changed its character*—it has become a good combing wool, instead of an inferior carding one; it has become more extensively useful, and therefore more valuable; and the time is not far distant when the sheepowner will be convinced that it is his interest to make the South-Down wool even longer and heavier than it now is. A sheep possessing such qualities must of course be valuable in upland districts, in the vicinity of markets. They have been introduced into every part of the British dominions, and imported into various other countries. The Emperor of Russia paid Mr. Ellman three hundred guineas for two rams, and in 1800, "a ram belonging to the Duke of Bedford, was let for one season at eighty guineas, two others at forty guineas each, and four more at twenty-eight guineas each." These valuable sheep were introduced into the United States a few years since by Col. J. H. Powell, of Philadelphia, and a small number were imported in 1834. The last were from the flock of Mr. Ellman, at a cost of $60 a head. Several other importations have since taken place.

The Cotswold Sheep.—The Cotswold is a large breed of sheep, with a long and abundant fleece, and the ewes are very prolific and good nurses. Formerly they were bred only on the hills, and fatted in the valleys of the Severn and the Thames; but with the inclosure of the Cotswold Hills and the improvement of their cultivation they have been reared and fatted in the same district. They have been extensively crossed with the Leicester sheep, by which their size and fleece have been somewhat diminished, but their carcasses considerably improved, and their maturity rendered earlier. The wethers are now sometimes fattened at fourteen months old, when they weigh from fifteen to twenty-four pounds per quarter, and at two years old increase to twenty or thirty pounds. The wool is strong, mellow, and of good color, though rather coarse, six to eight inches in length, and from seven to eight pounds per fleece. The superior hardihood of the improved Cotswold over the Leicester, and their adaptation to common treatment, together with the prolific nature of the ewes and their abundance of milk, have rendered them in many places rivals of the New Leicester, and have obtained for them, of late years, more attention to their selection and general treatment, under which management still farther improvement appears very probable. They have also been used in crossing other breeds, and, as before noticed, have been mixed with the Hampshire Downs. It is, indeed, the improved Cotswold that, under the term new or improved Oxfordshire sheep, are so frequently the successful candidates for prizes offered for the best long-wooled sheep at some of the principal agricultural meetings or shows in the kingdom. The quality of the mutton is considered superior to that of the Leicester, the tallow being less abundant, with a larger development of muscle or flesh. We may, therefore, regard this breed as one of established reputation, and extending itself throughout every district of the country.

The Cheviots.—This breed has greatly extended itself throughout the mountains of Scotland, and in many instances supplanted the black-faced breed; but the change, though in many cases advantageous, has in some instances been otherwise, the latter being somewhat hardier, and more capable of subsisting on heathy pasturage. They are, however, a hardy race, well suited for their native pastures, bearing with comparative impunity the storms of winter, and thriving well on poor keep. Though less hardy than the black-faced sheep of Scotland, they are more profitable as respects their feeding, making more flesh on an equal quantity of food, and making it quicker. They have white faces and legs, open countenances, lively eyes, without horns. The ears are large, and somewhat singular, and there is much space between the ears and eyes. The carcass is long; the back straight; the shoulders rather light; the ribs circular; and the quarters good. The legs are small in the bone and covered with wool, as well as the body, with the exception of the face. The Cheviot wether is fit for the butcher at three years old, and averages from twelve to eighteen pounds per quarter—the mutton being of a good quality, though inferior to the South-Down, and of less flavor than the black-faced. The Cheviot, though a mountain breed, is quiet and docile, and easily managed. The wool is coarse and inferior to that of the South-Down.

COMPARATIVE VALUE OF THE DIFFERENT BREEDS OF SHEEP.—On this subject we quote the careful, and to us convincing reasoning of H. S. Randall, Esq., contained in "The Sheep Husbandry:"

"In instituting a comparison between breeds of sheep for wool-growing purposes, I will, in the outset, lay down the obviously incontrovertible proposition that the question is not what variety will shear the heaviest or even the most valuable fleeces, irrespective of the cost of production. Cost of feed and care, and every other expense, must be deducted, to fairly test the profits of an animal. If a large sheep consume twice as much food as a small one, and give but once and a half as much wool, it is obviously more profitable, other things being equal, to keep two of the smallest sheep. The true question then is, with the same expense in other particulars, from what breed will the verdure of an acre of land produce the greatest value of wool?

"Let us first proceed to ascertain the comparative amount of food consumed by the several breeds. There are no satisfactory experiments which show that breed, in itself considered, has any particular influence on the quantity of food consumed. It is found, with all varieties, that the consumption is in proportion to the live weight of the (grown) animal. Of course, this rule is not invariable in its individual application, but its general soundness has been satisfactorily established. Spooner states that grown sheep take up three and one-third per cent. of their weight in what is equivalent to dry hay per day, to keep in store condition. Veit places the consumption at two and a half per cent. My experience would incline me to place it about midway between the two. But whatever the precise amount of the consumption, if it is proportioned to the weight, it follows that if an acre is capable of sustaining three Merinos weighing one hundred pounds each, it will sustain but two Leicesters weighing one hundred and fifty pounds each, and two and two-fifths South-Downs, weighing one hundred and twenty-five pounds each. Merinos of this weight often shear five pounds of fleece, taking flocks through. The herbage of an acre, then, would give fifteen pounds of Merino wool, and but twelve pounds of Leicester, and but nine three-fifths pounds of South-Down (estimating the latter as high as four pounds to the fleece)! Even the finest and lightest fleeced sheep ordinarily known as Merinos, average about four pounds to the fleece, so that the feed of an acre would produce as much of the highest quality of wool sold under the name of Merino, as it would of New Leicester, and more than it would of South-Down! The former would be worth from fifty to one hundred per cent. more per pound than either of the latter! Nor does this indicate all the actual difference, as I have, in the preceding estimate, placed the live-weight of the English breeds low, and that of the Merino high. The live-weight of the four pound fine fleeced Merino does not exceed ninety pounds. It ranges from eighty to ninety pounds, so that three hundred pounds of live-weight would give a still greater product of wool to the acre.* I consider it perfectly safe to say that the herbage of an acre will uniformly give

---

* It is understood that all of these live-weights refer to ewes in fair ordinary, or what is called store condition.

nearly double the value of Merino, that it will of any of the English long or middle wools.

"The important question now remains, What are the other relative expenses of these breeds ? I speak from experience when I say that the Leicester* is in no respect a hardier sheep than the Merino—indeed, it is my firm conviction that it is less hardy, under the most favorable circumstances. It is more subject to colds, and I think its constitution breaks up more readily under disease. The lambs are more liable to perish from exposure to cold, when newly dropped. Under unfavorable circumstances—herded in large flocks, pinched for feed, or subjected to long journeys—its capacity to endure, and its ability to rally from the effects of such drawbacks, do not compare with those of the Merino. The high-bred South-Down, though considerably less hardy than the unimproved parent stock, is still fairly entitled to the appellation of a hardy animal. In this respect, I consider it just about on a par with the Merino. I do not think, however, it will bear as hard stocking as the latter, without a rapid diminution in size and quality. If the peculiar merits of the animal are to be taken into account in determining the expenses—and I think they should be—the superior fecundity of the South-Down is a point in its favor, as well for a wool-producing as a mutton sheep. The South-Down ewe not only frequently yeans twin lambs, as do both the Merino and Leicester, but she possesses, unlike the latter, nursing properties to do justice by them. But this advantage is fully counterbalanced by the superior longevity of the Merino. All the English mutton breeds begin to rapidly deteriorate in amount of wool, capacity to fatten, and in general vigor, at about five years old, and their early maturity is no offset to this, in a sheep kept for wool-growing purposes. This early decay would require earlier and more rapid slaughter or sale than would always be economically convenient, or even possible, in a region situated in all respects like the South. It is well, on properly stocked farms, to slaughter or turn off the Merino wether at four or five years old, to make room for the breeding stock; but he will not particularly deteriorate, and he will richly pay the way with his fleece, for several years longer. Breeding ewes are rarely turned off before eight, and are frequently kept until ten years old, at which period they exhibit no greater marks of age than do the Down and Leicester at five or six. I have known instances of Merino ewes breeding uniformly until fifteen years old! The improved Cotswold is said to be hardier than the Leicester; but I have said less of this variety, throughout this entire letter, as from their great size† and the consequent amount of food consumed by them, and the other necessary incidents connected with the breeding of so large animals, the idea of their being introduced as a wool-growing sheep anywhere, and particularly on lands grassed like those of the South, is, in my judgment, utterly preposterous. There is one advantage which all the coarse races of

---

* I speak of full-blooded Leicesters. Some of its crosses are much hardier than the pure bred sheep.

† I saw two at the late New York State Fair, at Saratoga, which weighed over three hundred pounds each.

sheep have over the Merino. Either because their hoofs do not grow long and turn under from the sides, as do those of the Merino, and thus hold dirt and filth in constant contact with the foot, the coarse races are less subject to the visitations of the hoof-ail, and, when contracted, it spreads with less violence and malignity among them. Taking all the circumstances connected with the peculiar management of each race, and all the incidents, exigencies, and risks of the husbandry of each fairly into account, I am fully convinced that the expenses, other than those of feed, are not smaller *per capita*, or even in the number required to stock an acre, in either of the English breeds above referred to, than in the Merino. Nor should I be disposed to concede even equality, in these respects, to either of those English breeds, excepting the South-Down.

"You write me, sir, that many of the South Carolina planters are under the impression that coarse wools will be most profitably grown by them, *first*, because there is a greater deficit in the supply, and they are better protected from foreign competition; and, *secondly*, because they furnish the raw material for so great a portion of the woolens consumed in the South. Each of these premises is true—but are the conclusions legitimate? Notwithstanding the greater deficit and the better protection, do the coarse wools bear as high a price as the fine ones? If not, they are not as profitable, for I have already shown that *it costs no more to raise a pound of coarse than a pound of fine wool*. Nay, a pound of *medium* Merino wool can be raised *more cheaply* than a pound of the South-Down, Leicester, or Cotswold! This I consider clearly established.

"Grant that the South requires a much greater proportion of coarse than of fine wool, for her own consumption. If a man needing iron for his own consumption wrought a mine to obtain it, in which he should happen to find gold equally accessible and plentiful, would it be economical in him to neglect the more precious metal because *he* wanted *to use* the iron? or should he dig the gold, obtain the iron by exchange, and pocket the difference in value? Would it be economical to grow a surplus wool, wool for market, worth from twenty-five to thirty cents per pound, when it costs no more per pound to grow that worth from forty to forty-five cents? And even for the home want, for the uses of the plantation—for slave-cloths, etc.—*fine wool is worth more per pound than coarse for actual wear or use!* Is this proposition new and incredible to you? I challenge the fullest investigation of its truth, through the testimony of those familiar with the subject, or through the direct ordeal of experiment. It is true that a piece of fine broadcloth is not so strong, nor will it wear like a Chelmsford plain of treble thickness. The threads of the former are spun to extreme fineness to economize the costly raw material. To give it that finish which is demanded by fashion—to give it its beautiful nap—these threads are still further reduced by "gigging" and "shearing." But spin fine wool into yarn as coarse as that used in Chelmsfords, and manufacture it in the same way, and it would make a far stronger and more durable cloth. The reasons are obvious. Merino wool is decidedly stronger than the English coarse long and middle wools—or any other coarse wools—in proportion to its diameter or bulk. It felts far better, and there is therefore a greater cohesion between the different fibers of the same thread, and between the different threads. It is also more pliable and elastic, and consequently less subject to "breaking" and abrasion.

"Unless the views I have advanced are singularly erroneous, it will be seen that, for wool-growing purposes the Merino possesses a marked and decided superiority over the best breeds and families of coarse-wooled sheep. As a mutton sheep, it is inferior to some of those breeds, but not so much so as is generally supposed. If required to consume the *fat and lean together*, many who have never tasted Merino mutton, and, who have an unfavorable impression of it, would, I suspect, find it more palatable than the luscious and over-fat New Leicester. The mutton of the cross between the Merino and "Native" sheep would certainly be preferred to the Leicester, by any body but an English laborer used to the latter. It is short-grained, tender, and of good flavor. The same is true of the crosses with English varieties. These will be hereafter, more particularly alluded to. Grade Merino wethers (half-bloods) are favorites with the Northern drover and butcher. They are of good size—extraordinarily heavy for their apparent bulk*—make good mutton—tallow well—and their pelts, from the greater weight of wool on them, command an extra price. They would, in my opinion, furnish a mutton every way suitable for plantation consumption, and one which would be well accepted in the Southern markets.

"In speaking of the Merino in this connection, I have in all cases, unless it is distinctly specified to the contrary, had no reference to the Saxons—though they are, as it is well known, pure-blooded descendents of the former."

GENERAL MANAGEMENT OF SHEEP.—Their Summer Management.—The change in spring from dry to succulent food, produces in all sheep a certain degree of scouring, and which, if precautions have not been taken to guard against it, soils the wool on the hinder parts of sheep, and its subsequent removal becomes difficult. To prevent this, every sheep before being turned to grass in the spring should have that portion of the wool which is liable thus to become soiled carefully clipped away, including that which immediately surrounds the roots of the tail, covers the thighs, the bags of the ewes, etc. This operation saves the wool, which would otherwise be lost, the animal much subsequent suffering, and the owner much labor. *Tagging* sheep, therefore, should not be neglected by any careful shepherd.

It is scarcely necessary to say that the fields in which sheep are to run should be carefully cleaned of every variety of *burr*, by which so much wool is annually lost in this country, being so matted together with them as to be of little comparative value.

Care in the handling of Sheep should always be exercised. They never should be lifted by the wool, for, as the skin adheres so loosely, it is often separated from the body by the act of lifting, and blood has often been found settled beneath the parts thus improperly handled. The legs or necks of sheep are the parts by which only they should be seized;

---

* On account of the shortness of their wool, compared with the coarse breeds.

and for catching sheep the shepherd's crook is a very simple yet very convenient instrument. It is thus described by Mr. Stephens:

"The hind-leg is hooked in from behind the sheep, and it fills up the narrow part beyond while passing along it until it reaches the loop, when the animal is caught by the hock, and when secured, its foot easily slips through the loop. Some caution is required in using the crook, for, should the sheep give a sudden start forward to get away the moment it feels the crook, the leg will be drawn forcibly through the narrow part, and strike the bone with such violence against the bend of the loop as to cause the animal considerable pain, and even occasion lameness for some days. On first embracing the leg, the crook should be drawn quickly toward you, so as to bring the bend of the loop against the leg as high up as the hock, before the sheep has time even to break off, and being secure, its struggles will cease the moment your hand seizes the leg."

The Season of Lambing requires the shepherd's especial care. From the first to the middle of May is the best season. In the general course of breeding, however, it is desirable that the lambs should not fall until the cold of winter is over, and the pasture begins to afford some food for the little ones. This is peculiarly important in bleak and exposed situations. Thousands of lambs die every year from the cold to which they are exposed as soon as they are yeaned. On the other hand, there may be some inconvenience and danger if the period of lambing is too late. Hot weather is as fatal to the mother as cold is to the offspring. It frequently induces a dangerous state of fever; and both the mother and the lamb may be then injured by the luxuriance of the grass. If the lamb falls late in the season, it will be longer ere the ewe can be got ready for the butcher, and the ground cleared for other stock; and, in addition to this, the early lambs become larger and stronger, and better able to resist the cold of the succeeding winter. The yeaning time will, therefore, be regulated by the situation of the farm, the nature of the pasture, and the demand from the neighboring markets.

The duration of pregnancy is about five months, or one hundred and fifty-two days, with comparatively little deviation. As the end of this period approaches—and it should not be a matter of memory merely, but of record—the flock should receive the grazier's watchful attention. The ewes should be separated from the rest of the flock, and in an inclosure, in which is a shed or covert from the storms, which are so common, and so destructive to young lambs.

Care of the Lambs.—It is the duty, and would be the interest, of the farmer to attend to the comfort of his ewes and lambs at this period; the lambing-field should always be a sheltered one, and there should be a temporary or a permanent retreat for the weakly and the cold. The first care of the shepherd therefore should be to examine the newly-dropped lamb. If they are chilled and scarcely able to stand, he should give them a little of the milk, which he carries always with him, and then take them to some shelter, or place them in a basket well lined with straw. Nursing of this kind for an hour or two will usually give the animal sufficient strength to rejoin its mother.

Nature has given to the sheep, as well as to other animals, an instinctive and strong affection for its young; an affection which strengthens in proportion to the necessities of the parent and the offspring. The more inhospitable the land is on which they feed, the greater their kindness and attention to their little ones; nevertheless, it will occasionally happen that the young ewe, in the pain and confusion and fright of her first parturition, abandons her lamb. Some, when the udder begins to fill, will search it out again, and with unerring precision—others, severed from their offspring before they had become acquainted with its form and scent, are eagerly searching for it all over the field with incessant and piteous bleatings. Some will be hanging over their dead offspring, while a few, strangely forgetting that they are mothers, are grazing unconcernedly with the rest of the flock.

There is another circumstance that adds to the confusion. Some of the ewes have had twins; they have inadvertently strayed from one of them, or stupidly or capriciously have driven it from them; and the neglected one is wandering about, vainly seeking its parent, or angrily repulsed by it.

The first thing a lamber has to do is to remedy as well as he can this confusion. He first seeks out for those that have twins, and that have recognized both of their lambs, and, taking his little marking-bottle and marking-iron, he puts a particular mark on each of the twins, by which he may again recognize them, and on each pair he puts a different mark. If they are just dropped, and are weak, he leaves them for a while; but if they are able to travel a little, he drives them into a pound, or into a corner of the field with the other twins, or he at once removes them into another and somewhat better pasture, which he had destined for the twins.

He then looks for the lambs that have apparently been abandoned by the mother, and if, as he takes one of them up, it bleats, he will presently find whether there is any responsive call or gaze of recognition. If the mother eagerly calls to it, he has but to put it down, and she will speedily rejoin and suckle it, if it is strong enough to raise itself from the ground for this purpose. If the animal is almost exhausted, he must catch the ewe, and assist her to suckle the lamb. It will soon revive, and her love for it will revive too. If she merely gives a careless look of recognition, he must suckle the lamb from his bottle of ewe's milk, and leave it for a while; perhaps her affection will return when her udder begins to be distended with milk; if not, he must drive her with others into a fold, and, suffering the rest to escape, try every means to induce her to let the little one suck. There may be considerable difficulty in this at first, but, by the exercise of some patience and tact, he will generally succeed. After all, however, he will probably have some lambs upon his hands for whom he cannot find a mother, or whose own mother will not suckle them.

On the other hand, he will find some ewes who are gazing mournfully on their dead lambs. With some contrivance, he will generally find in these foster-mothers for his abandoned ones. He ties a piece of cord round the hind feet of a dead lamb, and the mother, if she has not been unnecessarily frightened by the lamber, or his dog, will follow for miles with her nose close to the lamb, and may be led wherever the shepherd chooses.

The Substitute Lamb.—The bereaved and affectionate ewe is induced to follow the remains of her little one to the lambing pound, or to some other convenient place. A lamb that has lost, or been abandoned by its mother is then selected. The head, tail, and legs of the dead lamb are cut off; an incision is made along the belly, and the body turned out, and this skin is then drawn over the substitute lamb. The body of the dead lamb is opened, the liver taken out, and the head and legs of the living lamb, and what other parts the skin does not cover, are smeared with blood. In the darkness of the night, and after the skin has been warmed on it, so as to give something of the smell of her own progeny, the substitute is put to the bereaved ewe. In the majority of cases the fraud is altogether successful, and the impostor is at once received, and fondled, and suckled. This being effected, the shepherd hastens to remove the false clothing; the lamb is returned to her, and "whether it is from joy at this apparent reanimation of her young one, or because a little doubt remains on her mind, which she would fain dispel, cannot be decided; but for a number of days she shows more fondness by bleating over and caressing this one, than she did formerly over the one that was really her own."

If she does not take to it at first, she must be compelled to suckle it, and confined so that she shall not be able to kick or otherwise hurt it. In two or three days she will generally own it, and then they may be turned together into the field without any apprehension or trouble.

Care, however, should be taken that the age of the substitute lamb and that of the true one should correspond as much as possible. If a lamb lately dropped is put to a ewe whose young one would have been a week or two old, the milk will be too strong, and a purging will be set up, which, probably, no medicine can arrest. On the other hand, if the substitute lamb is a week or two old, and the foster-mother had lost hers in the act of yeaning, her milk will be injurious on account of that purgative quality by which the intestines of the newly-dropped lamb are first excited to action. Sometimes the foster-lamb, frightened or exhausted, will not readily take the teat, however disposed the ewe may be to adopt and feed it. Care should be taken to ascertain whether this is the case, and, if necessary, the lamb should be held while a little of the milk is pressed into its mouth from the udder. This will rarely need to be repeated, for instinct will teach it where to seek and how to obtain its proper nutriment.

After-Care of the Lambs.—In the course of a little more than a week, the great majority of the ewes will have produced their young, and the lamber will have more leisure for those cases which particularly require his attention. The twin field will particularly demand his care. He will seldom enter it on the morning without finding some degree of confusion. Some of the lambs will have strayed from or been abandoned by their mothers; and these twin-mothers are sometimes not a little capricious, and especially when, not having sufficient milk for the two, they are teased and worried by the incessant sucking of the twins. In such case they will, in the most determined and furious manner, repulse one of them. Amid the intermingling of the offspring of the different ewes he will find the advantage of having marked the respective twins, and thus, although not always without regularly drawing them off, he will be enabled properly to separate the respective families: he will relieve the weakly ewe from a burden which she cannot support; and, on the other hand, he will reconcile the deserted little one to its unnatural parent, or find a better mother for it. The ewes with their single lambs will not, after a few days, require any extraordinary degree of trouble, but those with twins must be carefully watched, at least until the lambs begin in good earnest to graze. Many a lamb has been stinted in its growth, and irreparably injured, by the insufficient supply of milk which the ewe with twins can afford.

Twins.—This is the proper place to speak of the desirableness of having many twins. Most breeders are partial to them, on account of the apparent rapid increase of the flock, or the additional quantity of lambs that can be prepared for the market. The question depends entirely on the quantity of land which the farmer holds, and the nature of the soil. If he has pasture enough, and good enough, twins are highly desirable; for at only the usual expense before the yeaning time, the number of his lambs is doubled, and, the pasture being good and the lambs well fed, there will be very little difference in health, condition, or value, between the twins and the single lamb.

The ewe seldom has twins at her first yeaning; and it is fortunate that she has not; for it is seldom that she has any great supply of milk then, and, consequently, the mother and her offspring would equally suffer. The twins are generally obtained from ewes that are three, four, or five years old. The disposition to twinning is undoubtedly hereditary. There are certain rams that have the credit of being twin-getters, and that faculty usually descends to their offspring; but this is oftener the case with regard to the ewe, agreeably to the old couplet:

"Ewes, yearly by twinning, rich masters do make:
The lambs of such twinners for breeders go take."

The female of every species of animal has far more to do with this unusual multiplication of the offspring than has the male; and the farmer who wishes rapidly to increase his stock through the medium of twins, may go some way toward the accomplishment of his object by placing his ewes on somewhat better pasture, or allowing them a few turnips when November approaches.

The Management of the Lambs.—We return once more to the lambs, now a few days old. The old ewes will prove assiduous and faithful nurses, but the young ones will occasionally wander from their lambs, and prove inattentive to or have not recognized their bleatings. Such mothers must be separated from the flock, and folded and confined with their young ones, until they appear to be disposed faithfully to do their duty. Some lambs refuse the attention of the mother, and lie weak or sullen, and droop away and die. Some of the mother's milk should be frequently introduced into the mouth; and, if that has not the desired effect, a foster-mother must, if possible, be found; or the little churl must be brought up by the hand. There will, generally speaking, be very little difficulty about this. If it is at first fed with warm sheep's or cow's milk, by means of a spoon, until it is old enough to suck out of a sucking-bottle, it will soon begin to bleat for its food, and greedily meet the bottle the moment that it is presented to it.

The *cuckoo* lambs will require the particular attention of the shepherd. They are those that are dropped later than the others, when the cuckoo is just making his appearance, and after whom they are named. They are usually the progeny of very young or very old mothers, who were not impregnated so soon as the others, and who generally are not so strong and so hardy as the rest of the flock. Care must be taken that they have sufficient, yet not too nutritive food; and that the diseases to which weakly lambs are subject are promptly attended to.

Some ewes will permit other lambs beside their own to suck them, and then there will possibly be one or more greedy lambs, who will wander about from ewe to ewe, robbing the rightful owner of the greater part of his share. He and his mother must be removed to another pasture, where he will soon learn to satisfy his voracious appetite with the grass. As the shepherd takes his round he should inspect every lamb. If one does not appear to thrive, he should endeavor to ascertain the cause. Has the mother any or sufficient milk? Are the teats free from disease? He should either supply the deficient nutriment, or provide a foster-mother. Does the milk disagree with the lamb? Is there any or considerable purging? The calves and sheep's cordial must be immediately resorted to; and, if necessary, nursing, or separation from the mother. In two or three weeks, and often considerably sooner, the lambs will begin to nibble a little grass. Is it too luxuriant for them, or has it been eaten down close by the ewes, and is the owner thinking of providing a fresh pasture? Let him beware! There is no situation in which the old advice of not making "more haste and good speed" should be more carefully heeded than in this. If one paramount cause of disease, and fatal disease to lambs, were selected, it would be a sudden change from bare to luxuriant pasture. It often sets up a degree of inflammatory fever, which no depletion will extinguish, or a diarrhœa which no astringent can check.

The technical term which the shepherd applies to the lamb diseased from this cause is *gall-lamb*. The liver seems to be the principal seat of inflammation, and a great quantity of bile or *gall* is found in the duodenum and small intestines; a portion of it has frequently regurgitated into the abomasum or fourth stomach, and some has entered into the circulation, and tinged the skin and flesh of a yellow color. It is a disease which very speedily runs its course; occasionally carrying off its victims in a little more than twelve hours, and seldom lasting more than three days. Immediate bleeding in the early stage, and afterward Epsom salts, with a small portion of ginger, will afford the only chance of a cure. The poor animal is often condemned and slaughtered at once—that is barbarous work.

Castration.—There is a great difference of opinion as to the time when the tup-lambs that are not intended to be kept for breeding should be castrated. Some recommend the performance of this operation as early as three days after the birth. Mr. Parkinson says that "he has several times cut a lamb the very day that it was lambed, when strong and healthy, and that he never knew one do ill from the operation." The proper period depends a great deal on the weather, and on the stoutness of the lamb, and varies from the third or fourth to the fourteenth or twenty-first day, the weather being cool or even cold, and somewhat moist. It would be highly improper and dangerous to select a day unusually warm for the season of the year. The absence of unusual warmth, and the health of the animal to be operated upon, are the circumstances which should have most influence in determining the time.

There are two methods of performing the operation. The lamb being well secured, the operator grasps the scrotum or bag, and forces the testicles down to the bottom of it. He then cuts a slit across the bottom of the bag, in a direction from behind forward, through the substance of the bag, and large enough to admit of the escape of the testicles. They immediately protrude through the incision, being forced down by the pressure above. The operator then seizes one of them, and draws it so far out of the bag that a portion of the cord is seen ; and then, if he is one of the old school, he seizes the cord between his teeth and gnaws through it. This is a very filthy practice, and inflicts some unnecessary pain. The testicle being thus separated, the cord retracts into the scrotum, and is no more seen. The other testicle is brought out and operated upon in a similar manner. Very little bleeding ensues—and the young one may be returned to its mother. An improvement on this operation, and which any one except of the lowest grade would adopt, is to use a blunt knife instead of the teeth. By the sawing action which such a knife renders necessary, the artery is even more completely torn than with the teeth; and yet without so much bruising of the part, and probability of ensuing inflammation. It is by the laceration, instead of the simple division of the cord, that after-bleeding is prevented.

Another way of performing the operation is to push the testicles up toward the belly, and then, grasping the scrotum, to cut off a sufficient portion of the bottom of the bag to admit of the escape of the testicles when they are again let down. They are, one after the other, pushed out, and taken off in the manner already directed. The wound is considerably longer in healing when the base of the bag is thus cut away, and the animal consequently suffers more pain. The first is the preferable way, if the incision is made sufficiently long to prevent its closure for two or three days, thus leaving an outlet for the escape of the blood and pus from the inside of the bag.

There is usually little or no danger attending the operation, and yet occasionally it is strangely fatal. In a whole flock not a single lamb will sometimes be lost; but at other times the deaths will be fearfully numerous, the same person having operated on both occasions. Much, probably, depended on some peculiar state of the atmosphere, of the actual nature of which we know nothing at all; and more probably might be connected with a disposition to inflammation in the patient proceeding from too high feeding, or from a debilitated state of the frame, and which had not been observed or properly estimated.

When fatal disease occurs after castration it usually assumes the form of tetanus, or locked-jaw. The village operator pretends to tell when this will or will not supervene. The usual struggles of the animal, or the usual expressions of pain, he does not regard; but when, as he is gnawing the cord asunder with his teeth, he feels a deep and universal shudder of the animal, he says at once that that lamb will die. He is often right about this, and when he is, it can be easily explained. By the fearful torture he has inflicted, he has caused a shock of the whole of the nervous system, from which the poor sufferer can never perfectly recover.

Occasionally, when the lamb that was selected as a breeder does not turn out well, it is necessary, in order to fatten him and to make his flesh salable, to castrate him. There are various ways of performing this operation on the young or fully adult sheep. Some proceed precisely as with the horse. An incision is made into the scrotum; the testicle is forced out, the iron clamps are put on the cord, which is then divided between the clamp and the testicle, and the cautery is had recourse to in order to sear the part and prevent bleeding. This operation usually succeeds well, but it is not every operator on sheep that has the clamps or the firing-iron.

The preferable way of operating is, to tie a waxed cord as tightly as possible round the scrotum above, and quite clear of the testicles. The circulation will here also be completely stopped, and usually in two or three days the scrotum and the testicles will drop off. Accidents have occurred, but which are attributable to the operator; he has included a portion of the testicle in the ligature, and thus laid the foundation for very great and fatal inflammation; or he has used too large a cord, and which could not be drawn sufficiently tight; or the knot has slackened and the ligature has pressed sufficiently to produce excessive inflammation and torture, but not completely to cut off the supply of blood. Care being taken in the application of the cord to the exact part, and the tightening of the ligature, the animal seems scarcely to suffer any pain; indeed, the nerves are evidently deadened by the compression of the cord, and no accident occurs.

Docking.—There is much variety of opinion among sheep-masters as to the time when this operation should be performed. Some, like Mr. Parkinson, think that it should be done within a very few days after the birth; the ewes on the first, second, or third day, and the male lambs when they are castrated. The author of the "Complete Grazier" would defer it until the lambs are three or four months old. This must depend on the state of the weather, and the health of the animals. No one should dock his lambs when the weather is very cold, because the bushy tails of the animals afford a great deal of warmth. On this account, in particularly exposed situations, it is deferred until the warm weather sets thoroughly in, and by some, and particularly with their ewes, not practiced at all. The tail certainly affords both protection and warmth to the udder, and likewise defense against the dreadful annoyance of the flies in hot weather; but, on the other hand, it permits the accumulation of a great deal of filth, and, if the lamb or the sheep should labor under diarrhœa, and the shepherd should be somewhat negligent, the tail may cling to the haunches, and that so closely as to form an almost insuperable obstruction to the passage of the fæces. It likewise can scarcely be denied that the removal of the tail very much improves the beauty of the animal, by the fullness and width which it seems to impart to the haunches.

The operation is a very simple one. An assistant holds the lamb with its back pressing against his belly, and thus presenting the haunches to the operator, who, with a knife, or a strong pair of scissors or forceps, cuts it off at the second or third joint from the rump. A few ashes are then sprinkled on the wound—common flour would do as well, in order to form a coagulum over the part and stop the bleeding. It is seldom that the bleeding will continue long; but, if the lamb should appear to be growing weak in consequence of the loss of blood, a piece of twine tied tightly round the tail, immediately above the dock, will at once arrest the hemorrhage; the twine, however, must be removed twelve hours afterward, otherwise some sloughing will ensue, and care must likewise be taken that the incision is made precisely in the joint, otherwise the wound will not heal until the portion of bone between the dock and the joint above has sloughed away.

Spaying.—A few weeks after castrating the spaying of the rejected ewe-lambs will succeed, an operation which will materially contribute to their increase of growth and disposition to fatten. It is singular that this practice should be almost confined to Great Britain and to Italy, for there can be no manner of doubt of the advantage of it. Daubenton, however, in his "Instructions to Shepherds," gives a useful account of the manner in which it is best performed.

At the age of six weeks, the ovaries are grown sufficiently large to be easily felt, and that is the time usually selected for the spaying, being immediately after the first formal examination of the flock. The lamb is laid on her right side, near the edge of a table, with her head hanging down by the side of the table; an assistant stretches out the left hind-leg of the animal, and holds it in that situation, with his left hand grasping the shank; and in default of a second assistant, he also holds the two fore-legs, and the other hind-leg with his right hand. The lamb being thus disposed, the operator, tightening the skin of the part, makes an incision of an inch and a half in length, midway between the top of the haunch and the navel, and penetrating through the skin; another incision divides the muscles of the belly and the peritoneum. A careful operator will, perhaps, make three incisions, the first through the skin, the second through the abdominal muscles, and the third through the peritoneum. He then introduces his forefinger into the abdominal cavity, in search of the left ovary, which is immediately underneath the incision; and, having found it, he draws it gently out. The two broad ligaments, and the womb and the right ovary, protrude at the same time. The operator cuts off the two ovaries, and returns the womb and its dependencies; he then closes the womb by means of two or three stitches through the skin, carefully avoiding the abdominal muscles below; and, last of all, he rubs a little oil on the wound, or he does nothing more, but releases his patient.

The lamb very probably will be unwilling, and perhaps will altogether refuse to suck or to graze during the first day, but on the following days he will feed as usual. In ten or twelve days the wound will have perfectly healed, and the threads may be cut and taken away. The only thing to be feared is inflammation of the peritoneum, which was divided in the operation; but this rarely occurs, and, on the whole, there is not so much danger in the spaying of the ewe-lamb, as in the castration of the tup.

Sheep-Washing.—This is best done in vats constructed for the purpose, and where large flocks are to be washed, the expense and care are well repaid. These vats are to be so located as that the water can be conveniently let into them by spouts, and a small stream, dammed up, will answer the purpose. The vat should be about three and a half feet deep, and of such size as to admit two spouts to flow into it at the upper end, at which two men can wash, while two others can be so employed at its lower end and over which the water flows. The vat should have a gate to draw off the water as often as fifty sheep are washed. A platform should connect the top of the vat with the sheep-yards, of which there should be two, one to contain the unwashed, and the other the washed sheep; lambs, on account of their liability to accident, should not be driven with the flocks to the washing-pens. The operation of washing is facilitated, and rendered much easier by heavy rains immediately preceding it, and which have thoroughly saturated the fleeces. Sheep are more generally injured while washing than in any other way, and hence, at this time the utmost care is needed in handling them.

Sheep-Shearing.—This, in fair weather, may be done in from five to six days after washing. The operation should always be carefully done, and by those only who are experts in the art. This is equally dictated by the true interest of the wool-grower—as by no others can the fleeces be kept and put into proper merchantable shape—and by humanity, as clumsy shearers clip and mutilate, and otherwise often shamefully abuse the uncomplaining sheep.

Every thing being arranged, a shearer seizes a sheep, and sets it on its rump, and keeps it in this position by resting the back against his own legs. He removes all straws, thorns burs, etc., that may have adhered to the wool. While thus held, the wool is removed from the head and neck as far as the shoulders, and also from the belly, the scrotum, and the edge of the thighs. The head of the animal is then bent down sidewise, and the shearer, placing a leg on each side of the neck of the sheep, pushes out the opposite ribs by pressing his knees gently against the ribs that are nearest to him. He next shears the wool from the far side with his left hand, from the belly to the middle of the back, and as far down as the loins. The sheep is now turned, and the right hand is employed to shear the wool from the near side. The sheep is then laid flat on its side, and kept down by the shearer with his face toward the rump of the sheep, resting his right knee on the ground in front of the neck, and his right toe being brought to the ground a little behind and below the poll; the head and neck of the sheep are thus confined by his right leg, while he uses his right hand to shear the wool from the hind quarter. In this way the clips of the shears will appear in concentric rings round the body of the sheep. The dirty portions of wool about the tail are then removed by the shears and kept by themselves; the outside of the fleece is folded inward, beginning at the sides, and narrowing the whole fleece into a strip about two feet wide. This strip is then rolled firmly up from the tail end toward the neck.

WINTER MANAGEMENT.—Sheds, to shield sheep from cold rains, sleety storms, and from piercing winds, are at once dictated by humanity and true economy; but every arrangement for thus housing sheep should provide for free ventilation, as the health of none other of our domestic animals is so entirely dependent on pure air as that of the sheep.

Winter Food.—Hay is the staple winter food of sheep in the United States. Morrell, in *The American Shepherd*, states the daily quantity, in cold weather, which a sheep weighing one hundred pounds will consume, at two and a half pounds; and if every one hundred sheep should have a daily supply of from six to eight quarts of corn, or its equivalent in cut potatoes or other roots, the increased thrift of the flock, and their larger return of better wool, would richly repay the extra cost and trouble.

When the foddering season arrives, the flock should be arranged into as many apartments as circumstances will admit. A small one of the oldest and poorest should have the preference as to accommodation and attention, and to it should be added occasionally such as may from any cause be declining; and such as have sufficiently recruited in this department may give place to them. This flock should be fed with grain and roots, as their condition and circumstances may require, through the winter. So with the lambs, a flock of the smallest and poorest should be managed in the same way.

When assorting and arranging for the winter, the feet and toes of all should be cut and trimmed to a proper shape; and the ends of the horns of all such as incline to branch out should be sawed off. The whole should have free access to water and salt through the winter, and should be fed with hay, in boxes, plentifully and regularly three times a day; under cover when cold or stormy, outside when fair, if more convenient; and in rain-storms should be confined under cover. It is convenient to let them have free access to straw, in boxes, at all times, and occasionally a change of the different kinds of hay and corn fodder. The sheds should at all times be well littered.

The proper time to put bucks with ewes is the first of December, which is generally after they are arranged for winter, and that arrangement should be made with reference to that object, allowing but one buck to a flock; and no wether should be allowed in a flock with a buck, as his presence creates suspicion, and disturbs the quiet so necessary to the desired performance. The number of ewes to a buck will vary according to his age, vigor, and keeping; a full-grown, vigorous one, well fed, will serve one hundred; the same, without extra feed, will serve fifty; young ones from thirty to forty. The bucks should be painted on the breast to make apparent their progress. Four weeks is sufficient time for them to remain with the ewes; after that, there is danger of the ewes being injured by their ungallant and knock-down propensities.

MEDICINES EMPLOYED IN THE TREATMENT OF SHEEP.—Simple medicines ought to be in the possession of the farmer for instant use in cases

of emergency; but the administration of the more potent drugs ought
to be intrusted to the veterinary surgeon, by whom alone all important
operations ought to be performed. Read's enema and stomach-pump
adapted to sheep, should be in every breeder's hands, and kept constantly ready for use. In the treatment of many of the diseases of
sheep, the advantages of purgative or of sedative injections are too much
overlooked. Aperient injections may consist of a handful of common
salt, or an ounce or two ounces of Epsom salts, with a wineglassful of
linseed oil, mixed in a pint of water or thin gruel. Sedative injections,
in cases of diarrhœa and dysentery, may consist of a pint of gruel or
starch, with three or four grains of powdered opium, or fifty drops of
laudanum.

Aperients.—In administering medicines to the sheep, the fluid should
be allowed to trickle slowly and gently down the gullet or œsophagus,
as we have already urged in the case of the ox, and for the same reasons—the structure of the stomach being in both animals on the same
plan. To give medicine in a hurried manner, so as to force the animal
to gulp it, is to defeat the very object intended; it will force the pillars
of the œsophagean canal, enter the insensible paunch, and there continue inert. It may here be as well to observe, that the doses of medicine for sheep, in general are about one-sixth in quantity of what are
usually given to cattle. Young lambs require only a third, or half the
quantity of medicine constituting a dose for an adult sheep.

The following medicines are the most valuable aperients:

Common Salt (Chloride of Sodium or Muriate of Soda).—Salt is a tonic
in moderate doses, and of great benefit in the rot. It should always
be accessible to the flock. In doses of one or two ounces, dissolved in
four or six ounces of gruel, it forms an excellent aperient.

Epsom Salts (Sulphate of Magnesia).—An excellent purgative, and that
which is most commonly employed. Its dose ranges from half an ounce
to two or three ounces. The repetition of small doses at intervals of six
hours will keep up the action of the first full dose when desirable; or
sulphur may be employed for this purpose.

Sulphur.—Sulphur, besides its value in cutaneous affections, is very
useful as an aperient, especially for keeping up the action of the bowels
after the operation of salts. Dose, from one to two ounces. Sulphur is
the base of every ointment for the cure of mange.

Aloes.—This drug is not only very uncertain in its operation in sheep,
but has often proved fatal, by inducing direct inflammation. It is invaluable as a horse medicine, but should never be administered to the
sheep.

Linseed Oil.—Linseed oil is occasionally used as a purgative; it is
given in doses of two or three ounces.

ALTERATIVES AND SPECIFIC MEDICINES.—These are medicines which
exert a peculiar influence on certain organs, altering their diseased action,
or stimulating their respective secretions. Some act more especially on
the liver, others on the glandular system, and some on the skin; while
one exerts a peculiar action on the muscular fibers of the uterus. A
knowledge of the effects of these medicines has been gained by experience; but we know nothing of their *modus operandi*.

Calomel (Submuriate or Protochloride of Mercury).—Calomel is seldom used in the treatment of the diseases of the sheep. In cases of rot, two or three grains of calomel, mixed with a grain and a half of opium, have been found beneficial; this dose may be repeated every day, or every other day, for several times, its effects being watched.

Sulphate of Mercury or Æthiops Mineral.—As an alterative medicine, useful in cutaneous disorders, Æthiops mineral has long enjoyed great reputation; it is usually combined with nitre and sulphur in the following proportions for a daily dose: Æthiops mineral, one scruple; nitre, two scruples; sulphur, four scruples.

Iodine.—Iodine is useful both as an external application, and also as a medicine taken internally, in cases of glandular affections and indurated swellings of the udder. Its most convenient form is the iodide of potassium. An excellent ointment is composed of one part of the iodide and seven of lard.

Iodide of potassium is strongly recommended in consumption, when tubercles have formed on the lungs. The dose is two grains, gradually increased to four or six, given morning and evening, in a little gruel.

Ergot of Rye.—In cases of lingering parturition, when the powers of the uterus are exhausted, ergot of rye is found very useful. It exerts a peculiar action on that organ, and arouses its dormant energy. It should be employed with caution. The dose is a scruple or half a drachm, repeated at intervals of half an hour, if necessary. An infusion of ergot of rye is used by lambers and shepherds, conjoined with a cordial composed of equal parts of brandy and spirits of nitre (*sp. æther nitrici*).

SEDATIVE AND FEBRIFUGE MEDICINES.—These are medicines calculated to allay fever and moderate the action of the arterial system. Among these, nitre or nitrate of potass, tartar emetic, or tartrate of antimony, and the powder of digitalis, *i. e.*, of the dried leaves of the foxglove, are chiefly in requisition. Opium, or tincture of opium (laudanum), is in a certain sense a sedative; indeed, in some diseases, its use in allaying irritation cannot be overrated.

Nitrate of Potass.—Nitre is used as a febrifuge with good effect, but generally in combination with other medicines. Its dose is from half a drachm to a drachm.

Tartrate of Antimony.—The effect of this medicine, in lowering the action of the heart and arterial system, is very decided. Hence in many inflammatory diseases it is of great importance. It is given to the sheep in doses of five or six grains.

Digitalis.—The powdered leaves of the dried foxglove have been long esteemed for their decided effects upon the action of the heart. They not only reduce the force of the pulse, but often render it intermittent. Digitalis, in combination with nitre and tartar-emetic or tartrate of antimony, forms an efficient fever medicine in cases of high inflammation, as pleurisy and similar diseases.

The following formula for sheep has been used with success: digitalis powder, five grains; tartrate of antimony, five grains; nitrate of potass, half a drachm; water, three or four ounces. Mix. To be given twice a day.

ANTISPASMODICS.—The great antispasmodic, the great allayer of pain, and of irritation of the alimentary canal, whether in cases of diarrhœa or dysentery, is opium.

Opium.—The dose of this all-potent medicine (when judiciously administered) is two or three grains. Combined with oil, it has been given in dysentery with the best effects. Mr. D. Sayer found in certain cases of dysentery the following prescription of great service:—linseed oil, two ounces; powdered opium, two grains. Mix in an infusion of linseed.

On the following day, .ie gave twice in the twenty-four hours this mixture:—powdered opium, two grains; powdered ginger, and powdered gentian, of each, half a drachm. Mix in linseed tea.

Afterward this draught was repeated once a day, with the addition of half an ounce of linseed oil. This was continued for four days, when the sheep recovered. In cordial and astringent medicines, opium is an essential ingredient, and it may also be combined with aperients.

Laudanum, or Tincture of Opium.—Tincture of opium possesses the same properties as the powder of opium, but is perhaps quicker in its effects. The dose for sheep is from twenty to sixty drops.

TONICS.—It is often necessary in cases of debility, when acute diseases have been subdued, to restore or invigorate the system by tonics. Of these, gentian is the best, and, indeed, will supersede every other.

Gentian.—Powdered gentian root may be given as a tonic in doses of from half a drachm to two drachms, in combination with a scruple or half a drachm of powdered ginger in gruel or water, or in a little ale.

Cordials.—Cordials, or stimulating drenches, are not so often given to sheep as to horned cattle. The best of these cordials are ginger, caraway-seeds, essence of peppermint, and carbonate of ammonia.

Ginger.—The dose of this root in powder is from a scruple to a drachm. It is generally mixed with aperient medicines, and aids their operation.

Caraway-seeds.—Bruised caraway-seeds are useful as a cordial, though inferior to ginger. Dose, half a drachm or a drachm.

Oil or Essence of Peppermint.—Peppermint water—that is, water in which the oil of peppermint is diffused—is a good vehicle for tonic and astringent medicines. It is never given alone.

Carbonate (Subcarbonate) of Ammonia.—In cases of repletion of the stomach by a mass of undigested curd (to which lambs are subject), carbonate of ammonia may prove very useful, both from its stimulating and its antacid properties. A drench, composed of a scruple of carbonate of ammonia, two drachms of carbonate (sesqui-carbonate) of soda, half an ounce of Epsom salts, and a scruple of ginger, in warm water, may be given every six hours. A solution of potash in lime-water is recommended in these cases. We here give the directions for making and administering this solution:—take a lump of quick-lime, of the size of an egg, and pour on it, in a convenient vessel, as much water as will slake it. This being done, then pour upon it one pint of boiling water; stir the whole up, and cover close. While this is allowed to stand for some time, take an eight-ounce bottle, and put into it two ounces of subcarbonate of potass, and fill up the bottle with the lime-water already made: pouring it off rather turbid than in a state of purity. Cork this up, and label it, "Solution of potass in lime-water." Of this "solution," a teaspoonful or two should be added to some warm water, together with half an ounce of salts and a scruple of ginger, and given every six hours, till good effects result. We can hardly call this a cordial medicine. Its effects, setting aside the Epsom salts, are chemical, and the same observation applies to chloride of lime given internally in cases of hoove. Its dose in the shop is about half a drachm. As a disinfectant and cleanser of foul ulcers, a solution of chloride of lime, applied externally, and used freely as a wash, is invaluable.

Chloride of Lime.—For its properties, see above. A solution of chloride of lime, for washing infected sheep-cotes, ulcers, etc., may be made with half an ounce of powder dissolved in a gallon of water. Taken inter⸺ly in hoove, it acts chemically as a cordial by secondary effects.

Carbonate (sesquicarbonate) of Soda.—Carbonate of soda is an antacid, and useful as a component in cordial draughts, where the correction of acidity in the stomach is desirable. Dose, about a drachm.

ASTRINGENTS.—Astringents are medicines which act upon the mucous membrane of the alimentary canal, and check diarrhœa. They consist of lime, or chalk, opium, catechu, etc., and are always combined with cordials. Of lime, or rather chalk, little need be said; it is given in doses of either half a drachm or a drachm. Of opium, we have already spoken.

Catechu.—This is an extract from a tree of the acacia tribe, and is very valuable. Dose, a scruple.

The following is a useful astringent cordial for sheep and calves:— prepared chalk, one ounce; powdered catechu, half an ounce; powdered ginger, two drachms; powdered opium, half a drachm; mucilage or gum-water, thick, two ounces; peppermint-water, six ounces. Mix. Dose: two tablespoonfuls twice a day.

Alum.—Alum is not often used in the treatment of sheep. Its dose is ten or twenty grains, according to age. The "sheep's cordial" renders it unnecessary.

EXTERNAL APPLICATIONS.—Setons are seldom used in the treatment of the diseases of sheep, and the wool prevents blisters from taking effect. With respect to chloride of lime, as we have noticed it under the head of cordials, we need not repeat our observations relative to its value as a disinfectant and cleaner of foul, sloughing fetid ulcers, when properly diluted with water (half an ounce to the gallon). The following external applications require a brief notice:—

Poultices.—Those of linseed-meal are best; it is often advantageous to mix with them a little chloride of lime, especially if they be applied to foul ulcerations. In accelerating suppuration, a little turpentine is a useful addition.

Stimulants.—Turpentine, camphorated oil, and hartshorn, form a good embrocation, useful in strains and chronic rheumatism. To two ounces of camphorated oil may be added an ounce of turpentine, and half an ounce, or even an ounce of hartshorn.

Ointments and Lotions, etc.—*Mercurial Ointment*, when rubbed down with five or seven parts of lard, forms a safe and almost certain cure for the scab. *White Lead* is often sprink⸺ ⸺er the part struck by the fly, in order to destroy the maggots bu⸺ the skin. It is superseded by the spirit of tar, or by the coarsest kind of fish-oil. *Corrosive Sublimate.*—A dangerous remedy, often employed in solution as a wash for scab. Washes, whether of a solution of arsenic, infusion of tobacco, or of hellebore, are equally objectionable. They are superseded by the diluted mercurial ointment. *Spirit of Tar.*—A useful application in foot-rot, and very serviceable when freely applied to parts that have been struck by the fly; it not only kills the maggots, but prevents the attacks of the insects, which are repelled by its odor. *Turpentine.*—Useful as a stimulant in ointments and embrocations. It may be mixed with linseed-meal poultices, in order to hasten the suppuration of sluggish tumors, and is a serviceable application to wounds of long standing which require a stimulus.

Dressings.—Among the dressings for wounds, tincture of aloes, tincture of myrrh, and tincture of benzoin, or Friar's Balsam, are chiefly in request. Tar mixed with lard is a useful dressing in foot-rot.

Caustics.—At the head of caustics stands nitrate of silver, or lunar caustic. It is to the free use of this that the veterinary surgeon will trust in probing the wounds in cattle caused by the bite of a rabid dog. It is very useful in removing warts and cutaneous excrescences. Other caustics, however, are in requisition. In cases of foot-rot, hydrochloric acid, or a solution of bichloride of mercury, is recommended by Mr. Read, as an application to the part affected. Butyr of antimony, or chloride of antimony, is a very useful and convenient caustic. It has been employed in foot-rot, and acts well where a superficial effect only is required. It does not produce any deep corrosion; hence in indolent ulcers, in foot-rot, and in the removal of fungous excrescences, it is of important service. Verdigris, or acetate of copper, mixed with sugar of lead, finely powdered, sprinkled on sluggish ulcers, sometimes acts with good effect. Blue vitriol, or sulphate of copper finely powdered, is frequently employed as an escharotic, in order to produce superficial sloughing. A saturated solution is recommended by some veterinarians as an application of great benefit in cases of foot-rot.

Fomentations.—The great benefit resulting from fomentations arises from the warmth of the water. In cases of inflammation of the udder or garget, fomentations are indispensable. Many have an idea that the good effects of fomenting depend on the herbs which, as is generally the case, are boiled in the water; but this is an error. Poppy-heads or a little laudanum in the water may be advantageous, from the known properties of opium in allaying pain. Slight fomenting is useless—it should be long kept up; but this is seldom done, for it requires no small degree of quiet patience.

Plaisters or Charges.—Plaisters, or charges, are in frequent demand. They are useful in cases of sprain or local debility, or as a covering and protection to sores or wounds, or the basal part of fractured horns. They form a good defense in case of travel-worn feet, and in various ways are serviceable. They consist of a mixture of pitch, wax, resin, lard, etc., in different proportions, thickly spread upon coarse cloth or leather. Tar, spread upon cloth, forms an excellent plaister, especially where the main object is to exclude the air. Their application requires some little dexterity of manipulation. Tar is a useful dressing in foot-rot, when the healing process has commenced. A plaister composed of a pound of pitch and two drachms of bees' wax, melted together, and spread while warm on soft leather or linen cloth, is applied with much advantage to the heads of sheep which are sore from the ravages of the maggots of the fly. Some, as a precautionary measure, smear the head in May with this composition, and scatter a little wool over it; others sew the plaister round the head.

Salving, or Smearing.—The practice of salving or anointing the skin of the sheep, after shearing, with some unctuous preparation, is not universal. It is, however, the ordinary custom in Scotland, and is, indeed, essential to the health and comfort of sheep exposed to bleak winds in open mountain districts, to heavy mists, and drenching and long-continued rains.

The primary object of smearing is the protection of the skin from wet and cold; and next, to promote the growth of the wool and improve its character. Besides these objects, there are others not unimportant—the prevention of the attacks of insects, the destruction of such as might adhere to the skin, and the healthy action of the skin or the removal of cutaneous affections, for which tar is very efficient. Tar, mixed with butter, in order to counteract its tenacity, is the ordinary salving material; and vast quantities of damaged butter are yearly sent to the grazing districts of Scotland, for the use of the sheep farmers. One serious disadvantage, however, attends the application of tar—it indelibly stains the wool; hence it cannot be used for white goods, and what is more, it will not take the finer and more brilliant dyes. Wool thus tar-stained is termed *laid* wool, and sells at a lower ratio than *white* or *unsalved* wool. Yet in exposed situations the necessity of salving is felt, and various unguents have been tried. Instead of butter whale-oil, as an adjunct to tar, has been used, and is recommended by the Hon. W. J. Napier in his "Treatise on Practical Store-farming;" but the tinge of the tar is not obviated by this admixture. Mr. Hogg says: "Of late, several compositions have been purposely and extensively tried, in which the spirit of tar has been substituted for tar itself. This has, in some cases, been complained of as too irritating; and there is no doubt that a too free use of spirit of tar is injurious and even fatal. Some of the salves, while they prove to be perfectly well adapted to flocks that are clean, have been found ineffectual either in curing or warding off the scab—a disease which the common salve made of tar and grease seems effectually to resist. When a flock is perfectly clean, olive-oil has been found to be the best substance for softening the fleece, and warding off rain and snow. For clean sheep, 'Taylor's salve' is also suitable, though some English staplers have condemned it. If a tar-salve were made so as to be free from the impurities of the tar, it might probably answer every purpose. The ordinary proportion of one cwt. of grease to a barrel of tar, might be increased to one and a half cwt.; and when melted together, the impurities of the tar might be suffered to subside and be separated. In this way the tar might not leave a stain upon the wool when scoured. Olive oil seems to impregnate the wool, or to adhere to it more firmly than any other kind of greasy matter; and it has been successfully employed by Mr. Sellar, of Morvich, a first-rate store-farmer in Sutherland."

Mr. Hogg recommends the following unguent to be rubbed over every part of the animal, after shearing, with a curry brush :—train or seal oil, four gallons; tar, half a gallon; oil of turpentine, one pint. Mix. Mr. John Graham, of Newbigging, perceiving the disadvantage of tar as a wool-stainer, and yet desirous of smearing his sheep, used the following preparation, in which the tar was omitted, yellow resin being used in its stead :—butter, eighteen pounds; hogs' lard, eighteen pounds; resin, twelve pounds; Gallipoli oil, one gallon. Mix. This quantity he found sufficient for fifty or fifty-five sheep, and the cost of smearing each sheep was about four and a half pence. He found this wool, when washed, equally valuable with the *white* wool : and it sold for a considerably higher price than the *laid* or tarred wool. The importance of smearing or salving is undeniable. The use of a small quantity of some oleaginous or greasy application immediately after shearing is now generally acknowledged. The protection which it affords to the almost denuded skin—its substitution for the natural yolk, which is not in its full quantity immediately secreted—and the softness which it will impart to the wool—are circumstances well deserving attention.

THE
DOMESTIC HOG:

TO

BREED, FEED, CUT UP, AND CURE.

THE DOMESTIC HOG:

TO BREED, FEED, CUT UP, AND CURE.

VARIETIES OF THE HOG.—There exist only THREE actual varieties of the domestic hog—the Berkshire, Chinese, and Highland, or Irish; all other breeds, described as separate varieties, are only offshoots from one or the other of these three main stocks.

The True Berkshire Pig is black, or black and white, short-legged, full and round in the loins, rather fine in the hair, the ears small and erect, and the snout not lengthy. This description of animal forms a striking contrast with the long-sided, convex-backed, lob-eared, long-legged, and shambling brute which was common in many parts of Great Britain, and almost universal in Ireland, thirty or forty years ago, and which still, without any improvement in form, is the general description of the pig throughout France and most of Germany.

In giving preference, however, to the Berkshire breed, it is not to be understood that we consider them handsome in a positive sense, or perfect models of good breeding and propriety in their habits and manners. No dumpy animal, with its belly near the ground, with four short crutches for legs, hair by no means silky, a little curled tail, and small, sunk eyes, peering into every hole and corner and never looking upward to the glorious firmament, can be called an absolute beauty; but, compared with other races of swine, the Berkshire are handsome; and, as to their habits and manners, they have no little merit; for, considering the natural dispositions of the hog family, and the contemptuous manner in which they are spoken of and treated everywhere (except in certain parts of Ireland, and the Highlands of Scotland, where pigs are privileged orders, and experience such respect as to be permitted, and even invited, to occupy the same room with their masters, by day and night, in consideration of their paying the house-rent, and supplying the means of purchasing salt, candles, and soap), the Berkshire race have unquestionable merit, and appear to respect the decencies of life. Their females have never been known to commit infanticide, as some other domesticated tribes of swine undoubtedly do, from what we consider a depraved taste; nor have either sex of this tribe been ever justly accused, or even suspected, of that cannibal propensity which has led individuals of certain other tribes of the great hog family to seize upon the tender babe in the cradle and devour it, "marrow, bones, and all!" They (the Berkshires) are so docile and gentle that a little boy or girl may drive them to and from the pasture-field or the common without having their authority disputed; and, when ranging about in the happy consciousness of liberty, though they may sometimes poke their noses where their interference is not desired, they do not perpetrate half the mischief to the turf which other classes of swine are prone to commit. They seem disposed to content themselves with the grass on the surface of the soil, without uprooting it in search of delicacies that may lie

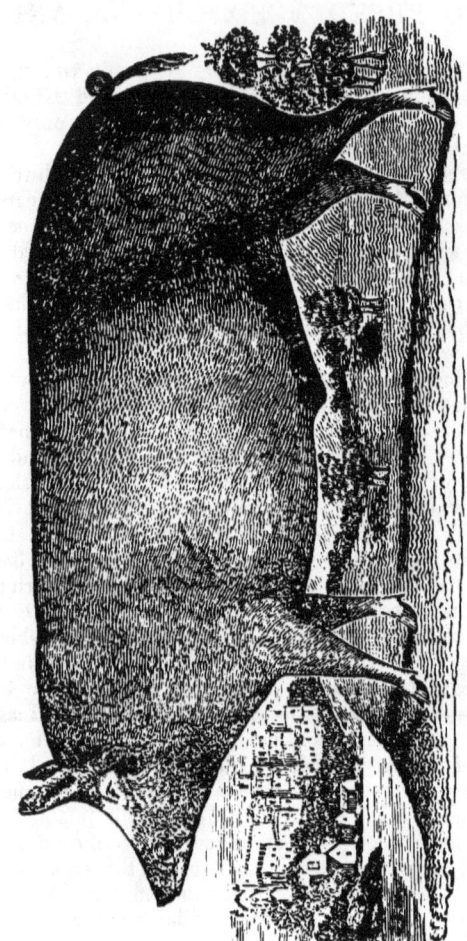

THE BERKSHIRE HOG.

beneath, as do some of the long-snouted tribes which plow the earth up in furrows. They seem to make it a point of honor, too, to become fat as fast as possible, in return for the food they have received, in order that thus they may be in condition to pay "the pound of flesh" which is "in the bond" against them. They never fret at trifles, and thereby impede their digestion, and lose health and flesh. They never sulk and refuse their meals; nor do they complain of the quality or scantiness of their food, like some of those ungrateful children of certain parochial asylums, who have fancied that they could have eaten a little more porridge if it had been ladled into the platter for them. I do not indeed say that the Berkshire swine are singularly neat in their personal habits, quite ceremonious at their meals, and free from the vice of gluttony, nor that they will not scramble and fight for the best bits, and exhibit their unseemly manifestations of self-indulgence; nor that they would be shocked at snoring aloud, even in the presence of royalty or nobility, if the inclination to fall asleep should seize them; but, then, it is to be remembered that every individual of the hog species would do the same things. In short, their peculiarities decidedly tend to the benefit of mankind; and, after all, their failings, like many of our own, proceed entirely from the stomach.

The capacious paunch of the pig, and its great powers of digestion, are what render it so beneficial to us; yet, though in a domesticated state, a pig will eat almost any sort of animal or vegetable food—raw or cooked, fresh or putrid—he is, when at large, as naturalists inform us, the most delicate and discriminating of all quadrupeds. If free to select his vegetable food, he will reject a greater number of plants than the cow, the sheep, the horse, the ass, or the goat will refuse; so nice does he become when luxuries surround him, that in the orchards of peach-trees of North America, where the hog has delicious food, it is observed by Goldsmith, " that it will reject the food that has lain but a few hours on the ground, and continue on the watch whole hours together for a fresh windfall."

The Hampshire.—This breed is often confounded with the Berkshire, but its body is longer and its sides flatter; the head is long and the snout sharp. The color is usually dark-spotted, but sometimes altogether black, and sometimes white. This variety has been produced by crosses with the Berkshire, Suffolk, Chinese and Leicester breeds.

The Yorkshire.—This is the product of a cross with the true Berkshire. They are quick feeders and fatten rapidly.

Herefordshire.—Generally supposed to be the result of a cross with the Shropshire; it is shorter in the body, carries less bone than that breed, has also a lighter head, a smaller ear, a less rugged coat, and is altogether a far more valuable animal. This hog is little inferior to the Berkshire breed.

Gloucestershire.—The Gloucestershire hogs are somewhat less in size than the preceding, and are also shorter in the body, rounder both in frame and limb, and altogether more compactly built. They make good store hogs, and their pork is of prime quality.

Northamptonshire, of a light color, of a handsome shape, light and small ear, little bone, deep-sided and compactly formed. This is a profitable porker and a good store, for he feeds well, fattens rapidly, and arrives early at maturity.

Norfolk.—A small breed, with pricked erect ears; color various, but generally white. The white-colored are said to be the best; when striated or blue, the breed is inferior, at least generally so. This is a short-bodied and compactly formed pig, and is an excellent porker. There is another Norfolk variety, of larger size, spotted, but inferior in point of delicacy.

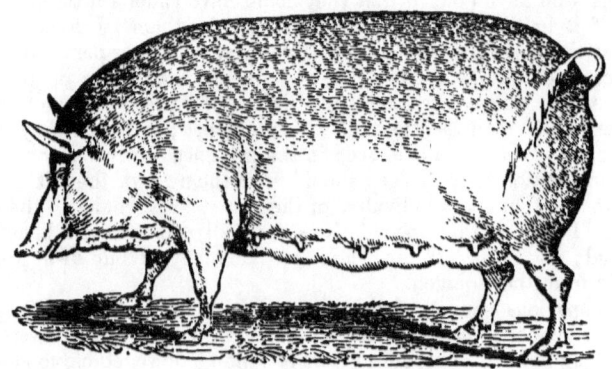

THE LEICESTER SOW.

Leicestershire.—An ancient breeding district, and once greatly celebrated for its swine. The old stock were large-sized, deep in the carcass, and flat-sided; the head and ear light and handsome, color light-spotted.

Lincolnshire.—The old Lincolnshire breed was light-colored, or even white, with, in most specimens, a curly and woolly coat, of medium size; good feeders, came early to maturity, and fattened easily.

The Essex was in former days a very capital hog, but degenerated, and, of course, lost the esteem of breeders. A recollection of the former good qualities which characterized the breed induced some persons of practical judgment to revive it, which was accordingly done; and now this hog, under the name of

The Improved Essex, ranks, most justly, very high amongst the British breeds of swine. The improvement of this hog is due to a cross with the Neapolitan; and this cross has been so frequently resorted to, that the pure Essex breed and the Neapolitan are so much alike that it is not every cursory observer who is capable of discriminating between them. It is probable, also, that the Chinese was employed in the regeneration. The Essex hog is up-eared; has a long, sharp head; also a long and level carcass, with small bone; color most frequently black, or black and white. This is a quicker feeder, but he requires a greater proportion of food than the weight he attains to justifies; besides which, he is troublesome in a fold, being restless and discontented. The pure breed should be almost bare of hair, and black in color.

There is another improved Essex breed called the *Essex half-blacks*, resembling that which we have described, in color, said to be descended from the Berkshire. This breed was originally introduced by Lord Western, and obtained much celebrity. They are black and white, short-haired, fine-skinned, with smaller heads and ears than the Berkshire, feathered with inside hair, a distinctive mark of both; have short, snubby noses, very fine bone, broad and deep in the belly, full in the hind quarters, and light in the bone and offal. They feed remarkably quick, grow fast, and are of an excellent quality of meat. The sows are good breeders, and bring litters of from eight to twelve, but they have the character of being bad nurses.

The Sussex.—Black and white in color, but not spotted, that is to say, these colors are distributed in very large patches; one-half—say, for instance, the fore-part of the body—white, and the hinder end black; sometimes both ends black, and the middle white, or the reverse. These are no way remarkable; they seldom feed over one hundred and sixty pounds.

The Chinese Hog.—This breed is of small size, yet its early maturity, the rapidity with which it takes on flesh, and the smallness of its bones, have induced many breeders to use it in crosses with larger and coarser breeds—one of the best results of which has been the production of a very popular variety, denominated *The Suffolk*.

The Suffolk Hog.—The Suffolk breed of swine are a small, delicate pig, thin-skinned, soft-haired, small, pricked ear; color white. They are in character like the Chinese, fed almost as easily, are more hardy, and possess more lean meat.

HOW TO CHOOSE A PIG.—How to choose a pig?—that is the question. To rely on the terms Berkshire, Essex, Suffolk, Improved Yorkshire, Improved Bedfordshire, etc., as guarantees of first-rate qualities, would be folly. In all countries, even those the most renowned for their breeds, there are both good and bad; and even of the best breeds some are inferior to the others, and ought to be rejected as unfit for becoming the parents of a lineage.

The following, the result of large and recent experience, are well worthy the attention of breeders:

Fertility.—The strain from which the farmer or breeder selects ought to be noted for fertility. In a breeding sow this quality is essential, and it is one which is inherited. The same observation applies to other domestic animals. But, besides this, she should be a careful mother, and with a sufficient number of dugs for a family of twelve at a single litter. A young untried sow will generally display in her instincts those which have predominated in the race from which she has descended; and the number of teats can be counted. Both boar and sow should be sound, healthy, and in fair but not over-fat condition; and the former should be from a stock in which fertility is a characteristic.

Form.—It may be that the farmer has a breed which he wishes to perpetuate; it is highly improved, and he sees no reason for immediate crossing. But, on the other hand, he may have an excellent breed with certain defects—as too long in the limb, or too heavy in the bone. Here, we should say, the sire to be chosen, whether of a pure or cross breed, should exhibit the opposite qualities, even to an extreme, and be, withal, ne of a strain noted for early and rapid fattening.

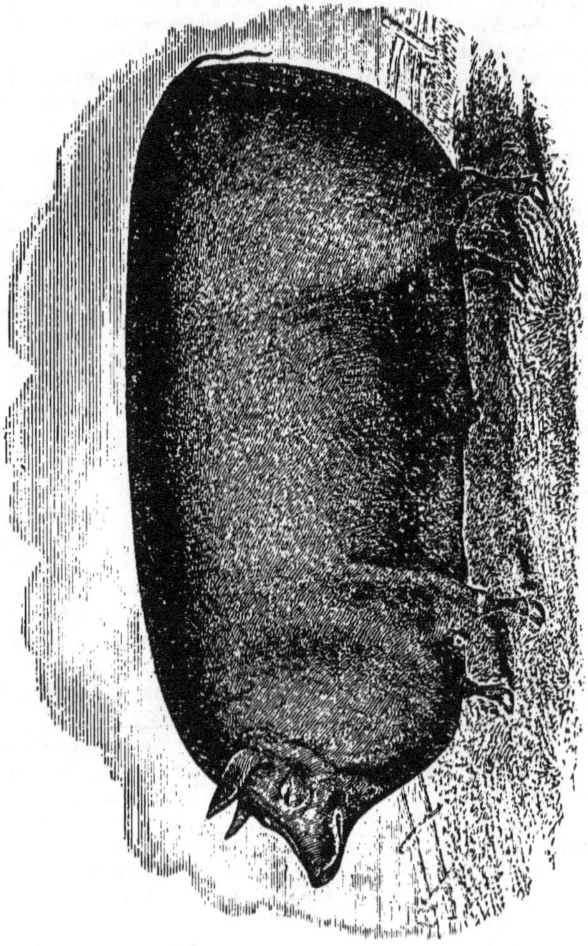

IMPROVED CHINESE HOG.

But what is meant by *form*, as applied to the pig? A development of those points connected with the profit of the owner. In these points high or low blood is demonstrated. The head should be small, high at the forehead, short and sharp in the snout, with eyes animated and lively, and thin, sharp, upright ears; the jowl, or cheek, should be deep and full; the neck should be thick and deep, arch gracefully from the back of the head, and merge gradually into a broad breast; the shoulders should be set well apart at the clavicular joint; the body should be deep, round, well-barreled, with an ample chest, broad loins, and a straight, flat, broad back; the tail should be slender; the hams should be round, full, and well developed; the limbs fine-boned, with clean, small joints; and with small, compact hoofs, set closely together, with a straight bearing upon the ground. If in perfect health, the animal will be lively, animated, hold up his head, and move freely and nimbly. We do not speak of fat hogs, for they are necessarily sluggish and unwieldy; nor yet of pregnant sows; but of young store-hogs, or of young stock selected for breeding.

The *skin* should be soft and thin, of a bright pink color; the neck short, the chest wide (which denotes strength of constitution); broad, straight back, short head, and fine snout, slightly curved upward; and in the large breed there is often a pretty prominent swelling on the snout, between the nasal and frontal bones. The legs and hoofs should be small. The sows should have at least twelve teats. In purchasing a prize animal, whether boar or sow, see that it can walk well. A lump of fat bacon may do to kill at Christmas, but will be of very little use until reduced to breed from; and in the journey and reduction you may lose your pig and your money.

For breeding sucking-pigs there is nothing better than the large English breed (they are prolific, and good mothers), crossed with a white Chinese boar. No other breed will raise sucking-pigs to the same size as this cross; they also form excellent porkers, speedily attaining from forty-eight to fifty-six pounds; but if required to be much larger, it will be found to pay better to treat them as stores, letting them graze, or run as "shocks" in the field after harvest, or rooting on the manure-heap, until they are ten or twelve months old, and then put them up to fatten. Still they are not so profitable as the improved Essex, and do not make such fine bacon as the improved Berkshire.

The improved Essex, if well fed from the first, arrives very early at maturity, as to its frame or bony structure, and is the best for making hobbledehoys of porkers from eighteen to twenty pounds' weight.

The improved Berkshire may be considered the more useful to a farmer who desires a sort useful in every stage of its growth. The Berkshire sow will suckle ten or a dozen sucking-pigs—even more if assisted by artificial means—and is very superior for large ham and bacon. The small breed is very well for porkers, but not for the flitch. A good little animal is good; but we want a good and big animal. The improved Berkshire realizes this desideratum, as it realizes the highest price from the bacon-curers, cuts up wide over the back, well interlarded with fat and lean. It is also more free from lameness than any other breed.

In a word, in choosing a pig, you must consider your climate, your means of feeding, and your market; whether you want sucking-pigs or hobbledehoy pork.

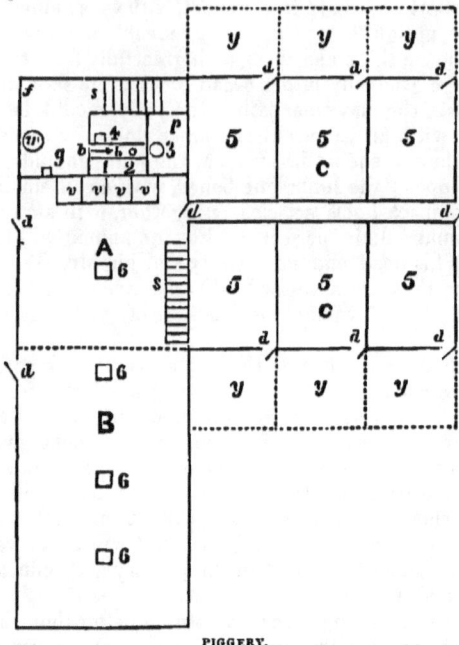

PIGGERY.

A, A, front; C, C, rear for pens; 5, 5, pens with alley between; r, r, r, v, vats on level with pens; 1, safety valve; 2, steam pipe; 3, supply barrel to boiler; b, boiler; f, furnace; p, platform partly over boiler; 4, chimney; t, drain; w, water-cistern; g, door to cellar; s, s, stairs; d, d, doors; 6, 6, scuttles to cellar; y, y, yards to pens.

HOUSES AND PIGGERIES.—An inclosure proportionate to the number of swine which you intend to keep, and, if possible, so managed as to admit of extending the accommodation, will be found the best for general purposes. It should be provided with a range of sheds, so situated as to be thoroughly sheltered from wind and weather, paved at the bottom, and sloping outward. Relative to the paramount necessity of cleanliness and dryness, let both inclosure and sheds possess the means of being kept so. In order to keep the sheds, which are designed as sleeping places, in a dry and clean state, an inclination outward is necessary; a shallow drain should run along the whole of their extent, in order to receive whatever wet flows down the inclined plane of the sleeping huts; and provision should also be made for this drain to carry off all offensive matters beyond the precincts of the piggery.

The ground on which the piggery is established should likewise be divided into two parts, by a drain, which should run through it; and toward this drain each section should slope. This the main drain should be carried beyond the fold, and fall into a large tank or pit formed for that purpose. The object in view is to keep the pig-fold and sties in a clean and dry state, and to preserve the valuable *liquid manure*, which comes from the animals you keep. Some will probably inquire whether it would not be better to suffer the moisture to soak into earth or straw, or other substances on the *floor* of the inclosure, and then to clear all away periodically, than to drain off the liquid into a tank. By drawing off the liquid you add to the cleanliness of your swine, and, in proportion, to their health and capacity for thriving; and the collection of the liquid manure into tanks is less troublesome than the removal of substances saturated with it, from the floor of the fold, would be.

The sties should be so constructed as to admit of being closed up altogether, when desirable; for swine, even the hardiest breeds, are susceptible of cold, and if exposed to it in severe weather, it will materially retard their fattening. The sty should be kept constantly supplied with clean straw. The refuse carted into the tank will, in the form of manure, more than repay the value of the straw. It has been asserted that swine do not thrive if kept upon the same ground in considerable numbers; this assertion rests on a want of ventilation and cleanliness.

As to *troughs*, let them be of stone or cast metal;—if of wood, the pigs will soon gnaw them to pieces;—and let them be *kept clean*. Before each feeding, a pail of water should be dashed into the trough; this may be deemed troublesome, but it will confer *golden returns* on those who attend to it.

A supply of fresh water is essential to the well-being of swine, and should be freely furnished. Some recommend this to be effected by having a stream brought through the piggery; and undoubtedly, when this can be managed, it answers better than any thing else. Swine are dirty feeders, and dirty drinkers, usually plunging their fore-feet into the trough or pail, and thus polluting with mud and dirt whatever may be given to them. One of the advantages, therefore, derivable from the stream of running water being brought through the fold is, its being, by its running, kept constantly clean and wholesome. If, therefore, you are unable to procure this advantage, it will be desirable to present water in vessels of a size to receive but one head at a time, and of such height as to render it impossible or difficult for the drinker to get his feet into it. The water should be renewed twice daily.

We have hitherto been describing a piggery capable of containing a large number; a greater proportional profit will be realized by keeping a number of swine than a few. It may happen, however, that want of capital, or of inclination to embark in swine-feeding as an actual speculation, may induce many to prefer keeping a small number of pigs, or even perhaps one or two, in which case such accommodations as have been described would be more than superfluous. In this case, a single hut, well sheltered from wind and rain, and built with a due regard to comfort, to warmth, with a little court surrounding its door, in which the tenant may feed, obey the calls of nature, and disport himself, or bask in the sunshine, will be found to answer; a small stone trough, or a wooden one, bound with iron, to preserve it from being gnawed to pieces, will complete the necessary furniture. The trough will serve alternately for food and drink. Even, however, when this limited accommodation is resorted to, a strict attention to cleanliness is no less necessary than when operations are carried on on the most extensive scale. Both the floor of the hut and that of the little court should be paved, and should incline outward; along the lowest side should be a drain, with a sufficient declination, and so contrived as to communicate with your dung-tank. The farther the manure-heap, or tank, from the dwelling, the better : vegetable matter, in progress of decomposition, gives rise to pestilential vapors, or miasmata.

When the weather is fine, a few hours' liberty will serve the health and the condition of your hog, and a little grazing would be all the better. Should you be desirous of breeding, and keep a sow for that purpose, you must, if you have a second hog, provide a second sty, for the sow will require a separate apartment when heavy in pig, and when giving suck. This may be easily effected by building it against that which you have already erected, thus saving the trouble of raising more walls than are absolutely necessary; and it need not have a court attached to it, should it be inconvenient for you to have one, as the best accommodation can be given up to the breeding sow, and your pigs will do well enough with a single apartment, if not too confined, and it have sufficient ventilation; and if you permit them the advantage of taking air for a few hours daily. The extensive feeder should have a boiler of large size, properly fitted up, and an apparatus for steaming, as some vegetables are cooked in this mode more advantageously than by boiling. The poor man can use a pot as a substitute for a boiler, remembering in every case to clean it before using. Food should be presented to swine in a warm state—neither too hot nor too cold.

A sty should be about seven or eight feet square, and the court about ten feet. The second sty need not be more than six feet square, and does not absolutely require a court.

Breeding, Rearing, and Feeding.—In the selection of a boar and sow for breeding, much more attention and consideration are necessary than people generally imagine. It is as easy, with a very little judgment and management, to procure a good as an inferior breed ; and the former is infinitely more remunerative, in proportion to outlay, than the latter can possibly ever be. In selecting the parents of your future stock, you must bear in mind the precise objects you may have in view, whether the rearing for pork, or bacon; and whether you desire to meet the earliest market, and thus realize a certain profit, with the least possible outlay of money, or loss of time ; or whether you mean to be contented to await a heavier although somewhat protracted return. If bacon, and the late market be your object, you will do well to select the large and heavy varieties, taking care that the breed has the character of being possessed of those qualities most likely to insure a heavy return, viz.: *growth* and *facility* of taking fat, relatively possessed by each. To that description we refer the reader. If his object be to produce pork, he will find his account in the smaller varieties; such as arrive with greatest rapidity at maturity, and which are likely to produce the most delicate flesh. In producing *pork*, it is not desirable that it should be *too fat*, without a corresponding proportion of lean ; and on this account, rather take a cross-bred sow than a pure Chinese stock, from which the over-fattening results might most naturally be apprehended. The Berkshire, crossed with Chinese, is about the best porker I can mention. In every case, whether your object be pork or bacon, the *points* to be looked for are— in the sow, a small, lively head, a broad and deep chest, round ribs, capacious barrel, a haunch falling almost to the hough, deep and broad loin, ample hips, and considerable *length* of body in proportion to *height*. One qualification should ever be kept in view, and, perhaps, should be the first *point* to which the attention should be directed, viz., *smallness of bone*.

Let the boar be less in size than the sow, shorter and more compact in form, with a raised and brawny neck, lively eye, small head, firm, hard flesh, and his neck well furnished with bristles—in other respects seek the same points we have described in reference to the sow. Breeding within too close degrees of consanguinity, or, *breeding in and in*, is calculated to produce degeneracy in size, and also to impair fertility; it is therefore to be avoided, although some breeders maintain that a *first cross* does no harm, but on the contrary, that it produces offspring which are disposed to arrive earlier at maturity. This may in some instances be the case; it is so with horned cattle, but as far as swine are concerned, it is not my own experience.

Differences of opinion exist as to the precise age of boar and sow, at which breeding is most advisable. They will, if permitted, breed at the early age of six or seven months; but this is a practice not to be recommended. My advice is, to let the sow be *at least* one year old, and the boar *at least* eighteen months; but, if the former has attained her second year, and the latter his third, a vigorous and numerous offspring are more likely to result. The boar and sow retain their ability to breed for about five years, that is, until the former is upward of eight years old, and the latter seven. I do not recommend using a boar after he has passed his fifth year, nor a sow after she has passed her fourth, unless she has proved a peculiarly valuable breeder; in which case, she might be suffered to produce two or three more litters. When you are done with the services of the boar, have him emasculated—an operation that can be performed with perfect safety at any age—fatten or sell him. When it is no longer desirable to breed from the sow, kill her. Before doing so, it is a good plan to put her to the boar, as she takes fat afterward more rapidly than she otherwise would.

If a sow be of a stock characterized by an unusual tendency to take fat, it is well to breed from her at an unusually early age—say eight or nine months; for this tendency to fat, in a breeding sow, is highly objectionable, as conducing to danger in parturition. Let her have the boar a couple of days after pigging, and let her breed as frequently as she is capable of doing. This will effectually check the tendency to fat; and, after having taken a few litters from her, you will find the rapidity with which, should you desire her for the butcher, she will take flesh quite extraordinary. In the case of such a sow, do not give the boar before putting her up to fatten.

Feed the breeding boar well; keep him in high condition, but not fat; the sow, on the other hand, should be kept somewhat low, until after conception, when the quantity and quality of her food should be gradually increased. The best times for breeding swine are, the months of March, and July or August. A litter obtained later than August has much to contend with, and seldom proves profitable; some, indeed, state that when such an occurrence does take place, whether from accident or neglect, the litter is not worth keeping. It is little use, however, to throw any thing away. Should the reader at any time have a late litter, let him leave them with the sow; feed both her and them with warm and stimulating food, and he will thus have excellent pork, with which to meet the market, when that article is at once scarce and dear, and consequently profitable. By following this system of management, he will not only turn his late litter to account, but actually realize most as good a profit as if it had been produced at a favorable season.

The period of gestation in the sow varies; the most usual period during which she carries her young, is four lunar months, or sixteen weeks, or about one hundred and thirteen days. M. Teissieur, of Paris, a gentleman who paid much attention to this subject, in connection not merely with swine, but other animals, states that it varies from one hundred and nine to one hundred and forty-three days; he formed his calculation from the attentive observation of twenty-five sows.

The sow produces from eight to thirteen young ones at a litter, sometimes even more. Extraordinary fecundity, is, however, not desirable, for a sow cannot give nourishment to more young than she has teats for, and, as the number of teats is twelve, when a thirteenth one is littered, he does not fare very well. The sufferer on these occasions is of course the smallest and weakest; a too numerous litter are all indeed generally undersized and weakly, and seldom or never prove profitable; a litter not exceeding ten, will, usually, be found to turn out most advantageously. On account of the discrepancy subsisting between the number farrowed by different sows, it is a good plan, if it can be managed, to have more than one breeding at the same time, in order that you may equalize the number to be suckled by each. The sow seldom recognizes the presence of a strange little one, if it has been introduced among the others during her absence, and has lain for half an hour or so among her own offspring in their sty.

While the sow is carrying her young, feed her abundantly, and increase the quantity until parturition approaches within a week or so, when it is as well to diminish both the quantity and quality. While she gives suck you cannot feed her too well. You may wean the young at eight weeks old, and should remove them for that purpose from the sow; feed them well, frequently, abundantly, but not to leaving, and on moist, nutritious food, and pay particular attention to their lodgment—a warm, dry, comfortable bed is of fully as much consequence as feeding, if not even of more. Should the sow exhibit any tendency to devour its young, or should she have done so on a former occasion, strap up her mouth for the first three or four days, only releasing it to admit of her taking her meals. Some sows are apt to lie upon, and crush their young. This may be best avoided by not keeping the sow too fat or heavy, and by not leaving too many young upon her. Let the straw forming the bed also be short, and not in too great quantity, lest the pigs get huddled up under it, and the sow unconsciously overlie them in that condition.

The young pigs should be gradually fed before permanently weaning them; and for first food, nothing is so good as milk, which may be succeeded by ordinary dairy wash, thickened with oat or barley-meal, or fine pollard; this is better scalded, or, better still, boiled. To the sow, some dry food should be given once daily, which might consist of pease, beans, Swedish turnips, carrots, parsnips, or the like, either well boiled or raw; but I prefer the food to be *always* boiled, or, what is still better, *steamed*. Some wean the pigs within a few hours after birth, and turn the sow at once to the boar. Under certain circumstances, this may be found advantageous; but I think that the best mode of management is to turn the boar into the hog-yard about a week after parturition, at which time it is proper to remove the sows for a few hours daily from their young, and let them accept his overtures when they please. It does not injure either the sow or her young if she take the boar while suckling, but some sows will not do so until the drying of their milk.

Castration and Spaying should only be performed on such as you intend to keep, as you do not know what a purchaser's wishes on the subject might be. It is, of course, unnecessary for me to give any directions as to the mode of performing this operatior, as no amateur should attempt it; and men who make the practice their means of livelihood are, in every district, not difficult to be got at, or exorbitant in their terms. The sow is, if desirable, to be spayed while suckling; the boar, as we have already stated, may be castrated at any age with perfect safety.

Ringing.—At weaning time, ring the young pigs. This operation must be a painful one, but scarcely so much so as the little sufferers would seem to indicate. Ringing is, however, absolutely necessary, unless the cartilage of the nose be *cut away*, a practice resorted to in substitution for it in some parts of England; the latter practice is, however, far more cruel than ringing, and its efficacy is by many stated to be at the best questionable.

After about five weeks' high and careful feeding subsequent to weaning, the young pigs may be put up for stores, porkers, etc., according to your views respecting them. Very young pigs, immediately after being weaned, if fed on the refuse of a dairy, will be brought up for delicious pork in five or six weeks; for the last week prior to killing, the addition of grains or bruised corn will impart a degree of firmness to the flesh, that is considered an improvement. This is called "dairy-fed pork," and it never fails to fetch an enhanced price, thereby amply remunerating its producer.

Hogs designed for pork should not be fattened to the same extent as those designed for bacon. We are aware that it will be vain for us to request the reader not to do so, as fat produces weight—weight, profit—and profit is the object of the feeder. But to those who feed for home consumption, we urge the suggestion, and they will find their account in following it. Porkers should be suffered to run at large. Grazing, or the run of a wood in which roots or nuts may be met with, is calculated in an eminent degree to improve the quality of their flesh. It will be necessary to give the hogs regular meals, independent of what they can thus cater for themselves; and the hours for so doing should be in the morning, before they are let out, and in the evening, before they are returned to the sty. Too many swine should not be kept in one sty; and if one become an object of persecution to the rest, he should be withdrawn. The introduction of strangers should likewise be avoided. Bacon hogs fatten best by themselves; they need no liberty; and it is only necessary to keep the sty dry and clean, and to feed abundantly, in order to prepare them for the knife. In order to fatten a hog, his *comforts* must in every respect be attended to.

Those who make pork-feeding a business, and consequently keep a number of these animals, should so manage as to be enabled to provide for their maintenance and fattening from the produce of their crops. They should therefore raise the potato, beans, pease, barley, buckwheat, flax, parsnips, carrots, cabbage, lettuce, Lucerne, Italian rye-grass, clover, rape, chiccory, and vetches. Nor are we to forget the important articles, mangold and Swedish turnips; the latter especially, as being an article that sad necessity has recently, for the first time, brought into the full degree of notice it has always deserved; and an article that is now found to be no less valuable for human food than it is admitted to be for the food of cattle.

The best possible mode of feeding hogs is with a mixture of two or more of the roots or plants enumerated, well steamed, and a little meal or bran added, or, instead of meal or bran, add brewer's grains, wash, half-malted barley, pollard, etc. Let these be well boiled and given moderately cool, and in a moist state.

The advantages derivable from the use of hay-tea in store-feeding hogs was, I think, for the first time demonstrated to the public, some years ago, by Mr. Saunders, of Stroud, in Gloucestershire. Mr. Saunders was induced to try this diet with hogs, from an observation of its efficacy in weaning calves; his experiments were attended with the most unqualified success.

The use of flax-seed, as an addition to the other food for fattening swine, has been recommended, but is found not to answer nearly so well in the crude state as previously kiln-dried, and well crushed, so as to crack the seed; otherwise the animal will pass a large proportion of the seed in a whole state; the whole seed acts as a purgative and diuretic, which will be opposed to the secretion of fat. To prepare the seed for food, steep them for twelve hours in water, which may be poured on them in a tepid state, but not at boiling heat; and, prior to giving the mess, add as much lukewarm wash as will bring it to the consistence of gruel. This wash may be produced from brewers' grains, or simply from mangold or Swedish turnips, well boiled and mashed, and given with the water in which they have been boiled; the addition of a proportion of bran improves the mess, and, when one has it, it should not be omitted.

The adoption of hay-tea as the vehicle for mixing these ingredients, will be found also advantageous. Do not boil the flax-seed—boiling will produce a coarse, tough, and not very digestible mass; but steeping, on the contrary, furnishes a rich and nutritious jelly. Linseed cake is a good substitute for the seed, and is to be given in a proportion of fourteen pounds for seventeen or eighteen pounds of ground seed. Neither should be given, except in combination with a large proportion of other substances, as they are of a very greasy nature, and are apt to impart a rank flavor to flesh, if given in an unmixed state, and are actually more efficacious in combination. If you have plenty of meal, the addition of a little to the daily feeds will be found to tell well, especially toward the close of fattening, a few weeks previous to transferring your stock to the butcher.

The refuse of mills forms a very valuable item in swine food, when mixed with such boiled roots as I have enumerated—as starch sounds, the refuse from the manufacture of that article; also the fibrous refuse remaining from the manufacture of potato-starch.

Swine are frequently kept by butchers, and are fed principally upon the garbage of the shambles—as entrails, the paunches, lights, and the viscera of sheep and cattle, as well as the blood. Swine are, like their human owners, omnivorous, and few articles come amiss to them. It must, nevertheless, be confessed, that the flesh of hogs fed on animal food is rank both in smell and taste, and readily distinguishable from that produced from a vegetable diet. I am not unnecessarily prejudiced, and it is on the merits of the case alone that I condemn butcher-fed pork. Pork butchers, resident in large towns, are very apt to feed chiefly on offal of all sorts, including that arising from the hogs daily slain and dressed for the market.

There is yet another description of feeding—I allude to the feeding of swine in knackers' yards. The animals are kept in considerable numbers, and are fed wholly upon the refuse of dead horses—chiefly the entrails, the carcass being in too great demand among those who keep dogs to permit of it being unnecessarily wasted. Nor are these horses always fresh, the swine reveling in corruption, and disputing with the maggot the possession of a mass of liquid putrefaction. And are we to say nothing of the number of horses who die of glanders, farcy, or some similarly frightful contagious and incurable disorder? How can we be certain that this is not one of the many sources whence occasionally spring apparently causeless pestilences or malignant epidemics? While such a practice is tolerated, with what caution should we not purchase bacon or pork, lest we should thus eat at second-hand of substances so revolting to the feelings, so dangerous to individual and public health!

Chandlers' Greaves are likewise objectionable as food for swine, unless given in comparatively small quantities, and mixed with bran, meal, and boiled roots. If fed wholly on either greaves, or oil-cake, or flax-seed, the flesh becomes loose, unsubstantial, and carriony; and gives out a flavor resembling that of rancid oil.

Hogs that have been fed chiefly on corn, alternated with the vegetable diet already described, produce pork nearly equal in delicacy of flavor, whiteness of color, and consequent value, to that well-known, delicious article, DAIRY PORK. Indian corn is most useful in feeding and in fattening pigs; it should be employed in conjunction with oat or barley meal, or some other equally nutritious matter.

Respecting the quality of food, vast numbers of bacon hogs are almost invariably fed upon potatoes; but however apparently satisfactory may be their weight and condition, yet, when slaughtered immediately, or before having several weeks of substantial food, to harden their flesh, they are always found inferior to corn-fed pork and bacon, the fat having a tallowy appearance, of an insipid taste, and shrinking for want of firmness; whereas, when boiled, it should be transparently hard, with a tinge of pink in its color; the flavor should be good, and the meat should swell in the pot. Potatoes, therefore, though fine food for stores, should never be used alone as sustenance in the fatting of bacon hogs; for, in proportion to the quantity employed, it will render the flesh and consequently the price, inferior to that of hogs which have been properly fed. They are, however, frequently employed, when steamed, in conjunction with either tail or stained barley, coarsely ground; and farmers who grow potatoes for the market may thus profitably dispose of the chats along with their unmarketable corn; but those persons who wish to acquire a reputation for producing fine bacon, should never use any thing for fatting but hard meat, together with skim-milk, if it can be procured.

When swine are not of very large size, and it is desirable to raise pork rather than bacon, a very economical mode of feeding may be advantageously employed:—it consists of equal parts of boiled Swedish turnips or potatoes, and bran. If it be desirable to render the accumulation of fat more rapid, let Indian meal be substituted for the bran, and in flax-growing countries, the seed prepared as already directed.

A hog washed weekly with soap and a brush will be found to thrive, and put up flesh in a ratio of at least five to three, in comparison to a pig not so treated. This fact has been well tried, there can be no possible question about its correctness, and the duty is not a very difficult matter to perform, for the swine, as soon as they discover the real character of the operation, are far from being disposed to object, and after a couple of washings, submit with the best grace imaginable.

BEWARE NOT TO SURFEIT your hogs. It is quite possible to give too much even to them, and to produce disease by over-feeding.

Many examples of great weights, produced by judicious feeding and management, are upon record. Mr. Crockford's Suffolk hog, at two years old, weighed nine hundred and eighty pounds; but I scarcely think it could have been true Suffolk, that being a small breed. Mr. Ivory's Shropshire hog weighed fourteen hundred, when killed and dressed, and there was, a short time since, a specimen of the improved Irish breed of hog exhibited in Dublin, at the Portobello Gardens, which weighed upward of twelve hundred weight; this, when killed, would have amounted to something over half a ton.

In conclusion, observe caution in conjunction with the directions already given relative to feeding.

1. AVOID FOUL FEEDING.
2. DO NOT OMIT ADDING SALT in moderate quantities to the mess given; you will find your account in attending to this.
3. FEED AT REGULAR INTERVALS.
4. CLEANSE THE TROUGHS PREVIOUS TO FEEDING.
5. DO NOT OVER-FEED; give only as much as will be consumed at the meal.

6. VARY YOUR BILL OF FARE. Variety will create, or, at all events, increase appetite, and it is further most conducive to health; let your variations be guided by the state of the dung cast; this should be of medium consistence, and of a grayish-brown color; if hard, increase the quantity of bran and succulent roots; if too liquid, diminish, or dispense with bran, and let the mess be firmer; if you can, add a portion of corn—that which is injured, and thus rendered unfit for other purposes, will be found to answer well.

7. FEED YOUR STOCK SEPARATELY, in classes, according to their relative conditions; keep sows in young by themselves; stores by themselves; and bacon hogs and porkers by themselves. It is not advisable to keep your stores too high in flesh, for high feeding is calculated to retard development of form and bulk. It is better to feed pigs intended to be put up for bacon, loosely, and not too abundantly, until they have attained their full stature; you can then bring them into the highest possible condition in an inconceivably short space of time.

8. DO NOT REGRET THE LOSS OR SCARCITY OF POTATOES, so far as swine-feeding is concerned. Its loss has been the means of stimulating inquiry and producing experiment, which has resulted in the discovery that many other superior vegetables have been hitherto neglected and foolishly passed aside.

9. DO NOT NEGLECT TO KEEP YOUR SWINE CLEAN, DRY, AND WARM. These are essentials, and not a whit less imperative than feeding, for an inferior description of food will, by their aid, succeed far better than the highest feeding will without them; and we would reiterate the benefit derivable from washing your hogs; this will repay your trouble manifold.

10. WATCH THE MARKETS. Sell when you see a reasonable profit before you. Many and many a man has swamped himself by giving way to covetousness, and by desiring to realize an unusual amount of gain; recollect how very fluctuating are the markets, and that a certain gain is far better than the risk of loss.

Time Requisite for Feeding Fat—Quantity of Food.—This will, of course, vary very considerably, according to the weight, age, breed, and condition of the store when first put up, as well as the description of food on which, up to that period, the animal has been fed. The same observations are applicable to the quantity of food required for the production of fat.

If a young store, five or six weeks may be sufficient; if older, six or eight; and if of the mature age, intended for a perfect bacon hog, of that moderate degree of size and fatness which is preferred for the general consumption of the middle classes, from twelve to fourteen. A bacon hog, if intended to be thoroughly fattened for farm use, should, however, be of a large breed, and brought to such a state as not to be able to rise without difficulty, and will, perhaps, require five or six months, or even more, to bring him to that condition. This, however, supposes him to be completely fat; to ascertain which with perfect accuracy, he ought to be weighed every week during the latter part of the process; for although his appetite will gradually fall off as he increases in fat, yet the flesh which he will acquire will also diminish, until at last it will not pay for his food, and he should then be immediately slaughtered.

The Chemestry of Pig-Feeding.—In 1851-2, with the view of ascertaining, among other points, the comparative value of various kinds of food used for fattening pigs, Mr. J. B. Lawes, of Rothamsted, Herts, the eminent chemist and manufacturer of super-phosphate of lime, undertook a series of experiments on a large scale, recorded in a paper illustrated by a series of elaborate tables, which occupy upwards of eighty pages of the fourteenth volume of the "Journal of the Royal Agricultural Society." This paper, of the highest possible value to the scientific agriculturist, few plain farmers or fancy pig-feeders would have the courage to read, or would be able fully to understand, if they did. We shall, therefore, endeavor to give the results briefly and plainly; they fully confirm the opinions of the most successful pig-feeders.

The food employed in these experiments was composed as follows:— 1. Equal weights of beans and lentils; 2. Indian corn; 3. Bran. The food was accurately weighed; and the animals were put into the scales every fourteen days.

For the first series of experiments, forty animals, as nearly as possible of the same character, and age about ten months, were purchased, and divided into twelve pens of three pigs each, and were all fed alike for twelve days, changed from pen to pen, and the unruly ones whipped, so as to put down the tyrants and enable them all to start fair in the feeding race for weight. When fairly started, twelve dietaries were prepared from three standard food-stuffs, arranged as follows:—1. Bean and lentil mixture, an unlimited allowance; 2. Two pounds of Indian corn per pig per day, and an unlimited allowance of the beans and lentils; 3. Two pounds of bran per pig per day, and beans and lentils unlimited; 4. Two pounds of Indian corn, two pounds of bran, and the bean and lentil mixture unlimited; 5. Indian corn alone, unlimited; 6. Two pounds of beans and lentils, and unlimited Indian corn allowance; 7. Two pounds of bran per day, and unlimited Indian corn allowance; 8. Two pounds of bean and lentil mixture, two pounds of bran, and Indian corn unlimited; 9. Two pounds of bean and lentil mixture, and bran unlimited; 10. Two pounds of Indian corn-meal, and bran unlimited; 11. Two pounds of bean and lentil mixture, two pounds of Indian corn, and bran unlimited; 12. Bean and lentil mixture, Indian corn-meal and bran, each separately and unlimited.

This food was duly mixed with water. The animals were fed three times a day; viz., early in the morning, at noon, and at five o'clock in the evening. The limited food was mixed with a small quantity of that given *ad libitum* in the first two feeds of the day. Great care was taken in the management of the supply of food, both that the troughs should generally be cleared out before fresh food was put into them, and that the pigs should always have a liberal supply within their reach.

In one of the pens two of the pigs having become unwell from large swellings in their necks, which affected their breathing, a mixture was prepared, consisting of twenty pounds of finely-sifted coal-ashes, four pounds of common salt, and one pound of super-phosphate of lime, and placed in a trough. The pigs devoured it with eagerness; and, from this time, the tumors began to diminish, and entirely disappeared in six weeks. Three pigs consumed nine pounds in the first fortnight, six pounds in the second, and nine pounds during the third.

Three sets of pigs, each divided into twelve pens of three pigs each, were devoted to three series of experiments, with the various quantities of the food mentioned; in one series barley-meal taking the place of Indian corn, and the third series being devoted to the trial of dried Newfoundland codfish—an article which could be supplied in large quantities at a moderate price, in connection with the other food named. The amount given varied from one to two pounds of codfish per day. It was in all cases boiled, and a portion of other food mixed with the soup thus obtained.

The following are the more simple of the conclusions at which Mr. Lawes arrived: Indian corn or barley-meal with a limited supply of bran is very good food, the bran adding to the value of the manure. Where the pigs had unlimited access to three kinds of food, viz., the highly nitrogenous pulse mixture, the non-nitrogenous Indian meal, and bran, which is moderately nitrogenous—they gradually discontinued the proportion of their consumption of the first, as they approached maturity, and throughout only consumed five per cent. of bran. The average consumption of corn per pig per week was sixty pounds, or about nine pounds per day, which produced ten to twelve pounds of meat per week, or about one and a half pounds per day. There was a very rapid decrease in the rate of consumption of food to a given weight of animal as it fattened. The nearer a fattening animal approached maturity, the greater was the proportion of fat in the gross increase obtained.

Indian corn and barley-meal contain less than two per cent. nitrogen, bran about two and three-quarters per cent., beans and lentils about four and a half per cent., and dried codfish about six and a half per cent. Dried codfish contains less than one per cent. of fatty matter, beans and lentils two and a quarter per cent., barley-meal about the same, and Indian corn and bran about five per cent.

It was found that "the larger the proportion of nitrogenous compounds in the food, the greater was the tendency to increase in frame and flesh, but that the maturing or ripening of the animal, in fact, its fattening, depended very much more on the amount of 'certain digestible non-nitrogenous constituents in the food.' It also appeared that some of the cheaper highly nitrogenous foods would produce a given amount of gross increase more economically than the expensive ones (peas, beans) which are usually preferred by pork-feeders.

"If the amount of gross produce in meat in return for a given amount of food, of a given money value—is alone to be taken into consideration, then, in addition to roots, wash, etc., it would be most advantageous to rely for fattening upon highly nitrogenous foods, such as dried fish, or animal refuse, or leguminous seeds, beans, lentils, and the like, because not only would the weight be obtained at less cost than by the use of cereal grains, but the manure—the value of which must never be lost sight of in calculating the economy of the feed process—would be much richer than if the latter were employed. But it is not a large amount of gross increase that makes the farmer's profit upon his sties. When pigs are fed freely upon highly succulent food, such as cooked roots, the refuse of starch, herbs, and the like, they are frequently found to give a very rapid increase. But pork so fed is found to sink rapidly in the salting process, and to waste considerably when boiled. And although the first batch of pigs so fed may fetch a good price, their character is at once detected, and the market closed against a second sale.

"On the other hand, when pigs are fattened upon the highly nitrogenized leguminous seeds—peas being, however, much less objectionable than some others—the lean is hard, and the fat wastes in cooking. Fish, flesh, and strong oily matters give the pork a rank flavor.

"Finally, it is the interest of the farmer to use highly nitrogenous leguminous seeds, and even refuse flesh, if at command, during the earlier and growing stages of his bacon hogs. But if a constant market is to be secured for pork, barley-meal or other cereal grain must supersede every thing else as fattening proceeds." Thus Mr. Lawes confirms Mr. Tyrrel, and gives us a golden maxim for making a pig pay—a little bran or bean meal, and plenty of Indian corn.

Diseases of Swine.—In order to prescribe with any reasonable hopes of success, for any animal, a knowledge of that animal's anatomy, physiology, and habits when in health, are indispensable, and an intimate acquaintance with the characters of the substances employed as remedies. we would not recommend you to place any confidence in books published by quacks, and purporting to contain infallible specifics for the several diseases to which live-stock are liable. Veterinary text-books, written by competent persons, are very different things. A host of honorable names stand upon record, on the face of their publications, in proof of the correctness of my assertion. By diligent study of these books, farmers might, I have little doubt, eventually arrive at a very respectable share of veterinary knowledge; acquire a tolerable idea of the internal structure of the several inhabitants of the farm-yard, and of their physiology; by practical observation they would become able to detect the presence of disease from the symptoms present, and be able to adopt such a course of treatment as might be suggested in the books they possessed. Under these circumstances, apply, if possible, to a regular veterinary surgeon.

Swine are by no means the most tractable of patients. It is any thing but an easy matter to compel them to swallow any thing to which their appetite does not incite them, and hence, "prevention" will be found "better than cure." Cleanliness is, in my opinion, the great point to be insisted upon in swine management; if this, and warmth, be duly attended to, the animal will not, save in one case perhaps in a hundred, become affected with any ailment.

As, however, even under the most careful system of management, an occasional disappointment may occur, the reader is furnished with the following brief view of the principal complaints by which some are, under the most unfavorable circumstances, liable to be attacked, and the plainest effectual mode of sanatory treatment, in such cases, to be adopted.

The principal diseases to which swine are liable are :—1. Fever; 2. Leprosy; 3. Murrain; 4. Measles; 5. Jaundice; 6. Foul skin; 7. Mange; 8. Staggers; 9. Cracklings; 10. "Ratille," or swelling of the spleen; 11. Indigestion, or surfeit; 12. Lethargy; 13. Heavings; 14. "Diarrhœa;" 15. Quinsy; 16. Tumors; 17. Catarrh.

All which dangerous and often fatal maladies may be PREVENTED from occurring by the simple attention to cleanliness already recommended, with judicious feeding. A hog can be relieved by bleeding, when such an operation will effect relief, whether he like to submit or not; but it is very questionable whether he can be compelled to swallow medicines without his perfect consent and concurrence; these, therefore, will best be administered by stratagem, and the hog's *appetite* is the only assailable point he has.

Fever.—The symptoms are, redness of the eyes, dryness and heat of the nostrils, the lips, and the skin generally; appetite gone, or very defective, and the presence, usually, of a very violent thirst. Of course, no symptom can be regarded as individually indicative of the presence of any particular disease; these, which I have named, might, individually, indicate the presence of many other disorders, nay, of no disorder at all, but collectively, they point to the presence of fever as their origin.

Let the animal, as soon as possible after the appearance of these symptoms, be bled, by cutting the veins at the back of his ears. The pressure of the finger raises the vein, and you can then puncture it with a lancet. If the bleeding from this channel be not sufficiently copious, you must cut off a portion of his tail; and after bleeding let him be warmly housed, but, at the same time, while protected from cold and draughts, let the sty be well and thoroughly ventilated, and its inmate supplied with a constant succession of fresh air. The bleeding will usually be followed, in an hour or two, by such a return of appetite as to induce the animal to eat a sufficient quantity of food to admit of your making it the vehicle for administering such internal remedies as may seem advisable. The best vehicle is bread steeped in broth. The hog, however, sinks so rapidly, when once he loses his appetite that no depletive medicines are in general necessary or suitable; the fever will usually be found to yield to the bleeding, and your only object need be the support of the animal's strength, by small portions of nourishing food, administered frequently.

Do not, however, at any time suffer your patient to eat as much as his inclination might prompt; the moment he appears to be no longer *ravenous*, remove the mess, and do not offer it again until after a lapse of three or four hours. It is a singular fact, that as the hog surpasses every other animal in the facility with which he acquires fat, he likewise surpasses all others in the rapidity with which his strength becomes prostrated when once his appetite deserts him. The French veterinarian practice recommends the addition of peppermint to the bread and broth. If the animal be not disgusted by the smell, it may be added; and if the bowels be confined, the addition of castor and linseed oil, in equal quantities, and in the proportion of two to six ounces, according to the size of the hog, should not be omitted.

If you find yourself unable to restore the animal's appetite, the case is nearly hopeless, and you may regard its return as one of the most infallible symptoms of returning convalescence. It is, however, *possible* to administer medicine to the pig by *force;* although, for my own part, I cannot say that I have ever found it practicable.

There is a description of fever that frequently occurs as an epizootic. It often attacks the male pigs, and generally the most vigorous and the best-looking, without any distinction of age, and with a force and promptitude absolutely astonishing; for in the space of twelve hours, I have sometimes seen a whole piggery succumb: at other times its progress is much slower; the symptoms are less intense and less alarming; and the veterinary surgeon, employed at the commencement of the attack, may promise himself some success.

The Causes of the Disease are, in the majority of cases, the bad sties in which the pigs are lodged, and the noisome food which they often contain. The food which the pigs meet with and devour, are the remains of mouldy bread and fruit, especially those of pease and lentils— the fermentation and decomposition of which farinaceous substances, and especially the bran which is too frequently given to them, and the prolonged action of which determine the most serious in the whole economy. In addition to this, is the constant lying on the dung-heap, whence is exhaled a vast quantity of deleterious gas; also, where they remain far too long, on the muddy or arid ground, or are too long exposed to the rigor of the season.

As soon as a pig is attacked with disease, he should be separated from the others, placed in a warm situation, some stimulating ointment to be applied to the chest, and a decoction of sorrel administered. Frictions of vinegar should be applied to the dorsal and lumbar region. The drinks should be emollient, slightly imbued with nitre and vinegar, and with aromatic fumigation about the belly. If the fever now appears to be losing ground, which may be ascertained by the regularity of the pulse, by the absence of the plaintive cries that were before heard, by a respiration less laborious, by the absence of convulsions, and by the non-appearance of blotches on the skin, there is a fair chance of recovery. We may then be content to administer, every second hour, the drinks and the lavements already prescribed, and to give the patient his proper allowance of white water, with ground barley and rye. When, however, instead of these fortunate results, the symptoms are redoubling in intensity, it will be best to destroy the animal; for it is rare, that, after a certain period, there is much or any chance of recovery. Bleeding, at the ear or tail, is seldom of much avail, but occasionally produces considerable loss of vital power, and augments the putrid diathesis.

Leprosy.—The symptoms of this complaint usually commence with the formation of a small tumor in the eye, followed by general prostration of spirits; the head is held down and the whole frame inclines toward the ground: universal languor succeeds; the animal refuses food, languishes, and rapidly falls away in flesh; blisters soon make their appearance beneath the tongue, then upon the throat, the jaws, the head, and the entire body. The flesh of a leprous pig is said to possess most pernicious qualities, and to be wholly unfit for human food If the animal be killed in the very first stage of the disease, however, the affection is only superficial, the flesh nothing the worse, but rather improved in tenderness, and indeed, not to be distinguished from that of a perfectly sound animal. The cause of this disease is want of cleanliness, absence of fresh air, want of due attention to ventilation, and foul feeding. The obvious cure therefore is—first, bleed; clean out the sty daily; wash the affected animal thoroughly with soap and water, to which soda or potash has been added; supply him with a clean bed; keep him dry and comfortable; let him have gentle exercise and plenty of fresh air; limit the quantity of his food, and diminish its rankness; give bran with wash, in which you may add, for an average-sized hog, say one of one hundred and sixty pounds' weight, a tablespoonful of the flour of sulphur, with as much nitre as will cover a sixpence, daily. A few grains of powdered antimony may also be given with effect.

Murrain.—Resembles leprosy in its symptoms, with the addition of staggering, shortness of breath, discharge of viscid matter from the eyes and the mouth. The treatment should consist of cleanliness, coolness, bleeding, purging, and limitation of food. Cloves of garlic have been recommended to be administered in cases of murrain. Garlic is an antiseptic, and as, in all these febrile diseases, there exists more or less a degree of disposition to putrefaction, it is not improbable that it may be found useful.

Measles.—This is one of the most common diseases to which hogs are liable. The symptoms are redness of the eyes, foulness of the skin, depression of spirits, decline, or total departure of the appetite, small pustules about the throat, and red and purple eruptions on the skin. These last are more plainly visible after death, when they impart a peculiar appearance to the grain of the meat, with fading of its color, and distension of the fiber so as to give an appearance similar to that which might be produced by puncturing the flesh.

Suffer the animal to fast, in the first instance, for twenty-four hours, and then administer a warm drink, containing a drachm of carbonate of soda and an ounce of bole Armenian; wash the animal, cleanse the sty, and change the bedding; give at every feeding, say thrice a day, thirty grains of flour of sulphur, and ten of nitre. It is to dirt, combined with a common fault too little thought of, viz., giving the steamed food or wash to the hogs at too high a temperature, that this disease is generally to be attributed. It is a troublesome malady to eradicate, but usually yields to treatment, and is rarely fatal.

Jaundice.—Symptoms—yellowness of the white of the eye, a similar hue extending to the lips, with sometimes, but not invariably, swelling of the under part of the jaw. Bleed behind the ear, diminish the quantity of food, and give a smart aperient every second day. Aloes are, perhaps, the best, combined with colocynth: the dose will vary with the size of the animal.

Foul Skin.—A simple irritability or foulness of the skin will usually yield to cleanliness and a washing with solution of chloride of lime, but if it has been neglected for any length of time, it assumes a malignant character, scabs and blotches, or red and fiery eruptions appear, and the disease rapidly passes into mange.

10*

Mange.—If the foul hide already described had been properly attended to, and the remedies necessary for its removal applied in sufficient time, this very troublesome disorder would not have supervened. Mange is supposed, by most medical men, to owe its existence to the presence of a minute insect, called "*acarus scabiei*," or "mange-fly," a minute creature, which burrows beneath the cuticle, and in its progress through the skin occasions much irritation and annoyance. Others, again, do not conceive the affection styled mange to be thus produced, but refer it to a diseased state of the blood, which, as is usually the case, eventually conveys its morbid influences to the superficial tissues. Much has been, and still more might be said on both sides of the question, but such a discussion is scarcely suitable to the pages of a popular work. The symptoms of the disease are sufficiently well known, consisting of scabs, blotches, and sometimes multitudes of minute pustules, on different parts of the body. If neglected, these symptoms will become aggravated; the disease will rapidly spread over the entire surface of the skin, and if suffered to proceed upon its course, unchecked, it will ere long produce deep-seated ulcers and malignant sores, until the whole carcass of the poor affected animal becomes one mass of corruption.

The Causes of Mange have been differently stated; some referring them to too high, and others to too low a diet. The cause is to be looked for in *dirt*, accompanied by *hot-feeding;* hot-feeding alone would, perhaps be more likely to produce *measles* than *mange,* but *dirt* would unquestionably produce the latter disease, even if unaided by the concomitant error of hot-feeding.

Hogs, however well and properly kept, will occasionally become affected with this, as well as with other disorders, from *contagion.* Few diseases are more easily propagated by *contact* than mange. The introduction of a single affected pig into your establishment may, in one night, cause the seizure of scores, and probably furnish you with a three months' hospital experience. Do not, therefore, introduce any foul-skinned pigs into your piggery; in fact, it would be a very safe proceeding to wash every new purchase with a strong solution of *chloride of lime.* This substance is very cheap, and a little trouble, when applied as a preventive, is surely preferable to a great deal of both trouble and *disappointment* when you are compelled to resort to it to cure.

If a hog be only afflicted with a mange of moderate virulence, and not of *very long standing,* the best mode of treatment to be adopted is:

1. Wash the animal from snout to tail, leaving no portion of the body uncleansed, with *soft soap* and water.

2. Put him into a dry and clean sty, which is so built and situated as to command a constant supply of fresh air, without, at the same time, being exposed to cold or draught; let him have a bed of clean, fresh straw.

3. Reduce his food, both in quality and in quantity; let boiled or steamed roots, with buttermilk or dairy wash, supply the place of half-fermented brewers' grains, house-wash, or any other description of feeding calculated to prove of a heating or inflammatory character. It is, of course, scarcely necessary to add, that those who have been feeding their swine on *horse-flesh,* or chandlers' greaves, cannot be surprised at

the occurrence of the disease; let them, at all events, desist from that rank and nasty mode of feeding, and turn to such as has been indicated.

4. Let your patient fast for five or six hours, and then give, to a hog of average size—Epsom salts, two ounces, in a warm bran wash. This quantity is to be increased or diminished as the size may require. The above would suffice for a hog of 160 lbs. It should be previously mixed with a pint of warm water. This should be added to about half a gallon of warm bran wash. It will act as a gentle purgative.

5. Give in every meal afterward—of flour of sulphur, one tablespoonful; of nitre, as much as will cover a sixpence, for from three days to a week, according to the state of the disease. When you perceive the scabs begin to heal, the pustules to retreat, and the fiery sores to fade, you may pronounce your patient cured. But before that pleasing result will make its appearance, you will perceive an apparent increase of violence in all the symptoms—the last effort of the expiring malady, as it were, ere it finally yields to your care and skill.

6. There are, however, some very obstinate cases of mange occasionally to be met with, which will not so readily be subdued. When the above mode of treatment has been put in practice for fourteen days, without effecting a cure, prepare the following: train oil, one pint; oil of tar, two drachms; spirits of turpentine, two drachms; naphtha, one drachm; with flour of sulphur, as much as will form the above into the consistency of a thick paste. Rub the animal, previously washed, with this mixture—let no portion of the hide escape you. Keep the hog dry and warm after this application, and suffer it to remain on his skin three entire days. On the fourth day, wash him once more with soft soap, adding a small quantity of *soda* to the water. Dry the animal well afterward, and suffer him to remain as he is, having again changed his bedding, for a day or so: continue the sulphur and nitre as before. I have never known any case of mange, however obstinate, that would not, sooner or later, give way before this mode of treatment.

7. Your patient being convalescent, whitewash the sty; fumigate it, by placing a little chloride of lime in a cup, or other vessel, and pouring a little vitriol upon it. In the absence of vitriol, however, boiling water will answer nearly as well.

Finally, all mercurial applications are, as much as possible, to be avoided; but, above every thing, avoid the use of ointments composed of hellebore, corrosive sublimate, or tobacco-water, or, in short, any *poisonous* ingredient whatever; very few *cures* have ever been effected by the use of these so-called remedies, but very many *deaths* have resulted from their adoption.

Staggers, caused by excess of blood to the head; bleed freely from behind the ears, and purge.

Crackings will sometimes appear on the skin of a hog, especially about the root of the ears and tail, and at the flanks. These are not at all to be confounded with mange, never resulting from any thing but exposure to extremes of temperature, without the suffering animal being able to avail himself of such protections as, in a state of nature, instinct would have induced him to adopt. They are peculiarly troublesome in the heats of summer, if the hog be exposed to a hot sun for any length of time, without the advantage of a marsh or pool in which to lave his parched limbs and half-scorched carcass. Anoint the cracked parts twice or thrice a day with tar and lard melted up together.

Ratille, or Swelling of the Spleen.—The symptom most positively indicative of this disease, is the circumstance of the affected animal leaning toward one side, cringing as it were, from internal pain, and bending toward the ground. The cause of the obstruction on which the disease depends is over-feeding, permitting the hog's indulging its appetite to the utmost extent that gluttony may prompt and the capacity of its stomach admit of; a very short perseverance in this mode of management will produce this, as well as other maladies deriving their origin from a depraved condition of the secretions and obstruction of the excretory ducts.

On first perceiving the complaint, clear out the alimentary canal by means of a strong aperient. If you think you can manage it, you may administer this forcibly, by having the mouth kept open by two cords, that attached to the upper jaw being thrown across a joist, and drawn just so tight as to compel the patient to support himself on the extremities of his fore-toes; or allow the animal to fast for from four to five hours, he will then take a little sweet wash or broth, and in it you may mingle a dose of Epsom salts, proportioned to his bulk. This will generally effect the desired end of a copious evacuation, and the action of this medicine on the watery secretions will further relieve the existing diseased state of the spleen. Many recommend *bleeding ;* and if the affection have continued for any length of time, it should be resorted to at once; when the disease is, however, discovered ere it has attained any considerable head, the aperient will suffice. The French veterinarians recommend the expressed juice of the leaves and tops of wormwood and liverwort to be given, half a pint for a dose. The decoction of these plants produced by boiling them in soft water for six hours, may be given in doses of from half a pint to a pint and a half, according to the size, age, etc., of the patient.

Scammony and rhubarb, mixed up in a bran mash, or with Indian meal, may be given with advantage the following day, or equal portions of blue-pill mass and compound colocynth pill, formed into a bolus with butter, and the animal, having been kept fasting the previous night, will probably swallow it; if he will not do so, let his fast continue for a couple of hours longer. Lower the animal's diet, and keep him on reduced fare, with exercise, and if you can manage it, *grazing,* until the malady has quite passed away; if you then wish to fatten, remember to do so gradually; be cautious of at once restoring the patient to full diet.

Surfeit.—Another name for indigestion; the symptoms are such as might be expected—panting, loss of appetite, swelling of the region about the stomach, etc., and frequently throwing up the contents of the stomach. In general, this affection will pass away, provided it is only permitted to cure itself, and all food carefully kept from the patient for a few hours; a small quantity of sweet grains, with a little bran-wash, may then be given, but not nearly as much as the animal would wish to take. For a few days the food had better be limited in quantity, and of a washy, liquid nature. You may then resume the ordinary food, only observing to feed regularly, and remove the fragments remaining after each meal.

Lethargy.—Symptoms, torpor, and desire to sleep, hanging of the head, and frequently redness of the eyes. The apparent origin of this disease is the same as the last, only in this instance acting upon a hog having a natural tendency to a redundancy of blood. Bleed at the back of both the ears as copiously as you can, and if you cannot obtain a sufficient quantity of blood from these sources, have recourse to the tail. Administer an emetic, of which a decoction of chamomile flowers will be found the safest; or a sufficient dose of tartar emetic, which will be far more certain. After this, reduce for a few days the amount of the animal's food, and administer a small portion of sulphur and nitre in each morning's meal.

Heavings, or Inflammation of the Lungs.—This disease, which has acquired its name from the principal symptom by which it is characterized, is scarcely to be regarded as curable. If indeed, it were observed in its first stage, when indicated by loss of appetite, and a short, hard cough, it might run some chance of being got under by copious bleeding, and friction with stimulating ointment on the region of the lungs, minute and frequent doses of tartar emetic should also be given in butter, all food of a stimulating nature carefully avoided, and the animal kept dry and warm. Under these circumstances, there would be no reason absolutely to despair of a cure, but it would be advisable at the same time, if the hog, when this primary stage of the malady was discovered, were not in very poor condition, to put him to death. If once the heavings set in, it may be calculated with confidence that the formation of tubercles in the substance of the lungs has begun, and when these are once formed, they are very rarely absorbed. The cause of this disease is damp lodging, foul air, want of ventilation, and unwholesome food. It is difficult to suggest what should be done when matters have reached this pass, or what remedies would prove of any service. It is now too late in most cases to resort to blood-letting, and the hide of the hog is so tough that it is not easy to blister it, for the purpose of counter-irritation; you may, however, try the following, though perhaps the knife might be best, if only to relieve the poor sufferer, and provide against the danger of infection; for it may be as well to state that, once tubercular formation becomes established, the disease may be communicated through the medium of the atmosphere, the infectious influence depending upon the noxious particles respired from the lungs of the diseased animal. Shave the hair away from the chest, and beneath each fore-leg; wet the part with spirits of turpentine, and set fire to it; you will, of course, have had the patient well secured, and his head well raised, and have at hand a flannel cloth, with which to extinguish the flame, when you conceive it has burned a sufficient time to produce slight blisters; if carried too far, a sore would be formed, which would be productive of no good effects, and cause the poor animal unnecessary suffering. Calomel may also be used, with a view to promote the absorption of the tubercles, but the success is questionable.

Diarrhœa, or Looseness.—The symptoms, of course, require no comment, as they constitute the disease. Before attempting to stop the discharge—which, if permitted to continue unchecked, would rapidly prostrate the animal's strength, and probably terminate fatally—ascertain the quality of food the animal has recently had. In a majority of instances, you will find this to be the origin of the disease; and if it has been perceived in its incipient stage, a mere change to a more binding diet, as corn, flour, etc., will suffice for a cure; if you have reason to apprehend that acidity is present, produced in all probability by the hog having fed upon coarse, rank grasses in swampy places, give some chalk in the food, or powdered egg-shells, with about half a drachm of powdered rhubarb; the dose of course varying with the size of the hog. In the acorn season, and where facilities for obtaining them exist, they alone will be found quite sufficient to effect a cure. When laboring under this complaint, dry lodging is indispensable; and diligence will be necessary to maintain it and cleanliness.

Quinsy, or Inflammatory Affection of the Glands of the Throat.—Shave away the hair, and rub with tartar emetic ointment. Stuping with very warm water is also useful. When external suppuration takes place, you may regard it as rather a favorable symptom than otherwise. In this case, wait until the swellings are thoroughly ripe; then, with a sharp knife, make an incision through the entire length, press out the matter, wash with warm water, and afterward dress the wound with any resinous ointment, or yellow soap with coarse brown sugar.

Tumors, or Hard Swellings, which make their appearance on several different parts of the animal's body. It would not be easy to state the causes which give rise to these tumors, for they vary with circumstances. They are not formidable, and require only to be suffered to progress until they soften; then make a free incision, and press out the matter. Sulphur and nitre should be given in the food, as the appearance of these swellings, whatever be their cause, indicates the necessity of alterative medicines.

Catarrh, an inflammation of the mucous membranes of the nose, etc., if taken in time, is easily cured by opening medicine, followed up by warm bran-mash, a warm, dry sty, and abstinence from rich grains or stimulating farinaceous diet. The cause has probably been exposure to drafts of air—see to it.

The instructions given comprise all that the amateur will ever find necessary for domestic practice, and far more than he will ever find occasion to follow, if he have attended to cleanliness, dry lodging, regularity of feeding, the use of salt in the food, and the addition of occasionally a small quantity of sulphur and nitre to the morning's meal.

Medicines Employed in the Treatment of Swine.—Few medicines are requisite in the treatment of swine. Of these the chief are common salt, Epsom salts (dose, from one-half to two ounces); sulphur (dose, one-half to one and a half ounces); useful as the basis of ointments for cutaneous diseases; nitrate of potass (dose, one scruple to one drachm); ginger (dose, one scruple to one drachm); croton-oil (dose, one to three drops); castor-oil (dose, one-half to two ounces); jalap (dose, one scruple to one half-drachm). Besides these, we may mention oil, mercurial ointment, and turpentine, as ingredients in ointments, mixed with sulphur, for cutaneous affections. Turpentine, it may be observed, is useful in cases of worms; it may be given in doses of about half an ounce or more, in gruel.

SLAUGHTERING AND CURING.—The Almighty Creator, when he had formed man, and placed him upon the earth, gave him power of life and death over all the inferior animals. This power was, however, given to him to be used, not to be abused; while permitted to slay for food, clothing, or other necessaries—nay, luxuries of life—it was never designed by our all-benevolent as well as omnipotent Lord that this power should be converted into a medium of cruelty, or that life should be taken away from any of his creatures in any other than the most humane manner possible. The necessity of humanity toward animals thus stands as not only a high moral duty, but one absolutely enjoined as a divine ordinance; it is also a part and parcel of all that is noble or excellent in human nature.

It is a mistake to suppose that this poor animal is insensible to pain. The poor hog does indeed feel, and that most acutely; well would it be for him that he did not, for then what miseries would he not be spared!—he would not then care whether he was put out of pain at once, or suffered to hang up by the hind-legs, the limbs previously dislocated at the hocks, between the tendons and the bone of which has been passed the hook by which he is suspended. Were he indeed insensible to pain, it would of course be a matter of indifference whether or not he were suffered to die first, or—as soon as he had bled a sufficient quantity—was, still living and breathing, plunged into boiling water, in order to remove his hair; or then, with a refinement of cruelty that would not even permit of his being put out of his misery so soon, removed from the cauldron, ere life or feeling had yet departed, opened, and disembowelled alive.

We should be sorry to give pain to the feelings of any of our readers, but we had rather hurt their feelings than leave a suffering, a tortured quadruped, and that, too, one so useful to us, to experience such an ungrateful return, in the shape of such terribly revolting miseries. We have described only what we have personally witnessed, and we trust that what we have said may lead master-butchers and others to ascertain the conduct of their slaughterers, and the manner in which they perform their necessary but-painful duty.

The usual mode of killing a hog in the country parts of England is, or used lately to be, by fastening a rope around the upper jaw, and throwing it across a joist or beam; this is hauled by an assistant just sufficiently tight to compel the animal to support himself upon the extremities of his toes, with his snout elevated in the air. The butcher then kneels in front of him, and taking a sharp and pointed knife, first shaves away the hair from a small portion of the front of the throat, then gently passing the sharp-pointed steel through the superficial fat, gives it a plunge forward, a turn, and withdraws his weapon. A gush of blood follows, which is usually caught in proper vessels, for the purpose of forming black puddings. The rope is somewhat slackened— the victim totters, reels, the eye glazes—his screams cease—he falls, and life would speedily become extinct; but, alas! the butcher is paid by the job, he is in a hurry, and ere the breath is out of the poor brute's carcass—nay, ere he ceases to struggle or moan—he is tumbled into the scalding tub; he is then withdrawn in a second, placed upon a table, the hair and bristles carefully removed by scraping with a knife; disembowelling follows—and it is well if the poor wretch has perished before that process commenced.

In olden times it would appear that our butchers were less hasty, or more merciful. All the skulls of hogs were broken in upon the frontal bones, precisely in the same manner as are now the skulls of oxen and other animals. Were the hog first deprived of sensibility by compression of the brain, as produced by a violent blow upon the forehead, he would be a passive victim in the butcher's hands, who could not only perform all the remainder of the process with more humanity, but—and think well of it, such of you as might probably be swayed by no other consideration—with more dispatch and less trouble.

We are happy in being able to add, that a humane custom of knocking the hog on the head before cutting his throat is rapidly gaining ground, and that no respectable butcher will allow it to be dispensed with. In the country parts of both England and Ireland, however, the old abuses are still permitted to exist; and we are grieved to say that everywhere, with a very few honorable exceptions, the barbarous practice of plunging the hog into the scald while yet living, is still systematically and designedly adopted. A very respectable man surprised us the other day by deliberately telling us that "a hog will no way scald so well as when the life is in him." This is, however, a mistake. It is only necessary not to suffer the animal to become cold and stiff. Readers—we raise our voice in behalf of a very useful and most cruelly-treated animal—may we beg of all to unite with us in the cause of humanity, and then we shall not have raised our voice in vain.

And now, having supposed the animal killed and dressed, let us proceed to inquire into the most approved modes by which its flesh may be converted into bacon and ham. The hog should be left fasting for full twenty-four hours before killed; and after the carcass has hung all night, it should be laid on its back upon a strong table. The head should then be cut off close by the ears, and the hinder feet so far below the houghs as not to disfigure the hams, and leave room sufficient to hang them up by; after which the carcass is divided into equal halves, up the middle of the back-bone, with a cleaving-knife, and, if necessary, a hand-mallet. Then cut the ham from the side by the second joint of the back-bone, which will appear on dividing the carcass, and dress the ham by paring a little off the flank, or skinny part, so as to shape it with a half-round point, clearing off any top fat that may appear. The curer will next cut off the sharp edge along the back-bone with a knife and mallet, and slice off the first rib next the shoulder, where he will find a bloody vein, which must be taken out, for, if left in, that part is apt to spoil. The corners should be squared off when the ham is cut out.

This passage is quoted because it describes a novel mode of cutting bacon, and which we have not as yet seen practiced. The ordinary practice is to cut out the spine or back-bone, and, in some English counties, to take out the ribs also. It is only in porkers that the backbone is thus divided.

The most approved mode of saving bacon, as practiced by a majority of those extensive curers who have kindly favored us with the necessary details of this portion of our subject, is as follows: if the swine you design killing have been a recent purchase, and have been driven from a distance, so as to have become winded or jaded, it is right that they should be kept up for a week, or perhaps more, until the effects of the journey have been entirely removed, and the animals restored to their original tranquillity and primeness of condition; during this interval they should be fed upon meal and water. A difference of opinion exists, as to whether this food should be given in a raw state or boiled. We have taken some pains to ascertain the truth, and have no hesitation in pronouncing in favor of the latter; at the same time, however, the mess should be given in a perfectly cold state, and not of too thick consistence. Some recommend that a small dose of nitre should be given daily in the food for a fortnight previous to killing; others pronounce this to be unnecessary; but all unite in recommending a very considerable reduction in the animal's food for two or even three days before killing, and a total deprivation of food for at least the last twelve hours of life.

In the country districts of Ireland, the hog is usually secured by the hind-leg to a post or ring, the head is fastened to another; the animal is thus securely strapped down upon a sloping slab or table, and the head is severed from the body by means of a sharp knife. I am informed that the bacon of a hog thus killed is more easily saved, and is superior in flavor and color.

The ordinary mode of killing a hog is, we are most happy to say, gradually approximating to such as humanity would dictate. It is thus: a flat stage or table, inclining downward in one direction, is prepared; the pig receives a powerful blow with a mallet upon the forehead, which effectually deprives him of sensation; he is then thrown upon the stage, and a knife plunged into the chest, or rather into that spot where the chest meets the neck. The blood flows freely, and is received into vessels placed for the purpose. A large tub or other vessel has been previously got ready, which is now filled with boiling water. The carcass of the hog is plunged into this, and the hair is then removed with the edge of a knife. The hair is more easily removed if the hog be scalded ere he stiffens or becomes quite cold, and hence some butchers cruelly conceive it advisable to scald him while yet there is some life in him. The animal is now hung up, opened, and the entrails removed; the head, feet, etc., are cut off, and the carcass divided, cutting up at each side of the spine. A strong knife and mallet are necessary for this purpose, and will be found to answer better than a saw.

HOW TO CURE BACON AND HAMS.—One and a half pounds of salt and one ounce of saltpetre are enough to salt fourteen pounds of meat, or two hundred weight of meat will require twenty-four pounds of salt.

The following is Mr. Rowlandson's plan :—" Having cut up a well-fed hog, which absorbs much less salt than an ill-fed animal, and runs very little risk of being over-fed, salt, and saltpetre, in the proportions described, must be sprinkled over the flitches, etc., and then they must be laid one over the other in a slate trough, or a wooden trough lined with lead, to the number of half a dozen; in the course of twenty-four hours, or forty-eight hours, according as the salt is converted into brine (and this will depend on the weather—in frosty weather the meat will not take the salt, and in moist weather it is apt to spoil), the sides are removed, rubbed, replaced in inverse order, the top at the bottom, with a little fresh salt sprinkled between each course, and the brine thrown over the whole. In favorable weather for curing, once turning and replacing will be found enough, and will not occupy more than a week.

Bacon is cured in very different ways. For domestic use, it is usually laid upon a table, and salt, with a little nitre added, well rubbed in, first on one side and then on the other, either with the bare hand or the salting-glove. Some straw is then placed upon the floor of an out-house, a flitch laid thereon, with the rind downward—straw laid above this, then another flitch, and so on; above the whole is placed a board, and heavy stones or weights above all. In three weeks or a month the meat is sufficiently salted, and is hung up on hooks in the kitchen rafters. The general practice of burning wood and turf in Irish kitchens, imparts a sweetness to the bacon thus saved that is not to be met with in any which you can purchase.

Another method is as follows:—prepare a pickle, by boiling common salt and nitre in water; mix, for a single hog, of tolerable size, one pound of coarse brown sugar, with half a pound of nitre; rub this well in with the salting-glove, then put the meat into the pickle, and let it lie in this for two days; afterward take it out of the pickle, and rub it with salt alone, then put it back into the pickle.

For a *mild cure*—form *sweet pickle*, by boiling molasses with salt and water; rub the meat with sugar and nitre—add a small portion of strong pickle to the meat—put the meat into this, and let it lie in it for about three weeks. If there be any spare room in the cask, fill up with molasses—eight pounds of salt; one pound of nitre, and six pints of molasses will about suffice for each hundred weight of meat; and will take about five gallons of water.

In about three weeks—less or more time being required according to size—take the meat out of pickle, and hang it in the drying-house. While in the drying-house, the flitches should be hung, neck downward. You may cut out the ham, and trim the flitch according to fancy—nearly every county in England has in this respect a fashion of its own.

You then remove your hams and bacon to the smoking-house; they should not be suffered to *touch each other;* with this precaution you may hang them as close as you please. Smoke-houses are of every dimension, but the smallest answer as well as the most extensive. Before suspending the meat in the smoke-house, it should be previously well rubbed over with bran. The fire is made of saw-dust, which burns with a low smouldering glow, giving out far more smoke than if actually flaming.

In the process of smoking, your meat will lose from about fifteen to twenty pounds per hundred weight—a fact necessary to be borne in mind.

Sometimes the hogs are killed before they arrive at full size, and their hair removed by singeing; the bacon and hams of these are said to possess peculiar delicacy of flavor.

The best saw-dust for smoking hams or bacon is that made from oak, and it should be thoroughly dry. The saw-dust of common deal imparts a flavor of a disagreeable character, not unlike that of red herrings.

Westphalian Hams.—The *genuine* Westphalian bacon is particularly good, but all sold under that name is not genuine; spurious Westphalian hams are manufactured to a considerable extent. The process of imitation is not difficult, and none but one of the trade can detect the imposture. The fine quality of Westphalian bacon depends on several causes: the healthy and semi-wild life the swine are permitted to enjoy —their relationship to the wild boar—they are not fattened to the fullest extent previous to killing. A large proportion of *sugar* and *juniper-berries* are used in curing—the proportion being usually one and a half pounds of sugar to three of salt, and two ounces of nitre. The *smoke* is also applied in a *cold state*. This is, perhaps, the principal secret. The hams are all hung at the top of a very lofty building, and by the time the smoke reaches them it is perfectly cold.

The ham of the Westphalian hog closely resembles that of the common old Irish breed; and the hams of that animal, when cured as has been described, could not be distinguished from those of Westphalia by the nicest judge.

Limerick.—The hams cured in Limerick have long enjoyed considerable celebrity, and are supposed to be superior to any others—those of Westphalia and Hampshire alone excepted. Their excellence appears chiefly to depend upon the sparing use of salt, and the substitution for it, to a great extent, of coarse sugar, with judicious smoking. Some of the Limerick smoking-rooms are upward of thirty feet in height.

Hampshire.—The Hampshire bacon is in greater esteem than even the Westphalian—a circumstance attributable to the superior excellence of the New-Forest swine to those of that country, while they share equally with them the privilege of a forest life and acorns. The Hampshire curers smoke with saw-dust. In both this county and in Berkshire, *singeing* is adopted more generally than scalding, and this process is considered superior to scalding, the latter being supposed to soften the rind and render the fat less firm.

The Wiltshire bacon is of peculiarly delicious quality, but the cause is obvious, and is not to be referred to any of the details of the curing process. This bacon is prepared from *dairy-fed* pork—this is the true secret.

In some counties the pig is *skinned* prior to curing. Some amount of additional profit is of course derivable from this practice, but the bacon is inferior, being liable to become rusty, as well as to waste in the boiling.

Hams and flitches should always be hung up in a *dry* place, indeed it will be found useful to sew up the former in pieces of canvas or sacking, as is practiced with the Westphalian.

It is difficult to save bacon in summer time, or in warm climates, but a machine has recently been invented, for which a patent has been obtained, which renders the saving of meat under the most adverse circumstances perfectly easy. The machine acts as a force-pump or syringe. Its extremity is inserted into the meat, and the handle worked; the brine, which must be very strong, is thus *forced through* the grain of the meat, and it is effectually impregnated with it, and well cured long ere it could turn: there can be no doubt but that this instrument is, under the circumstances described, eminently useful—but it is no less certain that meat so cured is not equal to that saved under ordinary circumstances and in the ordinary manner; the *grain of the meat* is too much loosened by the use of the machine, and the texture is thus deteriorated; it should therefore only be used when *necessity* requires, and never by *preference*, where the ordinary process can be adopted.

To extract the superabundant salt from your meat, prior to use, has long been a desideratum. The steeping it in water to which carbonate of soda has been added, is found useful; so is the addition of the same substance, or of lime, to the water in which it is boiled; so is changing the water, after the meat has been about half-boiled. Sailors find washing the meat in sea-water very efficacious, but I have made the discovery that this object can be attained to a far fuller extent by a very simple chemical process.

Put your meat to steep in tepid water, and after it has lain in it for some hours, add a small quantity of sulphuric acid. In three or four hours take it out, and wash it two or three times in water; to the third water add a small portion of carbonate of soda. Take your meat out, wash it again, and boil it for dinner. You will find the salt nearly, if not wholly discharged; but you need not be surprised should the *color* of the meat be somewhat darkened—the deterioration does not extend farther; the flavor remains the same as when first corned, and the article becomes as wholesome as fresh meat. It is possible that this simple process may be found useful in long voyages, for a long-continued use of salted animal food, without a free use of vegetables, is found to contribute to the production of many diseases.

The following communication, coming from a curer by profession, will be found at once interesting and useful:

"The hog is usually kept fasting for twenty-four hours previous to being killed. He is then brought to the slaughter-house, and dispatched in the following manner: the butcher takes a mall (a hammer with a long handle, like those used for breaking stones on a road), and with it strikes the hog on the forehead; if he be an expert hand, a single blow will suffice to knock the hog down and render him quite senseless. A knife is then taken, and the butcher sticks the animal in the lower part of the throat, just between the fore-legs. A boiler or tub, full of very hot or boiling water, is then prepared, in which the hog is immersed until the hair becomes so loose that it can be scraped off with a knife quite clean; where there is no convenience of this kind, the same effect may be produced by pouring boiling water over the hog. The hog is then hung up by the hind-legs, cut up the middle, and the entrails taken out; after this, the carcass is left there for about twelve hours, to cool and become firm, when it is fit for boning or cutting up. Sometimes, instead of scalding, the hog is singed by fire—burned straw is generally used for this purpose; and this is called 'singed pork.'

"The following is the mode of boning or cutting: the pig is placed on a strong table or bench; the head is then cut off close to the ears; the hog is then opened down the back, a cleaver or saw is used for the purpose, and both back-bone and hip-bones are taken out, except in one or two places yet to be spoken of, where a different system is pursued. The hind-feet are then cut off, so as to leave a shank to the ham. The fore-legs are then cut round at the hough, the flesh scraped upward off the bone, and off the shoulder-blade, which is taken out quite bare, under the side. The saw is then run along the ribs, so as to crack them; they then lie quite flat. The hog is then divided straight up the back, and the sides are ready for salting, the ham still remaining in.

"When the sides are ready for salting, they are well rubbed on the rind side, and the space from which the shoulder-blade was taken out is filled with salt. The sides are then laid singly upon a flagged floor, and salt is shaken over them. In a day, or two days if the weather be cold, they must again be salted in the same manner; but now two sides may be put together, and powdered saltpetre shaken over each side, in the proportion of about two ounces to each side, if of average bacon size. After three or four days, the sides are to be again changed, the shanks of the hams rubbed, the salt stirred on, a little fresh salt shaken over them, and five or six sides may now be placed over each other. The sides may then be left thus for a week, when they may be piled one over the other to the number of ten or twenty sides, if you have killed so many hogs. Leave them so for above three weeks, until they get firm; they may then be considered saved, and will keep so for six or eight months, or according to pleasure.

"When required for use or for market, the sides are taken out of the salt, well swept and cleaned—the ham taken out, hung up, and dried with turf smoke; if a brown color be desired, a little saw-dust of hard wood may be thrown over the turf. If hung up in a kitchen where turf is burned, and suffered to remain, not too near the fire, the same effect will be produced; and if the bacon have been well saved in salt, it will be excellent.

"The Belfast and Limerick methods of cutting differ from what I have described, inasmuch as the hip-bones are left in, and the hams are cut out, while the hog is fresh, and saved separately. In some cases, also, the ribs are taken out of the sides, and, in Belfast, the shoulder-blade is taken out over the side.

"Both the Belfast and Limerick hams are cured in the same mild manner; they are, as I have stated, cut out of the hog when fresh, cured separately, and only left a sufficient time to be saved, and no more. They are not suffered to become too salty, a fault sometimes perceptible in the Wicklow hams. The Limerick and Belfast curers also make up different other portions of the hog separately, as long sides, middles, and rolls, for the English market.

"Sometimes the ribs are taken out, and sometimes not, according to the market for which they are intended.

"Limerick and Belfast hams are cured in the following manner:— They are cut fresh from the pig, with the hip-bones left in them, and are placed on a flagged floor, the front of the second ham resting upon the shank of the first, and so until all are placed; they are then sprinkled with strong pickle from a watering pot, and a small quantity of salt is shaken over them. Next day, the hams are taken up, well rubbed with salt, and laid down as before, when saltpetre is shaken over them in quantities proportionate to their size; they are left so for two days, and then taken up and rubbed as before, when they are laid down again, according to the space they have to fill—from three to six hams in height, with layers of salt between. After six days, the hams are reversed in the piles, that is, those that were packed on the top are put at the bottom. They then remain for six days longer in the pile, when they are considered cured. They are then taken up, and washed, and hung up to dry in the air. When they are to be smoked, they should be placed in a house made for that purpose, and smoked—in Belfast, with wheaten straw and saw-dust, in Limerick with peat or turf.

"The English method of cutting up and curing is similar to that practiced in Belfast and Limerick, with the difference that, with the exception of Hampshire and I believe one other county, they never smoke their bacon.

"We have, this season, had imported a great quantity of hams and other bacon from Cincinnati and Baltimore, in America. They are cut in the same manner as the Limerick, and are in much esteem. The cured shoulders of the hog have also been imported—cut straight across, with the blade in, and the shank left attached. We have also received middles, and quantities of pork, in barrels, which is merely the hog cut up in pieces, and pickled.

"I have reason to know that there are at the present time numbers of curers emigrating from our best curing districts to America, and we may accordingly expect, ere long, to find our American hams surpassing, owing to the quality of the hogs they will have to operate upon, even our long-famed Limerick hams."

LIVE-STOCK—NUMBER TO BE KEPT, ETC.

The animals necessary for the stocking and cultivation of a farm, and those which are kept on it for profit, or for the sake of their dung, are called the live-stock of the farm, in contra-distinction to the dead-stock, which consists of the implements of husbandry and the produce stored up for use.

The live-stock on a farm must vary according to circumstances. The number of horses or oxen kept for the cultivation of the land and other farming operations should be exactly proportioned to the work to be done. If they are too few, none of the operations will be performed in their proper time, and the crops will suffer in consequence. If there are too many, the surplus beyond what is strictly required is maintained out of the profits of the farm. To have the exact number of animals which will give the greatest profit is one of the most important problems which a farmer has to solve: what may be very profitable in one case may be the reverse in another; and, as a general maxim, it may be laid down, that the fewer mouths he has to feed, unless they produce an evident profit, the less loss he is likely to incur. But this rule admits of many exceptions. It is of great importance, in taking a farm, to calculate the extent of the arable land, so that it can be properly cultivated by a certain number of pairs of horses or oxen. It is an old measure of land to divide it into so many plows, that is, so many portions which can be tilled with one plow each. When there are several of these, it is useful to have an odd horse over the usual number required for two or three plows, to relieve the others occasionally. The work is thus done more regularly and with greater ease. Where there are two plows with two horses each, a fifth horse should be kept, and so in proportion for a greater number. The odd horse will always be found extremely useful, if not indispensable, and the expense of his keep will be amply repaid by the regularity and ease with which the whole work of the farm will be done, and the relief which occasional rest will give to the other horses.

The other part of the live-stock kept on a farm must depend on various circumstances. Where there is good grazing land, the profit on the improvement of the live-stock, or their produce, is evident and easily ascertained. But where animals are kept upon artificial food or fatted in stalls, it is often a difficult question to answer, whether there is a profit on their keep or not. In most cases the manure which their dung and litter afford is the chief object for which they are kept. If manure could be obtained in sufficient quantities to recruit the land, at a reasonable price, it might often be more advantageous to sell off all the hay and straw of a farm, and to keep only the cattle necessary to till the ground or supply the farmer's family. But this can only be the case in the immediate neighborhood of large towns. In the country at a greater distance no manure can be purchased; it must consequently be produced on the farm; and for this purpose live-stock must be kept, even at a loss. The management and feeding of live-stock is therefore an important part of husbandry. The object of the farmer is principally to obtain manure for his land, and if he can do this, and at the same time gain something on the stock by which it is obtained, he greatly increases his profits. Hence much more skill has been displayed in the selection of profitable stock than in the improvement of tillage. Some men have made great profits by improving the breed of cattle and sheep, by selecting the animals which will fatten most readily, and by feeding them economically. It requires much experience and nice calculations to ascertain what stock is most profitable on different kinds of land and in various situations. Unless very minute accounts be kept, the result can never be exactly known. It is not always the beast which brings most money in the market that has been most profitable; and many an animal which has been praised and admired has caused a heavy loss to the feeder. Unless a man breeds the animals which are to be fatted, he must frequently buy and sell; and an accurate knowledge of the qualities of live-stock and their value, both lean and fat, is indispensable. However honest may be the salesman he may employ, he cannot expect him to feel the same interest in a purchase or sale, for which he is paid his commission, as the person whose profit or loss depends on a judicious selection and a good bargain. Every farmer therefore should endeavor to acquire a thorough knowledge of stock, and carefully attend all markets within his reach to watch the fluctuation in the prices. It will generally be found that the principal profit in feeding stock is the manure, and to this the greatest attention should be directed. A little management will often greatly increase both the quantity and quality of this indispensable substance, and make all the difference between a loss and a profit in the keeping of stock.

THE "CREAM-POT" BREED OF CATTLE.—This is a valuable dairy-breed and promises to exceed all other breeds in this country, in the quantity and richness of the milk it furnishes, and the extraordinary amount of butter which it yields. This breed originated in New England, and was produced by Col. Jaques, of Ten Hills Farm, Somerville, Mass., by crossing the improved short-horns with the most valuable native breed. Col. Jaques thus speaks of the origin of this breed:—" Hearing of cows that produce seventeen pounds of butter each per week, the inquiry arose, why not produce a breed of such cows that may be depended on? This I attempted, and have accomplished. I have made from one of my Cream-Pot cows nine pounds of butter in three days on grass feed only.

"The bull Cœlebs, an imported thorough-bred Durham, and Flora, a heifer of the same breed, and imported, and a native cow, whose pedigree is entirely unknown, comprise the elements of the Cream-Pot breed of cattle. The native cow was bought in consequence of her superior quality as a milker, giving eighteen quarts a day, and averaging about fifteen. In the month of April, the cream of two days' milk produced two and three-fourths pounds of butter, made of two and one-sixteenth quarts of cream, and required but two minutes' churning. Thus much for the mother of the Cream-Pots.

"I have bred my Cream-Pots with red or mahogany-colored hair and teats, and gold-dust in the ears, yellow noses and skin, the latter silky and elastic to the touch, being like a fourteen-dollar cloth. My Cream-Pots are full in the body, chops deep in the flank, not quite as straight in the belly, nor as full in the twist, nor quite as thick in the thigh as the Durhams; but in other respects like them. They excel in affording a great quantity of rich cream, capable of being converted into butter in a short time, with little labor, and with a very small proportion of buttermilk, the cream producing more than eighty per cent. of butter. I have changed the cream to butter not unfrequently in one minute, and it has been done in forty seconds."

Henry Colman thus refers to Col. Jaques's stock:—"Mr. Jaques is entitled to great credit for his care and judicious selection in continuing and improving his stock. I have repeatedly seen the cream from his cows, and its yellowness and consistency are remarkable, and in company with several gentlemen of the Legislature, I saw a portion of it converted to butter with a spoon in one minute. The color of Mr. Jaques's stock is a deep red, a favorite color in New England; they are well formed and thrifty on common feed; and if they continue to display the extraordinary properties by which they are now so distinguished, they promise to prove the most valuable race of animals ever known among us for dairy purposes, and equal to any of which we have any information."

TO ESTIMATE THE LIVE WEIGHT OF CATTLE, etc.—Drovers and butchers by long experience become very expert in estimating, by simple inspection, the weight of live cattle ; and in making purchases, they thus have a decided advantage over the less experienced seller. Hence, the importance to the latter of some means by which he can *know*, and not guess at the weight of his live animals.

The following rules, the result of careful experiments, and which we take from *The Valley Farmer*, will enable any one to ascertain the weight of live animals with a close approach to accuracy:—take a string, put it around the breast, stand square just behind the shoulder-blade, measure on a rule the feet and inches the animal is in circumference; this is called the girth ; then, with the string, measure from the bone of the tail which plumbs the line with the hinder part of the buttock; direct the line along the back to the fore part of the shoulder-blade ; take the dimensions on the foot-rule as before, which is the length ; and work the figures in the following manner:—girth of the animal, say six feet four inches, length five feet three inches, which multiplied together, makes thirty-one square superficial feet, and that multiplied by twenty-three, the number of pounds allowed to each superficial foot of cattle measuring less than seven and more than five feet in girth, makes seven hundred and thirteen pounds. When the animal measures less then nine and more than seven feet in girth, thirty-one is the number of pounds to each superficial foot. Again, suppose a pig or any small beast should measure two feet in girth and two along the back, which multiplied together makes four square feet, that multiplied by eleven, the number of pounds allowed to each square foot of cattle measuring less than three feet in girth, makes forty-four pounds. Again, suppose a calf, a sheep, etc, should measure four feet six inches in girth, and three feet nine inches in length, which multiplied together make fifteen and a quarter square feet; that multiplied by sixteen, the number of pounds allowed to cattle measuring less than five feet and more than three in girth, makes two hundred and sixty-five pounds. The dimensions of girth and length of horned cattle, sheep, calves, and hogs, may be exactly taken in this way, as it is all that is necessary for any computation, or any valuation of stock, and will answer exactly to the four quarters, sinking offal.

DOMESTIC POULTRY:

THEIR

BREEDS AND TREATMENT

IN

HEALTH AND DISEASE.

THE DOMINIQUE COCK.

DOMESTIC POULTRY.

" How grateful 'tis to wake
While raves the midnight storm, and hear the sound
Of busy grinders at the well-filled rack;
Or flapping wing or crow of chanticleer,
Long ere the lingering morn; or bouncing flails
That tell the dawn is near! Pleasant the path
By sunny garden wall, when all the fields
Are chill and comfortless; or barn-yard snug,
Where flocking birds, of various plume and chirp
Discordant, cluster on the leaning stack
From whence the thresher draws the rustling sheaves."

VIEW OF THE IMPORTANCE OF THE SUBJECT.—Poultry-keeping is an amusement in which every body may indulge. The space needed is not great, the cost of food for a few head insignificant, and the luxury of fresh eggs or home-fatted chickens or ducks not to be despised. In a large collection of poultry may be read the geography and progress of the commerce of the world. The peacock represents India; the golden pheasant and a tribe of ducks, China; the turkey, pride of the yard and the table, America; the black swan, rival of the snowy monarch of the lakes, reminds us of Australian discoveries; while Canada and Egypt have each their goose. The large fat white ducks—models of what a duck should be—are English, while the shining green black ones come from Buenos Ayres. And when we turn to the fowl varieties, Spain and Hamburg, Poland and Cochin China, Friesland and Bantam, Java and Negroland, beside Surry, Sussex, Kent, Suffolk, and Lancashire, have each a cock to crow for them.
VARIETIES OF THE DOMESTIC FOWL.—1. The MALAY FOWL, from its size and strength, is admirably adapted for crossing with the Dorking and other native breeds. 2. The JAVA FOWL, nearly resembling, and in the opinion of some, identical with, the Malay. 3. The COCHIN CHINA breed, equal in most respects, and more prolific than the Malay. 4. The SPANISH FOWL, perhaps the best breed known for laying. 5. The POLISH FOWL, a noble and very beautiful bird, and an excellent layer. 6. The SPANGLED VARIETIES, including the whole class of Gold and Silver Spangled, known in different countries as Spangled Hamburgs, Every-day Dutch, Bolton Bays, Bolton Greys, Chittyprats, Creoles, Corals, etc. 7. The SPECKLED and WHITE DORKING, the most delicate of all the varieties for the table. 8. The SUSSEX FOWL, most probably a variety of the Dorking. 9. The GAME FOWL, graceful of form and plumage, with undying courage, and excellent for crossing with common varieties. 10. The PHEASANT FOWL, erroneously said to originate in a cross with the Cock Pheasant. 11. The BANTAMS, more remarkable for their beauty than any other quality.
The Malay Fowl, called also the Chittagong.—This is a large and heavy fowl; it is a close and hard-feathered bird, from which circumstance it

often weighs more than it appears to do. It stands tall, with very upright gait. The legs are long, the thighs are remarkably long, strong, and firm; and the tarsi of moderate length, round, stout, and of a yellow color. The tail is long and drooping, the head snake-shaped, *i. e.*, with a great fullness over the eye, and of a flattened form above. The thick comb, scarcely rising from the head, has been compared to half a strawberry; so that the *natural* form of comb a little resembles that of the game-fowl when dubbed. The neck is rope-like and close-feathered, and the bird is almost without wattle.

The Malay should have a pearl eye, and a hawk bill free from stain.

The pullets commence laying early, and are often good winter layers. The egg is of medium size, with a tinted shell. The chickens when half-grown, are gaunt, ungainly looking young things, and, like many choice kinds, fledge slowly.

Height is a great point in a Malay. Old fanciers had a curious mode of comparing notes upon this point. They used to hold the bird out at full stretch, and measure the length, from beak to toe, on a table. Some of old Mr. Castang's breed are mentioned as having measured thirty-eight and a half inches. The cocks are said to have weighed from nine and a half pounds to eleven pounds, and the hens from eight pounds to ten pounds.

I have known a Spanish cock and a Malay hen produce excellent fowls for the table, being large, fleshy, and well-flavored.

The Malays are inveterate fighters; and this is the quality for which they are chiefly prized in their native country, where cock-fighting is carried to the extent of excessive gambling. Men and boys may be frequently met, each carrying his favorite bird under his arm, ready to set to work the moment the opportunity shall occur.

The Cochin China.—The history of the Cochin-China fowl might be the history of the poultry mania, an excitement which rivaled manias of greater importance in its strength. They were introduced some time about the year 1845, and soon became known and popular. Their large size, in the eyes of most persons, their handsome appearance, the brightness of their colors, the number of their eggs, and their gentle, quiet disposition, soon made their way; they were much liked, and were bought eagerly at from three to six dollars each; at that time a very high price for a fowl. Cochin China hens are excellent layers of medium-sized eggs, which they produce in great abundance at the season when they are of greatest value. The chickens, if bred from mature birds, are exceedingly hardy; and the fowls are of quiet, domestic habits, and easily kept within bounds. A first-class fowl should be compact, large, and square-built; full in the chest, deep in the keel, and broad across the loins and hind quarters. The best in form are as compactly made as Dorkings. The head is delicately shaped, with a short bill, and the comb fine in texture, rather small, perfectly single, straight, and equally serrated; the wings small and closely folded in, the tail short, and carried rather horizontally; the legs very short, yellow (according to rule) and heavily feathered. This fowl has, however, lost its earlier popularity, and is now generally discarded by good poulterers, being found a voracious feeder, and yielding a comparatively small return for the food consumed.

COCHIN CHINA, OR SHANGHAI FOWL.

Spanish Fowls.—The chief drawbacks in rearing Spanish are the delicacy of the chickens while young, and the length of time which elapses before the youngsters show their quality, unless they are bred from much better fowls than most persons can command; in which case the chickens develop their prize properties earlier. The combs of the hens shrink very much when they are not laying, and during the moulting season. In winter they should be protected from severe cold, which is very apt to seize the comb and wattles of the cocks.

The hens lay larger eggs than any other kind of fowl we have: they are non-sitters. The chickens hatch out black, with a little mixture of dull white, or yellow. They fledge slowly, and are very delicate while young.

The Minorca.—This is a plump-bodied, useful fowl, which would be a Spanish, if it could persuade its parents to bequeath it the white face which breeders and judges think so much of. The plumage is black, with metallic luster, and the hens lay fine large eggs. I believe they sit more than the Spanish.

The White Spanish.—The white-faced white Spanish I believe to be merely a sport of the white-faced black Spanish. The red-faced white Spanish, or white Andalusian, is really a Spanish fowl. They are good layers, and very precocious. The stock was brought from Spain.

Andalusian Fowls.—The birds which have been shown under this name are in color the kind of gray called blue, which is sometimes laced and shaded with black. Mr. Taylor, late of Shepherd's Bush, imported the original stock from Spain. They are good-looking fowls with large pendent scarlet combs like the Spanish, and are said to be good layers.

248   DOMESTIC ANIMALS.

THE SPANISH FOWL.

Polands.—With these fowls there has been much difference of opinion respecting the applicability of the name. Some, with apparent reason, would divide them into three families; the St. Jago, the Turkish, and

THE POLISH FOWL.

the Hamburg, or muffed kind. We rank as Polands all fowls with their chief distinguishing characteristic—a full, large, round, compact tuft on the head. It is a class of fowls, the beauty of which, united to their useful qualities, must make general favorites. All the sub-varieties are of medium size, neat compact form, with full plump bodies, full breast, lead-colored legs, and ample tails. The kinds more or less known are very numerous: they are all good layers.

The *White-crested Black Poland* is a fowl of a deep velvety black, with a large white tuft on the head. They should be without comb; but many have a little comb in the form of two small points before the tuft. The tuft, to be perfect, should be entirely white; but it is rare to meet with one without a slight bordering of black, or partly black feathers round the front.

The *Golden* and *Silver Polands* are, the one a gold color, the other white spangled with black: the tuft, as in the black, should be large and compact. The more completely the color in the tuft can partake of the character of feather in the rest of the bird, the better. Some persons admit white in the tuft of the golden Poland, but I cannot help thinking the mixture a great fault. Mr. Baily (well known as one of the best judges) would like to see the feathers of the tuft laced. This is very difficult of attainment. The marking of the bird is a black spangle on the golden or silver ground-color. The wings are barred, and the best judges admit lacing on the wing-coverts.

There are several other varieties of tufted fowls or Polands, and many intelligent breeders have devoted great attention to them.

The black and the white are both beautiful, with full tufts, muffs, and clean legs.

THE GOLDEN SPANGLED HAMBURG FOWL.

Hamburg Fowls.—The Hamburg is a medium-sized fowl, with a brisk and spirited bearing, a brilliantly red double comb, ending in a spike at the back, taper blue legs, ample tail, exact markings, and a well developed white deaf ear. They are profitable fowls to keep, being excellent layers, and not large eaters. They are what pigeon-fanciers would call good field-birds, delighting to wander far abroad, and to seek provender for themselves. The varieties are,

The *Spangled Hamburg*, or pheasant-fowls, the marking of which takes the form of a spot upon each feather. They are divided into gold and silver, according to the ground-color of the plumage.

The *Penciled Hamburg*, in which the marking is more minute. When seen at a distance, the hens have the appearance of being minutely speckled in plumage, and over this a pure white hackle falls and contrasts very prettily. When one feather is taken separately, the marking is very exact and beautiful, being a regular penciling; *i. e.*, the feather is divided by bars evenly arranged, of alternate white and gold color. Like the spangled, they are divided into golden and silver for the same reason—the ground-color of the plumage. In all these birds, exactness of the markings is a great point.

The Black Hamburg.—This is a very beautiful variety, being of a brilliant black, with metallic luster. The brilliancy of the plumage, contrasted with the coral-red of the spiked comb and the white earlobes, renders this fowl so attractive in appearance, that we cannot help wondering that it is not more general, particularly as, like all the Hamburgs, it is an excellent layer.

THE DORKING FOWL.

The Dorking Fowl.—The Dorking would appear to owe its name to its having been chiefly bred in a town of Surry, of the same appellation. That the peculiarity of five toes, or, in other words, of two hind toes instead of one, is to be regarded as a distinctive character of the breed, is by some writers questioned, and by others wholly denied. For my part, I should say, that whenever this characteristic is absent, a cross has been at work.

I do not, however, mean to assert that this possession of two hind toes instead of one, has never occurred in any other family of fowl except those bred at Dorking, in Surry, for Aristotle has mentioned the existence of a similar peculiarity among certain fowl in Greece, and both Columella and Pliny assert the existence of such in their time in Italy, so also does Aldrovand; and these authors lived hundreds of years ago; and, oddly enough, these breeds were remarkable, as are our own Dorking, for being good layers and good sitters.

The color of the Dorking is usually pure white, or spotted or spangled with black; these colors sometimes merge into a gray or grizzle. The hens weigh from seven to nine ponnds; stand low on their legs;

are round, plump, and short in the body; wide on the breast, with abundance of white juicy flesh. The hens are generally good layers, and their eggs, though smaller than the egg of the Spanish and Polish breeds, are of good size and well flavored. These birds have been long prized, and it is now many years since their superiority over our ordinary domestic varieties was originally discovered and appreciated; they were first noticed, and the variety adopted, by the Cumberland breeders, whence they were soon brought into Lancashire and Westmoreland, and gradually spread over all England. Whether, however, from injudicious treatment, or imperfect feeding, or change of climate, or from whatever cause, it is certain that, when met with far from their native place, they appear greatly to have degenerated from their original superiority of character. In this, and all other varieties of fowl, fresh blood should be introduced from time to time, or the breed degenerates.

The best breed of the gallinaceous fowls is the produce of the Dorking (Surry) cock and the common dunghill fowl. This cross is larger and plumper, and more hardy than the pure Dorking, without losing delicacy of flavor or whiteness of flesh.

The characteristics of the pure Dorking are, that it is white-feathered, short-legged, and an excellent layer. The peculiarity of this established variety, which has frequently five claws perfectly articulated (with sometimes a sixth springing laterally from the fifth, but always imperfect), is well known. The crossing with the Sussex fowl has however greatly diminished the monstrosity in the Surry pentadactylus variety. But though the true Dorking, which is white, is much esteemed, that color is rare, and prized for the ornament of the poultry-yard; speckled colors are most generally seen with the higgler.

The Sussex.—This is but an improved variety of Dorking, similar in shape and general character, usually of a brown color, but possessing the advantage of wanting the fifth toe; we say advantage, for the Dorking fowl frequently becomes diseased in the feet, the cocks especially, in consequence of breaking the supplementary toe in fighting.

The Game Fowl.—The game fowl is one of the most gracefully-formed and most beautifully colored of our domestic breeds of poultry; in its form and aspect, and in the extraordinary courage which characterizes its natural disposition, it exhibits all that either the naturalist or the sportsman recognizes as the *beau ideal* of high blood, embodying, in short, all the most indubitable characteristics of gallinaceous aristocracy.

We do not possess any very satisfactory record of the original country of the game fowl; but we are disposed to cede that honor to India, the natives of which country have always been remarkable for their love of cock-fighting; and we also know that there still exists in India an original variety of game cock, very similar to our own, but inferior in point of size. As to the date or occasion of their first introduction into the British islands, we know nothing certain; but it is probable that we owe it to the invasion of Julius Cæsar, the Romans having been very fond of the sport of cock fighting.

It is not only for its pugnacious qualities that the game fowl is to be noticed; it yields to no breed, nay, perhaps is superior to most, in the

THE GAME COCK AND HEN.

whiteness and sapidity of its flesh; the hens are excellent layers, and the eggs, though of moderate size only, are remarkable for the delicacy of their flavor. The game cock is very attentive to his female train, and ever ready to do battle in their defense; but not unfrequently he becomes savage and dangerous. A blow with his spur is no trifle. Children have been severely injured, and cases have been mentioned in which they have been killed. From these causes, and from the fact that the young broods, as soon as fairly feathered, begin to fight among themselves with desperate determination, blinding each other, stripping the skin from each other's heads and necks, and killing each other on the spot, many persons object to keep this breed; and it must be confessed that it occasions great trouble; it is not always convenient or possible to separate the young broods; and as the young cocks and hens fight indiscriminately, it not unfrequently happens that one-half is destroyed in the *mêlée*, while most of the survivors are so mangled as to render it necessary to put them out of pain, to the mortification of the farmer or breeder of fowls for profit; for not only are the broods lost, but the time also.

Of all breeds, the game breed is the most beautiful, whether we look to contour or coloring; the game cock carries himself proudly, and yet gracefully; his port and bearing proclaim his fiery spirit and undaunted mettle, which endure even to his last breath; for while prostrate and mortally wounded, he will answer the insulting crow of his victorious rival, and make a last effort to revenge himself before the spark of life is extinct. No wonder that the gallant cock should have been chosen as the emblem of courage.

Bantams.—The classes of Bantams are gold-laced, silver-laced, white, black, and one for "any other variety;" from which last may especially be selected the exceedingly beautiful game Bantams, and the once popular, but now rare, booted sub-variety. Diminutive size and bold carriage are important points in all Bantams; in other respects, the different kinds differ as much as distinct varieties of fowls can do. The Bantams are peculiarly fancy fowls; they have been accused of not being a useful kind, as of course there is little to eat in a fowl which, when full grown, should weigh, the cock about a pound, the hen less, the eggs

THE SEABRIGHT BANTAM.

being small in proportion. But how many hundreds of amateurs there are whose opportunities give them no room for full-sized fowls, but who, delighting in living things, can indulge their fancy and beguile many hours which would otherwise prove weary ones, by keeping a few Bantams. Their small eggs are delicacies which would tempt almost any invalid.

WHITE BANTAM COCK AND HEN.

The *gold and silver-laced, or Seabright Bantam*, is perhaps the most popular kind of all. The size should be quite diminutive, and the carriage saucy.

The *booted Bantam*, of which the most beautiful we have seen have been pure white, are completely feathered on the legs—not feathered down one side only, like the Cochin China.

Game Bantams are exact miniature representatives of game fowls, black-breasted reds, duck-wings, and other colors. An exact duck-wing game Bantam is the most beautiful little creature one can imagine.

BLACK BANTAM COCK AND HEN.

THE DOMESTIC TURKEY.—The domestic turkey can scarcely be said to be divided, like the common fowl, into distinct breeds, although there is, indeed, considerable variation in color, and also in size. The finest and strongest turkeys are said to be those of a bronzed black, resembling as closely as possible the original stock; they are reared the most easily, are large, and fatten rapidly. Some turkeys are of a coppery tint, others of a delicate fawn-color, others particolored, gray, and white, and some few of a pure snowy white. All these are considered inferior to the black; their color indicates something like degeneracy of constitution, and they are seldom very large-sized.

In the choice of store-birds some care is requisite; the stock should be of a good sort; the black Norfolk race is an excellent sort, probably produced originally by a cross with the wild breed of America.

Early in spring, generally speaking, the female commences laying; she indicates her intention by a peculiar cry, by strutting about with an air of self-satisfaction, and often by prying into out-of-the-way places. She should now be closely watched, and some management is required to induce her to lay in the place desired.

The nest should be prepared of straw and dried leaves; it should be secluded; and to excite her to adopt it, an egg, or a piece of chalk cut into the form of an egg, should be placed in it. When her uneasiness to lay is evident, and symptoms prove that she is ready, she should be confined in the shed, barn, or place in which her nest (in a large wicker basket) is prepared, and let out as soon as the egg is laid. It is generally in the morning that the turkey-hen lays, and mostly every other day, though some lay daily, until the number of eggs amounts to from fifteen to twenty. As the eggs are laid, it is as well to remove them (leaving the decoy egg or piece of chalk) until the number is complete; as they are liable to be broken, or to be sucked by rats or weasels. They may then be restored to her for incubation. The turkey-hen is a steady sitter, and in this respect resembles the wild bird; nothing will induce her to leave her nest; indeed, she often requires to be removed to her food, so overpowering is her instinctive affection. She must be freely supplied with water within her reach; should she lay any eggs after she has commenced incubation, these should be removed: it is proper, therefore, to mark those which were given to her to sit upon. The hen should on no account be rashly disturbed; no one except the person to whom she is accustomed, and from whom she receives her food, should be allowed to go near her, and the eggs, unless circumstances imperatively require it, should not be meddled with.

On the twenty-sixth day, according to some on whom dependence may be placed (the thirty-first according to others), the chicks leave the eggs.

The treatment of the chick now requires attention. As in the case of young fowls, the turkey chicks do not require food for several hours. It is useless to cram them, as some do, fearing lest they should starve; and besides, the beak is as yet so tender that it runs a chance of being injured by the process. When the chicks feel an inclination for food, nature directs them how to pick it up. There is no occasion for alarm, if for many hours they content themselves with the warmth of their parent, and enjoy her care only. Yet some food must be provided for them, and this should be, of course, suited to their nature and appetite. Here, too, let the simplicity of nature be a guide. We say this, because some have recommended spices, wine, and even bathing in cold water.

The first diet offered to turkey chicks should consist of eggs boiled hard and finely minced, or curd with bread crumbs, boiled nettles, and the green part of onions, parsley, etc., chopped very small, and mixed together, so as to form a loose crumbly paste. Barley or oatmeal, kneaded with a little water, and mixed with the pulp of potatoes and Swedish turnips, to which chopped beet-leaves are added, may also be given. They will require water; but this should be put into very shallow vessels, so as to insure against the danger of the chicks getting wet. Fresh milk is apt to disagree with the young birds, and is not needful. Both the turkey-hen and her chickens should be housed for a few days; they may then, if the weather be fine, be allowed a few hours' liberty during the day; but should a shower threaten, they must be put immediately under shelter. This system must be persevered in for three or four weeks. By this time they will have acquired considerable strength, and will know how to take care of themselves. On the first drops of a shower, they will run for shelter into their accustomed place of refuge, which should be warm and waterproof. As they get older, meal and grain may be given them more freely. They now begin to search for insects, and to dust their growing plumage in the sand. At the age of about two months, or perhaps a little more, the males and females begin to develop their distinctive characteristics. In the young males the carunculated skin of the neck and throat, and the horn-like contractile comb on the forehead, assume a marked character. This is a critical period. The system requires a full supply of nutriment, and good housing at night is essential. Some recommend that a few grains of cayenne pepper, or a little bruised hempseed, be mixed with their food. The distinctive sexual marks once fairly established, the young birds lose their names of *chicks* or *chickens*, and are termed *turkey poults*. The time of danger is over, and they become independent, and every day stronger and more hardy. They now fare as the rest of the flock, on good and sufficient food, if their keeper is alive to his own interest. I again repeat it, that a man who keeps poultry on meagre, spare, innutritious diet, will never rear fine poultry, and never repay himself even for his niggardly outlay. Poultry should never be in bad condition: let them not be kept at all, unless they are kept properly.

THE WILD TURKEY is a noble bird, far exceeding its domestic relative in neatness of form and beauty. Crosses in America often take place between the wild and tame races, and are highly valued, both for. external qualities and for the table. In districts where the wild turkey is common, such crosses are quite frequent; the wild male driving away his domesticated rival, and usurping the sultanship of the seraglio. Eggs of the wild turkey have frequently been taken from their nests, and hatched under the tame hen. The young preserve a portion of their uncivilized nature, and exhibit some knowledge of the difference between themselves and their foster-mother, roosting apart from the tame ones, and in other respects showing the force of hereditary disposition. The domesticated young reared from the eggs of the wild turkey are often employed as decoy-birds to those in a state of nature. Mr. William Bloom, of Clearfield, Pennsylvania, caught five or six wild turkeys when quite chickens, and succeeded in rearing them. Although sufficiently .ame to feed with his tame turkeys, and generally associate with them, yet they always retained some of their original propensities, roosting by themselves, and higher than the tame birds, generally on the top of some tree, or on the house. They were also more readily alarmed. On the approach of a dog they would fly off, and seek safety in the woods. On an occasion of this kind, one of them flew across the Susquehanna, and the owner was apprehensive of losing it. In order to recover it, he sent a boy with a tame turkey, which was released at the place where the fugitive had alighted. This plan was successful. They soon joined company, and the tame bird induced his companion to return home. Mr. Bloom found occasion to remark that the wild turkey will thrive more and keep in better condition than the tame turkey, on the same quantity of food.

The native country of the wild turkey extends from the northwestern territory of the United States to the Isthmus of Panama, south of which it is not to be found, notwithstanding the statements of authors, who have mistaken the curassow for it. In Canada, and the now densely-peopled parts of the United States, wild turkeys were formerly very abundant, but, like the Indian buffalo, they have been compelled to yield to the destructive ingenuity of the white settlers, often wantonly exercised, and seek refuge in the remotest parts of the interior. Although they relinquish their native soil with slow and reluctant steps, yet such is the rapidity with which settlements are extended, and condensed over the surface of this country, that we may anticipate a day, at no distant period, when the hunter will seek the wild turkey in vain.

The wooded part of Arkansas, Louisiana, Tennessee, and Alabama; the unsettled portions of the states of Ohio, Kentucky, Indiana, and Illinois; the vast expanse of territory northwest of these states, on the Mississippi and Missouri, as far as the forests extend, are more supplied than any other parts of the Union with this valuable game, which forms an important part of the subsistence of the hunter and traveler in the wilderness. It is not probable that the range of this bird extends to or beyond the Rocky Mountains. The Mandan Indians, who a few years ago visited the city of Washington, considered the turkey one of the greatest curiosities they had seen, and prepared a skin of one to carry home for exhibition.

In Florida, Georgia, and the Carolinas, the wild turkey is not common, and still less so in the western parts of Virginia and Pennsylvania. Some, however, are said to exist in the mountainous districts of Sussex county, New Jersey.

The wild turkey is irregularly migratory, as well as irregularly gregarious. Whenever the forest fruits (or mast) of one portion of the country greatly exceed those of another, thither are the turkeys insensibly led, by gradually meeting in their haunts with more fruit, the nearer they advance toward the place in which it is most plentiful. Thus, in an irregular manner, flock follows flock, until some districts are deserted, while others are crowded with an influx of arrivals. "About the beginning of October," says Audubon, "when scarcely any of the seeds and fruits have fallen from the trees, these birds assemble in flocks, and gradually move toward the rich bottom-lands of the Ohio and Mississippi. The males, or, as they are more commonly called, the *gobblers*, associate in parties of from ten to a hundred, and search for food apart from the females; while the latter are seen either advancing singly, each with her brood of young, then about two-thirds grown, or in union with other families, forming parties, often amounting to seventy or eighty individuals, all intent on shunning the old cocks, which, when the young birds have attained this size, will fight with and often destroy them by repeated blows on the head. Old and young, however, all move in the same course, and on foot, unless their progress is interrupted by a river, or the hunter's dog force them to take wing.

" When they come upon a river, they betake themselves to the highest eminences, and there remain often a whole day, and sometimes two, as if for the purpose of consultation. During this time the males are heard gobbling, calling, and making much ado, and are seen strutting about, as if to raise their courage to a pitch befitting the emergency. Even the females and young assume something of the same pompous demeanor, spread out their tails, and run round each other, purring loudly, and performing extravagant leaps. At length, when the weather appears settled, and all around is quiet, the whole party mount to the tops of the highest trees, whence at a signal, consisting of a single cluck, given by a leader, the flock takes flight to the opposite shore. The old and fat birds easily get over, even should the river be a mile in breadth, but the younger and less robust frequently fall into the water—not to be drowned, however, as might be imagined; they bring their wings close to their bodies, spread out their tails as a support, stretch forward their necks, and striking out their legs with great vigor, proceed rapidly toward the shore; on approaching which, should they find it too steep for landing, they cease their exertions for a few moments, float down the stream till they come to an accessible part, and by a violent effort generally extricate themselves from the water. It is remarkable that, immediately after crossing a large stream, they ramble about for some time as if bewildered. In this state they fall an easy prey to the hunter.

" When the turkeys arrive in parts where the mast is abundant, they separate into smaller flocks, composed of birds of all ages and both sexes, promiscuously mingled, and devour all before them. This happens about the middle of November. So gentle do they sometimes become after these long journeys, that they have been seen to approach the farm-houses, associate with the domestic fowls, and enter the stables and corn-cribs in quest of food. In this way, roaming about the forests, and feeding chiefly on mast, they pass the autumn, and part of the winter."

The season of courtship begins about the middle of February. The females now separate from the males, whom they endeavor to shun, but by whom they are perseveringly followed.

It is generally about the middle of April that the female begins to select a site, and arrange her rude nest, which consists chiefly of withered leaves, in some depression on the ground, amidst dense brushwood, or in such an obscure place as the locality affords. The eggs, like those of the domestic bird, are of large size, and of a dull cream-white, minutely freckled or dotted with reddish-brown; their average number varies from ten to fifteen. While the gradual addition of egg to egg is going on, the hen displays surprising instinctive caution. On leaving her charge, she is careful to cover the whole with dry leaves, so artfully disposed as to render it difficult, even for one who has watched her movements, to find the nest; and on returning to it she varies her rout, scarcely ever returning to it twice by the same course. Hence it is mostly by accident that the nest of the hen is discovered. It not unfrequently happens that several hens associate together and form a common nest, probably for mutual aid and assistance, and rear their broods together. Audubon says that he once found three hens sitting on forty-two eggs. In such cases one of the females at least is ever on guard, no raven or crow then daring to invade the nest. While in the act of incubation, the hen is not readily driven from her nest by the appearance of danger. A person walking carelessly along as if taking no particular notice, may pass a nest within five or six paces, the female crouching low to avoid observation; but, as Mr. Audubon has ascertained, if a person make his approach in a stealthy searching manner, she will quit it while he is yet thirty yards distant, and assuming a stately gait, will move away, uttering every now and then a clucking note, probably hoping by this means to draw off the intruder and baffle his search. The same writer says that the hen seldom or never abandons her nest if it has been discovered by man, but that if a snake or any other animal has sucked any of the eggs, she leaves it altogether. Under such circumstances, or when the eggs have been removed, she seeks the male, and recommences the preparation of another nest; but, as a rule, she lays only a single batch of eggs during the season. When the eggs are on the eve of hatching, the female will not leave her nest under any circumstances while life remains; she will even allow an inclosure to be made around her, and thus be, as it were, imprisoned, rather than seek her own safety by flight.

Before leaving the nest with her young brood, the female shakes herself, adjusts her plumage, and appears roused to the exigencies of the occasion; she glances upward and around her, in the apprehension of enemies, and as she moves cautiously along, keeps her brood close about her; her first excursion is generally to a little distance only from the nest, to which she returns with her brood at night. Subsequently they wander to a greater distance, the hen leading her charge over dry undulating grounds, as if aware of the danger of damp and humid spots. Wet, indeed, is fatal to young turkeys while covered only with down; hence, in very rainy seasons the brood becomes greatly thinned, for the young, if once completely wetted, seldom recover; their vital energies sink under the abstraction of caloric during evaporation.

At the age of a fortnight, the young birds begin to use their wings; hitherto they have rested on the ground, but now they begin to roost on the low branch of some large tree, crowding close to each side of the mother, and sheltered beneath her broad wings. They now wander about more freely, visiting the glades and open lands bordering the woods, in search of wild strawberries and other fruits, grasshoppers, the larvæ of ants and other insects; and roll themselves in the sand and dust, in order to clear their glowing feathers of loose scales and parasitic vermin : deserted ants' nests are favorite dusting-places.

By the month of August, the young birds acquire considerable growth, and use their wings and legs with great vigor and readiness, so that they are able to escape the sudden attack of foxes, lynxes, and other beasts of prey, by rising quickly from the ground and mounting the tallest branches of trees. The young cocks now begin to show their distinctive characteristics, and even to utter an imperfect gobble, while the young hens purr and leap. Several broods flock together, and so continue united, till after the October migration, and through the winter, when the males leave the females.

Turkeys, though extremely delicate in their infancy, become very hardy, and, if permitted, will roost on the highest trees, in the cold dry nights of winter, without suffering injury. The hen, which lays many eggs early in spring, sits thirty days, and covers from twelve to fifteen eggs. It is unnecessary for the turkey cock, as is the case with gallinaceous fowl, to be in constant intercourse with the hen during her period of laying. Two visits from him in that season are sufficient to impregnate all the eggs. She is a very steady sitter, and must be removed to her food and supplied with water, for she would never leave her nest. She wants the alertness and courage and sagacity of the common hen, and might be called a fool with much more propriety than the goose, which is an intelligent bird. The turkey hen is incapable of teaching her young ones how to pick up their food, on which account a poultry-maid should always attend them until they are reared.

The author of "*Tabella Cibaria*" proves it upon the bird that it is "so stupid or timorous that if you balance a bit of straw on his head, or draw a line of chalk on the ground from his beak, he fancies himself loaded, or so bound that he will remain in the same position till hunger forces him to move. We made the experiment." We never did; but we doubt it not, though we cannot accept it as a proof of stupidity. How much wit may be necessary to balance a straw may be doubtful; but gallant chanticleer has never been charged either with fear or folly, and yet you have only to take him from his perch, place him on the table by candle-light, hold his beak down to the table, and draw a line with chalk from it, so as to catch his eye, and there the bird will remain spell-bound, till a bystander, rubbing out the line, or diverting his attention from it, breaks the charm. Many a fowl have we fascinated in our boyish days.*

The Guinea-Fowl. —The Guinea-fowl is slightly larger than the ordinary barn-door fowl, but is inferior in size to the larger foreign breeds, as the Malay and Spanish ; in both aspect and character it appears to occupy a position between the pheasant and the turkey. Although long familiarized, the Guinea-fowl has never been fully domesticated, still retaining much of the restlessness and shyness of its primitive feral habits. It is very courageous, and will not only frequently attack the turkey, but even prove victorious in the encounter.

The cock and hen are so nearly alike, that it is not easy to distin-

---

* "*Tabella Cibaria.*"

THE GUINEA-FOWL.

guish them; there is sometimes a difference of hue in certain parts; but this difference only occurs occasionally, and indeed it is on gait, voice, and demeanor that we must chiefly depend. It must be remarked that they pair; therefore a second hen will be neglected and useless except for eggs.

Like all the gallinaceous birds, the Guinea-fowl is esteemed for its flesh and its eggs, which, though smaller than those of the common fowl, are very excellent and numerous, the hen commencing to lay in the month of May, and continuing during the entire summer. After the pheasant season, young birds of the year are, on the table, by no means unworthy substitutes for that highly-prized game. Such birds are acceptable in the London market, and fetch a fair price. The Guinea-fowl is of a wild, shy, rambling disposition; and, domesticated as it is, it pertinaciously retains its original habits, and is impatient of restraint. It loves to wander along hedgerows, over meadows, through clover or corn fields, and amidst copses and shrubberies; hence these birds require careful watching, for the hens will lay in secret places, and will sometimes absent themselves entirely from the farm-yard until they return with a young brood around them. So ingeniously will they conceal themselves and their nest, so cautiously leave it and return to it, as to elude the searching glance of boys well used to bird-nesting; but it may always be found from the watchful presence of the cock while the hen is laying. There is one disadvantage in this, the bird will sit at a late period, and bring forth her brood when the season begins to be too cold for the tender chickens. The best plan is, to contrive that the hens shall lay in a quiet secluded place, and to give about twenty of the earliest eggs to a common hen ready to receive them, who will perform the duties of incubation with steadiness. In this way a brood in June may be easily obtained. The young must receive the same treatment as those of the turkey, and equal care; they require a mixture of boiled vegetables, with curds, farinaceous food, as grits, barley-meal, etc.; they should be induced to eat as often and as much as they will. In a short time they begin to search for insects and their larvæ; and with a little addition to such fare as this, and what vegetable matters they pick up, will keep themselves in good game condition, without cramming or overfeeding. For a week or two before being killed for the table, they should have a liberal allowance of grain and meal.

Guinea-fowls mate in pairs; overlooking this circumstance frequently occasions disappointment in the broods. The period of incubation is twenty-six days. Though they are not unprofitable birds, as they are capable of procuring almost entirely their own living, they are rejected by many on account both of their wandering habits, which give trouble, and their disagreeable voice, resembling the noise of a wheel turning on an ungreased axletree.

THE PEA-FOWL.—A peacock in full feather, parading on a green lawn, or from the extremity of a terrace-wall, displaying the full length of his gorgeous tail, is one of the most beautiful living additions to garden landscape. But of fruit he will prove a devourer, not to be guarded against, and both he and his mate are not unfrequently murderous assassins of the young of other fowl.

In domestication it is a rambling bird, unsuited to confined premises; it requires lawns, shrubberies, and wide pleasure-grounds, to which it is an appropriate ornament, whether it moves about with its tail expanded, or walks trailing it along down avenues of smooth turf, or amongst the woodland glades. Semi-wild as the peacock is, it is disposed to become familiar, and if encouraged will visit the windows of the house, in order to receive an accustomed dole of bread, and when displaying its plumage seems to be aware of the admiration it inspires.

Grain of various kinds, mast, fruits, insects and their larvæ, together with small reptiles, constitute its food. It is not until the third year that the male acquires his glorious plumage; the aigrette on the head in this species (but not in the Japan peafowl) is composed of miniature plumes similar to those of the train. The tarsi are spurred, and when irritated, the peacock can use them with full effect.

For roosting, the peacock affects still higher branches than the turkey, and, failing these, the gable end of a house or barn, or some elevated situation; and here, through summer and winter will it take its station, defying the rain and the cold. Strange that a bird originally from India should be so hardy! It would seem as if Providence had expressly given to the gallinaceous birds that quality of constitution which fits them for accompanying man into regions far remote from their natural *habitat*. Such is the case, indeed, with all animals essentially subservient to his welfare; and we cannot but see in this fact a proof of the wisdom and goodness of that God who commanded man "to replenish the earth and subdue it."

Though the peafowl roosts in trees, the female incubates on the ground, making in her natural state a rude, inartificial nest, in some secluded spot, under cover of the dense jungle. The eggs vary in number from five to ten. This concealment, as in the instance of the turkey, is necessary; for, actuated by a strange jealousy, the male will break all the eggs if he discovers them; and this feeling actuates our domestic birds, insomuch that the female, during incubation, must be placed in such security as to prevent the access of the male to the nest. Eggs, grayish white; period of incubation, from twenty-seven to thirty days.

MUSK OR BRAZILIAN DUCKS.

THE DOMESTIC DUCK.—Ducks cannot be kept to advantage unless they can have access to water. This need not be in large quantities. A tub, holding a few gallons, set in the ground, and daily renewed, answering for a large flock. They are gross feeders, and excellent "snappers up of unconsidered trifles." Nothing comes amiss to them: green boiled vegetables, the waste of the kitchen, meal of all sorts made into paste, grains, bread, animal substances, worms, slugs and snails, insects and their larvæ, are all accepted with eagerness. Their appetite is not fastidious; in fact, to parody the line of a song, "they eat all that is luscious, eat all that they can," and seem determined to reward their owner by keeping themselves in first-rate condition, if the chance of so doing is afforded them. They never need cramming—give them enough and they will cram themselves; yet they have their requirements and ways of their own, which must be conceded. Confinement will not do for them: a paddock, an orchard, a green lane, and a pond; a farmyard, with barns and water; a common, smooth and level, with a sheet of water, abounding in the season with tadpoles and the larvæ of aquatic insects,—these are the localities in which the duck delights, and in such they are kept at little expense. They traverse the green sward in

Indian file (an instinctive habit still retained), and thus return at evening to their dormitory, or emerge from it to the edge of the pond or sheet of water, over which they scatter themselves; thus also they come to the call of their feeder.

Ducks should always have a lodging-place of their own; they should be separated from fowls, and never housed beneath their perches; yet where fowls are kept, a little contrivance would suffice to make them a comfortable berth in a fowl house. In winter, a thin bedding of straw, rushes, or fern-leaves, should be placed on the floor of their dormitory, and changed frequently. More than four or five females should not be allowed to a single drake. The duck lays a great many eggs in the season; there are instances in which one has laid as many as eighty-five eggs; but these cases are rare; the female will cover with comfort twelve or fourteen, and in most cases is a steady sitter. When she inclines to sit, give her a plentiful nest, with some broken straw or hay near at hand, with which to cover the eggs when she leaves them; as nature instructs her to use this precaution, no doubt it is best to give her the opportunity. Let her be supplied with food and water directly she leaves her nest; and if she choose to take a bath it will do no harm. It is common to put ducks' eggs under hens, and it is ludicrous, though somewhat painful, to see the trepidation and anxiety of the foster-mother on the edge of a pond, into which the young ducks have plunged, regardless of her feelings and incessant clucking, a language they do not understand. At what age young wild ducks are taken by their parents into the water we cannot say; but this is certain, that if young tame ducks visit the water too early, they are very apt to become cramped and perish. If very young ducklings once become *saturated* with water, they invariably perish; they are in this respect as tender as young turkeys. Ducks, although they float on the water, never become wet (that is, when properly fledged), for their plumage throws off the fluid, and they return dry from the pond; but ducklings, while yet in the down, get wet, and should therefore have sparing access to water until the feathers supply the place of the early down. Young ducks are easily reared, being fed on meal mixed with potatoes and green meat boiled; they are useful in gardens, which they clear of slugs and snails, without injuring the crops of vegetables. As a caution, we would here observe, that the ponds to which they are allowed access should contain neither pike nor eels; and rats should be extirpated. Rats and weasels often thin flocks of ducklings, to the great loss and vexation of their owner.

The Varieties of the Domestic Duck, are *the White Aylesbury*, large, plumage perfectly white, feet yellow, and a flesh-colored bill. This is one of the best varieties. *The Rouen duck*, a large dark-colored variety, is also highly esteemed. The *Hook-billed*, remarkable for the peculiar form of its beak. The *Penguin duck*, which walks, or waddles in an upright position, like the penguin; the *Musk duck*, so termed from the strong scent of musk which its skin exhales. This duck is of large size, and its plumage of a glossy blue-black. The *East Indian*, or *Buenos Ayres duck*, is a small and very beautiful variety, black, with a brilliant metallic luster on the feathers. These, and the various colored call-ducks, are highly ornamental.

The egg of the duck is by some people very much relished, having a rich piquancy of flavor, which gives it a decided superiority over the egg of the common fowl; and these qualities render it much in request with the pastry-cook and confectioners—three duck eggs being equal in culinary value to six hen eggs. The duck does not lay during the day, but generally in the night; exceptions regulated by circumstances, will, of course, occasionally occur. While laying, the duck requires more attention than the hen, until she is accustomed to resort to a regular nest for depositing her eggs—once, however, that this is effected, she will no longer require your attendance.

THE DOMESTIC GOOSE.—The best variety of the domestic goose is that which varies least in color. Gray is the best color. Mixed colors should be rejected.

As to breeding geese. These birds, as has been ascertained by M. St. Genis, will pair like pigeons; and even if the number of ganders exceeds that of the geese, no noise or riot takes place, mutual choice being evidently the ruling principle. Amongst other experiments tried by M. St. Genis, he left, besides the patriarch of the flock, two of the young ganders, unprovided with mates, but still those couples that had paired kept constantly together, and the three single ganders never attempted to approach any of the females during the temporary absence of their lords. M. St. Genis also remarked, in the course of his observations, that the gander is more frequently white than the goose.

The goose deposits from ten to twenty eggs at one laying; but, if you do not desire her to sit, you may, by removing the eggs as fast as they are laid, and at the same time feeding her highly, induce her to lay on from forty-five to fifty. This is, however, unusual, and it is unprofitable. When tolerably well cared for, geese may be made to lay, and even hatch, three times in the year. This care consists merely in high feeding and good housing early in the spring, so as to have the first brood early in March; but we would rather have two good broods reared than three bad ones, and we are, therefore, more disposed to recommend patience and moderation.

The goose will, when left to the unassisted promptings of nature, begin to lay about the latter end of February, or the beginning of March. The commencement of the laying may be readily foreseen by marking such geese as run about carrying straws in their mouth. This is for the purpose of forming their nest, and these individuals are about to lay. They should, then, of course, be watched, lest they drop their eggs abroad. Once a goose is shut up, and compelled to lay her first egg of that laying in any particular nest, you need be at no further trouble about her; for she will continue to lay in that spot, and will not stray on any account elsewhere.

We can always detect the inclination of the goose to sit or hatch. This is known by the bird keeping in the nest after the laying of each egg longer than usual. The hatching nest should be formed of straw, with a little hay as a lining; and so formed that the goose will not fling the eggs over the side when in the act of turning them. You need not banish the gander; on the contrary, let him remain as near the nest as he chooses; he will do no mischief, but will act the part of a most vigi-

EMBDEN OR BREMEN GEESE.

lant guardian. About fifteen eggs will be found as many as a good-sized goose can properly cover. Do not meddle with the eggs during the incubation, and do not meddle with the goose; but, as she is somewhat heavier than the hen, you may leave her food and drink rather nearer to her than is necessary with common poultry, as, if she chanced to absent herself from the eggs sufficiently long to permit them to cool, she might become disheartened, and desert her task altogether. It is, however, unnecessary to put either vinegar or pepper in her food or water, as recommended by some, or, in short, to meddle with her at all.

The goose will sit on her eggs for nearly two months; but the necessary period of incubation being but one, the early hatched goslings must be removed lest the more tardy might be deserted. About the twenty-ninth day the goslings begin to chip the shell; and if their own powers prove inadequate to their liberation, aid may be rendered them, and that, also, with much less risk than in the case of other young birds, the shell and its membranes being very hard and strong, and the young themselves also hardy, and capable early of enduring hardship. The best plan is to have the eggs set, of as nearly as possible equal freshness, that they may be hatched at one time.

On first being hatched, turn the goslings out into a sunny walk, if the weather will permit of such procedure; but do not try to make them feed for, at least, twelve hours after leaving the shell. Their food may then be bread soaked in milk, porridge, curds, boiled greens, or even bran, mixed with boiled potatoes, taking care not to give the food in too hot a state, while you equally avoid giving it cold. Avoid rain or cold breezes; and see, therefore, that the walk into which you turn the young goslings be sheltered from both wind and weather. The goslings should also be kept from water for at least a couple of days after hatching. If suffered too early to have free access to water, they are very liable to take cramp—a disease which generally produces permanent lameness and deformity, and but too frequently proves fatal.

Geese should have an inclosed court or yard, with houses in which they may be shut when occasion requires. It is better, however, to confine them as little as possible; and, by suffering them to stroll about, and forage for themselves, the expense of rearing them will fall comparatively lightly on you, so that you will not be conscious of any outlay. Geese require water, and cannot be advantageously kept when they cannot have access to it; still, however, we have known them to thrive where they had no access to any pond or river, but had only a small artificial pool, constructed by their owners, in which to bathe themselves. When geese are at all within reach of water, they will, when suffered to roam at liberty, usually go in search of, and discover it, and will, afterward, daily resort thither. Though the birds are thus fond of water, all damp about their sleeping places must be scrupulously guarded against. Grass is as necessary to the well-being of geese as water; and the rankest, coarsest grasses, such as are rejected by cattle, constitute the goose's delicacy.

THE WILD GOOSE.—Canada Goose, or Cravat Goose (*Anser Canadensis*), *Neescash* and *Mistchaynceseah* of the Cree Indian, *Wild Goose* of the Anglo-Americans. Hearne, Wilson, Audubon, Bonaparte, and others have given us full accounts of the habits and manners of the Canada goose in a state of nature. It is the common wild goose of the United States, and its regular periodical migrations are the sure signals of returning spring, or of approaching winter. The tracts of their vast migratory journeys are not confined to the sea-coast or its vicinity, for, in their aerial voyages to and from the north, these birds pass over the interior on both sides of the mountains, as far west, at least, as the Osage River. "I have never," says Wilson, "yet visited any quarter of the country where the inhabitants are not familiarly acquainted with the regular passing and repassing of the wild geese." It is an opinion in the states that they visit the lakes to breed. Most, however, it would appear, wing their way much farther northward, for from the Canadian lakes they migrate to still higher latitudes on the setting in of spring. Hearne saw them in large flocks within the arctic circle, pushing their way still northward. Captain Phipps observed them on the coast of Spitzbergen, in latitude 80° 27′ N. Audubon found them breeding on the coast of Labrador, and states that the eggs, six or seven in number, of a greenish white, are deposited in a roughly made nest. Bonaparte states that they breed everywhere throughout the Hudson's Bay territory, and have been observed in the middle of July on the Copper-mine river, not far from its debouchure, accompanied by their newly-hatched young. The cry of the species is imitated by a nasal repetition of the syllable *wook*, or, as Wilson writes it, *honk*.

The destruction of the Canada geese during their migrations is enormous: the autumnal flight lasts from the middle of August to the middle of October; those which are taken in this season, when the frosts begin, are preserved in their feathers, and left to be frozen for the fresh provisions of the winter stock. The feathers constitute an article of commerce, and are sent to England. The vernal flight of these geese lasts from the middle of April until the middle of May. Their arrival in the fur countries from the south is impatiently expected; it is the harbinger of spring, and the month is named by the Indians the goose-moon. Dr. Richardson, in his *Fauna Borcali-Americana*, describes as follows the interest caused by the appearance of the flocks:—" The arrival of this well-known bird is anxiously looked for and hailed with great joy by the natives of the woody and swampy districts, who depend principally on it for subsistence during the summer. It makes its first appearance in flocks of twenty or thirty, which are readily decoyed within gunshot by the hunters, who conceal themselves and imitate its call. Two, three or more are so frequently killed at a shot, that the usual price of a goose is the single charge of ammunition. One goose, which when fat weighs about nine pounds, is the daily ration of one of the Company's servants during the season, and is reckoned equivalent to two snow-geese (*Anas hyperborea*), or three ducks, or eight pounds of buffalo and moose-meat, or two pounds of pemmican, or a pint of maize and four ounces of suet.

"About three weeks after their first appearance, the Canada geese disperse in pairs throughout the country, between the fiftieth and sixty-seventh parallels, to breed, retiring at the same time from the shores of Hudson's Bay. They are seldom or never seen on the coasts of the arctic sea. In July, after the young birds are hatched, the parents moult, and vast numbers are killed in the rivers and lakes, when (from the loss of their quill feathers) they are unable to fly. When chased by a canoe, and obliged to dive frequently, they soon become fatigued, and make for the shore with the intention of hiding themselves; but as they are not fleet, they fall an easy prey to their pursuers. In the autumn they again assemble in flocks on the shores of Hudson's Bay for three weeks or a month previous to their departure southward."

The Canada goose feeds on aquatic vegetables and their roots, and delicate marine plants of the genus *ulva*. To this diet they add grain and berries in their season.

The flight of this species is laborious and heavy, and generally in single file, or in the form of two sides of a triangle, the leader, some old gander, being the *apical* bird. From time to time this leader utters his deep "*honk*," which is responded to by the rest of the flock, and which may be translated, "What cheer, ho?" "All's well!" Very often, however, all is not well, for the line is scattered by the fire of the gunner; often, too, they meet with dense fogs, in which they become bewildered, and after wheeling about alight on the ground, where the gunners give them a warm reception. In some districts the sportsmen take with them into the marshes one or two of the domesticated race, which by their call attract the flocks passing overhead, and allure them to destruction.

Wilson says that, except in calm weather, the flocks of Canada geese rarely sleep on the water, generally preferring to roost all night in the marshes. When the shallow bays are frozen, they seek the mouths of inlets near the sea, occasionally visiting the air-holes in the ice; but these bays are seldom so completely frozen as to prevent them feeding on the bars at the entrance.

The Canada goose is a beautiful species, and its flesh is excellent. The head, two-thirds of the neck, the greater quills, the rump, and tail are perfectly black; the back and wings brown, edged with wood-brown; the base of the neck anteriorly, and the under plumage generally, brownish gray; a few white feathers are scattered about the eye, and a white cravat of a kidney shape forms a conspicuous mark on the throat; upper and under tail coverts pure white; bill and feet black. Such is a brief sketch of the Canada goose in a state of nature. Man, however, has appreciated its value, and it is kept domesticated not only in America, but in many parts of Europe where it breeds freely. In America the ordinary gray goose of Europe is very common; but this bird does not thrive there so well as in Europe; hence many prefer the Canada goose, which is as familiar, and its equal in other points.

This species will breed with the common goose; and it is asserted that the hybrid progeny is far superior in the flavor and sapidity of its flesh to the unmixed progeny of the common goose. Buffon, in whose time the Canada goose was kept in a domestic state in France, says: "Within these few years many hundreds have inhabited the great canal at Versailles, where they breed familiarly with the swans." That is, we suppose, interbreed with the swans, an instance of which has not come under our own notice; the intermediate position, however, of this species renders the fact probable.

Like the duck and the common goose, the Canada goose under domestication ceases to be as strictly monogamous as it is in its wild state —a circumstance which, in our tame *anatidæ*, may result from the plan of keeping but few males, and these in association with a flock of females, so that the ordinary results of pairing—that is, retiring from the rest to a secluded spot, which the mated pair exclusively occupy—are interfered with. Yet, as may be seen in the instance of the common goose, the male generally attaches himself to a particular female, while she is followed by her brood of goslings over the common, and is energetic in their defense. The instinct is not quite obliterated—there is a reigning sultana.

It is a question worth attention, whether the Canada goose might not with advantage be more extensively kept in our country than it is at present; it is common as an *ornament* to sheets of water in parks, gardens, and pleasure grounds, but is too much neglected as a bird of *utility*; it is alike valuable for flesh and feathers; it is not so decided a grazer as is the common goose; the precincts of marshes and ponds which abound in aquatic vegetation, for the procuring of which its strong bill and long swan-like neck afford it facility, offer the most advantageous sites for its establishment, and in such localities we strongly recommend its adoption. With regard to its management little is to be said; the sitting females require secluded nests, free from intrusion; and the flock, in addition to the vegetables they pick up, require an allowance of grain.

Like most birds known both in a wild and domestic state, the latter exceed the former in weight and magnitude.

FEEDING POULTRY.—It is a bad practice to under feed poultry. From the very first they should have good and solid food. Steamed potatoes and other roots mixed with meal of the various grains, form a cheap and excellent food. It is not necessary to soak, grind, or boil the grains for fowls, however, where they can have free access to pebbles to supply their own grinding-mills, by which they turn their own grain into flour. But when pent up and unable to procure what they so much need, meal, and boiled and crushed food should then be given them. The poultry-house, however, should be constantly supplied with fine gravel, lime, and pulverized charcoal—articles indispensable to the health and improvement of fowls. Green food should be given them daily. Cabbages hung where the fowls can pick at them are a good article. In winter, chopped potatoes, turnips, etc., are the only convenient green food. When practicable, fresh animal food should be frequently given fowls that are shut up, or at seasons when they cannot procure insects or worms. A bullock's liver, thrown in the yard, is a cheap and good food for them. Indian corn is an excellent food, and may be freely given.

Cayenne pepper, indeed all descriptions of pepper, especially the cayenne in pods, will be found a favorite with fowl, and will be greedily devoured by them; it acts as a powerful stimulant, and remarkably promotes laying; and, when mixed in a ground state with boiled meal, will be found productive of the best effects. In this, however, as in every thing else, let moderation be your ruling principle.

A different system should be adopted in treating poultry for the table, and for the laying and breeding department.

With regard to feeding fowls for the table, much depends on circumstances. Spring chickens may be put up for feeding as soon as the hen ceases to regard them, and before they lose their first good condition. In their fattening-pens they will have no opportunity of picking up little pebbles; their mills, therefore, will be inoperative, and the diet must consequently be pultaceous, viz., bread and milk, barley-meal, or oatmeal and milk, and meal of steamed potatoes mixed with barley-meal. Some recommend the occasional addition of a few grains of cayenne pepper, or of dried nettle-seeds, which the foreign feeders are in the habit of giving. Where chickens have the run of a good farm-yard, and plenty of food, it is a work of supererogation to pen them for fattening; they will be ready at any time for the table, and their flesh, being in its healthy state, will be sweet and juicy, delicately tender, and sufficiently fat. Some, indeed, prefer fatted fowls; but this is a matter of taste; to many the greasy fat of poultry is very disgusting.

The practice of cramming poultry by the hand is quite common, though not to be recommended. In France they have machines by which one man can cram fifty birds in half an hour. It is somewhat on the principle of a forcing-pump. The throats of the birds are held open by the operator until they are gorged through a pipe, which conveys the food from a reservoir below placed on a stool. In fifteen days, fowls are said to attain the highest state of fatness and flavor by this feeding. In addition to the ordinary paste of barley-meal, or meal made into little balls with milk, the dried seeds and leaves of nettles have been recommended by the continental poulterers, some of whom give a little henbane-seed to induce sleep, while others put out the eyes of the prisoners as the most effectual way of keeping them in a state of darkness, which is considered essential to their becoming rapidly fat; and under the pretext of relieving them from the irritation of vermin, they pluck the feathers from their heads, bellies, and wings. While fowls are thus preparing for the knife, though their bodies are closely confined, their hinder parts are free for evacuation and cleanliness, and their heads are at liberty to take in fresh supplies of nutriment.

Poultry are the better for high feeding from the very shell, and on this account the heaviest corn is often far cheaper for them in the end than tailings, as regards the flesh, or the size and substantial goodness of the eggs. Young chickens may be put up for feeding as soon as the hen has ceased to regard them, and before they lose their first good condition. When chickens are wanted for domestic purposes, they are often left at liberty in the farm-yard, and if they have plenty of good food, they will be in the most healthful state for the table, and rich and juicy in flavor.

POULTRY-HOUSES AND YARDS.—Those who intend to rear fowls or any kind of poultry on a large scale, should have a distinct yard, perfectly sheltered, and with a warm aspect, well fenced, secure from thieves and vermin, and sufficiently inclined to be always dry, and supplied with sand or ashes for the cocks and hens to roll in, an operation necessary to disengage their feathers from vermin: running water should be especially provided; for the want of water, of which all poultry are fond, produces constipation of the bowels and inflammatory diseases; and for geese and ducks, bathing is an indispensable luxury. A contiguous field is also necessary, for free exercise, as well as for the supply of grubs and grass to the geese. The fowl-house should be dry, well-roofed, and fronting the east or south, and, if practicable, at the back of a stove or stables; warmth being conducive to health and laying, though extreme heat has the contrary effect. It should be furnished with two small lattice windows, that can be opened or shut at pleasure, at opposite ends, for ventilation, which is frequently necessary; and the perches should be so arranged, that one row of roosting fowls should not be directly above another.

M. Parmentier has shown* by what arrangement a house twenty feet long and twelve feet wide may be made to accommodate one hundred and fifty hens at roost. The plan is simply this: the first roosting-perch (rounded a little at the upper angles only, for gallinaceous fowls cannot keep a firm hold on perfectly cylindrical supporters) should be placed lengthways and rest on trestles in each end wall, six feet from the front wall, and at a convenient height, which must depend on the elevation of the house from the floor, which should be formed of some well consolidated material that can be easily swept. Another perch should be fixed ladder-ways (*en échelon*) above this, but ten inches nearer to the back wall, and so on, until there are four of these perches, like the steps

---

* "*Dictionnaire d'Agriculture.*"

of a ladder when properly inclined, but with a sufficient distance between the wall and the upper one to allow the poultry-maid to stand conveniently upon when she has occasion to examine the nests, which it is her duty to do every day at least once, and in the forenoon. The highest of these she can reach by standing on a stool or step-ladder. By this contrivance the hens, when desirous of reaching the nests, have no occasion to fly, but merely to pass from one stick to another. If the size and form of the house permit, a similar construction may be made on the opposite side, care being taken to leave an open space in the middle of the room, and a sufficiently wide passage for the attendant to pass along the walls. It is not at all required to have as many nests as hens, because they have not all occasion to occupy them at the same time; and besides, they are so far from having a repugnance to lay in a common receptacle, that the sight of an egg stimulates them to lay. It is however true, that the most secluded and darkest nests are those which the hens prefer.

The nests, if built into the wall, are in tiers from the bottom to the top, the lowest being about three feet from the ground, and a foot square. If the laying-chambers consist of wooden boxes, they are usually furnished with a ledge, which is very convenient for the hens when rising. But the best receptacles for the eggs are those of basket-work, as they are cool in summer, and can easily be removed and washed. They ought to be fastened not directly to the wall, as is generally the case, but to boards fixed in it by hooks, well clinched, and with a little roof to cover the rows of baskets. They will thus be isolated, to the great satisfaction of the hen, which delights in the absence of all disturbing influences when laying. All the ranges of nests should be placed chequewise, in order that the inmates, when coming out, may not startle those immediately under: those designed for hatching should be near the ground (where instinct teaches the hen to choose her seat), and so arranged that the hens can easily enter them without disturbing the eggs.

Wheaten or rye straw is the most approved material for the bedding, being cooler than hay: the hens are sometimes so tortured by lice as to forsake their nests altogether, in an agony of restlessness. A Dorking housewife has assured us that she once lost an entire clutch, from having, as she believes, given a bed of hay-seeds to her sitting hen. The chicks were all glued to the shells, and thus destroyed, owing, as she thinks, to the high temperature occasioned by the fermenting seeds.

For all purposes two cocks in a good run are considered in the poultry counties contiguous to London as sufficient for twelve or fourteen hens, but in France they allow twenty mistresses to each cock, which no doubt is on account of the high temperature there. In a confined yard, five hens are sufficient for one cock in our cold country, and a double set will not answer in very limited space. When there are two or more cocks, care should be taken not to have them of equal age or size, for in this case they are always jealous and quarrelsome; if one is decidedly ascendant, the other will never presume to dispute with him. It will be judicious also to avoid the introduction or changing of cocks in the breeding season, for the hens require constant intercourse with them, and several days frequently elapse before they become familiarized with a stranger. The best way is to bring in the new cock in the summer, either as a chick, or late in the year in the moulting season, when he will not take too much notice of the hens. As a general rule it would be well to have one a yearling and the other a year older. In the third year, the cock, who then becomes lazy and excessively jealous, should be killed.

In selecting eggs for hatching, care should be taken that they are not at the utmost more than a month old, but their condition for hatching will greatly depend upon the temperature of the weather: vitality continues longest when the weather is cool.

It has been asserted that the future sex of the bird is indicated by the shape of the egg; the round producing the female, and the oblong the male. But this is contradicted, and, we believe, with sufficient reason, and it is impossible not only to foretell the sex, but even to ascertain whether the egg be fecundated. This however is certain, that if the air-bag (at the obtuse end), which has been mistaken for the germ, and the purpose of which is to oxygenate the blood of the chick, be perforated even in the least conceivable degree, the generating power is lost altogether. Those eggs only which have been fecundated by the male are possessed of the vital principle. The number of eggs for a hen should not exceed sixteen, as she cannot impart the necessary warmth to more. It is by no means uncommon with experienced breeders to place two hens on the same day on their respective eggs, and then on the twenty-first day when the broods are out, to give the maternal charge of both to one of the hens, removing the other to another set of eggs, which, if she be a steady setter, she will hatch as in the first instance. This, however, must be deemed a cruelty, though some hens would instinctively continue to sit until death. They would, however, become so attenuated by continued sitting, as to lose the power of communicating to the eggs the necessary degree of warmth. The practice of the Surry breeders is to feed the hen on oats while sitting, as less stimulating than barley, which they give to the laying hens on account of this very quality.

CAPONIZING.—The making of capons, that is, emasculating the males, is practiced a little in some of the English counties, and very much in France, where the females are also rendered incapable of breeding, and termed in their unsexed condition *poulardes*, in order to give them the tendency to fatten. An incision is made near the parts, and through this the finger is introduced to take hold of and bring away the genitals, but so carefully as not to injure the intestines: the wound is then stitched up and rubbed with oil or grease; and the comb (which appears to be an unnecessary and gratuitous pain and insult to the sufferer) is often cut off. The females are treated much in the same way, when they do not promise well for laying, or when they have ceased to be fertile; they are deprived of the ovarium. The subsequent treatment is similar to that in the former case. Care is taken to give them good food for three or four days, and during that time to keep them in a place of moderate temperature, to avoid the danger of gangrene, which, considering the time of the year—midsummer, when the operation is usually performed —is a very probable consequence. Pullets of the largest breed are selected for the purpose, as they yield the greatest weight to the poulterer; and if employed in hatching, cover the greatest number of eggs.

DISEASES OF FOWLS.—Fowls and poultry in general are subject to various diseases; as, *apoplexy, diarrhœa, rheumatism*, the *pip* or *thrush*, the *croup* (often termed *roup*), the *gapes, inflammation of the tail gland* (also called the *roup*, though the term is improperly applied), and other diseases which are not understood. Great difficulties attend the treatment of poultry diseases. Who attends to them? what complaint do they make? and when they die, how few persons acquainted with the symptoms before death make *post-mortem* examinations, and then refer those symptoms to the morbid appearances which his scalpel reveals? The following are the chief *active* disorders among them; *apoplexy*, evidenced by inflammation of the membranes of the brain, or by effusion of blood within or upon it; *peritoneal inflammation*, rapidly fatal; *inflammation of the lungs*, including the bronchial tubes; *tracheal inflammation* (or *gapes*) with parasitic worms in the windpipe; *inflammation of the mucous membrane of the intestines*, evidenced by previous dysentery; and *inflammation or intumescence of the rump gland*, symptomatic of a *febrile condition*. But what can be said as to the treatment of poultry under disease? Very little. To speak the truth, neither are their diseases well understood, nor is the treatment of them generally successful. A few observations on particular complaints may, however, be useful.

Apoplexy makes its attack in most instances without the slightest previous warning. Could it be known that a bird was in danger of an attack, means might perhaps be taken to insure safety. Aviary birds, in the finest health apparently, will drop dead from their perch from this cause. They are often over-fed; they have not to exercise themselves in the task of seeking for food; they have an allowance in unlimited measure, but have no according measure of muscular exertion; they "do not earn their bread before they eat it," as wild birds do. "*Experientia docet.*" The best advice to give, as to the means of *prevention*, is to feed birds a little in proportion to the exercise which they have the power to take.

The Pip, or Thrush, may be regarded as a token of derangement of the mucous membrane of the alimentary canal generally, and not as a local disease; it is *symptomatic*. Its cure will be effected by low diet; that is (in the case of fowls), by an allowance of fresh vegetable food, mixed with potatoes and a little oatmeal, granting at the same time a plentiful supply of pure water. Give of castor oil a teaspoonful, or thereabouts, according to age and strength. Do not scrape the tongue, nor use rough modes of cleaning it, but apply a little *borax*, dissolved in tincture of myrrh and water, by means of a camel-hair pencil, two or three times a day. The symptoms of *pip* consist in a thickening of the membrane lining the tongue and palate, which causes an obstruction of the free inspiration, and makes the poor sufferer gasp for breath; the plumage becomes ruffled, the bird mopes and pines, the appetite fails, and is at last utterly extinguished, the bird at length dying, worn out by fever and starvation.

Gapes (Inflammation of the Trachea) is a very fatal disease, to which all our domestic gallinaceous birds, as well as pheasants and partridges, are subject, and which often occasions great mortality. In the first instance it appears to arise from a croupy or catarrhal affection, which is indicated by running at the nostrils, watery eyes, alteration of voice, and loss of appetite and spirits. The bird dies. If the trachea be examined, it will be found replete with narrow worms, about half an inch in length, imbedded in slimy mucus. This singular worm is the *Syngamus trachealis,* or *Distoma lineare.* It consists of a long and a short body united together; the long body is the female, the short body the male; each, were it not that they are permanently united together, being an animal distinct and perfect in itself. Whether these parasitic worms are the cause or consequence of the disease, we pretend not to say, nor can we tell how they become introduced into the trachea; this, however, seems to be certain, that their removal is requisite to give the feathered patient a chance of recovery. This can be done by means of a feather, neatly trimmed, which is to be introduced into the windpipe, and turned round once or twice, and then drawn out. It will dislodge the worms, and bring back many of them adhering with slime unto it. This plan requires great dexterity, and some knowledge of the anatomy of the parts; a slow, unskillful operator may kill the already half-suffocated bird, instead of curing it. Another mode of destroying these worms is, by putting the birds in a box, and making them inhale the fumes of tobacco, thrown into it through the stalk of a tobacco-pipe. Some recommend the forcing of tobacco-smoke down the bird's throat, and others that the mouth be crammed with snuff; while many place faith in the efficacy of a pinch of salt, introduced into the back part of the mouth. Something like a scientific mode of treatment may, however, be suggested. Give a grain of *calomel,* made up with bread into a pill, or two or three grains of Plummer's pill (*pil. hydr. submur co.,* London Pharmacopœia); after which let flour of sulphur be administered, with a little ginger, in pultaceous food composed of barley-meal. In the mean time let the bird be kept in a dry warm shed or room, apart from the rest of the fowls, as the disease may be infectious. Let the mouth and beak be washed with a weak solution of chloride of lime. A correspondent, who dates his letter from Wootton, Christchurch, speaks of turpentine as the only remedy on which to depend. His words are: "Half a teaspoonful of spirits of turpentine, mixed with a handful of grain, is a certain cure in a few days, giving a handful of such grain to a couple of dozen young chicks each day. It is the most perfect and unfailing remedy. I communicated this receipt to the 'Gardeners' Chronicle' (No. xxix., July 17, 1847, p. 476), and I understand it has been found by other persons besides myself to be successful —perfectly so. In this part of England it is the only disease of chickens; and for two seasons the number that died of it was very great." The *rationale* of this mode of treatment is as follows:—the turpentine is absorbed into the system, and so brought into contact with the parasitic worms in the windpipe, to which it is speedily fatal; they are then ejected with the mucus; and the cause of irritation being thus removed, the bird speedily recovers. Wet, ill-feeding, an ill-ventilated fowl-house, confinement on a spot or plot of ground tenanted year after year by fowls, without attention to cleanliness, to renovation of the soil, and a proper allowance of gravel, ashes, fresh vegetables, etc.; these are the causes which produce this and many other diseases. The gapes is an epidemic disease, which often thins the preserves of pheasants and the coveys of partridges.

Inflammation of the Lungs, including the bronchial tubes, is not uncommon. Its symptoms are quick breathing, often with a rattle or râle very audible, dullness, disorder of plumage, vacancy in the eye, and indisposition to stir. In this, death can hardly be prevented. Human patients can explain their feelings—cattle, to a certain degree, indicate them, and speak in dumb eloquence; but birds give little indication, by voice or manner, leading to what the medical man calls *diagnosis*. The persevering use of cod-liver oil will give relief, and even effect a temporary, or at any rate an apparent cure; but who would like to breed from the bird.

Peritoneal Inflammation, or Peritonitis.—This disease runs so rapid a course, that death not unfrequently occurs before any marked symptoms have appeared indicative of active disease. The bird perhaps appears a little drooping—it refuses to eat; but as it is highly fed, this circumstance occasions no surprise; it retires to its roost, and is found dead in the morning. Examination at once reveals the cause of death—the peritoneal membrane exhibits all the indications of active inflammation. We have noticed the occurrence of the same disease among carnivorous mammalia. An animal appears to be as well as usual—at least it attracts no observation—but it dies suddenly. On opening the body, the cause is manifest—*Peritonitis* has done its work.

Inflammation of the Mucous Membrane of the Intestinal Canal is usually evinced by *dysentery*. The bird pines; it is purged; in a little time the evacuations become more or less tinged with blood, and death ensues. Damp and improper food are the causes of this affection. It can be treated with success only in the early stage. First give a small quantity of castor-oil. This will clear the bowels of irritating secretion. Afterward let the bird have doses of the *Hydrargyrum cum cretâ* (of the London Pharmacopœia), rhubarb, and laudanum :—of the hydrargyrum cum cretâ, three grains; rhubarb, two or three grains; laudanum, two, three, or four drops. Mix in a teaspoonful of gruel or gum-water. To be given every alternate day for a fortnight.

Simple Diarrhœa may be generally cured by a change of diet, and a little chalk given in gruel.

Constipation of the Bowels will yield to castor-oil, and a diet upon oatmeal porridge and green vegetables.

Asthma.—Both fowls and pigeons are affected with this complaint, which is evidenced by difficulty of breathing and a wheezing, rattling noise on inspiration. It is the result of a thickening of the bronchial tubes from previous inflammation, often accompanied by an alteration in the structure of the cellular tissue of a portion of the lungs. There appears to be no rational plan of treatment likely to effect a cure.

Inflammation and Intumescence of the Rump Gland is generally symptomatic of a febrile condition of the system. To this affection the term *roup* (an indefinite term for all the diseases of poultry) is often applied.

The treatment is simple. Let the swelling be opened by a lancet, and the matter gently squeezed out; afterward foment well with warm water; put the bird upon a diet of oatmeal and green vegetables, and, if necessary, give a teaspoonful of castor-oil. Be sure that the roosting-place is clean and well ventilated.

Moulting.—This process is natural, and consists in the gradual exchange of old feathers for new ones. Nevertheless it often happens that birds in a state of domestication have not sufficient vital energy for the accomplishment of the change. They require improved diet, warmth, and good water. Of course their roosting-place must be properly sheltered and ventilated. A grain or two of cayenne pepper, made into a pill with bread, may be given daily with advantage. Saffron is useless; but a nail, or any bit of iron may be put into the drinking-trough, in order to render the water chalybeate.

Fowls are subject to a loss of feathers, which must not be confounded with moulting. At first the plumage appears ruffled and disarranged; then the feathers begin to drop out; and continue to fall till the bird is greatly denuded. In the mean time it is dull and destitute of appetite, and becomes thin and feeble. This disease is most common among poultry kept in a limited space, debarred from exercise and fresh air, with a wet soil beneath them, having little or no gravel, nor any dusting-place in which to clean their plumage: it is analogous to the mange in cattle, and is not easily cured. A change of diet, good air, cleanliness, and a dusting-place (or, as some call it, a dust-bath), are essential. Some recommend small quantities of sulphur and nitre mixed with butter to be daily given.

As the successful treatment of diseases may sometimes depend on promptitude, it may be useful for every poultry-keeper to have a convenient supply of a few simple medicines. The following may be named as rather suggestive than complete:—1. jalap, in fifteen-grain powders; 2. hydr. cum cretâ, in three and five-grain doses; 3. cod-liver oil; 4. cocoa-nut oil; 5. flour of brimstone; 6. Baily's roup pills.

In cases where inflammation is suspected, the hydr. cum cretâ is pronounced by the best judges to be a valuable medicine. To a grown fowl five grains, with from five to fifteen grains of jalap (according to the strength of the dose required), may be given. Jalap is a very good poultry medicine. Cocoa-nut oil and flour of brimstone make perhaps the best ointment for white comb, and one which is less disfiguring to the plumage than turmeric. Baily's roup pills are almost universally known and appreciated.

SHIPPING POULTRY AND EGGS.—Messrs. Charles R. Huntington & Co., produce commission merchants in New York, give the following directions as to slaughtering and shipping poultry and eggs:—

Food in the crop injures the appearance, is liable to sour, and purchasers object to this worse than useless weight: therefore keep from food twenty-four hours before killing. Opening the veins in the neck is the best mode of killing. If the head be taken off at first, the skin will recede from the neck-bone, presenting a repulsive appearance. Most of the poultry sent to this market is "scalded" "or wet-picked," but "dry-picked" is preferred by a few, and sells, to a limited extent only, at good prices. Poultry may be picked dry without difficulty, if done immediately after killing. For scalding poultry, the water should be as near the boiling point as possible, without actually boiling; the bird, held by the legs, should be immersed and lifted up and down in the water, three times—the motion helps the hot water to penetrate the plumage, and take proper effect upon the skin. Continue to hold the bird by the legs with one hand, while plucking the feathers with the other without a moment's delay after taking out—if skillfully handled in this way, the feathers and pin-feathers may all be removed without breaking the skin. A torn or broken skin greatly injures the appearance, and the price will be low in proportion. The intestines or the crop should not be "drawn." After removing the feathers, the head may be taken off and the skin drawn over the neck-bone and tied; it should next be "plumped" by being dipped into water, nearly or quite boiling hot, and then at once into cold water about the same length of time. Some think the hot plunge sufficient without the cold. It should be entirely cold but not frozen before being packed. If it reaches market without freezing it will sell all the better. In packing, when practicable, use clean hand-threshed rye-straw; if this cannot be had, wheat or oat straw will answer, but be sure that it is clean and free from dust of any kind. Place a layer of straw at the bottom, then alternate layers of poultry and straw, taking care to stow snugly, back upward, legs under the body, filling vacancies with straw, and filling the packages so that the cover will draw down very snugly upon the contents, so as to prevent shifting or shucking on the way. Boxes are the best packages, and should contain from one hundred and fifty to three hundred. Large boxes are inconvenient, and more apt to get injured. Number the packages, mark the contents, the gross weight, and the tare of each on the cover; mark plainly to our address, placing your own initials also on the package, and send invoice and railroad receipt by mail, to avoid errors or delay in reporting sales.

Eggs require special care in packing. First—secure strong and substantial barrels, either good second-hand barrels, or new split-stave oak ones. Commence by putting a small quantity of clean wheat or oat straw at the bottom of the barrel; cover this with dry, sound oats, as clean, bright, and as free from dust as you can get them, say about two inches of uniform depth. Then pack eggs on the side, leaving a space of three-quarters of an inch between the outside tier and the staves; fill up the layers by making regular tiers. Carefully avoid packing so close together as to crowd them. Use plenty of oats, and shake the barrel well after covering each layer with oats. Leave a space of about three inches at the top, and cover the top layer of eggs with about two inches' depth of oats. Cut, of brown paper, a circle sheet that will just fit the barrel, and lay it on the oats. Then put on this a sufficient quantity of wheat or oat straw, or dry hay, to require a strong pressure to get the head into the crozen. Examine eggs closely, and be particular in counting. Always mark the quantity of eggs in dozens, and the number of bushels of oats contained in each barrel upon the head, and also upon the side of each barrel, with the initials of your name or firm. Eggs packed in this manner will command ready sale in this city, at the

278 DOMESTIC ANIMALS.

current market price, without any deduction for broken or rotten eggs, at all times. In order to avoid claims for rotten eggs it is desirable to ship frequently.

THE SILVER-SPANGLED HAMBURG FOWL.

BEES:

THEIR

HABITS AND MANAGEMENT.

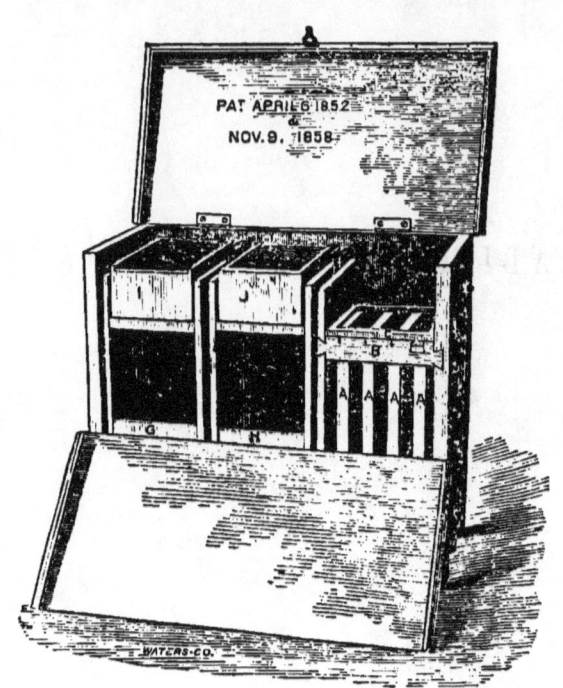

BEES.

THEIR HABITS AND MANAGEMENT.

THREE CLASSES OF BEES.—The **Queen Bee** is the sovereign, and literally the prolific parent of all her subjects. She is the sole monarch. Her body is longer, larger, and more pointed than that of the others, and her wings are much shorter than theirs, hardly reaching beyond her middle, whereas those of the others cover the entire body; her belly and legs are of a deep golden color, and the latter are not furnished with the little brushes which those of the workers have, to help them in collecting the floury matter which they require for making honey.

Anecdote of two Queen Bees.—The queen bears no rival authority. If there should be a second queen, she is either sent forth with an attendant swarm of colonists, or put to death by the other bees.

Huber gives an account of a duel between two queens, who, issuing from their nurseries in the same hive, rushed into deadly conflict, catching each other with the teeth. As if they dreaded the fatal consequences to themselves, which would follow from unsheathing their darts, they had the prudence to separate at the height of their fury and fly away. But the other bees compelled them to decide the point of sovereignty on the spot, and then forced them to the contest again. This was done repeatedly, after intervals of breathing time, until the stronger of the two, seizing the other by the wing, stabbed her to death.

The queen-bee commences depositing her eggs when about five days old; during the heat of the season she lays from one hundred and fifty to two hundred eggs per day, and lays with little or no intermission from early spring to the middle of autumn.

Drones.—The second class of bees are the drones. They are bulkier in the body than either the queen or the working-bee. Their head is rounder, proboscis shorter, eyes fuller, an additional articulation to the antennæ, and *no sting*. They also make more noise in flying than the other bees. The drones are the *males* of the hive; by them the royal mother is impregnated and her eggs fertilized. How or when this intercourse takes place has long furnished philosophers with a subject for controversy and inquiry; and it has not even yet been set at rest in such a manner as to admit being proved to a positive demonstration.

The drones form about a tenth part of the population of a hive. They are certainly idle and lazy, as are the husbands of other queens; yet they fulfill the objects of their creation. They cannot collect honey, for they have not the necessary organs for the purpose; their teeth are too little and too short for breaking off the capsules, their mouths are not well formed for sucking the sweets of flowers; and their legs have not those brushes or powder-puffs which enable the other to bring home the farina wanted for making wax. During the summer they find food for themselves, and pass their time in lounging from flower to flower, and they are not found in the hive during the winter. By an extraordinary instinct, they are massacred without pity by the females before this period, in order to save the winter stock of honey, until they have departed voluntarily to some nook where they may rest until wanted in the next spring. These poor things have no weapons of defense.

Working Bee.—The third class is the working bee. The working bee is considerably less than either the queen bee or the drone. It is  about half an inch in length, of a blackish brown color, covered with closely set hairs all over the body, which aid it in carrying the farina it gathers from the flowers; and on the *tibia*, or *forearm*, as it were, of the hind leg, is a cavity of cup-like form, for the reception of the kneaded little ball of pollen. It is the working bee which collects honey and pollen, and which forms the cells, cleans out the hive, protects the queen, looks after the condition of the young brood, destroys or expels the drones, when these are no longer necessary to the well-being of the community; who, in short, performs all the offices connected with the hive and its contents, save only those which have reference to the reproduction of the species. The working bees are of no sex, and are furnished with a horny and hollow sting, through which poison is ejected into the wound it makes; this poison is of an acrid character, and of great power in its effects, proving fatal to any insect, and instances are on record of its proving so to horses and cattle, nay, even to human beings: when human beings, however, are stung (an accident that will happen very seldom, if they use the precautions in manipulating with their bees, that shall be detailed in the course of this volume), they can instantaneously obtain relief by pressing upon the point stung with the tube of a key; this will extract the sting and relieve the pain, and the application of common spirits of hartshorn will instantaneously remove it; the poison being of an acid nature, and being thus at once neutralized by the application of this penetrating and volatile alkali.

WONDERFUL INSTINCTS AND CONTRIVANCES OF BEES.—The contrivances of bees in the construction of their combs are amongst the most wonderful works of God, as regards insect creation. "The form of the comb is in every country the same, the proportions accurately alike, the size the same, to the fraction of a line—go where you will, and the form is proved to be that which the most refined analysis has enabled mathematicians to discover, as of all others the best adapted for the purpose of saving room, work, and materials. This discovery was only made about a century ago; nay, the instrument that enabled us to find it out was unknown for half a century before that application of its powers. And yet the bee has been for thousands of years, in all countries, unerringly working according to a fixed rule, which no one had discovered until the eighteenth century."

We may instance among other surprising illustrations of the ingenuity of these wonderful creatures, that they lay the foundations of their cities at the top of the hive, and build downward. They have straight passages, or lanes, across their different dwelling-places, wide enough for two bees to pass.

ADVANTAGES OF KEEPING BEES.—It is strange, that though the expense of establishing stocks of bees, where there is a garden, is so trivial, and the possible gain so great, few people take the trouble of keeping them. Country cottagers too generally neglect to take advantage even of an adjoining common or lonely garden, which specially invite to bee-keeping. Where cottage gardens are very small and crowded, and multitudes of children swarm, it is certainly difficult, if not dangerous, to introduce tens of thousands of bees, with their formidable stings; but in numberless instances where bee-husbandry is neglected, it might be pursued with some profit.

No farmer, nor even humble cottager, who has a patch of garden, and lives near commons, heath-covered hills, or woods, should be without hives, as the great supply of bees' food is obtained by their own exertions. It is not the rarest and most beautiful flowers which afford the best honey, but those which abound in the open fields as well as in the garden; the flowers of mountain heath, clover, trefoil, beans, vetches, wild thyme, turnips and cabbages, privet, elder, bramble, rue, and, above all, the blossoms of the common furze, are among the best materials for honey. The cost of food is scarcely any thing, and the return may be considered clear gain.

The trouble of rearing bees, compared with the pleasure or the profit, is nothing.

MANAGEMENT OF BEES.—To him who is about engaging in bee-keeping, the first question of interest is, how to select his stock. As a rule, the spring is the best season to purchase a stock of bees, as they have then passed the casualties of the winter; and the question of profit, so far as the first year is concerned, is quite clear, if the swarms are judiciously chosen. Their value depends upon the health and number of bees, and the time they have occupied the hive. The number in a colony can be judged of with comparative accuracy by raising the hives and examining them, or by the hum produced on giving them slight taps; and by the weight, as shown either by lifting or weighing. The age of a swarm is told by the color of the comb; in new swarms the color being white, and varying from that to nearly black, in very old swarms. The brood combs grow thicker with age, and the cells and the bees hatched in them are therefore smaller, and the latter feebler. It is poor economy to purchase a colony more than two years old.

Transporting Bees.—Let the hive be placed on a cloth, the ends of which must be carefully tied over the top; if it is to be taken to a distance, the hive so tied up may be swung on a pole fastened across a cart from side to side; this prevents the jolting to which it might otherwise be subject, which would disturb the bees, and probably shake down the comb. When arrived at its destination, let the hive be placed on the stand, and if any of the bees have fallen out on the cloth, place them near the entrance, and they will soon find their way in.

SPRING MANAGEMENT.—As soon as the weather is fine examine your hives by lifting them carefully from the stand. Clear away all the dead bees and refuse matters which have collected during the winter. Rub the mouldiness and damp from the floor-board, and let it be well dried. The bottoms of the combs often become mouldy in the winter, especially in light stocks, and it will be a good thing to cut off the lower portions, which may be done with a table-knife, and without danger, by turning the hive on one side, in the evening or early in the morning, or at any time, if you take the precaution of wearing a bee-dress, hereafter described. The bees will soon renew the combs, and their health will be improved by the removal of the decayed portions.

Feeding.—Many swarms die in spring for want of food, and the wise apiarian will therefore feed his bees liberally, bearing in mind that what he gives them is not lost, as they can fully store for their owners' use what is not needed for their own support.

Begin to feed the light stocks; a liberal supply of food will be amply repaid by the consequent health and vigor of your bees, and the abundant store they will collect for your future benefit. And do not prematurely encourage the bees to go in search of food, but rather confine them to their homes. Guard against the admission of stranger bees while yours are feeding. Give honey now, if you can, rather than syrup, as it forms a better ingredient than sugar in the jelly which supports the young brood.

The consumption of food in a hive is now perhaps greater than at any period of the year. The queen lays from one hundred to two hundred eggs daily, and the increase of the brood is so prodigious, that it is impossible for any except a well-stored hive to meet the demand for food. Many persons wonder that their bees die in the spring, when they have survived the winter; but the food consumed during the cold weather is comparatively very small to what it is during breeding time. On this ground, then, feed abundantly all the stocks, but especially the light ones.

Feeding outside the hive, by placing food at the entrance, is a bad method, as stranger bees are attracted, which deprive your bees of a proportion of that which you have provided for them. Feeding at the bottom disturbs the bees, lowers the temperature of the hive when the food is introduced, and thus occasions loss of life; therefore, to obviate these evils, ingenious feeding-pans have been invented for supplying food at the top of the hive.

The following directions for feeding bees are from "The Bee-Keepers' Chart:" "Before feeding is commenced the hives should be set down upon the floors and the entrances for the bees so closed as to admit only one or two at a time. Two or three inch auger holes may be bored in the top, and the feeder placed by the side of them and covered with a small box, and this covered with an old carpet to prevent other bees from scenting the feed." Phelps's *Bee-Feeder* is thus figured

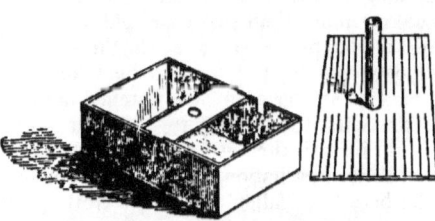

PHELPS'S BEE-FEEDER.

and described, and it may lead the ingenious to adopt it on a better plan :

"It consists of a tin pan, or tray, placed in a wooden box, with a float to fit, and a tin tube passes through the float and is secured to it on the under side. The float may be raised at any time, even if it is covered with bees, by means of the tube, and the syrup poured into the pan through the tube by inserting a funnel in the top of it. The float supports the bees and prevents them from getting into the syrup, and as they consume the syrup it settles down with them. A piece of wood across the top of the box, with a hole for the tube, keeps it in its place, and a pane of glass on each side of this confines the bees, and affords an opportunity to observe their operations while feeding."

The same author recommends the following compositions for feeding bees :

First: two pounds West India or Orleans sugar; three gills ale; one gill Malaga wine; (if the ale and wine cannot be had, use sap or water,) one teaspoonful fine salt. Mix together in a tin or copper vessel ; set it over a slow fire; stir occasionally until it arrives to a boiling point; set it off, and let it cool, remove the scum, and it is fit for use.

Second: one gallon (or twelve pounds) of West India or any other honey; four pounds West India or Orleans sugar; one gallon maple sap or water ; half a pint ale; two tablespoonsfuls fine salt. Heat and mix as above. This composition may be made without the ale by using water.

It is however doubted by some experienced bee-keepers, whether the general feeding of bees is, upon the whole profitable. It is argued that while it is wise to feed bees that have not sufficient food to keep them alive, any thing given them beyond that is unprofitable, and produces an inferior article of honey, if any thing but pure honey be fed. The following is Mr. Eddy's argument:

"The theory of feeding bees on a large scale has had its day. It has presented splendid results for a time, and resulted at length in splendid failures. Cheap honey, or a composition, has been used, and the bees have been fed freely, under the impression that whatever they stored in their cells must of course be honey of the first quality. I would ask why Cuba or Southern honey is not made of the first quality when it is stored up for the first time in Cuba or Florida, if bees have the power of converting an inferior article into one of superior quality. The true reason is, that much of this so-called honey is taken from the sugar plantations, or from flowers which do not furnish the best honey. And the second transportation, although done by "Yankee" bees, does not produce any chemical change in the article which is fed. Honey is gathered, not made by the bees. Those who purchase in market Cuba honey which is packed up in "Yankee" boxes, do not get the best end of the bargain. They have yet to learn that the packing or transportation does not make it the fine-flavored and wholesome article which is found in white clover upon all our hills in New England. The feeding of the bees on a large scale, or with a view to secure larger quantities of surplus honey, operates unfavorably upon the bees in a variety of ways, and the principal objections to it are the following; 1. There is no profit in it. No man gets the quantity of honey which he feeds. 2. It prevents the bees from going abroad to gather honey from the fields. 3. If the bees are fed liberally late in the fall and early in the spring, there will be very few empty cells in which to rear young bees. 4. It is deceptive, because a cheap and inferior article is sold for one of superior quality. 5. It results, in the process of time, in the extinction of the bees. The feeding of the bees may be practiced with advantage whenever they are not amply supplied with winter stores, a thing which happens to late swarms and to those from which large quantities of honey have been taken. For this purpose a cheap article may be used to help them through the winter. It may be desirable to take from the bees all the white clover honey which can be obtained in boxes with a view to supply the bees with a cheaper article."

Daily Examination of the hives for the removal of all filth tends to domesticate the bees, and if done gently the effect is to so accustom them to their keeper that he can handle them with perfect impunity.

The Position of the Bee-House should be free from exposure to the north and west winds, and from the morning sun. A southwest exposure is recommended by the best authorities.

SUMMER MANAGEMENT.—Preparations for Swarms.—Every thing necessary should now be prepared for the establishment of swarms, which may be expected during the next two months, else there may be running hither and thither, while the swarm takes wing and is lost through your delayed preparation. Hives, or boxes if you intend to make use of these, must be kept dry and sweet; stands or stools to place them on must be prepared, and a hand-brush, leather gloves, crape, or other covering for the face, placed in readiness.

As bees require water to drink, especially through this and the next month, it is necessary to place some for them, if there is no pond or rivulet near. Cotton says that, in the Isle of Wight, the people have a notion that every bee goes down to the sea to drink once a day. Water is needful for them in the breeding season, and they will drink water with salt in it, and like it better than the freshest brook that runs. It is very curious to see how they will flock by thousands to the drinking-troughs in April, May, and part of June; and then their thirst seems to be quenched all of a sudden, for not one will be seen at them. The reason seems to be that they do not want so much water after the greater part of the young brood is hatched.

Shallow dishes or plates filled with water, and having thin boards, pierced with small holes, floating on it, from which the bees may drink without fear of drowning, are convenient. Small pebbles or moss, placed in the plates with the water, will answer almost as well.

The hives, if old, should be scalded to destroy the larvæ of insects. If new, the only preparation is to wet the inside with salt and water, sweetened with either honey, molasses, or sugar.

Indications of Swarming.—The most certain indications of swarming are, the hive appearing full of bees—clusters of them gathering on the outside, and sometimes hanging from the alighting-board; they also neglect their daily toil and refrain from going abroad in search of sweets, even though the weather be ever so inviting. Just before they take flight, the hive is hushed, the bees are silent and carefully loading themselves with provender for their journey. For two or three nights prior to swarming, you will also hear a peculiar humming noise within the hive; the second swarm is announced by a different sort of buzzing, being, according to some writers, the result of a contest as to which of the two queens shall lead off from the hive. It is the old queen who leads off the first swarm.

If a swarm be about to quit the hive, the slightest change of weather will prevent their doing so, but nothing so effectually as a shower of rain; hence an excellent mode of preventing it, when the bees cluster on the outside of the hive, by syringing them with water from a common metallic syringe. When a swarm leaves the hive, if it do not settle on some tree or bush, but remains in the air, and you fear its going off to too great a distance, if not evading you altogether, you may bring it down by throwing up sand or dust, which the bees mistake for rain, or by firing a gun, which they mistake for thunder; hence the old fashion of the country people following a swarm with the noise of fire-shovels and frying-pans. You must be the more diligent in at once securing your swarm, for it is a fact that the bees send out scouts previous to swarming, whose duty it is to select a proper habitation for the colony. It is, on this account, a good plan, when you anticipate a swarm, to leave an empty hive, previously smeared on the interior with honey, in some convenient place, but not too near the old one.

When the swarm settles, the bees collect themselves in a heap round the queen, hanging to each other by means of their feet. When thus suspended from a tree, they may be secured by simply holding an empty hive under them, and tapping the branch from which they are suspended. They should, in this case, be sprinkled with honey and water, and confined for about twelve hours. When a swarm divides into two or more bands, and settle separately, it is probable that there are two queens. In this case you must secure one of them.

If, through your inattention, a second swarm comes off, you should, as soon as you have hived it, secure its queen, and return the swarm to the hive; indeed, when deprived of its queen, it will usually immediately return of its own accord. Swarming is a subject, we have reason to believe, which is very generally misunderstood, most persons desiring to promote it, conceiving that the greater the number of swarms the richer will the hives be in August. The very reverse of this is the case; for, when a hive is weak in numbers, a sufficient number of bees cannot be spared to go forth for honey; and hence they will be scarcely able to collect enough for their actual support, far less to collect any surplus for their master's benefit. Hear Mr. Briggs:

"The swarming of bees is a subject on which much misconception prevails. Most persons who keep their bees in the old straw-hive plan, and suffocating system, appear to anticipate their swarming with much anxiety, and to be of opinion that the greater number of swarms—firsts, seconds, thirds, etc.—they obtain from their old hives during the summer, the more remunerative will they prove to the owner at the end of the season; whereas the reverse of the above practice is much nearer of being the best system to follow, which I shall endeavor to elucidate. It has been proved from observation, that the average percentage of swarms have been twenty-four in May, sixty in June, fourteen in July, and two in August; from which it will appear that June is the principal month for swarming, in ordinary seasons; and it is in June and July that the greatest quantities of honey are stored up by the bees, when managed in a judicious manner.

"When the swarming is assisted and encouraged during June and July, the old stocks are considerably weakened, and the swarms are employed in building combs in their new hives, collecting pollen, and attending to the young brood, until the best part of the honey-storing season is over; so that, at the honey harvest in autumn, it will frequently require the contents of five or six old stocks, or late swarms, to produce as much pure honey as might have been obtained from one colony on the system of management which is recommended."

In collateral boxes, and in capped hives, swarming may be prevented by affording the bees additional accommodation, and reducing the temperature; and, for this end, it is recommended, by most apiarians, that the hive or box should be furnished with a thermometer as well as ventilator. We think, however, that even those who do not possess these accommodations may manage well enough by proper observation and attention to the symptoms we have detailed. When these appear in a collateral box-hive, open one of the partitions, and admit the bees into a new apartment; if all be full, take off a box, empty and restore it. In the case of a capped hive, remove the bung, and admit the bees to the cap; if full, remove, empty, and restore it. On this subject Mr. Briggs says:

"The most favorable degrees of heat for the prosperity of the brood are from 75° to 90° in the stock hive, and from 65° to 75° in the side boxes. The heat in a prosperous hive is sometimes upward of 70° at Christmas, and will, in hot summer weather, sometimes rise to near 120°, at which time the combs are in great danger of being damaged, and of falling to the floor of the hive; this may, however, be prevented, by giving extra room when required, and by shading the hives from extreme heat, as previously directed. It should always be borne in mind that all operations with bees should be performed as carefully and as speedily as circumstances will permit. The late Mr. T. Nutt remarked, in a conversation with him a few months previous to his decease, 'that in removing boxes, glasses, slides, etc., the apiarian should proceed in a manner so steady and cautious, that the bees should scarcely know that their habitation had been meddled with;' in which remarks I fully concur."

After having a new swarm, you must also recollect, that if unfavorable weather follow their departure, you must feed them, otherwise they will be starved; indeed, it would be well if each new swarm were always fed for a few days, as this will assist them in gaining strength in numbers and in store, before the principal part of the honey season goes over. In conclusion we would merely say, that the weight of a good swarm should be from five to seven pounds, and that all under five pounds in weight should be united to others, as being too weak in numbers to support themselves.

Bee Dress.—In hiving a swarm it is as well to be protected with a proper bee dress. *Prevention is better than cure,* and it is *better to be sure than sorry;* yet bees are certainly less apt to sting at this time than any other.

Some persons are particularly unhappy in possessing those qualities which render them disagreeable to bees. The main objections are, excessive timidity, and likewise, with some, an unpleasant odor, in some instances the result of personal negligence, but frequently of peculiarity of constitution. The remedies are a *bee-dress* for the former, and the use of some strong perfume which the bees like, and which will effectually conceal whatever is offensive to them.

"I have gone among them," says Mr. Worlidge, "in their greatest anger and madness, only with a handful of sweet herbs in my hand, fanning about my face, as it were to obscure and defend it. Also, if a bee do by accident buzz about you, being unprovided, thrust your face amongst a parcel of boughs or herbs, and he will desert you. But the most secure way of all, and beyond the completest harness yet published, is to have a net knit with so small meshes that a bee cannot pass through, and of fine thread or silk, large enough to go over your hat, and to lie down to the collar of your dress, through which you may perfectly see what you do without danger, having also on a pair of woolen gloves."

Mr. E. W. Phelps describes the following form of a bee-dress, which may be procured at an expense not exceeding twenty five cents: "Take one and a half yards of thin, light, three-quarter muslin, and a piece of wire-cloth (such as is used for meal sieves) about six inches square; it may be obtained of wire-weavers in most of our large towns and cities, or of hardware dealers. Lay the muslin over the head, with the ends down over the shoulders, with one end of the selvedge in front and the other back. The back part may be cut and fitted to the head, and a cord run in to gather it around the neck, and the wire-cloth sewed in over the face, first rounding the corners in shape of the face. It should extend down below the mouth, to afford free respiration, and the muslin sewed together below the wire-cloth, sufficient to extend below the vest. It may be worn under a coat, but it is not the best way, as it is usually warm weather when it is worn, and with the head-dress and a coat over it, a person will be very uncomfortable on account of the heat; besides, the bees will crawl up under one's coat and vest, and when in close quarters will often prick through the shirt, and tickle a person under the ribs. To prevent this and the other difficulty, I have prepared myself with a garment made of the same kind of material as the head-dress, and in the form of a hunting-shirt, open before, with buttons close together, to button up tight. I first put on my head-dress, and then over this my hunting-shirt, buttoned under my pants; and with a pair of thick woolen gloves, with stocking legs sewed to the wrists, to draw up over my sleeves, and my pants tied over my boots, I can defy all the forces they choose to bring against me.

Clustering Shrubs and Bushes, placed in the vicinity of the apiary, are recommended by experienced bee-keepers, as tending to diminish the difficulties of hiving bees. Mr. Phelps directs to "take the *seed-ends* of mullen-stalks about a dozen in number, and tie these to the tops of poles; the poles should be set in the ground so as to be easily taken up after the bees have settled on them; by managing in this manner, the hive may be set in the apiary, before hiving, and the bees may be carried on the pole and laid by the side of the hive, when they will enter it; this saves the trouble of moving the hive after hiving, and consequently no bees will be lost. The mullen tops should be attached to the poles so as to lie nearly horizontally. What there is in the mullen-stalks so attracting to the bees I know not, unless it is their rough, uneven surface, which affords the bees security against falling; old dry weather-beaten stalks are as good as any."

Mr. Weeks directs that "when there are no fruit-trees nor shrubbery in the immediate vicinity of the bees, it is found that they will cluster on bushes artificially set down about the hives; say, take hemlock, cedar, or sugar-maple bushes six, eight, or ten feet high; sharpen the largest end, with the foliage remaining on the top, and set them down like bean-poles promiscuously round about the hives, two, three, or four rods distant; when the bees swarm, they will usually cluster in a body on some one of them, which may be pulled up, and the bees shaken off for the hive. Some apiarians confine a bunch of the seed-ends of dry mullen-stalks near the top of the bush, so as to represent, at a little distance, a cluster of bees: this is said to be unfailing in catching swarms. Others recommend to drive down two stakes, two or three feet apart, and confine a stick of sufficient strength to each stake two or three feet from the ground, forming a cross-bar, so that, when a board twelve feet long is laid, one end resting on the cross-bar and the other on the ground, the bees will cluster under it, admitting it is at a reasonable distance, and yet so far from the old stock as to be out of hearing of their hum. Any one will know how to turn the board over, and set an empty hive over the bees.

"The hiver is made of three rough boards, half an inch thick, seven inches wide, twenty-four inches long, nailed together like a common trough, open at both ends,—a strap of iron riveted on its outside, across the center of each board, with a shank or socket to insert a rod to handle it with, so that when inverted by means of the rod, and placed over the bees when alighting, it forms a kind of half hive, which they readily enter. There should be from a dozen to twenty half-inch holes bored through the top board, so as to let the alighting bees enter through the holes. When a small proportion of the bees are found in the hiver, it may be moved a few feet from the limb, which may be shaken with another rod with a hook on its end, which disengages the bees, and in a few moments the whole swarm will be found in the hiver. By the addition of ferules and joints, the hiver may be raised to any reasonable height. Thus the labor of climbing, the use of ladders, and cutting the limbs of precious fruit-trees, is entirely dispensed with. It likewise enables the apiarian, in large establishments, to divide out and keep separate his swarms, which might otherwise alight many in one body."

Management of Black Combs.—The combs in hives that have stood for several years become black and useless, because the bees never clear out the cells in which the brood has been reared, and the skins which the young bees cast gradually fill up the cells until they are too small for breeding in; in consequence the hives get weaker and weaker; swarming cannot take place, and at last the bees die.

To prevent this fatal end, you may in spring, before breeding-time commences, after fumigating the bees a little, turn up the hive and cut out half the comb; put the bees in again, and during the summer they will fill up the vacancy, and have room for breeding. Next spring take out the remainder of the old comb in the same way. One stock treated in this manner is said to have been kept for the long period of sixty years. Sometimes, when a stock has not swarmed, it is desirable to remove the bees altogether from the old hive into a new one. This must only be done during the first week in July; if attempted earlier, the new brood not being all hatched, many bee-grubs would be destroyed, and you would have a weak stock. On the other hand, if transferred later, there would not be time for them to make their comb and lay up winter store. Fumigate or intoxicate the bees at night, and put them while stupefied into a new hive, taking care that the queen is among them; place the hive on the stand in the same position the old one occupied, and on the morrow they will commence their labor as a new swarm. If the weather be fine, they will do well; but if they are found to be weak in autumn, take them up and unite them with another stock.

September is the proper time for carefully inspecting your stocks, to ascertain which will stand the winter, for feeding those which have not sufficient food, and for uniting weak stocks to strong ones, as previously recommended.

By gently striking the hives, you may judge whether they contain many or few bees, from the greater or lesser noise they make in the buzzing which immediately follows. Do not leave any to remain for the winter but such as weigh about twenty pounds.* But recollect that a hive with two thousand bees will be more likely to survive than one with only one thousand, even if the latter have much more honey. On this account it is important to ascertain the number of bees, and to make your standing stocks as strong as possible, to maintain sufficient heat in the hives.

FALL FEEDING.—Whatever food is required must be given now, as bees should not on any account be fed in winter. Those who have not the convenience of the feeding-pans for the top of the hive, should provide little hollow troughs made of elder, or a split bamboo stopped at the ends. These must be filled with honey or syrup, and then pushed into the mouth of the hive at sunset, the entrance being carefully closed, to prevent other bees from entering. Feeding should not take place in the daytime, as the hive will then be subject to the depredations of wasps and robber-bees which are attracted by the scent, and not unfrequently devour the whole of the honey. In the morning, a little before sunrise, remove the troughs. Continue this operation nightly until you are sure

---

* *Age* will cause hives to weigh heavier than their *legitimate* contents would call for; this is occasioned by an accumulation of *bee-bread* and the cast sloughs which had formerly served as envelopes to the young. In the case of old hives, you must, therefore, allow from two to five pounds, according to age, for these matters.

your bees have sufficient winter provision. Do not be stingy: as we have said before, you will reap the profit of liberality to your bees in the rich return they will make.

HOUSING, etc., IN WINTER.—When there is snow upon the ground, the entrances of your hives should be entirely closed, and a screen or shade should be placed before the hive, in case of an accidental sunny day occurring, in order to prevent the bees from encountering even a single deceptive ray.

Another danger from which you are imperatively called upon to protect your bees during winter is *dampness*. It is to this cause that the loss of many a stock is to be attributed—an *internal dampness*, generated within the hive itself. This is best remedied by careful ventilation, placing a bell-glass, well covered with flannel, over the aperture on the top of your hive or box, removing it from time to time, and carefully wiping away from its interior the damp formed by condensed vapor; this remedy is at once simple and efficacious.

It will, perhaps, appear to some of our readers a singular experiment, resorted to by some bee-keepers, viz., *burying the hives*. When this is to be attempted, the hive should be buried in a cool, dry, shady place, among leaves, about a foot deep, and the interment should be performed during the first or second week of November.

A friend buried a hive of bees in the first week of November, about a foot deep, amongst dry leaves, etc., and disinterred it in the last week of February, when it was just *two pounds lighter than it was in November*, and the bees in *a lively and healthy state*. Another person immured a hive of bees in the earth four feet deep, in the second week of November, and at the end of January it was removed, and weighed *only three ounces less than it did before it was buried*.

The above experiments are worthy of attention; a shed having a northern aspect, and which is as dry as possible, would be a suitable place for further trials. The principal points by which there might be cause for fear of failure, would, as in other cases, be from dampness, disease for want of fresh air, and attacks from vermin, etc. To prevent the former I would recommend that the hives be placed on a long frame of wood, covered by a web of closely worked wire, and raised a few inches from the ground, the ends of which should communicate with and be occasionally opened to the fresh air. A long tube should also be placed from the hole at the top of each hive to the open air of the shed, from the upper end of which any dampness might be condensed by bell-glasses, and conveyed away as already directed.

Among other obvious mistakes, I may mention the recommendation to give the bees an opportunity of leaving the hive, and going abroad every fine day, already detailed. What advantage is expected to be derived from thus permitting the insects to go forth? They may be supposed to want exercise. This is a mistake; for the bees naturally crowd together, and remain in a sort of torpor during winter, and every thing that could tend to interfere with, or arouse them from it, must, of course, prove contrary to their natural instincts, and consequently, prejudicial. During winter the bees are inactive.

HIVES AND BOXES.—By having proper hives and boxes for bees, the following advantages are obtained:—First—the power of depriving bees of honey at pleasure, without injuring them. Secondly—obtaining it in larger quantities, and of finer quality. Thirdly—The means of a more thorough ventilation, the keeping of the bees cool, and of enlarging their accommodations at pleasure, and the power to control swarming at will.

ENEMIES OF BEES.—These are far more numerous than their diseases, and are as follows:

Poultry, mice, toads, frogs, snails, slugs, caterpillars, moths, millipedes, wood-lice, ants, lice, spiders, wasps, hornets.

Fowls should not be permitted in any apiary. They will kill and eat the bees, and such as they do not destroy they will annoy and disturb —besides, your bees will probably occupy a stand in your garden, a quarter whence other reasons should necessarily exclude poultry.

Mice.—While the bees are vigorous, the field-mouse does not dare attack the hive; but as the cold approaches, and the bees become less active, he enters, and commencing with the lower comb, ascends by degrees as the bees become torpid, until he either clears all away, or by the smell of the honey he has wasted on the board, induces other bees to come and plunder. As soon as the warm weather returns, the surviving bees will leave the hive in disgust. The remedy is easy. By having your straw hives, if you use such, coated on the exterior with Roman cement, you will prevent mice from nestling in the straw, whence otherwise they would speedily eat their way into the interior, and by narrowing the entrance of the hive in the manner already described, you will effectually keep out these little intruders. If your stands be placed on a single foot, or if the feet are so placed under the foot-board as to leave a wide, projecting ledge, no mice can arrive at the hive.

Toads will kill bees occasionally, but not in sufficient numbers to excite our alarm; but the toad is rather to be regarded as a friend to the bees —one of their enemies, the spider, being his favorite food.

Frogs may be classed with toads.

Snails and Slugs.—These creatures are not absolutely enemies of bees, as they have no design upon them or their honey in entering the hive, but merely do so from accident. The mischief done by them consists in the alarm and confusion they occasion. The bees first attack the unfortunate intruder and kill him with their stings, after which they carefully incase him in propolis, effectually preventing putrefaction or the production of maggots.

Caterpillars.—The most dreaded is the caterpillar of the wax-moth, so called from the ravages it makes amongst the combs as soon as it obtains entrance. By having the legs of the stand placed as we have already described, no caterpillar can climb up to the hive; but this will not prevent the moth herself from entering and depositing eggs in the hive; and so prolific are these moths, that a single brood would suffice to destroy a whole stock. Periodical fumigation, and cutting away such combs as contain the grubs, are the remedies to be adopted. Moths are only *nocturnal* enemies. During the day you have nothing to fear from their attacks. Let the entrance to the hive, therefore, be nearly closed in the evening, and you will protect your bees from their ravages. Columella recommends, as a trap for moths, a bottle, or other vessel, with a long and narrow neck increasing gradually to a wide mouth, and having a light in the neck, to be placed under the hive in the evening. We can vouch for the efficacy of this trap—it will destroy numbers. Another particular to be attended to is to have your stocks sufficiently strong; and for this purpose, if the hive attacked be weak, unite it to the bees of another hive, in the manner already described. The bees are themselves, if sufficiently strong in numbers, both willing and able to destroy the intruders. If weak, they will necessarily fall victims.

Millipedes, or Wood-lice, are often produced by the stands being made of decayed wood, or the hive being placed too near an old hedge. Let the stand be of new wood, and strew soot on the ground under and about the hive. This will also serve in part as a protection against the attacks of ants.

Ants.—You should always destroy such ants' nests as you find in the neighborhood of a hive. In the West Indies, glass-feet are used to prevent these insects from getting into furniture, etc. Might not such be used with advantage for bee-hives?

Lice.—These are small parasitical insects of a red color, which adhere to the body of the bee, and derive their nourishment from their juices. They are about the size of a grain of mustard-seed, or rather smaller.

Reaumur and others tried many remedies for these troublesome insects, but in vain, till at length Madame Vicat discovered that Morocco tobacco will kill the lice without injuring the bees.

Spiders.—Brush away their webs wherever you meet with them near your stand.

Wasps and Hornets.—These insects are most noxious to bees. Dig up and destroy their nests wherever you meet with them; but you will most effectually get rid of them by offering a reward for every queen wasp brought to you in spring. The destruction of each queen is tantamount to that of an entire nest; and if this plan were generally adopted, wasps would eventually be extirpated.

Birds.—Among those which are the greatest enemies to bees, we may mention sparrows and swallows. Set traps near the hives, baited with dead bees; shoot the birds; and hang up a few of such birds as you kill, on trees near the stands. Perseverance for a time in this will rid you of the annoyance.

Bees.—Bees are amongst the most dangerous foes of their own kind, being bold and resolute plunderers. It is only weak stocks, however, that suffer, so that union is the obvious cure. Avoid also placing your hives too close together; and also avoid at any time placing a weak stock near a strong one.

BEE-FLOWERS.—Conspicuous among all the plants loved by bees (for the best of reasons, that they get the most honey or other substances from them), are clover, wild-thyme, heath and broom, borage, French buckwheat, and *Melilotus leucantha*. This last may be usefully grown for the bees' especial gratification. It is easily cultivated, blooms from June to November, and is ornamental in addition to its other good qualities. But the most important qualification of bee-pasturage is, that there shall be always something for the bees, from the very earliest spring to the very latest autumn. It will be useful, therefore, to append a list of bee-flowers.

Spring.—Erica carnea,* winter aconite,* rosemary,* laurustinus, hazel,* snow-drop, crocus,* willow,* osier,* primrose, hepatica, violet, almond, wallflower* (single), borage,* onion, gooseberry, apricot, peach, apple, gooseberry,* currant,* laurel, turnip,* cabbage, etc.,* strawberry, tulip, hawthorn, gorse or furze, columbine, laburnum, berberry,* ribes sanguineum, Dutch clover.*

Summer.—Syringa, helianthemum, annual poppy,* sea-kale, French willow, sweet-brier, bean, yellow lupine, mignonette,* blackberry, chestnut, mallow, lime,* hyssop, teazle, nasturtium, yellow vetch, sainfoin, broom, wheat, viper's bugloss,* raspberry,* symphora, racemosa.

Autumn.—Michaelmas daisy, winter savory, purple houseleek, ivy, honeysuckle, French buckwheat* sowed at midsummer, Spanish broom,* hollyhock,* heath,* sunflower, lemon thyme,* St. John's-wort, melilotus leucantha.*

Those marked with an asterisk are understood to be the flowers especially favored by the bees. What a choice little garden for himself, as well as for his bees, the apiarian may make from the above list, if he does not choose to leave the bees dependent upon the stores of the neighborhood at large!

TRANSPORTING BEES.—Though few, in this country, it is presumed, will adopt the plan recommended in the following paragraphs, yet they are interesting as showing the pains taken elsewhere in the keeping of bees:

"Should the surrounding neighborhood not furnish a sufficiency of flowers, the practice of transportation, or shifting, is strongly recommended by many authors. It is not in the power of every bee-keeper, but as those whose home is placed by a river or canal, have a means at hand for transporting their hives, we have chosen to mention it here. In some countries, boats are built expressly for this purpose. They receive a very large number of hives in each boat, and by traveling for a few hours at night, the bees find themselves in a new country during their working hours, and the hives are rapidly filled with honey and wax of the best quality. The boatmen receive a small sum for each hive that they transport, but we rather fancy that their ingenuity does not rest until it has extracted some portion of the honey from the best-filled hives. The Nile is much used for this purpose, and bees traverse the entire length of Egypt during the summer. In China ducks are subjected to the same migratory life, and thrive amazingly. Hives may easily be carried on men's shoulders, as that mode of conveyance shakes them less than carriage by wagon. Heaths are the best places that bees can possibly live in, and in Scotland there are people who make their living by taking care of hives during the time that the heath is in blossom, a period of about two months, for which time a rent of from one shilling to eighteen pence is paid by the proprietor. It is always necessary while the bees are migrating, to take them at least ten miles during the nocturnal journey, as they are otherwise apt to fly back to the former position of their hive, and to lose themselves in searching for it. The distance to which bees can fly for food is shown in the following anecdote, which has been recently published:

"'A man who kept bees in Holborn, wishing to find out where they worked, sprinkled them all with a red powder as they came out of the hive in the morning. As the heath and thyme were now in full bloom, he at once thought that Hampstead, being the nearest heath, would be the likeliest place to find his bees. As soon, therefore, as his bees were gone away, he hastened to the heights of Hampstead. The walk was a long and toilsome one, of at least four miles, in a July sun. But he trudged manfully on, soon left behind him Camden and Kentish towns, and at last was refreshed with the soft summer breeze sweeping across the purple and golden bloom of the heath. After a few minutes' rest on the green sward, he began his search, and before long was delighted to find there, among thousands of other busy bees, his own little fellows in the dusty red coats, which he had given them in the morning.' Many of the bees made the journey more than twice in each day, thus piloting themselves through sixteen miles of smoke and dust within the twelve hours.

"If the hives are taken by water, they should always be placed on the shore at some distance from the bank, before opening the doors, as they will very probably when returning home, wearied and laden with their burdens, fall into the water before they can reach the hive. If the hives are placed for the season, they should be kept at some little distance from other hives, as if they are weak, their more powerful neighbors will inevitably plunder them."

FUMIGATION.—The following particular description of the manner of fumigating or stupefying bees will enable any one to practice it.

Fumigation implies directing certain smoke of a stupefying character into the hives, so as to render the bees harmless while their combs are being removed, while at the same time no injury is done to the bees themselves. There are several substances which stupefy; tobacco is one, but it is apt to give the wax and honey an unpleasant flavor, and we will, therefore, say nothing about it. The best material that can be used for this purpose, is the lycoperdon, or common puff-ball. A fine specimen of this fungus will grow as large as a child's head. It may be found in almost any field where mushrooms grow. It should always be gathered when nearly ripe, in dry weather, and either exposed to the heat of the sun or placed in an oven until it turns brown and leathery. Some always squeeze it flat during the drying process, as it then can be packed easier, and appears to take fire sooner than if left to dry in any shape it chooses to take. In order to insure its burning freely when lighted, some recommend that when dried, it should be dipped in a very weak solution of saltpetre, and again dried. There are many ways of applying the smoke, but all are useless unless the fungus is retained outside the hive, and only the smoke permitted to enter, as the bees are sure to fall on the burning mass, and thus many will be killed or maimed. Moreover, the operator ought to be able to regulate the amount of smoke poured into the hive. Mr. Cotton, the author of "My Bee-Book," managed it by having a tin box made to fit the nose of a pair of bellows, in which was placed a piece of lighted fungus about twice the size of a hen's egg. There were two openings in the box, one to admit the nose of the bellows, and the other immediately opposite, from which the smoke poured. The box being fixed on the nose of the bellows, and the end being placed against the entrance of the hive, a few vigorous puffs soon fill the hive with the stupefying smoke, under whose effects, after a brief buzz of indignant astonishment, the bees are heard falling as thick as hail, and in a few minutes all is still within.

In performing the work of fumigation, many failures have occurred, from setting about the operation too hastily, or from the non-observance of a few rules that can be easily remembered, and as easily put in practice. In the first place, great care must be taken that the smoke of the fungus or other material used for the purpose is not admitted into the hive at too high a temperature. If this is the case, the heat of the smoke will in the first place scorch and kill the bees, who will rush to the entrance of the hive on the first intrusion of the fumigating tube, and will also melt the wax of the combs, and do considerable mischief. The tube, therefore, should be a very long one, and small in diameter. There is no hurry about the operation, work the bellows quite deliberately, and the danger of burning the poor bees, or spoiling the combs, will be avoided. There is hardly a more pitiable sight than to find on turning up the hive a number of bees lying on the board, with scorched and shriveled wings—a loss of no small importance, as you will want every bee to set to work immediately, to repair the devastations committed in the hive. Another mistake not unfrequently occurs in following Mr. Cotton's directions too literally. It is not sufficient to have the fumigating box made merely of tin, as will most certainly be done if that order is sent to a tinman, for the heat of the ignited puff-ball will speedily melt the solder, and the whole apparatus will fall to pieces. A case of this kind occurred very recently. The box and tube were made according to order, the clay prepared for stopping the entrance of the hive round the tube, the fungus was duly lighted, placed in the box, the bellows fitted, and then vigorously worked. Suddenly, while the operators were complacently puffing away at the bellows, and congratulating themselves on securing both honey and bees by this method, the box fell in pieces, the tube consequently was drawn out of the hive door, and out rushed the bees in a tumultuous state of indignation, thereby putting their would-be captors to an ignominious flight. So, lest you meet with a similar misfortune, give particular orders to have the whole affair made fire-proof, and then you may proceed without the least danger. Of course this must all be done some hours after dark, or the bees who are already out will soon signify their dislike of finding intruders when they return to the hive. It is also necessary to be very quick in cutting out the combs, as the bees do not remain long in their state of torpor or intoxication, and are quite ready on their revival to employ their stings. Always examine the combs that are removed, to see if any bees are left in them, as not unfrequently, when they begin to find that they cannot overpower the vapor, they dive to the bottom of an empty cell, and sometimes are so protected by this precaution, that they revive rather sooner than their less fortunate companions. The wax of the combs thus obtained is much whiter than if sulphur is used, and of course, will fetch a higher price in the market, besides being free from a slight tinge of sulphury flavor, which hangs about them for a long time.

13*

For fumigating, the circular bellows, set in motion by a winch, are much superior to the double bellows, as a constant stream of smoke is introduced into the hive, instead of a series of puffs. Mr. Pettigrew recommends (probably because they can more certainly be obtained when wanted), cotton rags, tightly rolled up in the form of a candle, and applied in the same way as the fungus. If so, it will be found advisable to steep the rags in a solution of nitre, as otherwise they are very apt to go out before a sufficiency of smoke has issued from them. The solution, however, must be weak also, or it may do mischief instead of good, for ignited nitre is apt to send forth sparks, especially if it is urged on by a draught of air. It may be possible that ether or chloroform may answer better than either fungus or rags, but the experiments do not yet appear to have been sufficiently numerous to enable one to speak with confidence. At all events, although chloroform and ether may not supersede fungus and nitre in stupefying bees, the smoke of puff-ball threatens to supersede chloroform and ether in their anæsthetic power as applied to human beings. We are bound to observe that fumigation may not be altogether so harmless as is supposed, and therefore should not be used without necessity.

When, after applying the fumigating apparatus, as has been described above, the stillness that reigns in the hive indicates that the bees are in a state of insensibility, the hive may then be turned up for any necessary operations. If honey is wanted choose the side combs, so as not to interfere with the brood in the center, and be moderate. Replace the violated hive carefully, and the bees will soon recover from their state of partial intoxication, and set to work to repair the ravages that have been made in their stores. Nor does fumigation injure the working power of the bees. Unlike the effects of alcoholic compounds, which when taken in an overdose, entirely prostrate the sufferer for some time, the smoke of the fungus causes a very transient intoxication, which in a few minutes passes away, and the bees appear rather refreshed than otherwise, after their involuntary debauch.

DRIVING.—In the hands of a skillful operator, driving will often be found useful, as it partly supersedes the necessity of fumigation. By driving, the bee-master induces his winged auxiliaries to change their position, by working on their fears instead of stupefying what brains they have. The best method of driving bees will be found in the pages of Bevan, who appears to think very highly of the operation. "Toward the dusk of the evening, when the family will be all, or nearly all at home, and no annoyance be experienced from stranger-bees, let the hive, or box, be raised gently from its floor-board, and supported on three thin wedges; let an assistant be at hand, provided with a tobacco-pipe, or the fumigating box and bellows, from one of which at the moment of raising the hive, let a few whiffs of tobacco smoke be blown into it all round, and a few more after it has been raised. This expedient will soon induce the bees to ascend and congregate at the upper part of the hive. It is next to be inverted steadily on a small tub or peck measure, puffed again, and then quickly and accurately surmounted by an empty hive or box, as nearly of its own diameter as possible. After securely closing the two hives, by tying a cloth firmly round them above and below the junction, so that not a bee may escape, it will be proper to place an empty decoy hive upon the stand where the full hive stood, to amuse any straggling bees that may have stayed out late, or that may escape during the operation. The conjoined hives are then to be removed into a darkened room, in the manner already described, when, if the hive be *well peopled*, and the *weather warm*, by drumming at first gently, and then smartly with the open hands or a couple of sticks on the outside of the hive, the bees will be so alarmed, that in a few minutes they will have ascended into the super. The ascent may always be ascertained by the humming noise attending it. The impulse thus communicated to the bees should be given in the direction of the combs, and by no means upon those parts of the hive which are opposite to their sides, as it might separate them from their attachments."

"The exchange of habitation having been effected, the ulterior proceedings must be regulated by the object in view. If it be wished to have possession of the full hive, it will be simply necessary to leave the decoy-hive in its place, and after covering the honey-combs with a cloth to prevent them from being scented, to carry the bees with their temporary abode toward their usual place of entrance, when, by spreading a cloth on the ground, or on a table, all the bees may be dislodged and made to fall upon it, by a smart stroke with the hands upon the top of the hive, and if one side of the cloth be raised to the resting-board, the bees will gradually ascend, and reoccupy their original station."

Driving is made use of by the Persian villagers, whose hives are made in a cylindrical form, and built horizontally into the walls of their houses, the bees' entrance being outside the wall, and a movable door inside, the end of the hive projecting more than a foot into the room. When the villager wishes for some honey, he drums smartly upon the end of the hive which projects into his room, which causes the bees to withdraw to the other end. The circular lid is then quickly opened, as many combs as he wishes for cut out, and the lid closed again.

No one should be without spare hives or boxes ready to be used when required, even if they do not at the outset fit up a complete apparatus. Thus—

1. A spare box or hive will be ready to receive a swarm obtained in the ordinary manner, with all its picturesque but inconvenient accessories: as, long watching to know the moment of swarming; long runnings, perhaps, to overtake the vagrant young colony, over hill and valley, brake and brier, and amid interminable ear-splitting tumult, which the bees have the bad taste, it is supposed, to like; and the race often ending in seeing the whole cluster safely deposited in a neighbor's apiary, who swears it went from his hive. If you wish to avoid all that kind of thing, do your best to give the bees no motive for such wanderings, and every conceivable reason to stay where they are. Put a decoy-hive ready, with a delicious piece of comb in it (an old hive, with its own combs, will be still more attractive), and it is most likely the scouts sent out to explore will return with such a glowing account of the land of milk and honey they have discovered, that the swarm will be impatient to be off and take possession. This must, however, be done with great care, and the decoy-hive not placed in the air too soon, as

its seductive stores will not only attract the bees who are intended to be its legitimate occupants, but also wasps, hornets, and robber-bees of all descriptions, so that the swarm will have to inaugurate their entrance by a battle.

2. Bees always will settle themselves as soon as possible after swarming, and if they have not already determined upon a new habitation, will fix themselves in the first place that they think will suit them. There are many instances known of bees having swarmed unexpectedly, and after escaping from their former owners, having made their habitation in a hollow tree in a wood, or in the roof of some deserted hovel. There have been several instances of bees choosing to make their nests in the roof or tower of a church, and an instance came very recently under the writer's notice. For several years the congregation had been considerably annoyed by the presence of bees during the service, but had made no particular endeavors to rid themselves of the plague. One summer, however, brought with it such an increase of bees that it was deemed necessary to institute an inquiry; for the winged intruders came in such numbers, and buzzed about so loudly, and frightened the juvenile portion of the congregation to such a degree, that the service could not proceed with any comfort. After some search, a hole was discovered in the roof of the church, through which the bees were constantly passing. This was accordingly stopped up, and the workmen retired, congratulating themselves on getting rid of their winged enemies so easily. They were, however, quite mistaken, for the bees descended in undiminished numbers. The roof was again examined, and found to be in such bad repair, that the colony of bees who had taken up their residence between the roof and the leads had found numerous openings, which they had enlarged for their own purposes. How to eject this formidable band was now the subject of deep consultation. Sulphur-smoke would not answer, because it would soon pass out through the apertures in the roof, and besides, there was a very prevalent alarm lest the church should be set on fire. At last a veteran apiarian was sent for from the next village. He immediately planted a ladder against the exterior wall, and examined the stones until he discovered the entrance to the bees' habitation. It was a mere fissure between two stones, where some of the mortar had fallen out, and the remainder been extracted by the bees for their own convenience. After surveying the prospect for some time, he declared that a stone must be taken out of the wall before the bees could be dislodged, and immediately began to loosen the stone which had already been partly deprived of its mortar. The bees, of course, were highly indignant at such an assault, but the man coolly proceeded with his work, not heeding their anger in the least. When the stone had been completely loosened, he laid by the crowbar, and deliberately pulled it out with his hands. Out rushed a perfect cloud of bees full in his face; but he quietly laid the stone down, and contented himself with brushing them off his face until he had made further investigations. All the spectators took to flight at the first appearance of the enraged bees; but their imperturbable enemy remained quietly at his post, and after descending the ladder pulled some eight or ten bees out of his hair, and remarked that they had not stung him so much as he expected.

It turned out that the man was almost invulnerable to stings; and although several dozen stings or so were in his face, they did not leave the slightest mark, and certainly did not appear to inconvenience him in the very smallest degree. He afterward in the same cool manner extracted the greater part of the combs, and the bees, taking the hint, speedily evacuated the premises. There was but little honey, but abundance of black, worn-out combs, and plenty of young bees in every stage of advancement. It is said that if any one is repeatedly stung by scorpions, the pain diminishes each time, and that at last the system is entirely uninjured by it. An English naturalist was bold enough to try the experiment upon himself, and found that after he had been stung four or five times the pain was comparatively trifling. Perhaps the same may be the case with regard to the bee-stings, and the old man just mentioned possibly owed his immunity to his frequent experience, as Mithridates was said to have completely fortified himself against poisons, by gradually imbuing his system with them.

3. Adopting as a rule the non-disturbance in any serious way of your stock hive, so that honey and brood shall there at least flourish together, when you think it is full (a solid sound from the hive, and a great long continued buzz from the bees in answer to a tap, is good evidence of that state), attach your side-box, open the communication, and make the bees enter and leave by the entrance to the side-box, which you will do by closing up the entrance to the other at night when the bees are all at home. A little piece of comb, fastened at the top of the side-box, may be at once a useful hint and a temptation to the bees. This box is to be kept solely for honey-combs by ventilation, which prevents the queen from laying eggs in it. When the heat in the side-box is 70°, you should admit air through the top by means of a piece of tin pierced with holes. A draft through the hive, from the entrance to the roof, now takes place. This must not be done until you see the bees have fairly passed the Rubicon, and have done and ventured too much to be inclined to retreat to the stock-hive. When the box is full, you can take it away, and replace it emptied, or by another, or by opening a communication to a similar side-box on the opposite side, as in Mr. Grant's hive. The bees in it will soon flock to the queen in the parent hive. This arrangement prevents swarming, or at least has a great tendency to prevent it; as the bees have more room given to them just when they want it. It also raises the stock itself to the highest state of prosperity, as only the surplus honey is taken away, and the brood is not interfered with.

4. But if you wish to have an increase of stock without the inconvenience of natural swarming, you may easily do so by treating the side-box exactly the same as the chief one—that is, by leaving it unventilated. Brood as well as honey will then be deposited in it, and you have only to watch for a favorable opportunity of securing two stocks. This should be a little before the natural period of swarming, of which the signs are, clustering on the outside, activity and commotion among the drones, inactivity of the workers, portentous silence in the hive in the day (during which the prudent bees are supposed to be filling their pockets with provisions for their journey), and a singular hum-

ming noise at night, presumed to come from the young queen-bees announcing their advent. But these warnings apply less to the first than to the subsequent swarms. However, there is a pretty good rule for effective action. As soon as you find the side-box is nearly full, watch for an opportunity when the queen, with about two-thirds of the bees of the colony, is in the side-box, then cut off the communication with, and remove, the parent hive three or four feet distant, and put an empty hive in its exact position. The returning bees will flock into the side-box as before, and that hive is done with. As to the parent-hive, the nurse-bees will take every care of the brood in it; in fact, they will be just as though a swarm with the queen had left them; and will proceed with due equanimity to supply her place in the approved way. This is the mode practiced with success by Mr. Grant, and may be varied according to circumstances. For instance, if the queen should not have been left in the side-box with the greater portion of the bees, and has, therefore, been removed with the parent hive, the rest must be in effect the same, as regards the two hives; most of the bees then might leave the side-box and flock to the queen in the parent-hive; but if there be a brood in the side-box, it appears that the nurse-bees will not desert it, and, therefore, there are still two communities, and both well provided with all they require for a new start in life.

5. There is also practiced, it is said with great profit, a more summary way of proceeding to make an artificial swarm, which consists in fumigating the bees, in order to divide them into two bodies as before. The period chosen is from the beginning of May to the middle of July, and when there are as many bees on the board at the bottom as will fill a thirty-two (eight and a half inches by six) sized flower-pot. To ascertain this, blow a little smoke into them and turn up the hive. Before commencing operations, place the hive intended for the new colony on the stand, with a bit of comb in its roof, and a stick across the middle to aid in the support of the combs. If you are short of hives, this one may be used instead of an additional empty hive in performing the operations about to be described. But the bit of comb may be somewhat in the way. The bees having been stupefied by the fumigation, the hive is turned up, its top rested on the ground, and an empty hive placed over it of exactly the same shape (at the edges at least), and a cloth tied round the circle of junction. Then tap or drum gently at the sides of the two hives for about ten minutes, in which time probably about two-thirds of the bees will have ascended into the upper hive. The queen, fortunately for the operation, is generally one of the first either to run away from or to confront the danger (we know not which it is) by ascending. If your hive have a glass window, as all should have, you can see when about the right proportion have ascended; if not, you must guess with the aid above given of the knowledge of the ordinary duration of time occupied. Now take off the top hive and reverse it also on the ground, while you make sure the queen is there, throwing, meanwhile, the cloth (that you have removed) over the exposed bottom of the parent hive. If the queen be there (and she is easily distinguishable) you have only to shake queen and bees into the prepared hive on the board, and restore the parent colony also to the ordinary resting-place, where the bees will soon rear

a new queen for it. If the queen be not there, then repeat the process with the prepared hive, and so you will catch her at last. You can then return the first batch of bees that were removed either to the parent hive or to the prepared hive, by simply shaking them into the one which most needs them.

Old hives thus deprived of their queens, and made to rear new ones, involve another important advantage. In twenty-one days the entire brood will be reared, no fresh brood having been deposited (through the absence of an old queen), and the young queen not having begun to lay, which they do in about ten days after they leave the cell. Here, then, where the hives are heavy, say forty or more pounds in weight, is an opportunity of removing the bees (by fumigation) into a new hive, and selling the contents of the old one. The honey is thus earlier than usual in the market, and fetches a higher price. Weak swarms should invariably be joined either to strong ones, or to each other, and as soon as possible after swarming. It is only a strong community that can so successfully establish themselves before winter, as to be in no danger from its severity. This junction may be performed by fumigation, and taking away one of the queens. A stock without a queen may by the same means be added to one that is more fortunate: and this applies even to the restoration of a swarm to its own parent hive if there be ample room in it.

We have said nothing of the plan of annually destroying the bees, for it is almost an insult to our readers to suppose they would approve of so senseless and unprofitable as well as cruel a practice. It is quite true that thus all the honey that is made in a season may be obtained at once, just in the same way that all the golden eggs of the goose in the fable were to be obtained at once. And if this wholesale deprivation be desired, it is perfectly obtainable without destroying the bees, by simply fumigating them, and removing them to another hive. And if you don't choose to feed the bees during the winter, let somebody else have them that will. It is possible, in a favorable late season, they may not need any assistance. At all events, let it be the golden maxim of bee management never to allow a single bee to be injured if you can help it.

We close our article upon bees with the quaint story of an o d English apiarian.—" In or about the year 1717, one of my swarms settling among the close-twisted branches of some codling-trees, and not to be got into an hive without more help, my maid-servant, hired into the family the Michaelmas before, being in the garden, very officiously offered her assistance, so far as to hold the hive while I dislodged the bees, she being little apprehensive of what followed.

" Having never been acquainted with bees, and likewise afraid, she put a linen cloth over her head and shoulders, concluding that would be a sufficient guard, and secure her from their swords. A few of the bees fell into the hive; some upon the ground; but the main body of them upon the cloth which covered her upper garments.

" No sooner had I taken the hive out of her hands, but in a terrible fright and surprise, she cried out the bees were got under the covering, crowding up towards her breast and face, which immediately put her into a trembling posture. When I perceived the veil was of no further service, she at last gave me leave to remove it. This done, a most affecting spectacle presented itself to the view of all the company, filling me with the deepest distress and concern, as I thought myself the unhappy instrument of drawing her into so great and imminent hazard of her life, which now so manifestly lay at stake.

"It is not in my power to tell the confusion and dis'ress of mind I was in, from the awful apprehensions it raised; and her dread and terror in such circumstances may reasonably be supposed to be much more. Every moment she was at the point of retiring with all the bees about her. Vain thought! to escape by flight. She might have left the place indeed, but could not the company, and the remedy would have been much worse than the disease. Had she enraged them, all resistance had been vain, and nothing less than her life would have atoned for the offense. And now to have had that life (in so much jeopardy) insured, what would I not have given.

"To prevent, therefore, a flight which must have been attended with so fatal a consequence, I spared not to urge all the arguments I could think of, and used the most affectionate entreaties, begging her, with all the earnestness in my power, to stand her ground, and keep her present posture; in order to which, I gave encouragement to hope, in a little space, for a full discharge from her disagreeable companions; on the other hand, assuring her she had no other chance for her life. I was, through necessity, constantly reasoning with her, or else beseeching and encouraging her.

"I began to search among them for the queen, now got in a great body upon her breast, about her neck, and up to her chin. I presently saw her, and immediately seized her, taking her from the crowd, with some of the commons in company with her, and put them together into the hive. Here I watched her for some time, and as I did not observe that she came out, I conceived an expectation of seeing the whole body quickly abandon their settlement; but instead of that, I soon observed them, to my greater sorrow and surprise, gathering closer together without the least signal for departing. Upon this I immediately reflected, that either there must be another sovereign, or that the same was returned. I directly commenced a second search, and in a short time, with a most agreeable surprise, found a second or the same; she strove, by entering further into the crowd, to escape me, which I was fully determined against; and apprehending her without any further ceremony, or the least apology, I reconducted her, with a great number of the populace, into the hive. And now the melancholy scene began to change, and give way to one infinitely more agreeable and pleasant.

"The bees, presently missing their queen, began to dislodge and repair to the hive, crowding into it in multitudes, and in the greatest hurry imaginable. And in the space of two or three minutes the maid had not a single bee about her, neither had she so much as one sting, a small number of which, would have quickly stopped her breath.

"How inexpressible the pleasure which succeeded her past fears! What joy appeared in every countenance upon so signal a deliverance! and what mutual congratulations were heard! I never call to mind the wonderful escape without a secret and very sensible pleasure. I hope never to see such another sight, though I triumph in this most noble stand and glorious victory."

HIVES AND BOXES.—Various improved hives and boxes have, from time to time, been invented and more or less used, giving greater or less satisfaction; yet among them all, we regard *E. W. Phelps's Combination Hive** as one of the best. It was first patented in 1852, and during the past year has been greatly improved. It is true that his hives are *patented*, and many are disposed to look with disfavor upon *all patents*. However, we are too much indebted to the protection afforded by our patent laws, for the many and important inventions in all the arts of life, to render any refutation necessary of the futile objection.

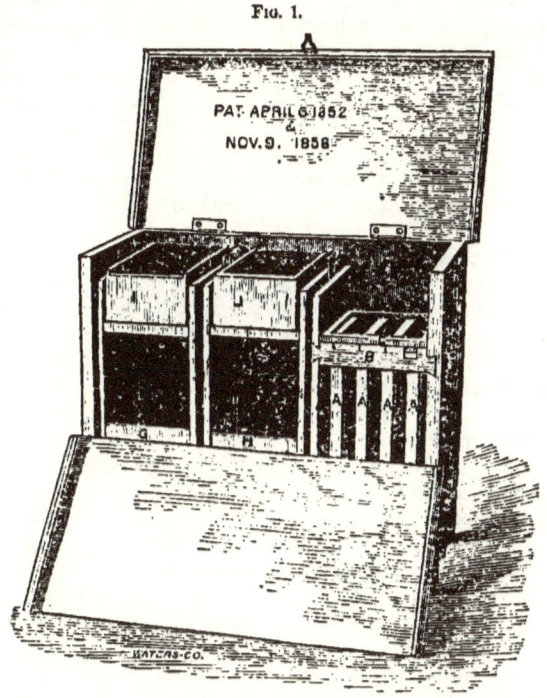

FIG. 1.

PHELPS'S COMBINATION HIVE.

These hives are made in four different forms and styles, to suit the views and wants of persons in different locations and circumstances, —the prices varying from $2.50 to $15.00. The latter is a "non-swarming hive," made with a mahogany or rosewood case in imitation of a beautiful wash-stand, and intended to be set in a gentleman's office or dwelling. The others include swarming and dividing hives, in different

---

* These hives are manufactured at Elizabeth, New Jersey, where information concerning them can be obtained.

styles and finish—some with boxes, others composed of "*improved, movable, sectional frames,*" and others combining the two principles—using a square box for the brood hive and "sectional frames," and small honey boxes for obtaining the surplus honey.

We believe the following illustrations and descriptions of these hives will be acceptable to our readers.

Fig. 1 is a hive containing the two principles combined; with the top and back opened, showing the internal arrangement. The boxes G and H, with the honey boxes I and J on the top, represent the "*Combination Hive,*" patented 1852. That part occupied with the "*Sectional Frames,*" AAAA is the late improvement of Mr. Phelps, also combining the two improvements, by using one box (H) for the *brood-hive*, with three or four of the frames, AAA, placed by the side (as seen in the engraving), with communications from the brood-hive to the frames, which are easily opened and closed at will, by means of a thin slide between the apartments. The advantages secured by the use of the small frames, in the place of a large honey box, as formerly used, is, in obtaining the surplus honey in a much more desirable condition, either for family use, or for market: as it is stored in the small frames in separate pieces, five or six inches square, in which condition it is taken from the hive without cutting or marring the combs, and can be kept in the frames until used.

The arrangement for freeing the honey and frames from the bees is a matter worthy of note, as all that is necessary to be done is, to close the communication between the apartments with the slides, and insert a long tin exit tube in the front of the hive, so that the bees must pass out *through the tube*, from the apartments containing the honey-frames, and in returning to the hive, will enter the *brood* apartment through a more open space. In this way the bees are soon cleared from the honey, leaving it free for removal, without resorting to smoking, driving, etc.

The main brood-hive (H) is occupied by the bees as their *permanent* residence, and is about one foot square in the clear, in the hives as now made. It is divided into two equal parts, and joined at the center by means of small dowels of wire, so as to be separated at will. In each apartment there is either a *sectional frame*, or *guide bars*, attached at the adjoining edges, in which the bees construct their combs, parallel with the separating joint, so that either half can be removed at will, without cutting or marring the combs, while at the same time there is no partition in the hive to separate the combs or bees; consequently, they construct their brood-combs equally in each half of the hive, and when either is removed, there is a certainty of obtaining about one half of the brood combs—an advantage not secured in any other arrangement that has come under our notice.

The tops of these hives are so constructed that by means of a late improvement the bees *cannot* construct their combs *across* the frames or bars. This is a very important feature in these hives, for, unless the combs are constructed straight on the frames or bars, and *parallel* with the joint of separation, the hive could not be taken apart without marring the combs and injuring the bees. It is also very important, in connection with the "movable frames," as here much difficulty has been experienced;

and in numerous instances the "movable frames," *as constructed in other hives*, have been rendered *entirely useless*, as far as removing the combs is concerned, on account of the bees building their combs *across* them, fastening them all together. It will be observed, that while the bees are altogether in this "*dividing-hive*," the same as in any square box-hive, and occupy the central part with their brood-combs, as is their custom, *either part* can be removed at will to obtain a portion of the honey or the old brood combs; or, the colony may be *divided*, at the proper season, and stocks multiplied without the trouble and risk attending swarming, whenever there is a sufficient quantity of bees to justify it

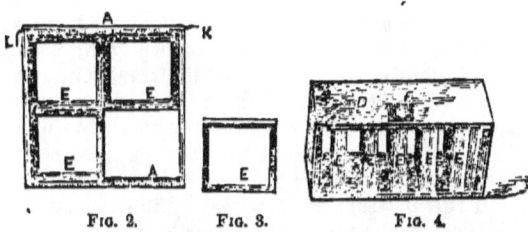

Fig. 2.   Fig. 3.   Fig. 4.

Fig. 2 is a side view of one of the frames (A) taken out. Inside of this are four smaller frames (EEEE), each one of which is about six inches square. The frame A is now dispensed with, and a more simple and cheap manner is employed of connecting the "*sectional frames*" by means of small wire hooks, thereby saving the space occupied by the large frame, and the expense of making it.

Fig. 3 is one of the sectional frames taken out.

Fig. 4 shows several of the smaller frames EEE, arranged in a box to be placed on the top of the hive when desired. In operating with the bees, the frames can be removed, replaced, or shifted, as circumstances may require.

We think every practical bee-keeper will see at once the advantage secured by the use of these small frames, over the large movable frame as constructed by others, for the honey taken from the hive, in the large frames, is in combs some twelve inches square, very inconvenient to handle or take to market, while in the small frames, the honey is in the most beautiful and convenient form possible, to use in the family, or retail in market; being in separate pieces about five inches square, weighing from one to one and a half pounds per frame, in which condition it may be kept until required for use; and one comb used at a time, without moving others. He also manufactures a plain low-priced *non-swarming hive*, the case constructed the same as shown in the engraving, only longer and higher, to afford ample space for all the bees to labor and store honey in one apartment. The interior of this hive is composed entirely of "sectional frames," placed side by side and one above the other, three or four tiers high, to the number of one hundred or more of the small frames, with no partitions or divisions between them, where the bees all labor in a mass, storing the honey in the frames; when at the close of the honey season it may be removed in the frames without moving the combs, or injury or exposure to the bees. This hive is so constructed, that, if desired, the bees may be confined to a space of one foot square, and the hive converted into a swarming hive.

The hives are all well ventilated at top and bottom, and the bottom being attached with butts and buttons, is easily let down and cleaned, without disturbing the bees. There is also a most ingenious and effectual device for destroying the bee-moth, attached to the bottom of the hive, affording the moth or worms a most convenient harbor, or hiding-place in which they are sure to secrete themselves, when the trap can be withdrawn and the worms destroyed without opening the hive or disturbing the bees.

A "*non-swarming hive*," combining the foregoing advantages has long been sought for, as there are many persons who have never kept bees, that would gladly do so, if swarming and the trouble attending it could be avoided. And as the backs of these hives are glass, they afford a good opportunity to observe the operations of the bees without exposure to them. It is an interesting sight to observe a good populous colony of "busy bees" at their labors in the hive, during the season for gathering honey, and the pleasure is increased by the reflection that we are to share with them in the products of their labors.

Another important advantage which these hives possess over those in common use, is, that the tops are composed of frames, or bars, on which the combs are attached, admitting a free circulation of air between all the combs, so that all the moisture and vapor, caused by the breath and warmth of the bees escapes freely up between them, keeping them dry and healthy, and free from mildew or mould; and it is strongly recommended to take off the honey boxes during winter, to give free ventilation, and prevent frost accumulating in the hive.

These hives are also well adapted to set in a building, on account of the peculiar construction of the entrance for the bees, and the alighting board, which forms a tube or spout to conduct the bees through the side of the building, or out at a window of a dwelling, without admitting them into it, to interfere with any one. Many persons are using these hives in their dwellings and offices. In most instances they are made in imitation of an inclosed washstand, and can be opened and all the operations of the bees observed without danger from them, and the honey obtained in tumblers or glass jars, or, in the small frames, or boxes.

We also give a brief description of Mr. Phelps's "bee-feeder." This is a very simple and practical arrangement for feeding bees; and as used in these hives obviates all danger of other bees robbing the colonies, or swarms, while being fed—a point of much importance, as generally, there is great danger of other bees being attracted to the hives by the scent of the feed, and, as it is the weakest and smallest families that usually require feeding, they are not able to defend themselves against the attacks of their more populous neighbors; and consequently, the robbers will enter the hives, and in a very short time, carry off all the honey it contains; and hence more injury than good has, in most cases, resulted from attempting to feed, for robbing one hive, does not satisfy the burglar bees, but encourages them to attack the next feeble colony, and not unfrequently several stocks will thus be destroyed before their depredations can be stopped.

This feeder is so constructed and arranged, and so harmonizes with the construction of the hives, that there is little or no danger to be apprehended from other bees being attracted to the hive or gaining access into it or to the feed, as the feeder is placed in the case, at the side of the brood-hive, near the top, with a small communication into the feeder, near the top of the hive, and therefore the robbers must pass up among the bees and combs through the body of the hive, to gain access to the feed. This they will not do, if the instructions are followed, which are : " *to nearly close the entrance tube while feeding,* leaving a space of only half an inch or so, that only one or two bees can enter at a time." In this condition a few bees are able to defend themselves against all intruders.

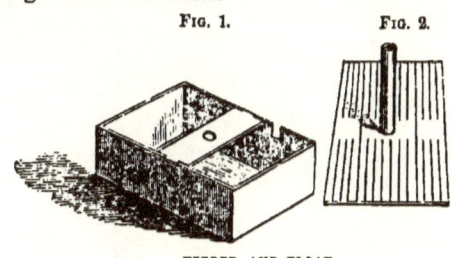

Fig. 1.   Fig. 2.

FEEDER AND FLOAT.

Fig 1 is a view of the feed-box. Fig 2, the *float* which is made to fit in it, to support the bees and prevent their becoming mired in the feed while feeding.

Fig. 1 consists of a wooden box made of half-inch boards, and is ten or twelve inches long, six inches wide, and four and a half inches deep, having one or two apertures an inch or so in diameter, near the upper edge, to communicate with the hive while feeding. A square tin pan, two inches deep, is made to fit closely in the box, even with the bottom, and secured there with small tacks.

The float, fig 2, is made of thin slats of light wood, about one inch wide, and one eighth of an inch thick, tacked on to a cross piece at the center, leaving a space between the slats of one eighth of an inch. The under side of the float is lined with strips of cork one eighth of an inch thick, tacked to the wood. A hole, five-eighths in diameter, is made in the center of the float, and a tin tube five inches long fitted in even on the under side. Another thin strip two inches wide is fitted across the top of the box, with a hole in the center one eighth of an inch larger than the tin tube, to receive it; and on each side of this top strip, a pane of glass is fitted to *confine* the bees, and afford means to observe their operations while feeding. By means of the tin tube, the float can be raised when the feed is put in the feeder, and the feed poured through it with a tunnel. The float can then be eased down on the feed, and the bees come on to it and feed through the apertures between the slats without being mixed and drowned in the feed. It is *surprising* and also *amusing*, to see how eager they are to remove the feed and store it in the hive. An ordinary family of bees will frequently remove a pint of the feed in an hour, and usually from one to two quarts during a night; and it does not retard them in the least from gathering from the field on the following day.

The feed may be made of poor, unmerchantable honey, or honey and sugar *mixed*, and prepared with water. Southern honey also answers a very good purpose for feeding, merely to sustain the bees through the winter; or, when cleansed and mixed with crushed sugar, makes a very good article for the table, *after being worked over* and stored in the combs by the bees. They also construct combs from the feed, as white and beautiful as any other. For feeding receipts see *ante*, page 285.

Household Menagerie and Museum,
OR THE
Encyclopedia of Animated Nature.

A BOOK THAT IS REALLY ALL LIFE—EVERY FAMILY SHOULD HAVE IT.

LIVING NATURE IN ALL ITS FORMS.

The only Book of its kind ever Published which gives Pictorial Representations and Popular Descriptions of the History, Habits, and Modes of Life,

OF ALL THE CLASSES OF

Living Beings on the Earth, in the Ocean, and
THE AIR.

1350 ENGRAVINGS OF MEN AND ANIMALS.

In One Quarto Volume, 1350 *Illustrations, Morocco, Gilt Back and Centre.—Price,* $3 50.

Books upon almost every other subject have been circulated among the people, except those relating to the very interesting and important one of NATURAL HISTORY. The books which have heretofore been published on this subject, have been adapted either to mere children, or to those who make it a thorough study. Hence, very few of the millions of readers in this country have within their reach anything satisfactory upon this subject. This indicates a great and an obvious want, as no subject is more intensely interesting, and none more improving, than that of the living beings that people the globe. This want we are confident we fully meet in the work we here offer to the public.

This subject is treated in a popular style; technical names and terms being carefully excluded, thus adapting it to the understandings and tastes of general readers, and making it one of

THE MOST INTERESTING AND USEFUL OF HOUSEHOLD BOOKS.

IT EMBRACES

I. **All the Various Races of Men,** with the varieties of each race, as the European, Mongolian, Malay, Negro, Indian, Australian, Negrillo, Telingin, Ethiopian, Hottentot, Abyssinian, &c., &c., with Engravings of each.

II. **All the Varieties of Land and Sea Animals,** including the various species of Monkeys, the Lion, Tiger, Leopard, and all the animals of the cat-kind, Jackall, Wolf, Bear, &c., &c., with their habits and the modes of taking them by hunting, trapping, ensnaring, &c., and also the animals living both in the Sea and on the Land, and those living exclusively in the former.

III. **All the Land and Sea Birds,** a list too numerous to repeat, correct Engravings of which constitute a very attractive feature of the work.

IV. **All the Various Tribes of Fishes,** of the Rivers, Lakes and Oceans.

V. **The Reptiles of the Globe.**

VI. **The Various Insects,** their habits, uses and modes of destruction, &c. &c.

VII. **Sea Insects, or Crustacea.**

VIII. **The Shell Animals, or Mollusca, &c., &c.**

All these various living beings are described, accurate Illustrations of each, and their habits, uses and modes of life are given; embracing over

THIRTEEN HUNDRED ENGRAVINGS OF MEN AND ANIMALS.

No work was ever issued that is more attractive to the young, none over whose pages they hang with deeper interest, or from which more that is instructive is derived.

It is the Book for the Young.

The Rapid Sale of over 12,000 Copies, shows the estimation in which it is held by the public; and is at once an index of the public want and of the complete adaptation of this work to meet that want.

PUBLISHED BY THE AUBURN PUBLISHING COMPANY, AUBURN, N. Y.

SOLD ONLY TO SUBSCRIBERS: is not therefore for sale in any Bookstore, and can be had only of our Canvassing Agents. And all who desire to engage in soliciting subscriptions for the above valuable work, will find immediate and profitable employment by addressing

E. G. STORKE, Publishing Agent,
AUBURN, N. Y.

Sold only to Subscribers.—Not for Sale in Book Stores.—No Library is complete without it.—It should be in every Family.

A MAGNIFICENT HISTORY,
Geography and Biography of all Nations,

COMPRISING, IN A SINGLE WORK,

THE HISTORY OF ALL NATIONS—THE GEOGRAPHY OF ALL COUNTRIES, AND THE BIOGRAPHIES OF THE PROMINENT MEN OF ALL TIME.

700 Engravings Illustrate its History,—200 Portraits its Biography,—and 70 Maps its Geography.

1235 DOUBLE-COLUMN IMPERIAL OCTAVO PAGES, COSTING OVER $11,000,

AND CONTAINING AS MUCH MATTER AS

TWENTY 12MO. VOLUMES OF ORDINARY SIZE!

THE WORK EXTENDS FROM THE EARLIEST PERIOD TO THE PRESENT TIME:

And in it the History of every Nation, Ancient and Modern, is separately given.

By S. G. GOODRICH, the Napoleon of the Pen,

Author of "Recollections of a Lifetime," "Peter Parley's Tales, &c., &c.

A New Revised Edition, including the Prominent Events of the Current Year.

It is believed that a UNIVERSAL HISTORY, suitable in form, extent and arrangement, to the wants of the mass of American readers has never before been presented to the public. For this reason, and in compliance with numerous suggestions from those entitled to respect, the author has undertaken the formidable task of supplying one of a popular character, and for general use.

The work presents a separate and distinct history, and also exhibits the present state of every Nation, Ancient and Modern, *including the recent revolutions in Europe*, and for the purpose of showing how nations have acted upon or influenced the destinies of one another, GENERAL VIEWS are given, at suitable periods, presenting the great movement of mankind as one family, in its onward march from the past to the present, combining A CYCLOPEDIA OF HISTORY AND UNIVERSAL GAZETTEER OF GEOGRAPHY AND BIOGRAPHY. With a view to render it more valuable, especially in the Family Library, an ample Chronological Table is given, *with a full Index*—containing upwards of *four thousand* Historical and Geographical Names; thus rendering it AVAILABLE, FOR DAILY AND FAMILIAR USE, AS A BOOK OF REFERENCE.

This work, by Mr. GOODRICH, must be very acceptable to the American public. It is the result of years of toil and labor, assisted in his researches by several scholars of known ability. It has been prepared at a great expense by the proprietors. No pains have been spared in the execution of the

ILLUSTRATIONS AND MAPS,

which were executed expressly for the work. Indeed all the other historical writings of Mr. GOODRICH sink into insignificance when compared with this, the result of his riper and maturer years. It is admitted that ONE HUNDRED DOLLARS could not purchase the same matter in any other shape; and the publishers confidently expect, in consideration of the great literary value of the work, the large sum expended in preparing it for the press, and the

EXCEEDINGLY MODERATE PRICE AT WHICH IT IS OFFERED.

that it will be favorably received by every lover of good books. Many of our first scholars, divines and gentlemen who have examined the work, have given it their UNQUALIFIED APPROBATION.

UNIFORM RETAIL PRICES:

In 2 Vols., Morocco, gilt backs and side dies, Marble Edges, ..$8 00
" Full Gilt Sides, and Gilt Edges,......................10 00

PUBLISHED BY THE AUBURN PUBLISHING COMPANY, AUBURN, N. Y.

☞ Canvassing Agents wanted for the above.

Address E. G. STORKE, Publishing Agent,
AUBURN, N. Y.

www.ingramcontent.com/pod-product-compliance
Lightning Source LLC
Chambersburg PA
CBHW031904220426
43663CB00006B/761